The Cambridge Introduction to
Theatre Directing

This *Introduction* is an exciting journey through the different styles of theatre that twentieth-century and contemporary directors have created. It discusses artistic and political values, rehearsal methods and the diverging relationships with actors, designers, other collaborators and audiences, and treatment of dramatic material. Offering a compelling analysis of theatre practice, Christopher Innes and Maria Shevtsova explore the different rehearsal and staging principles and methods of such earlier groundbreaking figures as Stanislavsky, Meyerhold and Brecht, revising standard perspectives on their work. The authors analyse, as well, a diverse range of innovative contemporary directors, including Ariane Mnouchkine, Elizabeth LeCompte, Peter Sellars, Robert Wilson, Thomas Ostermeier and Oskaras Korsunovas, among many others. While tracing the different roots of directorial practices across time and space, and discussing their artistic, cultural and political significance, the authors provide key examples of the major directorial approaches and reveal comprehensive patterns in the craft of directing and the influence and collaborative relations of directors.

CHRISTOPHER INNES is Distinguished Research Professor at York University, Toronto, and Research Professor at Copenhagen University.

MARIA SHEVTSOVA is Professor of Drama and Theatre Arts at Goldsmiths, University of London.

The Cambridge Introduction to

Theatre Directing

CHRISTOPHER INNES
MARIA SHEVTSOVA

CAMBRIDGE UNIVERSITY PRESS
Cambridge, New York, Melbourne, Madrid, Cape Town,
Singapore, São Paulo, Delhi, Mexico City

Cambridge University Press
The Edinburgh Building, Cambridge CB2 8RU, UK

Published in the United States of America by Cambridge University Press, New York

www.cambridge.org
Information on this title: www.cambridge.org/9780521844499

First published 2013

Printed and bound in the United Kingdom by the MPG Books Group

A catalogue record for this publication is available from the British Library

Library of Congress Cataloguing in Publication data
Innes, Christopher, 1941–
The Cambridge introduction to theatre directing / Christopher Innes, Maria Shevtsova.
pages cm. – (Cambridge introductions to literature)
Includes bibliographical references and index.
ISBN 978-0-521-84449-9 (hardback) – ISBN 978-0-521-60622-6 (paperback)
1. Theater – Production and direction. 2. Theater – Production and direction – History – 20th century. 3. Theatrical producers and directors. I. Shevtsova, Maria. II. Title.
PN2053.I525 2013
792.02′33–dc23 2012034004

ISBN 978-0-521-84449-9 Hardback
ISBN 978-0-521-60622-6 Paperback

Contents

Illustrations

Acknowledgements

The authors and publishers acknowledge the following sources of copyright material and are grateful for the permissions granted. While every effort has been made, it has not always been possible to identify the sources of all material used, or to trace all copyright holders. If any omissions are brought to our notice, we will be happy to include the appropriate acknowledgements on reprinting.

The authors wish to thank the photographers listed separately for their kind and most generous permission to publish the photographs selected for this book: figure 4 courtesy of Michèle Laurent, figure 5 courtesy of Thomas Aurin, figure 6 courtesy of Dmitrij Matvejev, figure 9 courtesy of A. Köhring © Theater an der Ruhr, figure 10 courtesy of Lesley Leslie-Spinks, figure 11 courtesy of Emmanuel Valette, figure 12 courtesy of Terry McCarthy, figure 13 courtesy of Pascal Victor, figure 14 courtesy of Viktor Vasilyev, figure 15 courtesy of Aleksandr Rysov © School of Dramatic Art, figure 16 courtesy of Sarah Ainsley, figure 17 courtesy of the Grotowski Institute, figure 18 courtesy of Irena Lipinska and the Grotowski Institute.

We wish also to thank Peter Sellars, Simon McBurney and Ariane Mnouchkine and the Théâtre du Soleil, and especially Franck Pendino and Charles-Henri Bradier; Audra Zukaityte and Agne Li of the OKT/Vilnius City Theatre; Judith Heider-Keßler and Helmut Schäfer of the Theater an der Ruhr; Dina Dodina at the Maly Drama Theatre in St Petersburg; and Anatoli Vassiliev and the School of Dramatic Art, as well as Aleksandr Shaposhnikov for his help in tracking down pictures. The contributions of Nicole Konstantinou and Barbara Shultz at the Volksbühne in Berlin have been precious, as has that of Johanna Lühr at the Schaubühne, also in Berlin; and many thanks to Thomas Irmer for his generosity. We are indebted to Eugenio Barba and the Odin Teatret, and to Magdalena Madra and the Grotowski Institute in Wroclaw. Thank you also Philippa Burt, Christina Korte, Sherena Aruldson and Sasha Shevtsova.

In addition, Christopher Innes would like to thank Lepage's associates at Ex Machina and McBurney's staff at Complicite, and particularly the director Peter Sellars, for their help with material for this book. He is also grateful to acknowledge the Canada Research Chair program, for enabling this research in terms of both funding and time. Maria Shevtsova, Fellow at the Research Centre, 'Interweaving Performance Cultures' at the Freie Universität in Berlin, wishes to thank the Centre for providing her with wonderful working conditions in which to write several sections of this book. The staff of this Centre which includes several angels without wings, has been admirable in its hospitable attention.

Introduction

Over the twentieth and twenty-first centuries, the director has come to be identified as a significant creative figure in European and North American theatre. Indeed, in festival, experimental and off-Broadway theatres, as well as in countries such as Germany, it can be argued that audiences are drawn to productions more by the name of the director than by the name of the author or the title of the play itself, or even by star actors. And it is to directors that the development of modern theatre can be traced in its varying manifestations. This book is a response to the emergence of such a vital artistic force, which makes it important to understand how the interrelationships now work between the different creative elements of the theatrical art, and what the guiding principles are, or how the contemporary stylistic forms are produced.

The function and position of the contemporary, twenty-first-century theatre director emerged (as discussed in Chapter 2 of this book) from the actor-manager of the nineteenth century and the pioneering endeavours, primarily in Europe, of Ludwig Chronegk at the Meiningen and Konstantin Stanislavsky at the Moscow Art Theatre. Other major figures in the first half of the twentieth century, from Max Reinhardt and Edward Gordon Craig to Bertolt Brecht, contributed, equally, to the transformations that are integral to modern directing. From these rich beginnings, numerous variations on the role of the director and how this person directs have followed, giving rise to complex interconnections of practice and thought in the making of theatre. The director has become an artistic figure in his or her own right: a figure who is not necessarily a manager or administrator, or an actor, nor one beholden to playwrights.

Already, in the opening decade of the twentieth century, Stanislavsky had insisted that the theatre was not literature, a conviction endorsed by Vsevolod Meyerhold through his highly stylized, theatricalized means, and reiterated in numerous different ways through the work of contemporary directors – in Germany, for instance, by Frank Castorf and Thomas Ostermeier. Yet Stanislavsky also notably collaborated with Chekhov, Meyerhold with Alexander Blok and Vladimir Mayakovsky, while others have also collaborated with writers who do not claim to be dramatists, like McBurney with the art critic, painter and novelist John Berger. Then, too, there are director-playwrights like Brecht and director-scriptwriters like Robert Wilson or Robert Lepage. Indeed, theatre *auteurs*, the subject of Chapter 5, not only create their own scripts, and design sets, costumes and accessories – the case of Robert Wilson and Lepage (and Wilson is a superlative light designer, as well) – but also at times perform in their own shows.

Examples of *auteur*-directors open up authorship questions of another kind, notably to do with group devising, examined in Chapter 7. Such groups devise verbal as well as physical and musical 'texts' or 'scores' and thus are what might be called performance authors, although co-authorship is far from a matter of 'writing' only with words, as this book amply demonstrates. As traced in the discussion of ensemble directing (Chapter 6), actors too are co-authors of productions with their bodies when they invent material *with* directors, some of which can also be dialogue. Such is the case of the Théâtre du Soleil with Ariane Mnouchkine, the Maly Drama Theatre of St Petersburg with Lev Dodin, Théâtre de Complicité (now known simply as Complicite) with Simon McBurney, and The Wooster Group with Elizabeth LeCompte. But the main point, regarding directors, is that no matter how many and varied their tasks may be, and how they may multi-task and come to dominate productions with their energy, directors' activities identify who directors are and what they do, specifically, when they work together with others. Directors cannot work alone. A solo director can only be, in fact, a solo performer.

While analysing the significance and influence of key innovators in the earlier part of the twentieth century – such as Stanislavsky, Meyerhold or Brecht, each identified with a different approach: the rehearsal processes for psychological realism (Chapter 2); pronounced theatricality and physical training (Chapter 3); epic-political staging (Chapter 4) – our main emphasis is on contemporary twenty-first-century directing. Following the historical overview, every chapter leads to the most contemporary examples of the particular trend or approach focused on there; and even though this is by no means a 'How-to' book for prospective directors, we intend its details of the working methods of directors, and especially of those elaborated by contemporary directors, to be inspirational for theatre professionals, students and general theatre-goers. We analyse the different forms and styles of theatre that twentieth-century directors have created, profiling specific productions to give their achievements concrete dimensions. Similarly, we consider the artistic, social and political implications of directors' work – which is not exclusively about directing – their approaches to actor training that, in several instances, is fundamental to their directorial work (demonstrated in the different approaches of Dodin, Anatoli Vassiliev, Jerzy Grotowski, Eugenio Barba), their rehearsal methods, their interaction with actors and their relation to spectators (exemplified contrastingly by Erwin Piscator, Peter Brook and Peter Sellars, among others). Several examples show the versatility of directors who stage opera, together with the challenges and opportunities of working within such a highly stylized form, while others focus on the genre of song theatre that, in part, grew out of Grotowski's research during what he termed the 'post-theatrical epoch'.

The area of directing is vast, and, in order to organize it, we have observed its variations, innovations and, in some cases, quite marked departures from established or even newly discovered practices. By noting these patterns, we reveal lines of directing that thread their way, whether through perceivable influence or in zigzags, across time and space and cultures. We have grouped directors along or in relation to these lines, giving them definition, as an etching might give definition, not because they sit attractively in the picture that takes shape overall, but because their distinctive characteristics are thrown into relief, acquiring strength from their 'place' in it. Lineages have developed over the past century, some indirectly, like the links between Craig, Norman Bel Geddes and Wilson. Others, which usually involve small performance groups, have more direct connections – the case of Gardzienice, Song of the Goat and Teatr ZAR, whose heritage comes from Grotowski. These latter groups speak of 'leaders' rather than 'directors', and their shift in vocabulary indicates, among other things, the paradoxical nature of collective improvisation that is finally orchestrated by one person. Certain types of ensemble theatre, several of which feature in this book, experience this same paradox, responding differently to it.

The patterns we have traced out show knots of interconnections, which means that a director whom we have grouped in one way belongs just as readily in another grouping: this is the case, noticeably, of Brook who appears in various chapters. Yet others could just as easily have crisscrossed our organization, not least Mnouchkine or Brecht, who are founders of ensemble theatres and could have figured in Chapter 6 as well as under the labels of 'theatricality' or 'epic' directing. In their case, as in several similar cases, we have grouped according to their predominant directorial principles.

What this wonderful tapestry of threads and knots shows is that not only discerning the coherent patterns of directors and directing is difficult, but so, too, is writing a history of directing, which, in some respects, we have also done. This has meant delving into the 'pre-history', if we may call it such, of the modern director, to which Chapter 1 is devoted. It has also meant remembering our *Directors/Directing: Conversations on Theatre* (2009), which, since it records the thoughts of living directors about their work, offers highly relevant documentation. As such, it contributes both to an understanding of the practical processes of directing in the present and to the history of directing as it may become in the future. Since the present book was conceived in tandem with *Directors/Directing*, it was logical that we should include those directors in it.

This book necessarily embraces more directors than the ones selected previously. However, quite a number of international figures have too few pages devoted to them, while others are merely referred to in passing. Of the latter, Krystian Lupa, key to the current high profile of Polish directors on the international stage, comes immediately to mind. Of the former, the Lithuanian Eimuntas Nekrosius and Oskaras Korsunovas (while discussed in terms of the political aspects of theatricality) deserve greater attention for their novel, surrealistic approaches, which have won them considerable reputations in Europe, spearheaded by resounding success in France, Italy and Germany. And then there are other innovative directors, some emerging in the international arena while others are already prominent, who are not named at all, but who were in our consciousness as we wrote.

In fact, the subject of Eastern European directors (described here by geographic location, certainly not in political terms) would make a book in its own right. So, too, would the missing link of this book, which is Asian theatre. Unfortunately, we have had to exclude a whole array of major Asian directors known across the world. The reasons are multiple. First, our task to unearth the roots of the modern director necessitated a European focus. Second, a mere acknowledgement of the names of Asian directors would have been nothing but lip service, or, worse still, a gesture towards the ultimately insulting 'politically correct'. Third, but not last, it would have been absolutely necessary to contextualize these directors: to show how, on the one hand, their modern perspectives are juxtaposed against their countries' centuries-old performance traditions and how, on the other, they have made methods developed in Europe uniquely their own, or have invented performance styles from which directors both in Europe and elsewhere are learning. Very often, this fruitful appropriation has generated a cross-cultural interpenetration of Asian and European ways of working, together with their artistic forms.

The type of contextualization outlined briefly here would have been indispensable for such directors of the past as Huang Zuolin, who was deeply inspired by Mikhaïl Chekhov (with whom he studied in the 1930s), Stanislavsky and Brecht, and who is possibly the most influential director on modern Chinese theatre. Looking at the past, a similar kind of contextualization would have been essential, for example, for the Bengali director Sombhu Mitra, who staged Ibsen's *A Doll's House* in the later 1950s. And only by means of intricate contextualization would it have been possible to do justice to such remarkable living directors as Yukio Ninagawa from Japan, or Oh Tae-Suk from Korea. Both explore their own cultural traditions in making modern Japanese and Korean theatre. The constraints of publishing have prohibited, here, anything like an adequate treatment of these figures, who are part of the world dynamics of directing.

Our study is, as it says, an Introduction to Theatre Directing, and it could not hope to be fully comprehensive from whichever point of view we took. In grouping the way we have, and in providing concrete details of many kinds – practical, aesthetic, theoretical, historical – our intention was to provide various vantage points from which our readers could begin their journey. It is they who must now take over and forge their own paths through the enormous, beautiful terrain fashioned by directors, directing.

Chapter 1

Traditional staging and the evolution of the director

While this book focuses on the work of contemporary directors and the directorial principles that have become defined over the modern period, it is useful to see these in the historical context. This broad overview not only allows a sense of both aesthetic and political perspective, but also suggests the need for the functions and position of the theatre director by illustrating the varied figures who assumed less defined even if possibly similar roles in specific eras. In addition, it demonstrates a long connection between innovations in performance, challenging or pre-empting the standard stage practices of a given age, and the activities of directorial prototypes: a connection that has become one of the defining factors of the contemporary director.

Theatre practice in the Western world evolved from two main origins. Firstly: the theatre in Ancient Greece, which was passed down in adaptations through Classical Rome to the *commedia dell'arte*, and was reintroduced – although in a very different form – during the Renaissance. Secondly: the medieval tradition of religious plays and royal pageants. Even back then there were almost certainly influences that flowed between Europe and other traditions: the theatre of Ancient Greece may well have borrowed from Asian traditions, or contributed to them (with miniature amphitheatres still surviving, carved into the hillsides across Asia Minor), while there are striking similarities between Persian Ta'zieh performance and the medieval Mystery play. However there is so little documentation of such interchanges that – while in discussing contemporary directors the influence of the twentieth-century Chinese actor Mei Lang-fan on Meyerhold and Brecht or the two-way street of Roberto Ciulli's 'Silk Road' are noted – this historical overview limits itself to the Western tradition.

The position of the actor in Europe was of course very different from period to period, depending on the society of the time, as was the function of the person responsible for orchestrating the staging, whatever his title. The style of performance varied even more widely, conditioned as it always is by the physical context of the production. Costuming (or in certain styles masking) has very specific effects on gesture, vocalization and indeed characterization. Open-air amphitheatres gathering thousands of spectators call for very different styles of expression from pageant wagon or a trestle platform in a town square, or from an indoor theatre – proscenium, or thrust stage, and so on – and each sort of venue makes different demands on the organizer of the show and therefore leads to a different type of job.

Classical Greek theatre: director as choreographer

For instance, in the Classical Greek theatre, commissioning a play was referred to as 'granting a chorus' – the chorus being the most numerous (and therefore most expensive) element of mounting a play, and dramaturgically the most important. This was not only because they represented the people, in other words the audience, or served as commentators and literally interposed between the spectators and the figures of the main characters, but also because of the perspective of the audience, whether in the relatively small Theatre of Dionysus under the Acropolis, or in far larger theatres like Epidaurus or Corinth. With the steep rake of the semi-circular ranks of stone benches set on the hill around the acting area, the majority of spectators looked down, and from quite a distance. As a consequence the patterns of movement of the chorus became the central communicative aspect.[1]

Theatre terms: Classical and modern

Many of our terms for parts of the stage come from the Classical Greek theatre, with *Theatron* – the word for all the elements of the Greek theatre building – carrying over almost unchanged. However, what most of these loan-words refer to in the modern theatre is significantly different. So, the Greek term *skene* (or scene) was a porticoed wall at the rear which acted as a backdrop, but the *proskenion* (from which we get our term 'proscenium') was the raised platform where the main characters performed – hence also called the *logeion*, or 'speaking place' – while the semi-circular or circular arena in front of this, the *orchestra*, in fact meant 'dancing space'. At the same time, we should remember that *auditorium*, the space for the public, meant 'hearing place' (while 'audience' of course means 'listeners', not 'viewers' like the modern 'spectators') and indeed even in the huge amphitheatre of Epidaurus the acoustics are so amazing that if a penny is dropped near a small hole in the stone that marks the centre of the *orchestra* – possibly the position of an altar – the clink can be clearly heard at the back in the highest rows of seats. The term for these, *kerkis*, or for the passages between the tiers, *klimakes*, have not carried through, since nowhere has the theatre changed more than in the arrangement of audience seating.

It is fair to assume that the actors playing the named roles – set upon the raised platform of the scene and wearing masks as well as *kothurni*, or platform shoes, to aid visibility – were presenting archetypal images, even though the characters in the scripts are to some degree individualized personalities. They therefore probably brought much the same expression to each role, so needing relatively little guidance, which would have been provided by the playwright. So the person with the most authority in the actual staging would be the choreographer for the chorus, who might again be the playwright. There would also have been a stage-manager or mechanic, since there was at least one piece of spectacle, the crane or lowering device for the *deus ex machina*, the 'god from the machine', together possibly with thunder-machines, and perhaps even lifts and traps, while particularly in the comedies of Aristophanes other stage effects were called for. Similarly the Greek theatre, being a permanent structure, required little or nothing in the way of specific scenery – although at some point in its history there were *periaktoi*, prismatic scenic units which could revolve to give different indications of stage location. Greek drama was generally performed at religious festivals, and presented as part of a competition, judged by the civic and religious leaders of the festival. Noticeably, the prizes were awarded jointly to the person who had sponsored the play (the *choregus*: literally the man who pays for the chorus) and to the poet – no mention of anyone else whose art added significantly to the performance, until after 448 BCE when a special acting prize was instituted signalling the growing importance of the actor vis-à-vis the chorus. The Greek theatre then, in the Classical period and at the major urban or festival centres, was as much a writers' theatre as were the later Elizabethan and Renaissance theatres.

Of course, not all Greek theatres were of the size and importance of a festival stage like Epidaurus, or the equally important stages of Athens: the Theatre of Dionysus built into the hill of the Acropolis in Athens, and renovated in stone in 362 BCE, or the Lycurgan Theatre, built about 330 BCE under Lycurgus, where all the major Classical playwrights whose work has survived competed. All these theatres of the Classical period, including theatres outside Greece like the one in Syracuse, built by Greek colonizers and taken over by the Romans, seem to have been designed to hold around 14,000 spectators. However, while records are scant, the earlier theatres were built of wood and significantly smaller, and the earliest surviving texts suggest that there was no separation between the chorus and the actors, and therefore no need of a structure or *skene* behind the orchestra, which was only bounded at the rear by a low wall. Indeed the chorus was the primary element of the drama at that period.[2] Then, in the later Classical period there seem to have been touring versions of plays, perhaps with only very few performers, since there are a scattering of tiny Greek theatres carved out of hillsides along the Mediterranean coast of what is now Turkey, one example being just outside

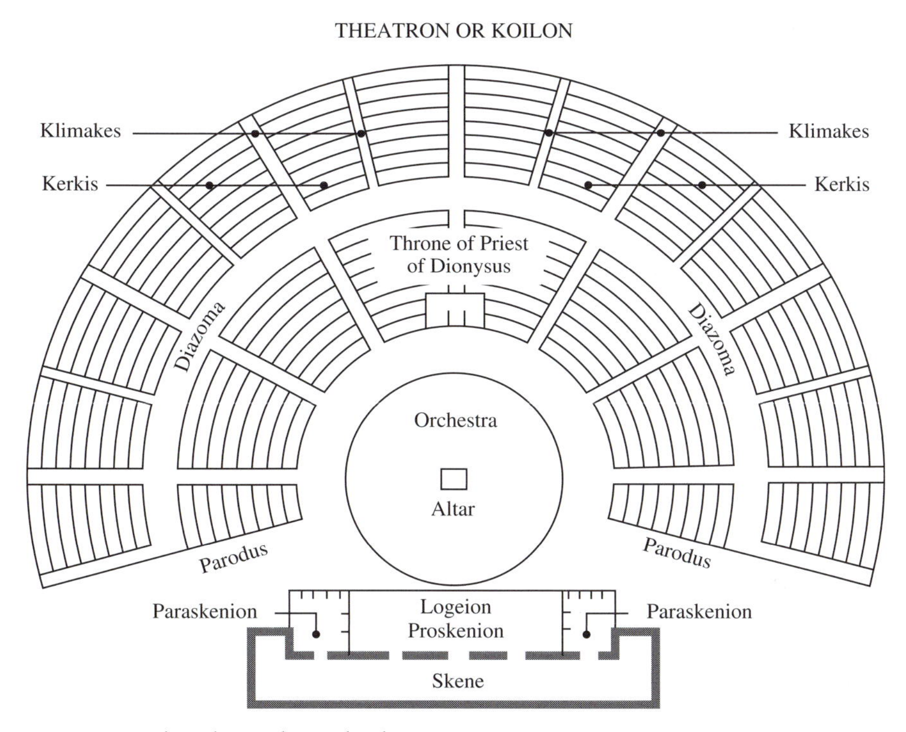

1 The Classical Greek Theatre

the walls of the castle at Alanya: high on a hill, the orchestra is barely 20 feet in diameter, bounded by a narrow platform just one step above the orchestra floor, with a small wall across the back over which the spectator looks out to the sea far below, and with just five semi-circular rows of seats carved into the rock. With such an intimate setting, it is hard to envisage the performance of the plays we know, developed as they were for the big theatres in Athens. However, it is clear that in both these forms of Greek theatre, it was the performers who would have controlled the staging. In the early period it is likely that the movements were based on folk dances, or even military manoeuvres. In the later travelling troupes, while they may have used codified gestures and moves, it is likely the group orchestrated their own staging. So the writers' theatre of the Classical period emerged from and was accompanied by actors' theatre.

From Greece to Classical Rome

The conditions on the Roman stage were widely different, even if their drama largely consisted of adaptations from the Greeks. Again the development was from temporary wooden stages, either in the public squares or – as part of the *Ludi* (Games) – in an arena, sharing the programme with horse-racing and gladiatorial combat. But instead of the Greek setting of a religious festival, in Rome theatrical performance was far more integrated with popular culture. Also in contrast to Athens, it was not until 55 BCE that Rome had a permanent stone theatre, although there were Greek-built theatres that had survived from the one-time Greek colonies in southern Italy. But the circumstances of its building show the status of drama as popular entertainment, since this theatre was constructed by Pompey the Great, during his second consulship, as a way of winning popular support against Julius Caesar (who was to be assassinated on its steps). Later Roman stages carried over the semi-circular shape of the Greek orchestra, but with variations, like the Roman theatre at Orange in France with its massive stone and brick portico towering across the back of the semi-circular stage, but with a relatively modest auditorium. At the same time, throughout the period, the more informal and intimate street theatre continued: particularly in perhaps the oldest type of drama, the Roman *mime*, boisterous and vulgar short farces of working-class life. While the actors were unmasked, the characters portrayed were almost always stock figures, and the action seems to have been generally improvised.

Most important from our perspective, there was a shift in the balance between writing and staging, which reflected the popular context of performance. For instance, from the reign of Augustus there was a vogue for dumbshows with a masked dancer – the *pantomimus*, from which we get our term 'pantomime' – accompanied by a chanted chorus, with subjects taken from Greek myths. The spectacle of the dance and the virtuoso performer was the primary element here; and indeed the Roman theatre produced 'star' actors, the most famous being Roscius (Roscius Gallus Quintus, 126–62 BCE) whose name is mentioned by Shakespeare and who, significantly, wrote a treatise on acting as rhetoric. The Roman theatre in general seems to have been an actors' theatre. Thus Plautus (c.254–184 BCE), the most popular Roman dramatist, whose plots are loosely adapted from Greek sources, mainly Menander (342–291 BCE), uses stock figures – the Cunning Servant, the Boastful Soldier, the Old Man, and so on – while continually breaking the dramatic illusion to allow direct address to the audience, frequently out of character, and also emphasizes the actor in other ways. So in one play a Sycophant, hired to deceive another character, recounts how he was selected because of his acting skills, was instructed in his role, and had a costume hired for him.[3] Plautus' dialogue is full of alliteration, puns and rhetorical tricks; but the plays, with loose ends to the plots and repeated farce situations, as well as long passages clearly designed for musical accompaniment, are scripts for performance, rather than literary texts. By contrast, Seneca's elaborately rhetorical tragedies (based largely on Euripides) focus so entirely on language, as the heightened expression of extreme emotions, that it is generally assumed they were designed for reading or recitation, rather than for performance.[4]

On one hand it was Seneca (4 BCE–65 CE) who influenced Elizabethan drama, creating a vogue for extraordinary violence and revenge tragedy. On the other, from the *mimes*, with their rough street-theatre tradition, and from the stock figures and farcical tricks (*lazzi*) of Plautus, combined with carnival masks from Venice, comes the popular tradition of the improvised *commedia dell'arte*, which appeared in the sixteenth century. Improvisation and masking, together with stock routines, are the signs of purely actors' theatre. However, the *commedia* form inspired the plays of the seventeenth-century French actor-manager Molière, and was to be revived as one of the bases of directorial theatre in the twentieth century, picked up by Meyerhold in his search for a physical and non-individualistic style of acting, by Jacques Copeau in France, and in Italy by Gorgio Strehler at his Piccolo Teatro di Milano and the anarchist playwright Dario Fo.

Medieval European staging

The alternate historical form of theatre that fed into the Western tradition, informing the plays of Elizabethan and Jacobean England (most obviously Marlowe's *Doctor Faustus*, with its Morality play Good and Evil Angels, or Ben Jonson's *Bartholemew Fayre*, with its setting of fairground booths), is the religious drama of the Middle Ages. This originated as liturgical homilies or dramatizations of the Easter ceremonies, performed by monks as part of a church service with liturgical costumes and props, and ritual movement and gesture. Dramatic elements were minimal and there would have been little space for interpretation. However, the long medieval period – over 600 years, a significantly longer time than the whole development of theatre since the Renaissance – engendered a remarkably wide range of performance, although little of it occurred in formal theatres.

When these liturgical performances moved outside the church, there seems to have been a gradually developing need for an organizing or directorial function focused on theatrical presentation, even if still very much under theological control. In some forms this remained minimal, as with Passion plays such as the one first presented at Oberammergau in 1633 and still performed today, where there is a script (based of course on the Bible) but the actions, broadly fixed by tradition, culminate in seventeen *tableaux vivants*. Yet in England the processional staging of Mystery cycles at York or Wakefield certainly needed overall coordination, with their forty-plus playlets covering Creation to Last Judgment on a single day, which toured from 'station' to 'station' through the town on separate wagons. But with each being financed and presented by a trade guild (bakers for the Last Supper, armourers for the Crucifixion, etc.) the presentation was probably fairly simple. Indeed with some scripts shorter than 100 lines, many episodes must have been primarily tableaux – although in the N. Town Cycle there are fairly full stage directions. Comic parts (episodes where evil was treated as farce or scenes of common people: e.g. Herod; the *Second Shepherd's Play*) clearly called for more activity and expressive interpretation, which would probably have been developed by the actors. Much of the widespread popular performance in Europe was either in the form of grand tableaux (as with royal processions) or as folk forms (e.g. mummers' troupes and disguisings, or, at the upper end of the social scale, tournaments and minstrels), and while the first certainly required artistic creativity, the second was largely an improvised performance.

There were also secular dramas: short secular farces and *sotties* (fools' plays), or iconic depictions of national heroes (e.g. Charlemagne in Germany; Robin Hood and St George in England) performed on the ground in the corner of a marketplace, or at country fairs on the sort of simple platform stage depicted by Breughel in his sixteenth-century painting of the *Village Festival*, where the tiny acting area made it a purely actors' theatre.

For *A Village Festival in Honour of St Hubert* by Pieter Breughel II (1632), see www.fitzmuseum.cam.ac.uk/pharos/images/collection_images/northern/1192/1192_SE.jpg.

However, where there was a specially constructed playing area (throughout the medieval era there were no permanent theatres, temporary wooden stages being built by local carpenters for particular performances then dismantled) some sort of a stage director would have been required. So in the German Passion plays, or English Morality plays, where multiple acting areas were constructed around a circular scaffold, allowing simultaneous action and broad patterns of movement, there needed to be more than just traffic-management – as indeed there did in French saints plays, such as the 25,000-line *Mystère de la passion* (c1450) by Arnoul Grébain, which took four full days to perform. Epic scope, whether in performance time or performance area, required complex orchestration. Thus, in the fifteenth-century English play *The Castle of Perseverance*, sketches of which show scaffold stages for World, Flesh and Devil set equidistant around a circular perimeter (a shape with symbolic connotations, where the audience was seated), the action flows from one perimeter stage to another and to the 'castle', built in the centre of the circle, with the dramatically complex 3,700-line script interweaving several different styles of interaction. Similarly in sixteenth-century Lucerne, where documents show a comparable distribution of scaffold stages (Heaven at one end of the Weinmarkt, Hell Mouth opposite) and where violent action in mimed dumb-show, for example Barrabas committing murder, took place at the same time as other more central scripted scenes, the names of specific directors are recorded. And a surviving prompt copy of Renward Cysat (who directed at Lucerne at least from 1583 to his death in 1614) gives details of how stage tricks were to be achieved, incorporating not only his own notes, but those of his predecessors. As this indicates, even in the early seventeenth century the director's function, while controlling the overall shape of the action and instructing the (non-professional) actors, was primarily seen to be repeating and expanding traditions of presentation.

It is worth noting that these forms of medieval drama lasted well into the Renaissance. Throughout the later fifteenth and earlier sixteenth centuries, there are works that serve as a bridge from medieval dramatic forms to the fully fledged Renaissance theatre. On a visual level there is Giorgio Vasari (1511–74), who created an early form of changeable perspective scenery with a system of rotating *periaktoi* in 1569 (multiplying the Greek triangular screen into a double series arranged in depth). His compatriot Filippo Brunelleschi engineered elaborate flying and lifting machinery for liturgical plays in Florentine churches, where lights on revolving wheels high above the altars represented heavenly choirs, and angels winged their way through a baroque Paradise. These led directly to the elaborate scenic effects for the court masques designed by Inigo Jones and coordinated by Ben Jonson (1572–1637) and others in the early seventeenth century. On a more literary level there were polemic propaganda plays – anticipating the eighteenth-century German Catholic counter-reformation drama – created for example by John Bale, bishop of Ossory in Ireland in 1553. Bale also wrote an early history play, *Kynge Johan* (just five years later in 1538) which combined symbolic morality figures and historical events with characters based on actual people, and may have served as a model for Shakespeare's *King John*. Similarly, *Magnyfycence* – a satire by John Skelton, printed in 1530 – or Sir David Lindsay's updated morality play, *A Satire on the Thrie Estates* (Edinburgh 1554) used old forms for contemporary criticism and commentary. There were also examples of developed drama like the anonymous *Everyman*, translated from Dutch to English in at least three versions from 1495 to 1595, where complex characterization was linked to symbolic figures and a liturgical plot. And indeed the Coventry Cycle – first recorded in 1392 – was last 'brought forth' in 1579, when

Shakespeare who lived in neighbouring Warwickshire was fifteen years old, while the final performance of Cysat's Passion play in Lucerne took place in 1616, the year of Shakespeare's death. Indeed Shakespeare was familiar with the style of acting in this type of performance, as can be seen from his comment on the passionate acting that 'out-Herods Herod' in *Hamlet* (III.ii.14).

So it is not altogether out of context to take Shakespeare's descriptions of actors as a model of how performances were prepared – and, allowing for the dramatic setting, of the minimal influence of a director during the medieval period, and even in Shakespeare's lifetime.

Playwright-managers: Renaissance and early seventeenth-century theatre

Much can be told of production methods and of the role of the prototype director versus the actors or the playwright, from the scenes in Shakespeare's plays where we are shown troupes of actors both rehearsing and performing: amateur in *A Midsummer Night's Dream* (1595); professional in *Hamlet* (1599–1600). While one is set in Athens of the legendary Theseus, and the other in a quasi-medieval Denmark, both are full of contemporary social reference; and even if the 'rude mechanicals' of *Midsummer Night's Dream* are represented satirically for comedy, each clearly describes staging situations that would be recognizable to an Elizabethan audience. At the same time, in each case the actors' texts are formalized, in comparison to the dialogue of Shakespeare's primary characters. Certainly in *Midsummer Night's Dream* this indicates an outdated dramatic style, although in *Hamlet* it is more setting off the artifice of performance.

The troupe that arrives in Hamlet's Elsinore is clearly run by an actor-manager, the Player-King. The stories they enact (for instance, of Dido and Aeneas, or indeed 'The Murder of Gonzago') are set pieces played for broad but realistic emotional effect, as we see from the tears the Player-King (as Aeneas) cries for Hecuba; and while they are certainly prepared to perform a play on demand and accept an inserted speech from their royal patron, the outer play seems to suggest that they perform it in a standard way, forcing Hamlet – as the author – to intervene during the performance because the point is apparently not being recognized by his targets (Gertrude and Claudius). The scene in which Hamlet instructs the players has often been seen as Shakespeare's own advice to the actors of his own day, while the play-scene can be interpreted as delineating the relative powerlessness of an author to control the expressive techniques of his actors in performance. In short Hamlet, as the author, is serving as a director, and, characteristically for Elizabethan theatre, his primary concern is with the delivery of the words.

> Speak the speech, I pray you, as I pronounced it to you – trippingly upon the tongue; but if you mouth it, as so many of our players do, I had as lief the town-crier had spoke my lines. Nor do not saw the air too much with your hands, thus, but use all gently; for in the very torrent, tempest, and as I may say the whirlwind of your passions, you must acquire and beget a temperance that may give it smoothness ... Suit the action to the word, the word to the action, with this special observance: that you o'erstep not the modesty of nature. For anything overdone is from the purpose of playing, whose end, both at the first and now, was and is to hold as 'twere the mirror up to nature, to show virtue her own feature, scorn her own image, and the very age and body of the time his form and pressure.
>
> *Hamlet*, III.ii.1–9 and 17–24

More directly, in *A Midsummer Night's Dream*, we are shown a rehearsal – albeit cut very short by Puck's intervention – as well as the performance of a play to celebrate a noble wedding, as continued to be common practice, at least up to 1634 when Milton's masque *Comus* was performed at Ludlow Castle with music by the court composer Henry Lawes. Despite the clearly satiric portrayal of this group of poorly educated tradesmen, whose script is described as incongruous nonsense, and whose incompetent acting transforms an intended tragedy into the farcical highpoint of the comedy, on a general level it still represents the functions of author and actors in the theatre of the period. Significantly Quince, the author, is a carpenter: the first of many self-designations of dramatists as construction experts (the most well-known being Ibsen's *The Masterbuilder*) and perhaps also pointing to the wooden construction both of the temporary medieval stages and of Elizabethan theatres like Shakespeare's Globe. For a start, when Quince complains that Flute (as Thisbe) speaks 'all your part at once, cues and all' we learn that the practice was to provide actors with cue scripts – where each actor only has a copy of his own speeches, plus the preceding actor's final words – a practice that continued to the end of the nineteenth century, long after the cheapness of printing removed its necessity. This had its effect on production, since none of the actors could have a complete overview of the play. And, as we see, the Elizabethan theatre could be labelled a playwright's theatre: it is Quince who has called and is running the rehearsal, not only distributing the parts, but instructing his actors in how to read them; and while taking suggestions, it is he who deals with scenic questions of location and time of day (his solution to representing the moon, deliberately farcical as it may be, is the one taken up). Effectively, as we are shown, the playwright functions as a director. In *A Midsummer Night's*

Dream he also appears in his own play, as Prologue – and there are records of Shakespeare too appearing on the stage as an actor – which links Quince to the actor-manager set-up: the standard for much of Western theatre from its earliest secular manifestations up to at least the twentieth century. Even so, Quince is hardly in control; and while the way his actors interrupt and call for script changes may be exaggerated into parody, undoubtedly there is some truth in the picture, as there is in the depiction of his lead actor, 'bully Bottom', taking over the performance.

Like Quince's group, Shakespeare's Lord Chamberlain's Men were required to perform at Court, where no scenery could be constructed, and while his Globe Theatre may have been richly decorated, its large thrust stage was bare except for the occasional piece of furniture. Similarly, while some costumes may have echoed a Roman toga, most characters, however historical, wore standard Elizabethan dress – as the record of scarlet satin breeches for Marlowe's *Tamburlaine* or the well-known sketch illustrating the staging of *Titus Andronicus* indicate.[5] This was an anti-illusionistic theatre, focused on language (to the extent that Shakespeare's audience are not intended to be surprised that Hamlet can repeat whole paragraphs of a speech, heard just once on the stage). Place and the positioning of characters within it are contained in the dialogue – almost all stage directions in Shakespearean or other Elizabethan drama have been added by later editors – and spectacle was extremely limited, where a whole army had necessarily to be represented by just one or two actors. The same applied generally to drama in the Renaissance, even where the stage was not bare – as for instance in Andrea Palladio's 1584 Teatro Olimpico in Vicenza. That indoor stage might represent an elaborately neo-classical architectural façade, in imitation of the Roman *scaenae frons*, with its trompe-l'oeil cityscape of sharply receding alleys in false perspective. The wood and plaster house-fronts that line these alleys are said to have been constructed as scenery for the first performance, *Oedipus Rex* in 1585; but the appearance is that of an Italian street with classical decoration. This setting was never changed, remaining exactly the same whatever the play being performed; and such an elaborate stage-scene must have been a limiting factor for the playwright, particularly by comparison with the imaginative freedom of the Globe or the Swan theatres in London. As the opening Prologue of *Henry V* clearly announces, Shakespeare's bare stage serves as a neutral field for the auditors' imagination:

> Can this cockpit hold
> The vast fields of France? Or may we cram
> Within this wooden O the very casques
> That did affright the air at Agincourt?

> O pardon: since a crooked figure may
> Attest in little place a million,
> And let us, ciphers to this great account,
> On your imaginary forces work.
> ...
> Piece out our imperfections with your thoughts,
> Into a thousand parts divide one man,
> And make imaginary puissance.
> Think, when we talk of horses, that you see them,
> Printing their proud hooves i' th' receiving earth;
> For 'tis your thoughts that now must deck our kings,
> Carry them here and there, jumping o'er times,
> Turning the accomplishments of many years
> Into an hourglass ... *Henry V*, I.i.11–31

This well-known passage is generally cited to illustrate the essential qualities of Shakespeare's drama – as indeed it does – but it can also be seen as an indication of the playwright's directorial function, which is clearly to orchestrate the actors' delivery of their speeches in such a way as to provide the most imaginatively and emotionally suggestive stimulus for the minds of the audience. At the same time it is probable, particularly with a troupe of actors stable enough for Shakespeare to write parts for particular performers, that moves and gestures were left for the actors to decide themselves – as indeed Quince does with his 'tedious brief scene of young Pyramus and his love Thisbe: very tragical mirth'.

That this absence of visual spectacle was to some extent a deliberate choice can be indicated by the existence of the court masque, which stands as the complete opposite of the public theatres. Already popular in France, this style of performance, which relied on scenes and elaborate stage machinery, was brought to its height in England by the collaboration of the playwright Ben Jonson with the architect Inigo Jones – which lasted from 1605 to 1634 – and by the musician Thomas Campion. Scenarios rather than plays, the aims of this type of performance can be seen from their titles: *The Masque of Blackness* (1605), where the light of royalty banishes the forces of night, *The Masque of Queens* (1609), where Jonson introduced the grotesque anti-masque, whose hideous disharmony dramatized the urgent need for harmony, which was then provided by the entry of the stately representatives of royalty, or *Pleasure Reconciled to Virtue* (1609). Moral allegories glorifying their royal audience, these included spectacular scenic effects of whole mountains opening up mechanically, realistic locations changing instantaneously through shutters, or elaborate perspective settings. The costumes were specially designed, splendid and fantastical. Movement was extensive and had to be carefully choreographed if the effects described in the texts were to be achieved, and while formal dances – which were a central part of the masque and symbolized the forces of harmony – would have been based on standard dance steps of the age, the grotesque capers of the anti-masques were almost certainly designed for the specific performance. In short, the masque required many of the skills and the sort of centralized control of the performance as a whole that we associate with contemporary directors. While Jonson was a playwright, and he was followed by other dramatists like William Davenant and James Shirley, masque scripts contained little in the way of dialogue; heavily poetic speeches were chanted or declaimed; and the main appeal to the ears was not words but music. Unlike the public Elizabethan theatre, then, this was not a playwright-manager's theatre (Shakespeare was also a stock-holder in the Globe); but for possibly the first time, responsibility for a production, and for coordinating the activities of the other experts, lay with a person whose primary job was neither as playwright nor as actor, but in a separate category: the masque presenter.

At the same time, masques began to appear as dramatic devices within ordinary plays, as in Cyril Tourneur's *The Revenger's Tragedy* (1606) or Thomas Middleton's *Women Beware Women* (1625), and in Shakespeare's last play, *The Tempest*, where there is both an anti-masque figure in Caliban, a discovery (a mountain opens to reveal the lovers playing chess in a cave) and a typical masque dance (goddesses summoned to bless the marriage), as well as significant use of music. Although remaining modest parts of Renaissance plays, in directorial terms this expansion of different theatrical elements is a sign of things to come. Masques were also theatres of high illusion, and have been suggested as the origin of the proscenium arch: a scenic innovation that became a standard part of theatre-building in the eighteenth and nineteenth centuries, as performances became increasingly illusionistic.[6]

The seventeenth and eighteenth centuries: Enlightenment and the actor-manager

If Shakespeare's was the prototype of the playwright-manager theatre – reviving the putative situation in Classical Greek theatre (and followed, of course, by Molière in France) – the dramatist William Davenant (1606–68), whose masques such as *Britannia Triumphans* (1638) were the last to be performed before the Civil War and Cromwell closed the theatres in England, continued this tradition after the Restoration. With a patent awarding his company a monopoly on theatre performance in London, Davenant founded the theatre in England with changeable scenery, in some ways a forerunner of the continental court theatres, the best preserved being Drottningholm in Sweden (1766) with its sliding scenery and stage machinery. But as well as producing his own plays and collaborating with Dryden, the leading neo-classical dramatist of heroic tragedy, Davenant also staged new works by younger playwrights. In staging scripts by others and coordinating the craftsmen producing scenic effects, Davenant is to some degree anticipating the role of a contemporary director. However, there is no record that he interpreted the plays or gave the actors detailed instructions about realizing their roles (both essential functions of the modern director), and while his scenery could be changed during a performance, the actual settings painted on the screens showed standard places that reappeared in play after play.

A similar evolution can be traced in France with Davenant's contemporary, Molière (the stage name taken by Jean-Baptiste Poquelin, 1622–73). Like Davenant, Molière also staged the plays of other dramatists, notably Corneille and the first two tragedies of Racine. But Molière was not only the manager of his own acting company. Also a brilliant comic actor, and author of *commedia dell'arte*-inspired comedies that became almost instant classics, which he produced in addition to performing the lead roles himself, Molière qualifies as the complete man-of-the-theatre: the prototype of the sort of theatrical *auteur* represented by a contemporary like the Quebec director Robert Lepage. What Molière's plays call for, from the 1659 *Les précieuses ridicules* (*The Affected Ladies*) to *The Imaginary Invalid* (1673, the year of his death), is a physical style of acting, aided only by costume, in which movements and physical display are defined by the dialogue. This *commedia*-based performance would have been pre-set, with stock characterization and gestures, removing the need for extensive acting rehearsals that are a large part of the modern director's function, while the lighting for Molière's productions was the standard candles of the time, and his scenery would have been stock sets. So while he combined the roles of actor and playwright-manager, Molière's significance is as dramatist, not director.

The first to be called a 'director' (albeit by a mid-twentieth-century theatre historian[7]) is the English actor-manager David Garrick (1717–79). Like Molière, he was a prolific dramatist as well as actor and manager of his own theatre, the Theatre Royal, Drury Lane, in which he was a shareholder as well as taking over as producer in 1747. At the same time, his plays were largely vehicles to showcase his own acting, and quickly vanished from the stage. His importance was as an actor and as a theatre manager; and his influence in eighteenth-century theatre, not only in England but also in Europe, was significant. He created what can only be called a personality cult, which restored moral respectability to the English stage, as well as setting standards of natural expression in acting on which whole treatises were based. So Dr Johnson quipped that 'his profession made him rich and he made his profession respectable', while after Garrick's death, no less than the statesman Edmund Burke eulogized him, as having 'raised the character of his profession to the rank of a liberal art, not only by his talents, but by the regularity and probity of his life and the elegance of his manners'.[8] For others it was Garrick's extraordinary acting talent, which appeared 'natural' according to the criteria of the time, yet was clearly controlled because of the extreme flexibility of his emotional expression, that made him a source for theoretical ideas. As the French philosopher and art critic Denis Diderot announced, witnessing Garrick perform 'alone made it just as worthwhile to make the journey to England as all the remains of ancient Rome made it worth the journey to Italy'.[9] Indeed Garrick was the first real-life actor to appear as the title character in a play, the part of Garrick being a vehicle for E. A. Sothern in 1864.

Garrick's acting was the culmination of a whole movement in the mid eighteenth century, which could be seen as a paradigm-shift in English theatre. The old style of acting, based on oratory and rhetoric, which had found its fullest expression in tragedy, had already been challenged by Charles Macklin (1699–1797), who made his name by a radically naturalistic portrayal of Shylock, based on research into Italian Jews, reversing the standard comic rendition. Garrick was coached by Macklin, and as another of Macklin's pupils describes: 'It was his manner to check all the cant and cadence of tragedy; he would bid his pupil first speak the passage as he would in common life, if he had occasion to pronounce the same words, and then giving them more force, but preserving the same accent, to deliver them on the stage.'[10] This naturalness was allied to sentiment (the sensibility of the age) and – just three years after his debut on the London stage – Garrick published *An Essay on Acting.* This links physicality with feelings in a phrase like 'bodily emotions' and suggests that he first built his roles with specific physical gestures expressing intense emotions, reacting to the character's situation, out of which he developed a rounded personality: an action-centred method creating character that has been seen as anticipating Stanislavsky's 'method'.[11]

Garrick on creating a role

Acting is an Entertainment of the Stage, which by calling in the Aid and Assistance of Articulation, Corporeal Motion and Ocular Expression, imitates, assumes, or puts on the various mental and bodily Emotions arising from the various Humours, Virtues and Vices incident to human Nature ...

> Now to Macbeth. – When the Murder of Duncan is committed, from an immediate Consciousness of the Fact, his Ambition is ingulph'd at that Instant, by the Horror of the Deed; his faculties are intensely riveted to the Murder alone, without having the least Consolation of the consequential Advantages, to comfort him in the Exigency. He should at that time be a moving Statue, or indeed a petrify'd Man; his Eyes must Speak, and Tongue be metaphorically Silent: his Ears must be sensible of imaginary Noises, and deaf to the present and audible Voice of his Wife; his Attitudes must be quick and permanent; his Voice articulately trembling, and confusedly intelligible.
>
> David Garrick, *An Essay on Acting*, London, 1744, 5, 7–9

While producing and acting in all his own plays – writing over twenty farces and social comedies between 1740 and 1775 – Garrick's main focus was on Shakespeare; and he is credited with restoring Shakespeare to the English stage, advertising his *Macbeth* as being 'revived as Shakespeare wrote it'.[12] But strikingly, apart from his Richard III, all his characters were in contemporary eighteenth-century dress, including Hamlet, Macbeth and Romeo, as well as Jaffier in Thomas Otway's *Venice Preserved.* And the settings for these plays seem to have been equally contemporary, with Romeo's discovery of Juliet (still alive in Garrick's version, allowing a sentimental apotheosis before death) taking place in a very eighteenth-century neo-classical mausoleum.[13] Even when the setting was a castle, as with Hamlet's Elsinore, stage-paintings show very contemporary ships in the background of the battlemented walls. This contemporaneity may have been largely due to the eighteenth-century theatre's use of stock scenes. As one manual stated: 'The stage should be furnished with a competent number of painted scenes, sufficient to answer the purposes of all the plays in stock, in which there is no great variety, being easily reduced to the following classes. 1st, Temples. 2ndly, Tombs. 3rdly, City Walls [etc.].'[14] However, the connection with the audience in terms of costume and setting also contributed to Garrick's naturalism. Naturalism of course is one of those terms that are relative, shifting its meaning with every historical period or even national context. Notions of historical authenticity are even more tendentious (an etching of Garrick in the title role of *The Roman Father* shows a fantastical neo-classical breastplate, with a highly decorated knee-length skirt standing out stiffly beneath and helmet surmounted by a fountain of feathers). It was particularly in his Shakespearean roles that Garrick made his reputation for both natural expression and intense emotion, but precisely here authenticity was communicated through illusion. The apparent naturalness of his acting was accompanied by the use of machinery and stage tricks: for instance, the invention of a 'wig-lifter' for his 1773 *Hamlet*, a mechanism hidden beneath his wig which gave a literal hair-raising effect when meeting the Ghost.

For David Garrick as Hamlet, Act I, Scene iv, engraving by James McArdell (1729–65) after Benjamin Wilson (1721–88), see http://hamletguide.com/film/images/David_Garrick_as_Hamlet.jpg.

As can be seen from the many stage-paintings of Garrick's performances by Wilson and Zoffany, the settings represented are painterly and realistic. Similarly for his 1748 *Romeo and Juliet*, in the final scene, moonlit trees and extremely naturalistic trailing foliage surround the tomb. In this, Garrick was echoing French scenic practice of the time, which he was soon to surpass.

In 1751 Garrick was responsible for reviving the Drury Lane pantomimes – a tradition that was to reach its highpoint in the 1880s and last into the 1920s. Started by John Rich, who had introduced the Harlequinade to England in 1717 (with Rich himself as a dancing Harlequin, a non-speaking role he continued to perform until 1760), these shows developed into lavish displays of stagecraft where whole battles or volcanoes and other natural phenomena were represented with lavish stage effects. Alexander Pope even included Rich in his satiric verse epic of 1729 *The Dunciad*, lampooning him as the theatre man who, instead of challenging the public intellectually, 'Rides in the whirlwind, and directs the storm'. And this style of spectacle was adopted in direct competition with Rich by Colley Cibber (playwright, adapter of Shakespeare, Poet Laureate and theatre manager – and the anti-hero of Pope's *Dunciad*), who preceded Garrick at Drury Lane. Just as with the Jacobean court masques, as grand visual pageant these pantomimes required more than simply a stage-manager, and Pope's verb would be accurate for today's use of the term 'director', although in a show that imported specialist acts there would have been little interpretative activity or rehearsing of actors.

But, in addition to orchestrating visual effects in his pantomimes, Garrick's own process of role-creation in which the pattern of his emotions would be developed through careful and detailed textual analysis in conjunction with his application of specific techniques of stagecraft, particularly for his Shakespearean roles, is also part of the technical preparation of the twentieth-century director. In addition, as Garrick's diaries and papers show, he was involved in all the daily duties of theatrical management. He was responsible for deciding the programme and negotiating with dramatists, casting, supervising rehearsals, and coordinating scenographers and tradesmen. He also wrote special prologues, provided critical assistance to contemporary editors of Shakespeare, and composed newspaper puffs to advertise his performances. Although he remained an actor and the focus of every performance, revolving his stagings around himself, he otherwise combined the duties and skills of several figures in the twentieth-century theatre: the contemporary director and the producer, with aspects of the dramaturge and the press agent.

Introducing scenery: Philip Jacques de Loutherbourg

With the emphasis on visual spectacle in the annual pantomime, as well as his use of stock but elaborately painted settings for the drama he produced, including Shakespeare, it is hardly surprising that Garrick hired the scenic innovator Philip Jacques de Loutherbourg, bringing him over from Switzerland, and paying him a princely salary of £500 a year to install his stage inventions at Drury Lane and superintend the scene-painting. De Loutherbourg had made his reputation for reproducing natural effects (particularly moon and stars or the illusion of running water) and his illusionary art was displayed in the December 1773 staging of *The Christmas Tale* (Garrick lifted the story from Purcell and Dryden's 1691 semi-opera of *King Arthur*), which included nightfall with the moon rising over a forest and the burning of an evil wizard's palace flaring sparks and flames. He used coloured glass slides through which lantern-light was projected to create atmospheric effects, developed the thin canvas we now know as a scrim, which was either solid or transparent depending on lighting, and specialized in creating eerie transformations through transparencies with different scenes painted on each side and oscillating between front and back lights. He invented clockwork stage machinery to create moving backgrounds that looked extremely realistic, and arranged wings and flats to create a convincing depth of perspective.

After Garrick's death de Loutherbourg went on to invent a purely mechanical theatre, albeit on a miniature scale, which gave the designer complete control of the performance and where no actors were required, in some important ways prefiguring Gordon Craig's theatrical ideas. This was the *Eidophusikon*, which he opened in 1781 in a house in Leicester Square with a show described in the *Public Advertizer* as 'various imitations of Natural Phenomena represented by moving pictures'. This has been described by several modern commentators as an early precursor of the movies. It seated around 130 people, who looked through a large square peephole at a miniature inner stage about 7 feet wide, 3 feet high and 8 feet deep.

For de Loutherbourg's *Eidophusikon* (Edward Francis Burney, 1782), see www.cichw.net/montheat/watershocon1.JPG.

The opening show was five scenes of picturesque landscapes with changing light or weather. Each scene used controlled lighting on three-dimensional models and clockwork automata, magic lantern slides, coloured silk filters and painted transparencies, as well as a sound system. The following year de Loutherbourg mounted what was his most admired piece, this time an exotic imaginary landscape: a Gothic movie scene giving physical form to the Pandemonium episode from Milton's *Paradise Lost.* As a newspaper review of 1782 described it:

> In the foreground of a vista stretching an immeasurable length between mountains, ignited from their bases to their lofty summits, with many-coloured flame, a chaotic mass rose in dark majesty, which gradually assumed form until it stood, the interior of a vast temple of gorgeous architecture, bright as molten brass, seemingly composed of unconsuming and unquenchable fire. In this tremedrous scene, the effect of coloured glasses before the lamps was fully displayed: which being hidden from the audience, threw their whole influence upon the scene as it rapidly changed, now to a sulpherous blue, then to a lurid red, and again to a pale vivid light, and ultimately to a mysterious combination of the glasses, such as a bright furnace exhibits in fusing various metals. The sound which accompanied the wondrous picture struck the astonished ear of the spectator as no less preternatural; for, to add a more aweful character to peals of thunder, and the accompaniments of all the hollow machinery that hurled balls and stones with indescribable rumbling and noise, an expert assistant swept his thumb over the surface of a tambourine, which produced a variety of groans that struck the imagination as issuing from infernal spirits.[15]

Then in 1786 de Loutherbourg created a true mechanized drama, which showed one of the great shipwrecks of the period – the sinking of an Indiaman, *The Halsewell*, in which over 300 people perished – complete with rising storm, the tempest-tossed vessel at sea, and 'close up' images of sailors struggling on the deck and fearful passengers praying below (represented by mechanical simulacra). The designer had become a director, at least of a toy theatre. But this was a one-off, and the *Eidophusikon* remains a unique oddity.

Settings and spectacle represent a divide between different types of theatre-manager. Typically it was the actor-managers – or, as here, a designer-manager – who emphasized spectacle, with poet-managers or (as we shall see) the German dramaturge-managers reacting against scenic realism. So the German *Intendant* Lessing cited Cibber, lamenting the new fashion for illusionistic settings (despite his own responsibility for competition in spectacle):

Gotthold Lessing

– Some have insinuated, that fine scenes proved the ruin of acting. – In the reign of Charles I. there was nothing more than a curtain of very coarse stuff, upon the drawing up of which, the stage appeared either with bare walls on the sides, coarsly matted, or covered with tapestry; so that for the place originally represented, and all the successive changes, in which the poets of those times freely indulged themselves, there was nothing to help the spectator's understanding, or to assist the actor's performance, but bare imagination. – The spirit and judgement of the actors supplied all deficiencies, and made as some would insinuate, plays more intelligible without scenes than they afterwards were with them. (Cibber's 'Lives of the Poets of G. B. and Ir.' Vol. II. p. 78.79.)

Hamburgische Dramaturgie, 5 February 1768, 80

Henry Irving: the nineteenth-century actor-manager

In England as much as in Europe, the nineteenth-century theatre was the province of great actor-managers, with Henry Irving – the most successful (and the first theatre artist to gain the recognition of a knighthood) – offering a good example of the type. Irving's training was typical, and demonstrates the continuity of theatrical tradition through the nineteenth century. His theatrical education was a roll-call of the actor-managers who had already won fame in the period. Starting off with R. H. Wyndham's company, Irving served his apprenticeship with E. A. Sothern, Dion Boucicault, Charles Fechter and Edwin Booth (who much later, in 1881, was to act in *Othello* at Irving's theatre, the London Lyceum, with the two of them alternating Iago and the Moor night by night). Brought to the Lyceum in 1871 by the manager H. L. Bateman, Irving made his mark in a role that was to become his signature piece: the villain in *The Bells* (an adaptation of a French melodrama, *Le Juif polonaise*). Three years later he was leading the Lyceum company, acting the title roles of Shakespeare's major tragedies – most notably Richard III in 1877 – and by 1878 he had taken over the Lyceum as 'sole Lessee and manager' (as proclaimed by the playbill for his December 1878 *Hamlet*).

Irving was hardly a matinee idol, and indeed his figure (as numerous cartoons attest) could verge on the grotesque. When explaining his acting, one witness from 1883 feels it necessary to start with a physical description of a face 'so finely and powerfully moulded that it is far from being plain ... a broad jaw, a low skull, and the eyes set close under the brows' while 'the singularity of its form startles us out of realizing that it is ugly'.[16] As all the critics of the time recognized, it was Irving's energy and intensity that focused attention.

His acting in *The Bells*, revived at the Lyceum in 1879 and still in the repertoire almost thirty years later, was hardly naturalistic. As one of the people who acted with him admiringly described it: 'Irving set out to wring our hearts, not to give us a clever exhibition of antics such as a murderer would be likely to go through.'[17] For Irving himself, the primary aim was 'the representation of passion', while an actor had to develop 'a double consciousness' – giving his emotions full rein while remaining aware of the communicative techniques for expressing such emotional states.[18] And this demonstrative and highly emotive style of performance was strikingly unique, as shown by the description of a scene in which the villain, Matthias, sits unlacing his boots while talk turns to the storm in which the Jewish traveller disappeared.

Melodramatic performance: the Victorian actor-manager

The way Irving did it ... was in every gesture, every half move, in the play of his shoulders, legs, head and arms, mesmeric in the highest degree ... We suddenly saw those fingers stop their work; the crown of the head suddenly seems to glitter and become frozen – and then, at the pace of the slowest and most terrified snail, the two hands, still motionless and dead, were seen to be coming up the side of the leg ... the whole torso of the man, also seeming frozen, was gradually seen to be drawing up and back.

Once in that position – motionless – eyes fixed ahead of him and fixed on us all – there he sat for the space of ten to twelve seconds, which, I can assure you, seemed to us all like a lifetime, and then said – and said in a voice deep and overwhelmingly beautiful: 'Oh, you were talking of that – were you?' ...

And then the next step in his dance began ... He glides up to a standing position: never has anyone seen another rising figure which slid slowly up like that: with one arm slightly raised, with sensitive hand speaking of far-off apprehended sounds, he asks, in the voice of some woman who is frightened, yet does not wish to frighten those with her: 'Don't you hear the sound of sledgebells on the road?'

Edward Gordon Craig, *Henry Irving*, 56–8

At the same time Irving was frequently criticized for putting himself in front of the play as a whole: 'Only too often does Mr Irving act his part while he does not act the play. He thrills, or touches, or terrifies the spectator by means which we know on reflection could not have produced the effects they are supposed to have had on the other personages of the story. To this we owe those grotesque mannerisms ... which would shock the public ... if it were not for the mysterious impression they produce of self-revelation in the actor.'[19] But this lack of psychological realism was the essence of the actor-manager; it was in fact a tribute to his cult of personality when Irving was attacked because he 'never succeeds in disguising himself for an instant' and 'plays entirely and solely to the audience'.[20]

In short, as with all other actor-managers, Irving's productions were organized almost solely around himself, as an anecdote about rehearsals for another standard Lyceum piece, *The Corsican Brothers*, illustrates: running through the duel scene, the actor fighting with Irving broke off and asked, 'Don't you think, Guv'nor, a few rays of the moon might shine on me – it shines equally on the just and the unjust.'[21] In this case, apparently, Irving agreed to share the limelight a little.

They also privileged spectacle. For instance, a play originally presented some decades before by Edmund Kean, *The Corsican Brothers* – where Irving played both twins – lacked the provocative effect it had had over a generation earlier; and Irving made up for the familiar text by scenic spectacle. So in one scene the audience were presented with a mirror image of the Lyceum auditorium, in full perspective with practicable boxes seating a whole stage audience, children representing adults at the rear; and this was changed – with the help of no fewer than ninety stagehands, thirty gas men to handle the flexible hoses and gaslights, and fifteen property men – in under forty seconds behind a front cloth that rose to reveal a forest with free-standing trees, in between and behind which actors could pass, with thick snow (salt) covering the whole stage floor.

The transition from traditional staging

The state of this traditional theatre that was to be superseded by the contemporary director is described by Gordon Craig: a rising young actor at the close of the nineteenth century who, in response to the shortcomings of the standard system, was to become the most extreme advocate of the director's art. Craig, the son of Ellen Terry, Irving's leading lady, served his theatrical apprenticeship at the Lyceum Theatre. His first independent position was with the W. S. Hardy Shakespeare Company, which he joined in 1894 to act the parts of Hamlet and Romeo; and as Craig recounts, no member of the cast had a complete text of the plays: only cue scripts. Still occasionally used in British provincial repertory theatre as late as the 1950s, these contained only the individual actor's lines, together with their cues. In addition, as Craig described the production process, at his arrival Mrs Hardy (who was playing Gertrude) asked him to 'tell us exactly what you want, and we will fit in' – following the standard practice where the lead actor controlled the tone and set the pace for the production – while the rehearsals for *Hamlet* took just three days, and for *Romeo and Juliet* just two. Craig went on to assert that, 'The actors between 1800 and 1900 never made new bits – it was ever the same old show done differently.'[22] Craig was exaggerating somewhat, seeking to justify his new Art of the Theatre by contrast, since actor-managers, as we have seen, did indeed foster new forms of stagecraft. Yet this still serves as a benchmark to illustrate the qualities brought to the theatre by the figure of the director.

Of course eras are not neatly divided; and the closer one comes to the present the more the history of theatre seems to bifurcate, even without taking account of the complex fragmentation and multiple rejection of tradition that characterizes the modernist movement and the whole twentieth- and twenty-first-century theatre. So, almost exactly 100 years before the beginning of Irving's career, as we shall see, the position of the independent director was beginning to take shape in Germany. Similarly, the traditional actor-manager continued to rule the stage in Britain, and to some extent in America, up until the mid twentieth century.

The continuation is most obvious in John Martin-Harvey (1863–1944), one of the most famous British actor-managers of the twentieth century, who started his career with Henry Irving's company, and continued the Victorian tradition up to the Second World War. Taking over the Lyceum after Irving's death in 1905, he continued to revive Irving's star vehicles – including *The Lyons Mail* and even *The Bells* – with himself in Irving's roles, and using the same props and settings; and like Irving, Martin-Harvey was knighted in 1921. He made his name with *The Only Way*, an adaptation of Charles Dickens' *A Tale of Two Cities* first produced at the Lyceum in 1899, where he played the young self-sacrificing hero, Sydney Carton: a role he continued to play until his retirement in 1939 at the age of seventy-six. He also transformed Bernard Shaw's American quasi-melodrama *The Devil's Disciple* into a vehicle for his romantic acting. Like other actor-managers, he made a career out of touring the United States and Canada (where he was particularly popular) as well as Britain, playing a limited repertoire that included *Hamlet* and *The Taming of the Shrew*, and always *The Only Way*, which he once claimed to have performed over 3,000 times. The equivalent in America would have been James O'Neill (1846–1920), memorialized in *Long Day's Journey into Night* by his son Eugene O'Neill. Having apprenticed as a Shakespearean actor with Edwin Booth (just like Irving), he took on the part of the quintessentially romantic hero, Edmond Dantes, in an adaptation of

Dumas' *The Count of Monte Cristo* in 1883 (dramatized by another actor-manager, Charles Fechter, who had died four years earlier), which became the only role he was identified with, playing it over 6,000 times.

Other actor-mangers included Herbert Beerbohm Tree (1853–1917), who designed and built his own London theatre, His Majesty's. While specializing in Shakespeare, Tree was best known for costume roles such as the evil hypnotist Svengali in *Trilby* or Fagin in his dramatization of Dickens' *Oliver Twist*, though he also premiered Shaw's *Pygmalion* as Henry Higgins – famously twisting the ending to suggest the romantic triumph of his role through the return of Eliza Doolittle, so demonstrating the typical type of distortion produced by the actor-manager.

Another who deserves mention as one of the originators of the modern musical theatre is Oscar Asche (1872–1936), who had trained with Beerbohm Tree, and acted in Gordon Craig's 1903 production of Ibsen's *The Vikings at Helgeland*. Together with the actress Lily Brayton, Asche founded his own theatre company in 1904, and began a series of famously spectacular exotic musicals with *Kismet* (1911), which could best be described as a modernization of the Victorian melodrama. Here musical accompaniment to the action and the occasional song had been introduced as a way of circumventing restrictive laws licensing plays in the early nineteenth century, with music being used to cover scene changes and songs not fully integrated with the dialogue or the action. The most extravagant of these was *Chu Chin Chow*, which set a record for the longest running show: 2,238 performances from August 1916 to July 1921. Asche, of course, played centre stage in the lead roles, together with Brayton, but the complexity of the spectacle together with the music (which in this show is almost continuous, with songs that define both character and action) and the dances required a great deal of technical orchestration. And a year after its London opening – anticipating the multiple international franchise productions of contemporary musicals – the show was franchised to New York, with costumes and scenery shipped from London, and with cloned blocking and choreography. As this sort of pre-fixed staging implies, Asche was here serving as one type of modern director; and while the New York version of *Chu Chin Chow* was very clearly identified with his name as its creator, Asche was not acting in it (he of course remained the centre of the stage in London). The reviews barely mentioned the name of the actor playing the main role. In New York all attention was on the spectacle, the camels and the exotic dancers – in other words on the staging and the nature of the piece itself, as is the case with director-driven productions – rather than, as generally with actor-managers, on the central figure and his performance.

The German stage and the function of the *Intendant*

Where the English and most of the European stages of the period were controlled through the eighteenth and nineteenth centuries by actor-managers, the situation in the German theatre was very different. This was largely due to the way Germany was divided into small dukedoms or princely states, which brought the theatres under the control of autocratic rulers. Having been shown the effectiveness of the stage for propaganda by the plays performed to promote the Catholic counter-reformation, these autocratic rulers, feeling the threat of the French Revolution – Pierre Beaumarchais' play attacking the aristocracy being popularly believed to have given impetus to the 1789 uprising – were as concerned to neutralize the potential radicalism of theatre as to control local newspapers. And the only practical way of ensuring a positive message from the stage (which subsequently led to theatre in Germany being seen as a 'Moral Tribune') was to have the theatre manager as part of their entourage.

The function of the director is usually thought of as called into being only in the latter part of the nineteenth century, by the emergence of naturalism as the dramatic form of the age. This style of drama, pioneered by Ibsen, required objectivity in presentation and individualized characterization, as well as placing significant emphasis on social context (both in environmental and biological terms). On the stage such qualities translate into scenic and psychological detail, creating a demand for something more than a stage-manager. And it is no accident that Germany was the first country outside Scandinavia to stage almost every one of Ibsen's naturalistic plays, since Germany had already introduced a close equivalent of the artistic director at the top of the theatrical hierarchy, long before Ibsen inaugurated the naturalistic movement with *A Doll's House* in 1879 (produced in Munich in 1880). These were the *Intendants*: superintendents, public bureaucrats appointed in practically all German court theatres after 1815.[23] One of the first of these *Intendants* was Wolfgang von Goethe, appointed to the position at the Weimar Court Theatre in 1791, because of his reputation as a dramatist (the Romantic *Sturm und Drang* play *Götz von Berlichingen*, 1771; and particularly the classical verse plays *Iphigenia auf Tauris*, 1787, and *Torquato Tasso*, 1790). While managing the Weimar Court Theatre, he wrote his influential ninety-one 'Rules for actors' that would set the standard for the acting of tragedy in Germany for almost a century.

Goethe's 'Rules for actors', 1803

Based on the premise that a performance should not simply copy nature but unite it with the ideal (and reflect hierarchical social concepts), Goethe's 'Rules for actors' are designed to encourage beautiful poses and smooth movements, with 'the chest always in full view of the spectator'. The Rules also clearly suggest that the staging Goethe developed was highly stylized, since his positioning of actors followed principles such as: 'the actor who stands on the left should be careful not to approach too closely the one on the right [because] the person of higher social scale (women, elders, noblemen) always occupies the right side' of the acting area. There was no attempt to create an illusionist stage picture: his actors were required always to show awareness of their audience, and speak directly to them, while 'The stage is to be regarded as a figureless tableau for which the actor supplies the figure.'

Goethe is frequently cited as the very first director in European theatre (although, as we have seen, Garrick has a slightly earlier claim in England). And indeed Goethe's 'Rules for actors' set out principles of aesthetic unity for stage production, anticipating Craig's demand over a century later. Other *Intendants* introduced different qualities. For instance, August Iffland (the actor who had created the role of Franz Mohr in Schiller's *Die Räuber* – appointed to the Berlin Royal Theatre in 1796) became known for a series of visually spectacular productions that set a standard to be emulated by subsequent German directors. By contrast, Gotthold Lessing, the *Intendant* of the newly founded Nationaltheater at Hamburg, was responsible for the development of a new style of drama – bourgeois tragedy – with his play *Miss Sara Sampson* (1755), as well as revolutionizing aesthetics with his cross-disciplinary book *Laoköon, oder Über die Grenzen der Malerei und Poesie* (1766). As the author of a collection of theoretical letters defining new forms of drama in the *Hamburgische Dramaturgie* (1767–69), he had particular influence.

Distance from the creative elements of the stage became almost standard over the nineteenth century. Being part of the bureaucratic hierarchy, these *Intendants* tended to come from outside the theatre, and – once appointed – to stay back-stage, unlike the earlier actor-*Intendants*. Not even playwrights, like Goethe or Lessing, they tended to be poets and novelists such as Heinrich Laube, who had been active in the Young German movement of the 1830s before becoming *Intendant* of the Vienna Burgtheater in the 1850s, or even librarians like Franz von Dingelstedt, who progressed from the Munich Court Theatre to the Weimar Court Theatre, then to the Vienna Opera and (following Laube) to the Burgtheater. Similarly Otto Brahm, who founded the Freie Bühne in Berlin in 1889 (in direct imitation of André Antoine's Théâtre Libre (1887)), to promote the new naturalistic drama, started off as a drama critic for the leading Berlin newspapers.

The critic as director: Gotthold Lessing at the Hamburg Nationaltheater

At the very beginning of the ascendance of the director-manager – in the shape of the German *Intendant* – we have Gotthold Lessing's theoretical journal, the *Hamburgische Dramaturgie*. Responding to the major theatrical issue of the time, these essays reinterpreted Aristotle to argue against the neo-classical tragedies of Racine, Voltaire and Corneille, and in favour of the contemporary bourgeois drama initiated by his own plays. To some extent this rejection of French neo-classicism was designed to encourage a specifically modern and German drama for the new Nationaltheater that Lessing helped to found and managed.

Gotthold Lessing on dramatic genres and contemporaneity

I would remind my reader that these pages represent nothing less than a dramatic system. (95th Piece, 29 March 1768)

When we find so little objectionable with the depiction of Roman or Greek manners and customs in Tragedy, why not also in Comedy? Where is the rule, if it is a rule at all, that the scenes of the first should be set in a faraway land, among foreign people, yet the scenes of the other in our home? Whence comes the compulsion, with which we burden the playwright, in that one to depict so precisely as possible the customs of those people, among whom he has set his action, when in this one we only demand to have our own customs represented? . . .

. . . Certainly local customs require local events too, yet even so, if only with these can Tragedy reach its goals most easily and surely, then it has to be better, despite all the difficulties that come from using such an action . . . Local customs are also easier in staging and promote the illusion for spectators.

So why should the tragic author give up this important double advantage? . . . Indeed, the Greeks themselves had nothing else than their own customs as a dramatic basis, not only in Comedy, but also in Tragedy. (96th Piece, 1 April 1768 and 97th Piece, 5 April 1768)

I have completely no idea from where so many comic playwrights have taken the rule, that at the end of the play evil characters either get punished or reform themselves. In Tragedy this rule might have more validity; it could reconcile us with Fate and transform disapproval into Pity. But . . . if the different characters that I bring together in an action just bring this action to a conclusion, why should they not remain as they were? Otherwise, of course, the action must consist of something more than a simple collision of characters: one which can be ended in no other way than through the yielding and changing of one part of these characters; and a play that has little or nothing more than this can never reach its goal. (99th Piece, 12 April 1768)

Hamburgische Dramaturgie, 1769

Lessing is sometimes hailed as the originator of the contemporary dramaturge (as known in the European theatre), or literary manager (the title of the equivalent post in British theatre), since he specifically said he was 'neither an actor nor a dramatist', pointing out that writing plays had never been his primary occupation.[24] Instead, Lessing designated himself as a critic; and his *Dramaturgie* is designed as a 'critical register of all produced plays [at the Nationaltheater under his tenure], accompanying every step of the art both of the playwright as of the actors' (102nd and 103rd Piece, 19 April 1768). It is divided into 104 sections or 'Stücke' (plays) although the actual number of plays considered and performed over the two years covered by Lessing's notes was actually fifty-eight – including three of his own plays.

Where Aristotle was the first known theatre theorist, basing his principles (the unities, the concept of *katharsis*, etc.) on the analysis of Classical Greek tragedies, Lessing (focused on dramatic genres) must count as the first modern theorist. His points, however abstract, are always attached to discussions of specific plays, and in a theatrical context where neo-classicism was giving ground to more naturalistic and contemporary works, this focus was at the centre of an aesthetic revolution paving the way for modern theatre. In a very real sense the next step was represented by Zola's theories on naturalism just a century later.

Styles and types of theatre management/direction through history

- Classical Greece: possibly the poet/playwright as orchestrator of the chorus, supplemented by a technician
- Classical Rome: the actor-manager, with the introduction of a star system (Roscius); possibly some control of staging by the playwright
- Medieval: a mix, depending on dramatic form – actor-manager for secular performances; a producer/coordinator for pageants, ranging to a director of the overall staging (possibly also blocking actors' moves, although much of the action would be traditional and pre-set) who manages stage effects.
- Renaissance: primarily a playwright-manager, recognizing the relative importance of the words over spectacle, but with largely independent acting, and in the court masques a presenter, choreographing movement and coordinating with the designer/architect.
- Age of Enlightenment: actor-manager – reintroduction of a star system. But the culture of sentiment, requiring emotional authenticity in acting, leads to the star actor directing the interpretation of a play and the acting of his troupe as well as scenic effects, establishing many of the techniques of the modern director. The introduction of realistic and illusionistic scenery suggests the possibility of a designer-manager/director.
- Nineteenth century: continuation of the actor-manager, but with the development of alternative structures towards the end of the Victorian period: the bureaucrat-manager (Germany: generally drawn from literary figures, like Lessing and Goethe); the commercial-manager or impresario, particularly in America; the artist-manager (Wagner); with each of these leading to prototypes for the modern director.

For the continuing development of the director's art, Lessing's theoretical context for the new forms of drama and performance had to be expanded. This was provided by three writers who, while steeped in theatre, only worked tangentially on the stage. It was Emile Zola (1840–1902) who offered a theoretical base for naturalism. While his output included a number of plays, the best known – *Thérèse Raquin*, 1873; *Nana*, 1881; *Germinal*, 1888 – are all dramatizations of his novels (the latter two being part of the immense *Rougon-Macquart* cycle for which he is most celebrated). By far the most significant offshoot from Wagner came through Adolphe Appia, whose whole concept of theatre was based on his designs for Wagner's operas – and on the complete repudiation of Wagner's staging. Yet Appia's actual theatre output was minimal: directing two productions for Dalcroze's institute in Hellerau (1912, 1913), one production of *Tristan* at La Scala (1923) and two from Wagner's Ring Cycle in Basle (both 1925), plus designs for just two produced pieces, Claudel's *Tidings Brought to Mary* at Hellerau and Aeschylus' *Prometheus* in Basle. Similarly Gordon Craig, who redefined theatre as an art and did more than virtually anyone else to justify the role of the modern theatre director, himself only directed six pieces after ceasing to act: two Purcell operas, *Dido and Aeneas* and *The Masque of Love*, followed by Handel's *Acis and Galatea* (1900, 1901, 1902), reintroducing baroque opera into the English repertoire, one Ibsen play and one Shakespeare (*The Vikings* and *Much Ado*; 1903), plus *Hamlet* for Stanislavsky (1912) and Ibsen's *The Crown Pretenders* (1926).

These three theorists, and their influence, mark a completely new departure in Western theatre: the dominance of the director. At the same time, while Zola represents the continuation of a movement started by Lessing over a century before, where dramatic themes and social commentary were the focus of naturalism, and the staging – developed by André Antoine and Konstantin Stanislavsky – was correspondingly realistic and psychological, the line initiated by Wagner and followed in their own ways by Appia and Craig, was primarily based on aesthetics, working towards a new definition of the theatre as art.

Further reading

While many studies of theatre history have been published, there are few books on the development of the director, or the historical position of the director. A signal exception is Kalman A. Burnim's *David Garrick: Director* (University of Pittsburgh Press, 1961), which deals in detail with eighteenth-century staging practices, and shows how these were employed by the greatest actor of the period. Almost all historical surveys deal with stage forms and styles of performance; and while there is generally little mention of directors before the twentieth century, this information is important as context. The standard overview is Oscar Brockett's *History of the Theatre* (Boston: Allyn and Bacon, first published in 1968 and continually revised, the most recent edition being 2008 with Franklin Hildy). There are also detailed studies of theatre in the various periods. Some of the most relevant are:

Beare, William. *The Roman Stage*, London: Methuen, 1968
Beer, Josh. *Sophocles and the Tragedy of Athenian Democracy*, Westport, CT: Praeger, 2004
Foulkes, F. J. *Lessing and the Drama*, Oxford: Clarendon Press, 1981
Hopkins, D. J. *City/Stage/Globe: Performance and Space in Shakespeare's London*, New York: Routledge, 2008.

Chapter 2

The rise of the modern director

Towards the end of the nineteenth century, theatrical conditions fostered the emergence of the modern director. Already foreshadowed by the *Intendant* system, established in Germany almost exactly a hundred years earlier, the earliest came out of that system: Georg II, Duke of Saxe-Meiningen (1826–1914). He was followed by a group of near contemporaries: André Antoine (1858–1943), working with Zola (1840–1902), Konstantin Stanislavsky (1863–1938), Adolphe Appia (1862–1928) and Gordon Craig (1872–1966). The first who qualify as modern directors, they created and represent the major lines of stylistic development at the beginning of the twentieth century. Each contributes different elements; but as we shall see, all share certain standards in dealing with dramatic material as well as common approaches to staging, and each combines theatre practice and theory: either developing theory from the work, or basing work on theory. Two – Antoine and Stanislavsky – continued to act major parts in the plays they directed, while Craig gave up an acting career specifically to reform the stage. One other influence needs to be noted: as a composer, Richard Wagner (1813–1883) conducted his own operas, and, in adding the function of commissioning settings and costumes as well as orchestrating the singers' moves, offered a model of the theatrical *auteur* that was to be picked up by Appia and Craig, working on principles of design.

The Meiningen Players and the conditions for naturalism

As the owner of his own court theatre, and taking over the position of *Intendant* himself, the Duke of Saxe-Meiningen had complete freedom to experiment. In contrast to the English-speaking theatre's focus on stars, in the form of the actor-manager, the *Intendant* system encouraged ensemble acting. And unity of expression on the stage, as well as ensemble work, was epitomized by his Meiningen Players.

When he inherited the small state of Saxe-Meiningen in 1866, Duke Georg set out to emulate the meticulous research and detailed accuracy that the famous English actor-manager Charles Kean (1811–68) had brought to his staging of historical drama. Kean had reproduced an authentic Norman castle for his 1852 *Macbeth*, and based his setting for Byron's *Sardanapalus* on a recently published account of the excavations at Nineveh in the same year – documenting the historical sources for each production with thirty- and forty-page pamphlets, which earned him election to the Society of Antiquaries in 1857. Similarly the Duke of Saxe-Meiningen anticipated Stanislavsky in creating an archaeologically authentic classical Rome for Shakespeare's *Julius Caesar* in 1874, even moving Caesar's assassination from Shakespeare's symbolically significant setting of the Capitol to its actual historic location at the Theatre of Pompey. As a skilful painter, Georg II is reputed to have designed the scenes, props and costumes for his early stagings at the Meiningen Court Theatre; and even after hiring a scenic atelier in 1872, he continued to influence the highly dramatic settings for the series of major productions that made the reputation of the Meiningen Company. But the Duke was also one of the first to pursue the ideal of unified harmony between the various elements of stage performance, one of his so-called 'Meiningen principles' being that scenery (however spectacular) must never overwhelm the rest of the work.

At the time the visual effects in the Meiningen stagings were seen as being extremely realistic, even though folds on the backdrops might be visible, while to modern eyes the sharp perspectives and strong colours look strikingly romantic. But this impression of pictorial illusion seems in fact largely due to the way crowd scenes were organized.

For an excellent impression of the backdrops painted by Max and Gotthold Brückner for the Meiningen productions, see www.meiningermuseen-thueringen.de/mmuseeneng/kerntext.html#ziel2.

The other major principle Duke Georg followed was that in any production a star, however famous, had to be ready to play a minor role if required. In addition, having the financial resources of a whole state behind the theatre allowed extensive rehearsal up till then unknown in European theatre. This made it possible to develop individual characterization for each of the figures in a crowd, while rehearsals – all conducted in full costume and with complete sets – enabled performers to become so accustomed to the dramatic environment that they could 'live' it. The impression of actuality was accentuated by the authenticity of the props and the costume materials. And there was one directorial innovation that contributed to this illusion of realism: Meiningen crowd scenes were orchestrated in a three-dimensional space extending diagonally from the audience or along multiple axes and off into the wings.

Although eventually becoming standardized, the greater complexity of this orchestration not only was closer to lived experience, but offered an aesthetic complexity that reinforced the harmony of other visual elements.

The major elements of Meiningen staging

- Choreography of crowds on the stage and individualization of the people in the crowds, together with the orchestration of their moves.
- Historically researched settings and costumes for each play (in contrast to the stock scenes and costumes still common at the time).
- Unified harmony in settings, costumes and acting. All aspects of a production should have the same tonal quality.
- Ensemble acting – with interchange of roles and a complete rejection of the star system – and long rehearsal periods with full costumes and sets.
- The human figure in movement as the primary visual unit in any scene.

The early Meiningen repertoire was almost entirely composed of Shakespearean and Romantic historical drama: the (mythical) Athens of *A Midsummer Night's Dream* or Illyria of *The Winter's Tale*; Bohemian castles and the besieged city of Pilsen for Schiller's *Die Räuber* and *Wallenstein*; the medieval cathedral of Kleist's *Käthchen von Heilbronn*; the archaic Jerusalem inhabited by Otto Ludwig's *Die Makkabäer*. And the scenic detail may not have been so different from that of the nineteenth-century English actor-manager Charles Kean. However, Duke Georg's antiquarianism extended beyond the scenery. Combining a similar pictorial accuracy with the realism of acting and placement that he introduced completely superseded his English model. What he achieved was to make the human figure in movement the primary visual unit.

Working together with his third wife, Helene von Heldburg, a former actress with a considerable reputation under the stage name of Ellen Franz, who served as his dramaturge as well as being responsible for actor training in the troupe, and with Ludwig Chronegk serving as tour manager, the Duke of Saxe-Meiningen set the standards for stage realism across Europe. And indeed the Meiningen troupe played a direct role in the development of naturalism. Ibsen's early heroic tragedy *The Pretenders* was entirely suited to the Meiningen historical realism, and after seeing their production in Berlin in 1876 Ibsen's own stage practice changed to incorporate authentic detail in the settings of the sequence of plays initiated by *A Doll's House* in 1879.

Arguably, without the Meiningen example there would have been little in the way of naturalistic stagecraft: the general widespread change it introduced is neatly measured by the difference in the Stockholm premiere of *A Doll's House*, for which the Royal Theatre allowed just two blocking rehearsals, eight general rehearsals and one dress rehearsal (with the inevitable recourse to acting clichés), and the production of *The Enemy of the People* at the same theatre just four years later, where the play was given thirty-two rehearsals, twelve of which (echoing Meiningen practice) were devoted solely to the crowd scene of Act IV. However, Duke Georg learned from Ibsen too, directing the original German production of *Ghosts* in 1886, where their correspondence dealt with the minutiae of wallpaper ('coloured, dark') and furnishings ('style of the First Empire; however ... consistently darker') to recreate the exact ambiance of a country house in western Norway.[1]

The Meiningen influence

The Meiningen Company example spread all through Western theatre, the techniques being also widely copied in America. The manager Augustine Daly became known as the first *régisseur* in the style of Duke Georg, while another manager – Steele Mackay – borrowed the Meiningen technique for presenting crowd scenes in his 1887 production of his own play *Paul Kauvar*; David Belasco was also influenced in his pursuit of realistic stage settings. Even if the star system was still the norm in America, as it was in England, commercial pressures and the requirements of touring the continent had brought a new style of management to theatre in the United States. Instead of the British actor-manager, or the German civil servant *Intendant*, America developed the role of the commercial manager: producer and impresario. The only equivalent in the London theatre of the time was D'Oyly Carte, who developed a company specifically dedicated to producing the Gilbert and Sullivan operettas. But in New York this became the norm, leading to several theatrical monopolies, chief among them the Syndicate (a national theatre and booking alliance, founded in 1896 by Daniel and Charles Frohman, which at its height is reputed to have controlled over 700 theatres in New York and across the United States) and the Shuberts, whose organization took over in 1913 and continued to dominate Broadway theatre until the 1950s.

Most of these impresario theatre-owners had purely commercial interests, but some of the earlier commercial managers became prototypes for the modern director. The best example is Daly, who founded his own acting company in the 1870s and opened Daly's Theatre in New York in 1879 (and another Daly's Theatre in London in 1893). Also an adapter and writer of over ninety scripts with theatrically effective scenes as vehicles for his company – for example the sensation-scene of his 1867 melodrama *Under the Gaslight*, which introduced the trope of the hero roped down to railway tracks with an approaching train thundering up while the heroine rushes to his rescue – Daly was concerned with the unified effect that came from ensemble acting, and rejected the star system. And while the drama he produced was anything but naturalistic, Daly rehearsed each of his plays with careful attention to the actors' interpretation of their roles as well as blocking, and also controlled the costuming and scenery. Because of the general habit of hiring others to stage the repertoire commissioned, the impresario system was also capable of developing the equivalent of the modern director far earlier than in England, as with David Belasco (1853–1931), who was brought to New York by the Frohmans in 1882, and might be seen as an American equivalent to Oscar Asche, the showman of *Chu Chin Chow*.

David Belasco was hired as stage-manager and resident dramatist for the Madison Square Theatre, then Daniel Frohman's Lyceum Theatre, where he produced *Madame Butterfly* (1900, which inspired Puccini). Belasco leased his own theatre where he directed the hit shows *The Darling of the Gods* (1902) and *The Girl of the Golden West* (1905, which Puccini adapted in 1910), finally achieving his own Broadway theatre in 1907. Co-written with Henry De Mille, his seventy or more scripts were primarily opportunities for stage effects, which he created and managed. He hired designers to create extremely realistic scenery, combining painted flats with three-dimension set pieces and actual objects as props, and rehearsed his pieces for ten weeks (instead of the standard four), allowing actors to develop their parts and creating an ensemble effect, which was praised for its realism. He also pioneered the development of electric lighting to create emotional moods. In staging his plays, Belasco was employing most of the techniques of a modern director, but while his staging was naturalistic, the dramatic material was highly stylized, even for his period. However naturalistic the visual appearances of his pieces may have been, the characters were idealized and sentimental, while most of the action was melodrama; and he had become outdated by the Provincetown Players and Eugene O'Neill's early naturalistic pieces, long before his death in 1931.

Arguably, the continuing dominance of the impresario-director in America, like that of the actor-manager in England, effectively prevented those countries from initiating any specific advance in staging or directorial innovation until at least the mid twentieth century. And these partial adoptions of the Meiningen style in America were eclipsed by its hugely productive influence in Germany, France and Russia.

At the same time as fostering Ibsen and the naturalist movement, there were close connections between Duke Georg and the composer Richard Wagner, who was driven to stage his own work because it was so different from the standard opera of the era. The two theatrical reformers exchanged views and saw each other's performances.[2] The Meiningen Company staged *Rheingold* and a series of *Tannhäuser* performances (1855 and again in 1866). When

Wagner rehearsed and staged the premiere of his 'Ring of the Nibelung' in 1875–76 almost half of his Festival Orchestra came from Meiningen, and when Wagner achieved his own theatre in Bayreuth he brought in the same scenic atelier as Duke Georg, giving Wagner's stagings a strong visual similarity to those of the Meiningen Company.

After the 1874 breakthrough in Berlin, the Meiningen Company toured throughout Germany, and from Stockholm (in 1888) via Vienna to Trieste, as well as London, St Petersburg and Moscow (where Stanislavsky saw their work in 1890). They also deeply influenced André Antoine, who spent time with the company in 1888 while touring one of his early Théâtre Libre productions in Brussels. For Antoine it was in particular the orchestration of crowd scenes and the realism of the costumes and settings that carried over into his own explicitly naturalistic theatre – even though he considered the Meiningen realism to be incomplete by the new standards of staging he promoted.

Similarly, the work of the Meiningen Company had significant influence on Konstantin Stanislavsky, who had closely studied their productions of Schiller and Shakespeare during their 1895 season in Russia.[3] In particular, as well as the Meiningen qualities of historical accuracy in set and costume, Stanislavsky took over the use of off-stage sound to create a wider illusion of realism, and the detailed choreography of crowd scenes. While he combined these with elements drawn from Antoine, whose work Stanislavsky had seen during his visits to Paris in the 1880s, his choice of name for the theatre he founded with Vladimir Nemirovich-Danchenko in 1898, the Moscow Art Theatre, specifically links it to the art theatre movement.

So it could be said that the Meiningen system had significant influence on all three of the major theatrical developments that created the modern director; and this tripartite influence will be followed in the next section: the line established by Zola and Antoine; the variation introduced by Stanislavsky, who influenced Lee Strasberg and Harold Clurman; and the alternative established by Wagner, followed by Adolphe Appia and extended by Gordon Craig.

The theory of naturalism: Emile Zola

Naturalism – as a specific focus for representing society, as well as a style of theatrical presentation – was first adopted in drama by Ibsen in Norway, and adapted variously by Anton Chekhov in Russia, Gustav Strindberg in Sweden, Gerhardt Hauptmann in Germany and George Bernard Shaw in England. A pan-European movement, it marked the opening of the modern age.

It corresponded with and responded to the key intellectual and scientific events that defined modernity: from Darwin's *Origin of the Species* or John Stuart Mill's *Essay on Liberty* (justifying the rights of the individual against claims of the state) both in 1859, together with the publication of *Das Kapital* by Karl Marx in 1867, Alexander Bell's invention of the telephone in 1876 followed by Thomas Edison's invention of the phonograph in 1877 and of the electric light in 1879, the same year as Nietzsche's *The Birth of Tragedy*, to Freud's *Interpretation of Dreams* in 1899 and Einstein's 1905 formulation of the theory of relativity. Promoted as a 'scientific' way of exploring moral questions and social conditions in this new scientific and industrial era, naturalism became the voice of modernity, thanks largely to the leading French author of the later nineteenth century, Emile Zola.

Published in French journals between 1875 and 1880, Zola's dramatic criticism was collected under the title *Naturalism in the Theatre* (1881). Together with his Preface to *Thérèse Raquin* (first published as a novel in 1867 then adapted into a play, first performed in 1873), these essays laid the theoretical basis for naturalistic drama.

The principles of naturalism

It seems impossible that the movement of inquiry and analysis, which is precisely the movement of the nineteenth century, can have revolutionized all the sciences and left dramatic art to one side, as if isolated ... An irresistible current carries our society towards the study of reality ... naturalism alone corresponds to our social needs; it alone has deep roots in the spirit of our times; and it alone can provide a living, durable formula for our art, because this formula will express the nature of our contemporary intelligence ...

Take our present environment then, and try to make men live in it: you will write great works ...

The formula will be found; it will be proved that there is more poetry in the little apartment of a bourgeois than in all the empty, worm-eaten palaces of history; in the end we will see that everything meets in the real ...

First the Romantic drama must be abandoned. It would be disastrous for us to take over its outrageous acting, its rhetoric, its inherent thesis of action at the expense of character analysis ... we must go back to tragedy – not, heaven forbid, to borrow more of its rhetoric, its system of confidants, its declaiming, its endless speeches, but to return to its simplicity of action and its unique psychological and physiological study of the characters ... and in a contemporary environment, with the people who surround us.

Emile Zola[4]

Naturalism had already become established in the novel (promoted in particular by Zola's twenty-novel cycle '*Les Rougon-Macquart*', written between

1871 and 1893, with a typically naturalistic subtitle: *Natural and Social History of a Family during the Second Empire*. Including novels like *L'assommoir* (*The Drinking Hole*, 1877), *Germinal* (*Spring*, 1885) or *La terre* (*The Earth*, 1887), the series was designed to show, according to Zola, 'how the race is modified by environment . . . My big task is to be strictly naturalist, strictly physiologist.'[5] The novel was a literary form that could be relatively easily transformed into naturalism, being solely the vision of a writer; but for Zola, the multiple means of expression inherent in theatre – actors, costumes, the settings and lighting – meant that the form itself had to be changed because, as he said, 'everything is interdependent'. As a result the revolution in staging that he called for paralleled Wagner's concept of the *Gesamtkunstwerk*, or 'Total theatre', although in different terms.

Costume, setting and the environment

Lifelike costumes look wrong if the sets, the diction, the plays themselves are not lifelike. They must all march in step along the naturalistic road. When costume becomes more accurate, so do sets; actors free themselves from bombastic declaiming; plays study reality more closely and their characters are more true to life . . . Most of all we would need to intensify the illusion in reconstructing the environments [on the stage], less for their picturesque quality than for dramatic utility. The environment must determine the character . . . Environment, the study of which has transformed science and literature, will have to take a large role in the theatre. And here I may mention again the question of metaphysical man, the abstraction who had to be satisfied with his three walls in tragedy – whereas the physiological man in our modern works is asking more and more compellingly to be determined by his setting, by the environment that produced him.

Emile Zola[6]

Without a naturalistic style of performance, there would be no naturalistic plays; without naturalistic plays there could be no reform in staging; and as Zola realized, acting and diction followed 'fixed traditional codes', as did each of the other expressive elements of theatre. Reform required someone who both wrote and staged plays; and the person who filled this requirement was Henrik Ibsen, who had been forced, by the failure of his first plays (tragedies in the heroic mould), to become a 'stage-manager' for the Norwegian Theatre in Bergen during the 1850s, transferring to a more senior position as *Intendant* for four years at the National Theatre at Christiana in 1858. Ibsen certainly produced well-made plays from France, and while the plays of his own that he staged in this period were all Viking history, his practical stage experience was to inform his later drama. It was no coincidence that, less than a year after the publication of *Naturalism in the Theatre*, Ibsen wrote a letter to actress Lucie

Wolf announcing his decision to abandon poetic drama. But the most direct disciple of both Zola's theories and the Meiningen staging techniques was André Antoine in Paris; and it was the influence of Antoine's staging, with its detailed realism, alongside his encouragement of new drama and new playwrights, that was decisive in making naturalism the default style for mainstream theatre through the twentieth century.

The naturalistic director: André Antoine and the Théâtre Libre

In France, Zola's call for a new theatre found an immediate disciple in André Antoine. Antoine's very first production, opening his new Théâtre Libre (1877), was the one-act *Jacques Damour*, an adaptation of one of Zola's short stories. Zola became an advisor to Antoine's theatre, and twenty years later was to preside at a banquet celebrating Antoine. At the same time, Antoine was also deeply influenced by the Meiningen Company, copying their crowd techniques for his productions after his contact with them in Brussels in 1888, while the Meiningen ensemble principle, and their rule that no actor had the right to refuse any role, was echoed in Antoine's 1890 manifesto, *Le Théâtre Libre*. But his aim was to go further than the Meiningen Company, by adding a detailed naturalism of appearance (costumes and make-up) to their lifelike organization of crowds.[7]

The authenticity aimed at in Antoine's productions is illustrated by reference to his opening production of *Jaques Damour*, where the stage furniture – being borrowed by Antoine from his mother's living room and wheeled across Paris on a hand cart – was clearly everyday, used and solid, while the stage properties and their precise placing were carefully listed on Antoine's copy of the script:

> 2 coffee cups on round table
> bottle cognac on round table
> death certificate in bureau drawer
> some small change on a plate on little cash table
> 1 bottle wine and 4 glasses on buffet
> 1 newspaper with Segnard [husband of the supposedly deceased Jacques' widow][8]

All this attention to accurate detail brought out the structural relationship between environment and character that is at the base of naturalistic drama; and in doing so, it underlines some of the key qualities that distinguish the modern director. To embody this nexus there must be coherence in all aspects of a production. Instead of simply coordinating the different elements of setting, lighting, stage movement, sound effects (as the old-style stage-manager), all of these together with casting and style of acting must be orchestrated for unified effect. In addition, Antoine was much praised as an actor for his emotional identification with the character of the unfortunate Jacques. Following the same principle, Antoine avoided type-casting and never allowed doubling of parts within a play because of his aim to have the actors absorbed in their roles. Particularly on the tiny and highly intimate stage of his first theatre (Passage de l'Elysée des Beaux Arts) actions had to be fully rehearsed, while his actors – observed in close-up – had to perform in a detailed, internalized and understated way, as well as creating a unified effect with others in the ensemble, all of which underscored the need for careful preparation, and the requirement for overall directorial control, even when (as here) Antoine was playing the main part.

Later, when he achieved a larger, proscenium-arch theatre, the Théâtre Antoine, with more scenic and technical resources, the realism became still more elaborate, reaching its pinnacle in the 1902 production of an adaptation of Zola's *La terre*. Here the set had a tactile solidity, the beams were real wood, the bales of hay were real. There were even live chickens, pecking at the straw strewn over the stage, and the lighting was carefully muted so that candles appeared to be the main source of illumination.

2 *La terre*, Act II, Théâtre Antoine. 1902

This apparent realism, of course, is paradoxical. It requires an intensification of illusion: while dialogue is made to appear spontaneous conversation, it is still scripted; even if the acting is internalized and avoids all declamation, the actor always represents a different figure in the character; the more accurately scenery embodies everyday settings, the more it disguises the theatrical actuality. And in the scene from *La terre* (see picture), despite all its apparent naturalness, the groupings are carefully balanced, giving prominence to the main figures. The more a stage picture appears to be actual life, the intenser and more detailed the orchestration of the various elements. And the maintenance of such illusion is one of the major elements justifying the modern director's function.

Prompt books survive even from these early productions, documenting Antoine's careful attention to the *mise en scène* with moment-by-moment stage directions and notes for actors' speeches, plus miniature sketched stage plans with blocking indicators, on plain sheets interleaved with the text. And from these first productions on the minimal stage up to productions like *Julius Caesar* or *Andromaque* at the Odéon (1906, 1909), Antoine created exactly the same sort of prompt book. As it has been argued, even though Antoine scrupulously followed the stage directions of naturalistic dramatists like Ibsen or Hauptmann, who were concerned with environment, this interleaving of blank pages and dialogue asserted the imaginative space of the director.[9] Later prompt books closely prefigure the modern 'director's book', with stage plans marking opening positions for each act, lists of movable props and their locations in extraordinary detail – showing the realistic representation of a whole material context – detailed annotations for each actor's movements, with specific gestures noted accompanying particular speeches, and miniature sketches of stage positions at key moments in the action. In many ways Antoine also introduced the typical working method of the modern director. Any new play was read to the whole cast, generally by the author, following which Antoine worked alone with the text, visualizing the action and the physical context in which it occurred, sketching plans, blocking, entries and exits, then discussing the requirements with a designer. Having prepared his detailed prompt copy, intensive rehearsals would start, with more detailed notes being recorded by assistant *régisseurs* as gestures, moves and changes of manner or tone were worked through; and as soon as costumes were available, they were used in rehearsal. There are also notes on colour in these prompt books, and on the lines and planes of stage space, as well as on lighting. However, these are always reinforcing the acting and bringing out the environment for the characters, and by no means the primary means of expression they would become in the hands of Appia and Craig.

While Antoine also produced symbolist and poetic dramas, where he experimented with new forms of staging, it was always to intensify the naturalistic representation of the action, as in his use of diagonal sets. For instance, in his 1893 staging of *Miss Julie*, where Strindberg's Preface calls for precisely this, Antoine's programme note remarks that 'décor arranged at an angle, the suppression of the ramp, lighting from above' were already standard at his theatre – the angling of the set both creating an impression of fluidity and also drawing the audience into the stage space, as though they were in a corner of the room instead of behind a fourth wall. In the same way, Antoine was the first to introduce the complete darkening of the auditorium in France (in 1888), where before the house lights had always only been dimmed. It also has to be remembered that Antoine was explicitly running a playwrights' theatre, continually commissioning new work from French poets and playwrights, making dramatic adaptations of naturalistic novels, and translating for his stage all the new naturalistic plays from Russia, Scandinavia and Germany. So, between March 1887 and May 1894 Antoine staged no fewer than 112 new dramas, among them plays by sixty-nine authors who had before that written nothing for the theatre. And it is equally true that reciprocally his realist stagings influenced the way these authors approached their material, although quite clearly Antoine saw his job as *régisseur* to be the interpreting of a script, both thematically and in translating text into action: one of the major functions of a modern director.

He also experimented with new dramatic material – most obviously in the 1888 staging of *La mort du Duc d'Enghien*, which, with a structure determined by historical event and dialogue largely reproducing speeches in actual records, counts as the first documentary drama. The minimalist scene and staging of the tiny Théâtre Libre, together with Antoine's use of coats and dresses that actually had been manufactured over eighty years earlier in 1804, the year of the action, intensified the factual effect. And Antoine's production of Tolstoy's *The Power of Darkness* in the same year has been described as epoch-making because of its influence. It provided an explicit model for Otto Brahm in opening his Freie Bühne in Berlin, while his touring production in Brussels directly led to the founding of the Belgian Théâtre Libre. It also toured to England, causing J. T. Grein to ask: 'Is a British Théâtre Libre, a theatre free from the shackles of the censor, free from the fetters of convention, unhampered by financial consideration – is such a theatre not possible?'[10] And when Grein founded the Independent Theatre (a name that recognized only relative freedom, since the censor remained a controlling factor in British theatre) his productions in its opening year (1898) copied Antoine's Théâtre Libre programme. Even so, as others have commented, Antoine occupies a position somewhere between the old-style actor-manager and the modern director, since – in addition to carrying out most of the functions of a director – he also acted in almost every one of his productions, usually in a major role: the title part of *Jacques Damour*, old Akim in *The Power of Darkness*, Oswald in *Ghosts*, Père Fouan (with 1,200 lines of dialogue) in *La terre*.[11]

As a signal of the level of realism attempted, and indeed of the scientific aspect of naturalism, one of Antoine's earliest productions (*La famille* by Oscar Méténier at the second soirée of May 1887) was photographed: the very first known photos of a play in performance. And Antoine prominently included photographic equipment in his 1891 production of Ibsen's *The Wild Duck* (illustrating Hjalmar's profession), drawing on the symbolic force of the camera as the only authentic way of reproducing reality, as well as a form of second-rate image-making. It is also no accident that Antoine was one of the earliest European film directors to attempt full-length serious feature films, for instance filming Zola's *La terre* in 1921 (building on his iconic naturalistic staging at the Théâtre Antoine in 1902).

A selected chronology of naturalism

(theatre events in bold type)

1859	Darwin, *Origin of the Species* John Stuart Mill, *Essay on Liberty* Invention of the panoramic camera
1866	**Henrik Ibsen, *Brand*** Alfred Nobel invents dynamite
1867	Karl Marx, *Das Kapital*
1869	Mill, *On the Subjection of Women*
1873	**Emile Zola, *Thérèse Raquin***
1874	**Meiningen Players first tour of Germany**
1875	**Zola begins calling for a naturalist theatre**
1876	Alexander Bell invents the telephone
1877	Thomas Edison invents the phonograph
1879	Edison invents the electric light **Ibsen, *A Doll's House***
1881	**Zola, *Naturalism in the Theatre*** **Ibsen, *Ghosts*** **Henry Becque, *The Crows***
1887	**Strindberg, *The Father*** **Ibsen, *The Pillars of Society*** **Anton Chekhov, *Ivanov*** **André Antoine founds the Théâtre Libre**

1888	**Strindberg, *Miss Julie***
	George Eastman introduces the Kodak camera
1889	**Gerhart Hauptmann, *Before Sunrise***
1890	**George Bernard Shaw, *The Quintessence of Ibsenism***
	Ibsen, *Hedda Gabler*
1893	**Hauptmann, *The Weavers* (Théâtre Libre)**
	Shaw, *Mrs Warren's Profession*
1895	Sigmund Freud, *On . . . Hysterical Phenomena*
1898	Zola, 'J'accuse!'
	Moscow Art Theatre: Chekhov, *The Seagull*
1899	**Chekhov, *Uncle Vanya***
1900	**David Belasco, *Madame Butterfly***
1902	Lenin, *What Is to Be Done?*
	Maxim Gorky, *The Lower Depths*
	Zola, *La terre* (Théâtre Libre)
1904	**Abbey Theatre (Dublin) founded**
	Chekhov, *The Cherry Orchard*
1905	Einstein, theory of relativity
	Harley Granville Barker, *The Voysey Inheritance*
	Mutiny on the battleship *Potemkin*

Naturalism was – and still is – focused on establishing a connection between theatre and society, in which the detailed reproduction of manners and behaviour, together with the accurate three-dimensional rendering of interiors (remarkably few of Ibsen's naturalistic plays have outdoor scenes) and gardens (even if Chekhov's characters talk of the forests, only Gorky's *Summerfolk* sets characters outside a controlled and socialized landscape), was combined to express a play script dealing with social issues in contemporary language. As a result, new standards of authenticity and individuality were developed in acting, based on emotional memory and subjective identification, while new standards of visual unity were required, with setting and lighting, costuming, moves and gestures all corresponding to evoke a facsimile of everyday life. (Aural unity was also involved – in the sense of vocal accents and environmental sound effects.) And together with the new emphasis on objectivity that the scientific claims of naturalism demanded, orchestrating all these elements required an outside eye, to develop a stageable interpretation of the script, and capable of controlling the whole process of production, which in terms of naturalistic expectations of the acting also included extensive rehearsals. That, of course, was the position and function defined by Antoine and developed for rather different purposes by Konstantin Stanislavsky, although both also included symbolist plays in their repertoire, with Antoine even directing the fairytale fantasy of Théodore de Bainville and the delicate imaginary spirituality of Villiers de l'Isle Adam.

Symbolist theatre: a call for directorial vision

Even before the realistic standards and illusionistic criteria of naturalism had been introduced to the theatre in the 1880s, with its implications for the function of the modern director, there was another – very different – style of theatrical production evolving in the nineteenth century: one that called for a unity which included still more expressive elements, requiring not only the same sort of control as exercised by a director in the naturalistic theatre, but also a wider range of expertise. Initiated by Richard Wagner, this style of theatre had already been established over thirty years before Zola's calls for the introduction of naturalism in the theatre, in works like *Rienzi* and *Tannhäuser* (staged in Dresden, 1840 and 1845). Indeed the full flowering of Wagner's theatrical concept, the massive opera cycle the Ring of the Nibelung, had begun as early as 1850, and all four parts were first performed the same year as Ibsen's earliest naturalistic drama *The Pillars of Society*, and a decade before the founding of Antoine's Théâtre Libre.

Integrating music with drama – the basis of Wagner's art – created a very different concept of theatrical unity, based on aesthetic grounds rather than realism, even if Wagner had close connections with the Meiningen Company. During his lifetime at least, the settings in his Festival Theatre in Bayreuth were as realistic (albeit in quasi-historic or mythically exaggerated rather than contemporary social terms) as any naturalistic staging. If the naturalists created an ensemble of realistic details (down to the dirt on the faces of Antoine's actors, or the sound of crickets in Stanislavsky's staging) where the aim was complete consistency to life, Wagner and those who followed him developed forms of 'total theatre' where the unity was created out of forms and light in purely aesthetic terms. And it is no accident that the two main theorists who subsequently challenged naturalism had their roots in opera. Adolphe Appia was specifically inspired by Wagner's works, developed his concepts around productions of Wagner's operas, and titled his most influential book *Music and Scenery*. Gordon Craig too used opera – the baroque operas of Purcell and Handel – to work out and test the ideas defined in his 1904 book on *The Art of the Theatre*.

Around the same time and in some ways informing the kind of theatre that Appia and Craig were working for, the symbolist poetic movement had transferred to the theatre. Maurice Maeterlinck's *Pelléas et Mélisande* opened the symbolist Théâtre de l'Œuvre, founded by Aurélien Lugné-Poë in Paris in 1893, and was turned into an opera by Debussy; Stéphane Mallarmé's *L'après-midi d'un faune*, translated into music by Debussy, came to epitomize symbolism in the notorious 1912 ballet choreographed by Nijinsky for the Ballets Russes; the Irish poet W. B. Yeats' Japanese-influenced *Plays for Dancers* formed part of the repertoire, along with naturalistic plays by J. M. Synge and Lady Gregory, at the Abbey Theatre that he had founded in Dublin. And the links with art theatre are clear in Craig's collaboration with Yeats, providing designs and a set of multi-use ivory screens for productions at the Abbey.[12] Significantly, all these key works of symbolist theatre have a musical or dance dimension, as did Oscar Wilde's *Salome*, adapted as an opera by Richard Strauss.

A selected chronology: symbolism, expressionism and art theatre

(theatre events in bold type)

1857	Charles Baudelaire publishes *Les fleurs du mal*
1872	Friedrich Nietzsche publishes *The Birth of Tragedy*
1876	**Wagner's Ring of the Nibelung cycle premieres in Bayreuth**
1886	Jean Moréas publishes 'Manifeste de symbolisme'
1890	**Maurice Maeterlinck, *Princess Maleine, The Intruder, The Blind***
1891	**Oscar Wilde, *Salome* (premiere 1896)** **Frank Wedekind, *Spring's Awakening*** Thomas Edison invents the Kinetoscope
1893	**Maeterlinck, *Pelléas et Mélisande***
1896	**Alfred Jarry, *Ubu Roi***
1898	**Stanislavsky founds Moscow Art Theatre**
1899	**Adolphe Appia, *Music and Stage Scenery*** Arthur Symons publishes *The Symbolist Movement in Literature*
1900	Sigmund Freud publishes *Interpretation of* Dreams **August Strindberg, *To Damascus***
1901	**Strindberg, *A Dream Play***
1902	Lenin publishes *What Is to Be Done?*
1904	**Abbey Theatre (Dublin) founded**
1905	Einstein, theory of relativity **Craig publishes *The Art of the Theatre*** Mutiny on the battleship *Potemkin*
1907	**Strindberg founds the Intimate Theatre**
1908	**Maeterlinck's *The Bluebird* staged by Stanislavsky at the Moscow Art Theatre** **Strindberg, *The Ghost Sonata***
1909	**Oskar Kokoschka, *Murderer, The Hope of Women***

1911	Maeterlinck awarded the Nobel Prize
1912	Hervath Walden coins the term 'Expressionism'
	Nijinsky, *L'après-midi d'un faune*
	Carl Jung publishes *Psychology of the Unconscious*
1914	The First World War breaks out
1916	**Georg Kaiser, *From Morn to Midnight***
1917	Communist Revolution in Russia
1920	Robert Wiene's film, *The Cabinet of Dr Caligari*
	Eugene O'Neill, *The Emperor Jones*

Aurélien Lugné-Poë's production of Maeterlinck's *Pelléas et Mélisande* underscores the different directorial approach required by the symbolists, with their use of myth and ritual to create hallucination and dreamscapes. Believing that reality is spiritual and only communicated by appeal to the imagination through the allusive language of symbols, while rejecting representationalism along with the validity of the material world, symbolist plays required a highly stylized and connotative staging. So in *Pelléas et Mélisande* most of the scenes were performed in semi-darkness, with actors moving slowly like sleepwalkers, gesturing with exaggerated solemnity, and speaking in a monotone staccato chant, marked by long pauses and repetitions, while the audience viewed the entire performance through gauze stretched across the proscenium as if 'through the mists of time'.

This corresponded to the aims expressed in Maeterlinck's 1896 essay 'The Tragical in Daily Life' where he called for a 'static drama'.

'The Tragical in Daily Life'

Indeed it is not in the actions but in the words that are found the beauty and greatness of tragedies that are truly beautiful and great; and this not solely in the words that accompany and explain the action, for there must perforce be another dialogue besides the one which is superficially necessary. And indeed the only words that count in the play are those that at first seemed useless, for it is therein that the essence lies. Side by side with the necessary dialogue will you almost always find another dialogue that seems superfluous; but examine it carefully, and it will be borne home to you that this is the only one that the soul can listen to profoundly, for here alone is it the soul that is being addressed . . .

Collected in *The Treasure of the Humble* (1916)

Characteristically in other productions, Lugné-Poë separated word and action – as in Henri de Regnier's *The Guardian* (1894) where the text was 'recited' by actors hidden in the orchestra pit, while on stage, behind a green gauze curtain, silent actors replicated emotions expressed from below in slow unsynchronized pantomime. Similarly, in Maeterlinck's *Interior* (1895), the action takes place in a house, seen only through windows from a garden where a Stranger, an Old Man and his two daughters discuss how to break the news of a child's drowning to the family inside, who are seen reacting to the conversation they cannot hear. Unspeaking, the interior family move and gesticulate in 'grave, slow, sparse ways' as though 'spiritualized by distance'.[13] This vocal and visual dichotomy, designed to intensify the sense of otherworldly remoteness aimed at by the symbolists, created the need for careful blocking of moves and orchestration of the separated elements of the performance.

Symbolist drama also explicitly challenged the dominant morality and materialism of nineteenth-century society. Originally written in French and first staged in Paris by the symbolist director, Lugné-Poë, Wilde's *Salome* (1896, censored in England until 1905) echoes Maeterlinck's *La Princesse Maleine* (1889). Both focus on a young heroine obsessed by a passion that can only be fulfilled in death, and use the repetition of simple phrases to create a dreamlike atmosphere. The Salome legend itself could be called the emblem of *fin de siècle* romanticism, recurring in Heine, Flaubert, Mallarmé, Huysmans and Massenet's *Herodiade*. In Wilde's interpretation, Salome's dance of the seven veils becomes a spiritual triumph over the incestuous and sterile social establishment, represented by Herod.

Everything represented is symbolic. The moon (which Aubrey Beardsley's illustrations show with Wilde's face, acknowledging the author's controlling consciousness) dominates the play. All the characters subconsciously perceive Salome's inner nature reflected in the moon; and Salome's passion and martyrdom, expressed in specifically Christian images, become the icon for a religion of aesthetics as well as sexual sublimation.

The antithesis of naturalistic theatre, *Salome* replaces plot and characterization (limited satirically to Herod and Herodias, who represent society) with the aesthetic values of colour and musical rhythms. Dialogue becomes incantation, invoking the dance, in which the unveiling of Salome's body is a metaphor for spiritual revelation. As Wilde himself had commented, he 'took the drama, the most objective form known to art, and made it as personal a mode of expression as the lyric or the sonnet' – all of which turned *Salome* into an icon of symbolist drama. And this has been reflected in the expropriation of the play by *fin de siècle* painters like Gustav Moreau, dancers such as Loie Fuller, and Richard Strauss's 1905 opera (the libretto of which uses Wilde's complete text and which has largely displaced it on the stage), as well as Alla Nazimova's films.

In terms of production, what these different adaptations emphasize is the degree to which symbolist drama requires interpretation to realize its dreamlike or visionary qualities in a stage presentation. And it is this interpretative function – together with the need for orchestrating movement and speech in precise and detailed ways that characterize naturalistic as well as symbolist staging – which defines the modern director, as well as the requirement for developing new approaches to acting grounded in the stylistic specifics of the type of drama being performed.

Richard Wagner: total theatre

In contrast to the court-controlled bureaucrat-managers, the *Intendants* of nineteenth-century Germany (see pp. 30–2 above), there is the towering figure of Richard Wagner, whose work was one of the major factors that made the modern director an essential figure in the theatre. Wagner was not only a socialist and supporter of the 1848 revolutions that spread across Europe, forcing him to take refuge in Paris. He was also the only creative artist, until Brecht, to found and run a theatre dedicated solely to his own works. Indeed Wagner functioned very much as a modern director in staging the operas he composed.

His major innovation in staging was the *Gesamtkunstwc* [illegible] 'total theatre' – which he outlined in his essays, as well as demonstrating at least partially in his productions of his operas.

The *Gesamtkunstwerk*

Artistic man can only fully content himself by uniting every branch of art into the common Artwork . . . in the common Artwork he is free and fully that which he has power to be . . . The highest conjoint work of art is the Drama; it can only be at hand in all its possible fullness when each separate branch of art is at hand in its own utmost fullness . . . In a perfect theatre edifice, Art's need alone gives law and measure . . . The spectator transplants himself upon the stage, by means of all his aural and visual faculties, while the performer becomes an artist only by complete absorption into the public . . . supplementing one another in their changeful dance, the united sister-arts will show themselves and make good their claim; now all together, now in pairs, and again in solitary splendour, according to the momentary need of the only rule – and purpose-giver, the Dramatic Action.

Richard Wagner, 'The Artwork of the Future', 1849

Indeed the concept of a *Gesamtkunstwerk* that Wagner called for – the 'Artwork of the Future' in which music, poetry and action (dance and gesture) would merge in a higher aesthetic unity[14] – was precisely what Duke Georg pursued so successfully in terms of action, scene and lighting. For Wagner,

Western performance art had been corrupted because (as he put it in the opening of *Opera and Drama*) 'a Means of Expression (Music) has been made the end, while the end (the Drama) has been made a means'.[15] Wagner's solution has been expertly summarized by a recent commentator.

> His vision is of a new kind of drama, rooted in mythical subject matter, which will restore the almost sacred relationship between author, performers and public (all as active participants) which Wagner believed to have obtained in the theatre festivals of Periclean Athens ... The time was now ripe to reunite the arts, to bring them together into a synthesis, into a *Gesamtkunstwerk* ('total work of art' is perhaps the least objectionable of possible translations) which would restore the Athenian spirit to the German people (for there was a vigorous nationalistic line in this too) ... The musical contribution, he argues, is never to be formal, decorative or self-sufficient. Its function is to breathe life into myth and present it directly to the senses. The words are to be clearly audible and comprehensible at all times. To the three arts of dance, music and poetry are to be added the visual arts of architecture, painting and sculpture. Architecture will again become beautiful and useful in the construction of theatres, painting will provide the scenery, while sculpture is to be reborn in moulding the living flesh of the singing actor.
>
> Carnegy, *Wagner and the Art of the Theatre*, 47–8

Arguably Wagner had just as much to do with the emerging prominence of the director in German theatre as the *Intendant* system. In the mid nineteenth century, when the mechanical hand of Eugène Scribe closed over the theatre in France and little original was being done on the English stage, Wagner's work presented a challenge and an opportunity unique to Germany (since the only one of his operas to be produced outside German-speaking countries during this period was a spectacular failure: the 1860 Paris *Tannhäuser*). From somewhat inauspicious beginnings in 1842 with the first performance of *Rienzi* in Dresden to the massive four-part cycle of the Ring of the Nibelung with which he triumphantly opened the Bayreuth Festival Theatre in 1876, Wagner became the driving force for renewal in German theatre: not as a model for other composers or dramatists – his vision being too idiosyncratic, too grandiose for others to try emulating – but with respect to staging. The mythic material and heroic treatment of his librettos, together with the overarching musical leitmotifs and sheer scale of his operas, absolutely required the kind of unified presentation provided by the control of an off-stage director. In a very real sense Wagner's work could only be theatrically realized by a production method such as the *Intendant* system, serving retrospectively as its artistic justification. And almost all the main *Intendants* of the time had some connection with Wagner.

Perhaps almost as important in setting the context for a new style of production was Wagner's actual design of his Festival Theatre in Bayreuth, which was to become a widespread model for theatres in the twentieth century.[16] The undivided (classless) raked seating focused spectator attention solely on a strictly perspective stage (instead of on other members of the audience, as with the standard boxes and tiers). It introduced a democratic symbolism into theatre that contrasted strongly with hierarchical architecture of all standard auditoriums of the time, as well as changing the relationship of each spectator to the scenic picture, since (as Wagner insisted):

> So soon as he has taken his seat [the spectator] truly finds himself in a 'Theatron', a room designed for nothing else than for looking. Between him and the visible picture nothing definite, tangible exists: instead the architectonic device of the double proscenium gives to the stage the remoteness of a dream.[17]

These new architectural qualities helped to enforce the new standards of unity and verisimilitude in stage presentation. However, it has to be said that the actual visual impression was anything but appropriate to the mythic material of Wagner's operas.

Going on the assumption that stage illusion should be so complete that an audience might lose themselves in the performance, the settings for his gods and heroes were all too naturalistic: trees painted with every leaf on cut cloths or flat backdrops; the Ride of the Valkyrie appearing complete with horses in mid-sky with the aid of a standard technique of Victorian spectacle; a rolling 'swimming apparatus' used together with clouds of steam for the Rhinemaidens. With nothing left to the imagination, there was no room for the spiritual reality expressed in the music. The elaborate pictorial romanticism that Wagner established was to remain a standard part of German stagecraft, reappearing for instance in the forest (complete with live rabbits) of Reinhardt's famous *Midsummer Night's Dream* production, which remained in his repertoire from 1905 right up to 1939.

Adolphe Appia: lighting and space

Along with Gordon Craig, Appia marks the emergence of a completely new type of director: the theoretician, who may only have a tenuous connection to practical stage performance but serves as a visionary catalyst, promoting ideals of directorial approach and theatrical presentation in the abstract. Both were in sharp opposition to the naturalistic movement, with Appia seeking to find a way of staging that would be as effective for more stylized or poetic drama, where realistic settings contradicted the symbolic level of mythic or Classical plays.

Beginning in the 1890s, Appia produced theoretical writings, scenarios and numerous designs for the Ring of the Nibelung, *Tristan und Isolde*, *Die Meistersinger* and *Parsifal* – but was only able actually to direct one of the operas over thirty years later. This was *Tristan*; when it opened in 1923 (on the stage of La Scala at Toscanini's invitation) the reception was mixed; and while his designs for *Rheingold* and *Die Walküre* were used by the Swiss director Oscar Wälterlin in Basle, these 1924 and 1925 productions caused such vociferous opposition that the plans to stage the rest of the Ring were abruptly cancelled, and Appia never worked in the theatre again. Indeed over his whole lifetime Appia directed a total of just three other productions, while his designs were only used for the staging of two non-Wagnerian pieces, most notably a version of Gluck's *Orfeo ed Euridice* staged with Dalcroze's eurhythmic-trained dancers at Hellerau (1912–13).[18]

However, in some ways this lack of stage work was an advantage. As his Wagner productions showed, radical experimentation aroused intense opposition, and would in any case be limited to a local audience, whereas publication and international exhibitions attracted far wider attention: a pattern that was also followed by Craig. And indeed, Appia's writings – from books such as *Staging Wagnerian Drama* (1895) and *Music and Scenery* (*Die Musik und die Inscenierung*, 1899), through his unrealized scenarios, to essays like 'Richard Wagner and the *mise en scène*' (1925) – spread his ideas and scene-sketches widely through the theatre world, while international theatre expositions in London and Amsterdam and Zurich showcased his designs, as did a series of exhibitions at Magdeburg and elsewhere through Germany.

Illustrating a radically non-illusionistic use of the stage, these exhibitions showed suggestive combinations of solid objects and empty space, light and shadow that substituted dynamic acting areas for the painted scene cloths which the Brückner brothers were providing both for the Meiningen Company and for Wagner at the time. If representing place at all, then only in the broadest strokes, in conscious opposition to the detailed visual realism at Bayreuth in the 1880s and 1890s, Appia's conceptual settings created an abstract but specifically theatrical environment from elements integral to the stage itself in a concrete realization of symbolist principles.[19]

For Adolphe Appia's 1892 design for *Die Walküre*, Act III (in later versions Appia cut the fir-tree branch (right), leaving only its shadow on the rocks), see www.monsalvat.no/appia-rock.jpg.

In place of realistic detail, Appia's settings are minimalist. So in his design for *Die Walküre* (published in *Music and Scenery*), the mountain is reduced to a cave and a slope rising to a peak, producing a stark profile against the sky. In contrast to the combination of painted flats and free-standing solid pieces standard at the time, the whole setting is designed to be solid, with every surface a space for performers, all unified; and changes of mood were to be achieved by lighting. And while his designs for Wagner are almost all contained within the stage space, Appia was concerned to break through the proscenium frame, as in his 1925 Basle production of Aeschylus' *Prometheus*, where his design called for a ramp to run all the way down over the orchestra pit and into the auditorium, although this proved impracticable.

For Appia, space had to be dynamic to facilitate the interaction of performer and spectator. Through his study of Wagner, and his scenarios accompanying the designs for the Ring, Appia concluded that the flat perpendicular scenery and horizontal stage floor with the actor moving in depth created jarring optical conflicts. To achieve visual unity the vertical and horizontal planes should be replaced by ramps, steps and platforms on different levels that would blend with the actor's moves, multiplying possibilities for movement through different dimensions and enhancing the dynamism of the human figure. Along with this, the backdrop representing the sky could be made into an area of visual movement through the shifting play of light; and the lighting would also unify the different elements of the stage image, casting a tonal chiaroscuro that made the whole emotionally expressive.

Appia on light

Like the actor, light must become active . . . Light has an almost miraculous flexibility . . . it can produce shadows and distribute the harmony of its vibrations in space exactly as music does. In light we possess all the expressive power of space, if this space is placed at the service of the actor . . .

'Actor, Space, Light and Painting'

Light, no longer constrained to illuminate painted canvas, can spread out into space, filling it with living colour and infinite variations . . . in delivering the *mise en scène* from the yoke of lifeless painting and illusion . . . in giving it thus the greatest possible flexibility and utmost liberty, we also set free the imagination of the dramatist . . . the influence of this scenic reform cannot even remotely be estimated.

'Eurhythmics and the Theatre'[20]

In addition to settings for particular plays, Appia also created designs specifically to demonstrate his principles of rhythmic dynamism, balance and visual unity. Although these were generally represented as empty stage spaces without the main element around which all these qualities were intended to intensify – the human figure – they were prepared for Dalcroze to base his school exercises on.

For an example of Appia's rhythmic design (1909) focusing on acting levels and light (notionally for a production of Sophocles) see www.hellerau.org/english/i/history_images/image/3.1.jpg.

Appia was moving towards an abstract theatre, in which music and light would give the singing/speaking, moving/dancing performers an atmospheric context, amplifying their emotional expression.

Appia on atmospheric settings

The second Act of *Siegfried* may serve as an example. How are we to present a forest on the stage? ... In order to create our setting we need not try to visualize a forest, but we have to imagine in detail the entire sequence of events that occurs in the forest ... [The stage director] will think of the forest as an atmosphere around and about the performer; an atmosphere that can be realized only in relation to living and moving beings on which he must focus ... the *mise en scène* then becomes the composition of a picture in time ... We shall no longer try to give the illusion of a forest, but the illusion of a man in the atmosphere of a forest.

'Comment reformer notre *mise en scène*'[21]

Appia's 'musical' dramaturgy of light, rhythmic space and three-dimensional staging had wide international influence, being taken up particularly in the work of the French director Jacques Copeau and Nicolai Okhlopkov's 'Realistic Theatre' in Russia; and it also had a more immediate impact in Germany, with the dominant flights of steps he had introduced for his production of *Orpheus and Eurydice* at Hellerau in 1913 becoming the signature stage-form for expressionist directors like Leopold Jessner (who had attended the Hellerau performance) in the 1920s. And even though Wagner's widow Cosima refused to allow any change in the way his operas had been staged by Wagner himself, Appia's concepts were gradually adopted piecemeal in the 1930s, although their importance was only acknowledged when Wieland Wagner took control in 1951, with the 'New Bayreuth Style' defined in the Souvenir Programme for 1955 as specifically deriving from Appia: 'a performance space fashioned out of the spirit of the music itself, and a sense of three-dimensionality ... the symbolic power of colour and of light, rhythmically coordinated with space'.[22] And all this had implications for the function of the director: the kind of function s/he would fill was what Appia himself, writing about the staging of Wagner's opera, labelled a 'word-tone-poet' – a sensitive creative interpreter of the dramatic work, capable of orchestrating all technical and design elements of production, to create a unified effect.

As Copeau wrote in a tribute where he accurately summed up the 'Master's' radical reform of the stage: 'For him, the art of stage production in its pure sense was nothing other than the embodiment of a text or a musical composition, made sensible by the living action of the human body and its reaction to spaces and masses set against it.'[23]

On Theory

There have always been writings related to theatre – from Aristotle's analysis of effective dramatic techniques for tragedy in Classical Greece, or the rhetoric-based concept of acting put forward by the Roman actor Roscius, through David Garrick's 'Essay on Acting' and Denis Diderot's 'Paradox sur le comédien' – with these in general reflecting both the aesthetic context of the time and the creative hierarchy in the theatre. In the heyday of the actor-manager, the theories are related to acting. With the rise of the dramaturge/director they become focused on structure, presentation or staging technique. The change comes with Gotthold Lessing's *Hamburgische Dramaturgie*. At the same time, rather than being descriptive (as with Diderot) or technically prescriptive (as with Garrick), theorists like Lessing and those who came later sought to change the nature of drama, and fostered revolutionary advances in stage presentation, dramatic focus and even the concept of theatre itself.

It is also noticeable that in each case the aim of the theorist runs counter to an immediately preceding reform. Under the Académie Française, founded by Cardinal Richelieu in 1635, the rules for neo-classical drama had been imposed on plays in France. This led to a strict division between Comedy and Tragedy (the only two genres recognized) and obedience to the unities, together with themes and subjects taken from Greek drama, as with the verse tragedies of Jean Racine, represented by *Phèdre* (1677). This style spread through Europe, becoming the dominant mode over the next century, just as the well-made play, a specific type of dramatic structure defined in France by the playwright Eugène Scribe, spread through Europe in the mid nineteenth century. Neo-classicism was challenged by Lessing. The well-made play, and the romantic style of performance that had preceded it, were rejected by Zola with the call for a naturalistic theatre that was answered by Ibsen, and is still the default mode for Western theatre. But hardly had naturalism become established than it was challenged by proponents of aesthetic unity: in particular Adolphe Appia and Gordon Craig.

Gordon Craig, Adolphe Appia and the theory of directing

It is hardly surprising if Gordon Craig shared many of the views of Appia, and arrived independently at similar conclusions, since both reformers were primarily designers – even though Craig had begun his career as an actor under Henry Irving, and achieved recognition as one of the leading young actors in Britain, before turning his energies to creating his new Art of the Theatre.

Paralleling Appia, Craig focused particularly on the importance of movement and light, to which he gave a spiritual value, together with even more radical changes to the stage space. Like Appia too, Craig's experience as an actual director was extremely limited. Craig's own stage directing – three groundbreaking stagings of baroque opera (Purcell and Handel) plus two other productions between 1900 and 1903, then a production of *Hamlet* for Stanislavsky's Moscow Art Theatre (1912), and a production of Ibsen's *The Crown Pretenders* at the Royal Theatre in Copenhagen (1926) – also seems minimal in comparison to Craig's immense influence.[24] But together with Appia, Craig was the first theatre artist to choose publishing to spread his message: Craig's first writings appeared in 1891 just three years after Appia's first foray into print. In addition to Appia's concentration on books, Craig also edited – and wrote all the pieces – for three journals, *The Page* (1899–1901), *The Marionette* (twelve issues, 1918–19) and most significantly *The Mask* (over forty issues in fifteen volumes between 1906 and 1929). Alongside this, Craig published a series of books outlining his theory of theatre: *The Art of the Theatre: The First Dialogue* (1905), *On the Art of the Theatre* (1911), *The Theatre Advancing* (1919), as well as *A Production: 1926*, several collections of visual material – including *Isadora Duncan: Six Movement Designs* (1906) and various *Portfolios of Etchings* (1908, 1910) – and *Towards a New Theatre* (1913). Unlike Appia's work during his lifetime, these were all translated widely, with *On the Art of the Theatre* appearing during the 1920s in French, Italian, Hungarian, Spanish, Polish, Russian and even Japanese.

Where Lessing's theoretical writings had taken the form of a journal, recording thoughts about the series of productions under his management that he considered in various ways failures, Appia's books – and even more so Craig's extensive publications – represent abstract theory, in important ways independent of the stage. Craig's books and journals laid out ideas through essays in dramatic form: Socratic dialogues and arguments (conducted by Craig through pseudonyms). Backed and extended by designs appealing to the imagination, which were available not only in published form but also through international exhibitions – which Craig was the first theatre artist to use extensively – both Appia's and Craig's visionary ideas and concepts had far wider currency than an actual production could have done, allowing different interpretations, and escaping from the problematic materiality of stage performance.

Based on his perception of the need for visual and tonal unity in performance, Appia established the need for a controlling consciousness in a production: the director. Working concurrently on similar principles, Craig outlined the director's functions, and provided a model where the director was the controlling artist of the theatre. On the English-speaking stage, whether in Britain or America, the figure of the actor-manager, and of the impresario or commercial manager, continued to loom large into the mid twentieth century. However, starting in 1900, Gordon Craig created a decisive break in this tradition, by asserting the need for a single, overarching theatre artist to control every aspect of a production.

Equally significant, Appia and Craig established the practice of directors publishing theatrical manifestos, books of theory or essays to explain/promote their practices and artistic principles. But while those who followed – from Bertolt Brecht to Eugenio Barba, Meyerhold to Marthaler – are writing in order to change the style of performance or reform the theatre in specific ways, Appia and Craig provided the broad theoretical stage context for the modern director. Stanislavsky, too, wished to reform the theatre, and his writings, which record his theatrical experiments, as well as his observations on himself as a developing director, were paths towards this desired change. Craig's concepts of an Art Theatre were highly influential during the 1920s and 1930s, providing justification for the position of the director, and for ideals of performance that were widely emulated. The writings of Stanislavsky influenced the working methods of many key directors after the 1950s and 1960s, who created some of the dominating developments in contemporary theatre. Among them are Ariane Mnouchkine, Jerzy Grotowski and Eugenio Barba, who all openly acknowledge their debt to Stanislavsky, or Peter Brook, who, more guarded about his reference points, nevertheless recognizes the general importance of Stanislavsky's work with actors.[25]

Stanislavsky and psychological realism

Konstantin Stanislavsky was, first and foremost, an actor who became a director largely because of the working circumstances of the new theatre, the Moscow Art Theatre, which he founded with Vladimir Nemirovich-Danchenko in 1897. He had relatively significant experience of directing in amateur theatre, but it was his many years of struggle there and afterwards to be a good actor – Stanislavsky was not a 'born' actor like Mikhaïl Chekhov – that guided his perception and practice of directing.[26] It was his unflagging commitment to what he regarded as his calling that fuelled his outburst to Nemirovich-Danchenko in 1905: 'There was never any jealousy [of Nemirovich-Danchenko] in my work as a director. *It is an activity I do not like* and I do it out of necessity.'[27] Further, asserting that he was not a director 'by nature': 'My success as a director is essential to the theatre [the Moscow Art

Theatre], not me . . . Think rather what it cost me to cede my pride of place as an actor to Kachalov and others.'[28]

By then, as is well known, Stanislavsky and his partner's relationship had deteriorated considerably, although each in his own way still held firmly to the ideals that had brought them together to establish their company. Stanislavsky and Nemirovich-Danchenko had met because they were dissatisfied with the standards of acting in Russia – the 'stock-in-trade' and ham acting that Stanislavsky despised as 'the theatre in the theatre' and combated all his life, gradually defining the acting principles that came to be known as his 'system'. Both men were deeply critical of the current star syndrome, which precluded ensemble work. Artistic cohesion was also impossible when actors chose costumes at will from their personal wardrobes, and sets were not constructed for a particular production but, like props, were recycled according to what was available in a theatre's storerooms. And they deplored the low status of actors in society, which, in their view, was tied up with their appalling working conditions and the fact that theatre was considered to be commerce and entertainment rather than a matter of serious art, like painting or music.

Stanislavsky on the failings of traditional theatre

He [Nemirovich-Danchenko], like me, took a bleak view of the theatre at the end of the century, when the shining traditions of the past had been turned into simple workable technical tricks. I am not talking, of course, about the outstandingly gifted actors who shone in the capital cities and the provinces. In the main, thanks to the drama schools, actors on the whole achieved a much higher intellectual level than previously. But there were few real 'God-given' talents, and the theatrical profession was, on the one side, in the hands of barmen and in those of bureaucrats on the other. How could the theatre flourish in such conditions? . . .

On general matters of ethics we agreed that before we could expect proper, decent behaviour from the actors we had to provide them with surroundings that were fit for educated human beings. Remember the kind of conditions actors live in, especially in the provinces . . . What space is left for the actor? One or two tiny rooms under the stage, which are more like stables, without windows or air, always filthy dirty because no matter how often they are cleaned there is corrosive dust from the ceiling, which is also the stage floor, mixed with dried paint from the sets which is bad for the eyes and the lungs . . . Not having a corner or a dressing room of their own, which did not exist at the time of which I write, the actors had nowhere to take shelter; these servants of beauty had to wander through dirty corridors and dressing rooms while waiting for their entrance. Endless smoking . . . gossiping, flirting, scandal-mongering, stories are the natural consequence of the inhuman conditions the actors are in. It is in such circumstances that the servants of the muses spend three-quarters of their lives.

My Life in Art, 159–62[29]

The role of the director, while apparently not of uppermost importance during their discussion about why they should form the Moscow Art Theatre, was understood to be essential for making a production a unified whole. Nemirovich-Danchenko was to write subsequently that the director was a 'triple-faced creature': an interpreter or pedagogue, who instructed actors how to play; a mirror 'reflecting the individual qualities of an actor'; and an organizer 'of the entire production'.[30] As for the production, 'its most crucial element' was 'its inner meaning, the strength and beauty of the total picture'.[31]

Stanislavsky's sense of himself primarily as an actor eventually led him to believe that an actor could not yield the best results unless he or she was the co-author of the theatre-making process; and it was to this end that, in 1905, after he had directed Chekhov's four great plays, he set up laboratory-type possibilities for the former MAT actor Vsevolod Meyerhold, in the Theatre-Studio. ('Theatre-studio' was a term coined by Meyerhold.) The venture failed for several different reasons, but the idea that the actor's ongoing input was necessary for the creative process of theatre was to grow in the years to come. The director in such a process was neither a tyrant nor a manipulator, but a collaborator whose task was to enable the actor: Stanislavsky observed in 1914 that the director could be compared to a midwife who 'guides the rightness of the birth in the right direction'.[32]

In Stanislavsky's focus on the specific role of the director, who is not above, but always active *in relation to* the actor, can be seen the modern ensemble director of the twentieth century and the twenty-first. This newly emerging kind of director, of whom Stanislavsky was the progenitor in and through his shifting, frequently contradictory variations on directing until his death in 1938, was a catalytic and sometimes even a revolutionary force in the very practice of theatre.

In the Russian school of directing, Stanislavsky's identification of the actor's creative responsibility for a performance was influential in different ways, going from Maria Knebel and Boris Zon, who were among Stanislavsky's last pupils, to Anatoli Vassiliev and Lev Dodin. The effects of Stanislavsky's emphasis on the creative responsibility of actors was equally influential beyond Russia, reaching Jacques Copeau, for instance, who was inspired by this and other MAT ideals to form his experimental group of actors 'les copiaux'. And it affected, to varying degrees, a whole range of major directors emerging as powerful innovators in the 1960s whose development of actors within closely knit groups was an integral part of their collective experiments. All of them gave rise to different artistic idioms, most having nothing to do with psychological realism in any way whatsoever. Take, among them, Ariane Mnouchkine, whose idea of actor-driven 'collective creation', as she called it at the beginning, came down the genealogical tree from Copeau, carrying Stanislavsky's laboratory/theatre-studio principle with it.

This, however, was the future. Stanislavsky's pathway goes back to the Meiningen Players whom he had seen on their second tour to Russia in 1890. He was impressed by the pervasive sense of harmony of the company's productions. Chronegk's handling of crowd scenes drew his admiration, but most inspiring of all was the picture-portrait historical accuracy of the costumes, which he copied into his notebooks, night after night, and which became his model for *Tsar Fyodor Ioannich*, his first production for the MAT in 1898. This type of verisimilitude of setting dovetailed with Zola's notion of 'milieu', a cornerstone of his theory of naturalism, which resonated with the left and liberal Russian intelligentsia all the more because it also promoted the idea of the social usefulness of art. Vestiges of the latter idea – which had taken root in the Russian context independently of Zola, aided by such radical texts as Nikolay Chernyshevsky's 1862 *What Is to Be Done?* and Leo Tolstoy's 1897 *What Is Art?* – surfaced in Stanislavsky's and Nemirovich-Danchenko's belief that the MAT should be 'accessible' to everybody (*obshche-dostupny*). However, the word was dropped fairly quickly from the proposed name of the theatre. Yet the goal of democratic access to *art* – MAT fare was decidedly not entertainment – remained in Stanislavsky's assumption that clarity of pictorial exposition (verisimilitude) on the part of a director, together with integrity of feeling (the Tolstoyan dimension of Stanislavsky's thought), provided the likelihood of understanding across a broad spectrum of people anticipated to be the theatre's audience.

Chronegk's imprint on Stanislavsky's first productions at the MAT is indisputable, as is also the case for his earlier productions, largely with amateurs, starting with the 1891 *The Fruits of Enlightenment* by Tolstoy. Whether Stanislavsky was directly influenced by Antoine is not known for certain, although he clearly adopted the concept of 'milieu' and so the exact reproduction of social and natural detail on the stage that was key to Antoine, as was the argument, spurred on by Zola, that the life of the lower social classes was a subject of vital importance for the theatre.

The sociopolitical thinking behind Stanislavsky's choice of plays is by no means transparent. He directed Hauptmann, Ibsen, Tolstoy and Gorky – playwrights selected by Antoine – because they were of his time; and staging contemporary writers and their concerns was integral to the goals of the MAT. As for Chekhov, the company's flagship author, Stanislavsky approached him at first with some trepidation, not experiencing ease with his elliptical ways until *The Cherry Orchard*, which he directed in 1904. Part of the problem for Stanislavsky, when directing Chekhov, was merging the plays' rich 'inner meaning', as Nemirovich-Danchenko put it, with tangible outer expression and, as well, tempering the 'outer' when the 'inner' could not be reached appropriately through illustrative, lifelike means.

He found this to be especially the case when he directed the symbolist playwright Maeterlinck, failing to communicate the mysterious world of Maeterlinck's *Les aveugles*, *Intérieurs* and *L'intruse*, which he staged as a triple bill in 1904. He was far more successful in 1908 with *The Blue Bird*, not least because he found, albeit by accident, the secret of making things disappear by using walls of black velvet, but also because he had, by then, fully realized the value of stylizing the actions of actors on the stage. This meant moving actors away from the performance of everyday behaviour, which was 'naturalism' in the strict sense of the word, and also away from the collocation of 'everyday behaviour' with 'milieu'. It also meant taking some distance from the notion that art was to reproduce things as they are – indeed, 'in nature'. After his work on Maeterlinck, both *The Blue Bird* and the short plays cited, Stanislavsky reflected on the inadequacies of directing to a formula, as if one applied to all. He thus noted in his journal in 1910:

> The appearance of stylization on the stage of the Art Theatre was not accidental. It was the natural step in the development of the theatre, in which we all shared. The Art Theatre was never a purely naturalistic theatre. It always conformed only to the spirit of the author, to his style. When the theatre mounted purely realistic drama, for example *The Power of Darkness* [1902], it was realistic in its detail, which the actor used to help himself; these were the demands of the author (the comments of the author himself).[33]

Then, in an uncanny echo of Konstantin's words in *The Seagull*, Stanislavsky observes that 'new drama appears – new forms appear'.[34] The search for new forms, including new methods of directing, was made necessary by Maeterlinck and, in another way again, by Chekhov, whose newness the Moscow Art Theatre had to learn to grasp.

Naturalism and realism

Although Stanislavsky seems to be using the terms 'naturalistic' and 'realistic' synonymously, a case is to be made for the difference between the two. The first refers to the surface of a production, and the second to a more comprehensive view that absorbs the inner justifications for outward appearance. It is the difference between the description of a phenomenon or state of affairs and an analysis, which situates and explains them. Stanislavsky recognized this distinction fully when he directed his actors, as early as *The Seagull* in 1898, to embody the psycho-emotional motives, conscious and unconscious, of their characters. His inspiration to search for this 'inner realism', as Stanislavsky termed it, which entailed coordination of psychological impulse, feeling, action and truthful rendition, came from Tommaso Salvini, whom he had seen in Russia, and the Russian actor Mikhail Shchepkin, who was reputed to have been without parallel in the immediacy and veracity of his characterization.

It was the surface, quasi-photographic 'setting' aspect of naturalism that so appealed to Stanislavsky that he drew the rooms, passages, furniture and gardens of his Chekhov productions in minute detail, adding soundscapes to complete the picture – the sound of frogs, crickets, corncrakes, dogs and distant bells, and anything else that built up a credible environment for the people in it and the events taking place there. Nemirovich-Danchenko complained to Stanislavsky about the croaking frogs during the performance of Konstantin's play, indicating that *The Seagull* was 'written in delicate pencil and demands, in my view, great care in the staging'.[35] He wrote to Chekhov about the opening night of *Uncle Vanya* (1899) noting that the actors' tendency to overplay was the fault of the director and his 'fondness for underlining things, for noise and external effects'.[36] In his letter to Chekhov about *The Three Sisters* (1901) he returned to the theme of 'clutter', his epithet for Stanislavsky's 'super-abundance of detail . . . all the moving around, the noises, the exclamations'.[37]

Chekhov, ever tremulous about the success of his plays, rarely missed an opportunity for ironicizing about Stanislavsky's preoccupation with 'noise', Olga Knipper's dismissive term, as well as that of Nemirovich-Danchenko. (Olga Knipper, MAT actress, who played Arkadina in *The Seagull*, was soon to become Chekhov's wife.) In response to Stanislavsky's request for permission to 'bring a train with little puffs of smoke across', Chekhov quipped that he could go ahead providing the train made its appearance 'without any noise, not a sound'.[38] The joke appears to have been on Stanislavsky, yet Stanislavsky was rather more than a director of external effects. 'Clutter' aside, he was looking, as a director, for a double solution to two problems: how to communicate the significance of scenic elements and how to concentrate the audience's attention. Accordingly, he pointed out to Nemirovich-Danchenko:

> Consider this, I put frogs in during the play scene to create total quiet. Quiet is conveyed in the theatre not by silence but by noise. If you don't fill the silence with noise you can't create the illusion. Why? Because people backstage (management, unwanted visitors) and the public in the auditorium make noise and break the mood on stage.[39]

Stanislavsky's remarks regarding quiet square with decidedly anti-realist director Robert Wilson's contention that seeing and hearing on stage is channelled best through the juxtaposition of opposites – in Stanislavsky's case, the perception of silence through noise.[40]

Here, as in other examples, Stanislavsky attempted to turn 'detail' into a directorial rather than pictorial device. So, for instance, the ploy of the 'fourth wall', which he borrowed from Antoine, the inventor of both the phrase and the convention. By seating the spectators of the play within the play of *The Seagull* towards the edge of the stage, with their back to the audience, he was able not only to gather energy within the stage and so establish what he called the 'circle of attention' of the actors, but also to set up the requisite tension between the actors/characters and between them and the audience.[41] As a consequence, he was able to follow the emotional tone established right at the start through the various scenes and structural 'bits' (Stanislavsky's terminology, translated also as 'units') that led to the conclusion, and the cohesiveness, of the production. Oleg Efremov, when he was the artistic director of the MAT, used Stanislavsky's device quite ostentatiously for his 1980 *Seagull* to demonstrate, with knowing humour, its boldness and efficacy.

Yet even the frogs and dogs that had provoked sarcasm were not merely illustrative, but provided a support for the actors, helping them to find, feel and express their characters in the prescribed contexts. The atmosphere created by a soundscape helped actors to penetrate their characters and identify not only their sensations, thoughts and mood (the inner journey necessary for embodying 'inner realism'), but also their possible actions in response to the given situation – what they might do and how they might do it in relation to other characters. Furthermore, this support helped actors to find the tempo-rhythm appropriate for their character in that precise situation at that precise moment. And a soundscape gave the musical key to a scene, sustaining its musicality – tempo-rhythm, beat, pace, intonation – which, while sustaining the work of the actors, guided the spectators, 'telling' them what kind of scene it was and arousing their emotions to interact with it. In other words, already at this early stage of his work as a director, Stanislavsky was intuitively looking for ways to help the actor in a *scenic* context where compositional elements, in this case the soundscape, were meant to operate together with the actors (and with each other) in an organically interconnected combination.

The Seagull

Stanislavsky's production score of *The Seagull* offers great insight into how he envisaged this process. Note that he called his director's manual or prompt book a score (*partitura*), exactly as in music, to suggest both the organicity and the structural formality of the process. Stanislavsky prepared this score in isolation (at his brother's house in the country) and handed it over, ready made, to the MAT actors, who were waiting to rehearse in a retreat at Pushkino, outside Moscow. The score makes it abundantly clear that Stanislavsky, here, was none other than the director-autocrat whom he was later to repudiate, fixing his interpretation of the play, allowing no scope whatsoever for the creativity of the actors and controlling sound, design, costume and every other production component. Here was the first incarnation of the new director with his pre-collaborative face, projecting his single, unified conception. Yet its pre-emptive strike and precision make it fascinating to observe at close quarters how such a director *imagines* a production; and the imaginative power of the score, for all its occasionally overwrought sequences, is compelling.

Take, for example, the close of Act I, which shows the very careful attention Stanislavsky pays to the opening and closing of acts: these are dramaturgical turning points, providing him with opportunities for heightened theatrical moments of revelation (of a character's hidden feelings), consolidation (of information), anticipation (of change), suspense, and so on. The example confirms a number of the points regarding soundscapes raised above. The scene itself could be taken as a climax, a 'summing up' of sorts, of the comparable situations in which all the protagonists find themselves. The chain of events leading up to it is, briefly: Konstantin's play has ended in a debacle; Arkadina suddenly has an inkling of Trigorin's and Nina's future love affair; Arkadina and her son have clashed, both fearing the loss of their love – Trigorin for Arkadina and Nina, Konstantin's love; spectators have begun to suspect Masha loves Konstantin; Masha and Dorn close the act. Stanislavsky places Chekhov's text and his own directorial commentary side by side in the production score, on opposite pages. The numbers in bold below provide a cross-reference between them and are consecutive for each act. In the Russian original, Stanislavsky numbers his interpolations afresh on each page, always starting from '1'. It is also to be noted, since this changes the scene's tempo-rhythm, that the English translator adds suspension marks not in Chekhov's text.

Chekhov's text:	**Stanislavsky's directions:**
MASHA: Oh, I'm so miserable! No one, no one knows how wretched I am! (*Puts her head on his chest. Softly.*) I love Konstantin! DORN: How overwrought they all are! How overwrought! And so much love,	**114**. Masha bursts into sobs, and, kneeling, buries her head on Dorn's knees. A pause of fifteen seconds. Dorn is stroking Masha's head. The frenzied waltz grows louder, sounds of the tolling of a church-bell, of a

too ... Oh, that spell-binding lake! (*Gently*) **114** But what can I do, my dear child? What? ... What? ... **115**	peasant's song, of frogs, of a corncrake, the knocking of the night watchman, and all sorts of other nocturnal effects **115** Curtain[42]

Clearly, Stanislavsky dictates the actors' actions and gestures, adding to Chekhov's stage directions (thus Masha moves from Dorn's chest to his knees) as Masha reveals and consolidates information. More significant is the long pause timed precisely to fifteen seconds after this action, first because it gives the actors space to affirm their play of emotions in relation to each other and, second because, like silence in a musical score, it is integral to the musicality of the piece. The musicality is striking for its contrast of tones and timbres (waltz, bell and frogs against each other, and so on) in which Masha's sobs are also a voice. This polyphonic nocturne assists the actors, especially Masha, to find their emotional tone (or tones) within themselves so that the sound of Masha's sobbing is not merely 'noise'. Worthy of attention, too, is the lyrical, poetic quality of the score, albeit potentially marred by Masha's exaggerated sobbing on Dorn's knees. Note, as well, that Stanislavsky has the curtain fall at a very precise point, straight after the second 'What?'

Take another example of Stanislavsky's imaginative response as a director, which, at the same time, translates as instructions to the actors. It concerns pauses, a prominent feature of his production scores for Chekhov in general. Most of them are timed exactly – five, ten, fifteen seconds and in fractional combinations – and all serve multiple purposes: psychological, emotional, structural, narrative, musical and, as well, the purpose of embracing the spiritual dimension of human life, which Stanislavsky, throughout his writings, called 'the life of the human spirit'. This example comes from a relatively short way into Act IV. Two years have passed since the end of Act III. Dorn has just asked Konstantin how Nina is 'getting on'. Dorn, to Konstantin's reply that it is a 'long story', asks him to 'make it short' – typical of Chekhov's dry humour. Chekhov follows this dialogue by 'A pause'. Stanislavsky's note to the pause goes as follows:

> **37.** A pause. Konstantin props his head up with his hands, his elbows resting on his knees. His gaze [is] fixed steadily at one point. Dorn is rocking himself in the chair and, as Konstantin's story grows sadder and sadder, his rocking grows slower and slower, until, at last, at the pause, he stops rocking himself altogether. The whole scene proceeds like that. All of them are motionless, as though frozen. Medvyedenko goes back to the stove. At the very beginning of Konstantin's story, Masha crosses over to Pauline, who puts her arm around her, strokes her head,

> pressing her close to herself. (I fancy both of them understand each other and each of them suffers in her own way.) The expression on Masha's face constantly changes.[43]

It is clear, from this direction, that Stanislavsky takes into account all the purposes referred to above, weaving them into each other in a living score, which, to be composed by actors, must breathe then and there in all its layers, like played music, in the moment of performance.

A third example from towards the end of Act IV foregrounds the psycho-emotional interaction between Konstantin and Nina in terms of 'inner' or 'psychological' realism:

Chekhov's text:

KONSTANTIN: Oh, Nina, I cursed you, hated you, tore up your letters and photographs, but every minute I was conscious that I belonged to you, that my heart was yours for ever. I find it impossible, Nina, to stop loving you. Ever since I lost you and my stories began to appear in print, life has been unbearable to me. I suffered agonies, agonies ... It was as though I were an old man of ninety. I prayed for you to come back, I kissed the ground you had walked on. Wherever I looked, I saw your dear face, your sweet smile, which brought so much sunshine into the best years of my life ...

NINA (*bewildered*): Why does he talk like this? Why does he talk like this?

KONSTANTIN: **119** I am alone in the world, Nina. I have no one whose affection might warm me. I'm cold, cold, as though I lived in some underground dungeon, and everything I write is dry, harsh, gloomy. Please, stay Nina, I implore you! Or let me go away with you!

Nina quickly puts on her hat and cloak. **120**

KONSTANTIN: Nina, why? For God's sake – (*Looks at her as she puts her things on; a pause.*) **121**

Stanislavsky's interpolations:

119. (Konstantin seizes her hand ecstatically and covers it with kisses. Nina tries to free her hand and turns away so that he should not see her face. Konstantin is drawn to her more and more.) [A note from the editor says that this was crossed out with a black pencil by Nemirovich-Danchenko. He was definitely 'keeping an eye' on Stanislavsky, as promised to Chekhov!]

120. Nina runs across the whole length of the stage to the french [*sic*] windows and puts on her hat and cloak there. Konstantin follows her.

121. No pause here under any circumstances.

122. She opens french [*sic*] windows to go out (noise of the wind rushing into the room). Then she stops – leans against the jamb of the door and bursts into sobs. Konstantin, who is leaning against the lamp-post, stands motionless, gazing at Nina. Whistling of wind from the open door. 'Could you give me some water, please?' Spoken between her sobs.

123. Konstantin walks off slowly (the jug of water is near the mirror in front of the stage), pours some water into a

NINA: My cab is waiting for me at the gate ... Don't see me out, please. I'll find my way alone ... (*Bursts into tears.*) **122** Could you give me some water, please? **123**

KONSTANTIN (*gives NINA a glass of water*): Where are you going now?

NINA: To the town. (*Pause.*) **124** Is your mother here? **125**

glass (sound of glass knocking against the jug), and gives it to her. A pause. Nina drinks. (Conversation in the dining-room.)

124. Nina wipes her tears with a handkerchief and smothers her sobs. Konstantin stands motionless, glass in hand, leaning against the lamp-post, staring lifelessly at one point. This is where he really dies.

125. Nina speaks restraining her sobs.[44]

What matters in this scene is the precision, complexity and nuance of characterization in action ('psychological realism') towards which Stanislavsky is groping, not always successfully. Successful or not, Nina's 'run across the whole length of the stage to the french windows' belongs to his preliminary attempts at merging inner psychological drive with outer physical expression. This is the precursor of the principle of psychophysical action which is part of the 'system' explored and noted down in the volume translated by Jean Benedetti as *An Actor's Work* (2008).

The 'How?' of Nina's run and similar questions regarding truthful execution led to Stanislavsky's technique of 'affective memory' (known also as 'emotion memory') which the actor was to draw from within himself/herself for the realization of the role; and what was truthful, for Stanislavsky, was tied up with acting that was unforced, organic, *natural*, but nevertheless fashioned through what he continually described as the 'laws' of art. The trick was to find the art of natural acting (which undoubtedly gave rise to the mistaken usage of the term 'naturalistic' for Stanislavsky's artistic objectives); and it was precisely for this type of performance that he began to devise the mental and physical exercises constituting the 'system'. Stanislavsky's remark about Konstantin, 'This is where he really dies', draws attention to the inner movement of 'the soul' – Stanislavsky's *dukh*, which he frequently links to *dusha*, meaning heart. And the prompt to the actor essentially to do nothing, but simply to stare 'lifelessly' at nothing in particular, is a call for natural acting. Stanislavsky is well aware, at this point, that the challenge for both the director and the actor is to embody the invisible moment when, somewhere in the interstices between what is said, unsaid, done and not done, the die for the character is cast. Note, also, Stanislavsky's rejection of Chekhov's pause, an uncharacteristic move, given his near-obsession with pauses. But here, the director in him appears to want the dramatic urgency of run-on movement.

3 *The Seagull*, Act IV (Moskvin as Medvedenko, Vishnevsky as Dorn, Meyerhold as Konstantin, Luzhsky as Sorin, Raevskaya as Polina, Lilina as Masha), Konstantin Stanislavsky, Moscow Art Theatre, 1896

Stanislavsky's capacity to shape 'bits' through physical movement is quite evident in this section from Act IV, and he gives it free rein in his scores for *Uncle Vanya*, *The Three Sisters* and *The Cherry Orchard*. Yet more, still, was involved than articulating sense through movement. Stanislavsky, in *The Seagull*, was in fact 'rephrasing the material, giving it a shape different from the author's',[45] and this was possible because Stanislavsky was already separating the theatre from literature, already working towards the distinction he made categorically in 1909 between 'literary theatre' and 'action theatre' when he staged *A Month in the Country* by Turgenev.[46] In this production, Stanislavsky replaced the logic of the text by the logic of stage action, which entailed deleting scenes from Turgenev and adding new ones for the dynamics of the stage work. Stanislavsky's operations demonstrated that theatre was an art in its own right, and that the director, in such a case, was not merely a translator of an author's ideas, but an independent creator of *another*, separate, entity.

Acting 'with the body'

The issue of both the status of the director and the identity of a directed production was the sticking point of his relationship with Nemirovich-Danchenko, latent at the time of *The Seagull* but reaching a point of no return with *A Month in the Country*, since Nemirovich, besides being a director with his own views on directing, was invested in the stakes as a playwright for whom the *playwright's* text was of paramount importance. Stanislavsky, by contrast, had begun to question the supremacy of the writer, observing in his notebook of 1902, after his production of *The Three Sisters*, that

> the author writes on paper. The actor writes with his body on stage.
>
> The score of an opera is not the opera itself and the script of a play is not drama until both are made flesh and blood on stage.
>
> The theatre is a synthesis of literature, music and the living word, living characters, living movement and dance against a life-size artistic background.[47]

Emphasis on the actor writing 'with his body' necessarily entailed a different perspective on the theatre, regarding not only its 'synthesis' – echoes of Wagner's *Gesamtkunstwerk* – but also its reliance on actors who were autonomous, that is, not imitators of an author's words, but creators of their own other-than-verbal compositions. Subsequently, in 1909, during the period of *A Month in the Country*, Stanislavsky wrote that such actors

> use a poet's work [that is, a creative writer's work] as a theme for their own creative work and carry it out no less independently than the poet does, although they do not do it in a verbal form, but in the form of images. The poet creates with words and lines, but the actor – creates without words and between the lines.[48]

The seeds of the 'system' are doubtless to be found in the framework of these thoughts, since all of its lures for the imagination and other psychophysical training techniques are intended to help actors write with their body and 'between the lines'.

By this time, Stanislavsky had come a long way from the 'director-dictator' he had once been, fashioned after Chronegk. For all his self-criticism, the Chronegk-type director was, in his view, the consequence of 'the absence of trained actors', and in their absence 'the centre of gravity of a production went over to the staging. The necessity of being creative on everyone's behalf turned the director into a dictator.'[49] (This, as will be observed in Chapter 5, was something Stanislavsky's contemporary Gordon Craig also experienced.) The more Stanislavsky worked on his 'system', the more, as a director, he shifted the centre of gravity back to the actors, eschewing the cover-up of poor acting by the 'director's talent'.[50] This not only meant removing the director's control through his reading and gloss of a play with his actors around a table, which was the accepted MAT practice, especially during Chekhov productions. It meant a different method altogether, that of actors working with their bodies, devising on the basis of *études*, on their feet, from the very beginning of a given project. It entailed, as well, a change of perspective away from 'affective memory' towards the 'method of physical action' by which the very act of doing, of physicality rather than of cognition, on the one hand, and the recovery of the unconscious, on the other, triggered off the self-awareness, sense of self in action, state of spirit, and the emotions appropriate and necessary for the role being played. The director, in this process, was a prompt, a help, a guide – indeed a 'midwife', in Stanislavsky's words.

Yet, with this method, Stanislavsky opened up another dimension of the director, that of the pedagogue. This was not Nemirovich-Danchenko's pedagogue who 'instructed actors how to play', but a pedagogue who prised individuality out of actors, facilitating their self-empowerment. Stanislavsky's last experiments with actors from 1934 to 1938 gave rise to an assiduous rehearsal method of action ('writing with their bodies'), which was a means of coming to grips with the structure and sequences of play texts. This approach, known as Action Analysis or Active Analysis, was the exact antithesis of the study of words on the page promoted by the 'around-the-table' discussions of Stanislavsky's early years. This legacy, transmitted by Maria Knebel and Mikhaïl Kedrov, both of whom became directors of the Stanislavsky Drama Theatre in 1948, attempted to fuse the Word and the actor, making the Word 'flesh and blood'. This mode of invention, based on *études*, like the preceding 'method of physical action', sought correspondence with the structure of the chosen text, but was owned by the actor. The director in this process was a vital presence, aiding actors to run their course in rehearsals so that the envisaged production could be alive, in the moment, on the stage: 'here, today, now', as Stanislavsky termed it. The director here might appear to have been effaced, but, in fact, his/her input was embedded in the production, since the actor was the vehicle of the production, and consequently, to borrow Stanislavsky's words, the 'centre of gravity' could not go over into 'the staging'. Outside Russia, the heir to this kind of seemingly invisible but wholly present directing was none other than Jerzy Grotowski, whom we will meet later in this book.

Further reading

Beacham, Richard. *Adolphe Appia: Theatre Artist* (Directors in Perspective), Cambridge University Press, 1987

Benedetti, Jean. *Stanislavsky: His Life and Art, A Biography*, London: Methuen, 1999

Carnegy, Patrick. *Wagner and the Art of the Theatre*, New Haven, CT: Yale University Press, 2006

Carnicke, Sharon Marie. *Stanislavsky in Focus: An Acting Master for the Twenty-First Century*, London and New York: Routledge, 2009

Chothia, Jean. *André Antoine* (Directors in Perspective), Cambridge University Press, 1991

Innes, Christopher. *Edward Gordon Craig: A Vision of Theatre*, Amsterdam: Harwood Academic Publishers, 1988

Knapp, Bettina. *The Reign of the Theatrical Director: French Theatre, 1887–1924*, Troy, NY: Whitston, 1988

Koller, Anne Marie. *The Theater Duke: Georg II of Saxe-Meiningen and the German Stage*, Stanford University Press, 1984

Merlin, Bella. *Stanislavsky*, London and New York: Routledge, 2003

Stanislavsky, Konstantin. *An Actor's Work*, trans. Jean Benedetti, London and New York: Routledge, 2008

My Life in Art, trans. Jean Benedetti, London and New York: Routledge, 2008

Worral, Nick. *The Moscow Art Theatre*, London and New York: Routledge, 1996

Chapter 3

Directors of theatricality

Vsevolod Meyerhold: *commedia dell'arte* to biomechanics

Meyerhold was one of the most daring experimenters of the twentieth century, exploring a breathtaking variety of ways of making theatre, and it is with him that the directorial line of theatricality begins. Like Stanislavsky, he was an actor, who had considerable success playing Konstantin Treplev in Stanislavsky's *The Seagull*, and performing in the provinces as well as in St Petersburg at the theatre of the renowned actress Vera Komissarzhevskaya. Despite his acclaim as an actor, he concentrated his efforts on directing, including productions at the Mariinsky Opera. His last stage performances were during the 1916–17 season of the Aleksandrinsky Theatre, an august establishment which, like the Mariinsky, was part of the group of imperial theatres of St Petersburg. However, he continued to act by proxy in so far as, in rehearsals, he 'demonstrated, demonstrated, demonstrated' to the actors.[1] His improvisation skills and capacity for 'instantaneous inspiration' made him an outstanding actor-demonstrator – a role of fundamental importance to his work as a director throughout his life. Meyerhold, unlike Stanislavsky, saw himself as a director, first and foremost.

Meyerhold was the stage director of the Aleksandrinsky from 1908 to 1917. His was an unlikely appointment given the theatre's strong links with the aristocratic elite, although, in fact, its liberal managing director had brought him in to breathe new life into this Tsarist institution. It was during his Aleksandrinsky period that, under the alias of Doctor Dapertutto, Meyerhold started the theatre-studios where he trained actors, a practice he was to continue after his return to Moscow. Many of his students were to become brilliant performers in his companies; and this actor training was also fundamental to his work as a director, since it provided him and his team with a common artistic understanding.

In 1920, after a number of vicissitudes following the 1917 Revolution, Meyerhold was called back to Moscow by the Soviet government, which he supported unreservedly. He directed almost exclusively in Moscow thereafter, with one or two exceptions in the 1930s in St Petersburg, renamed Leningrad. He went to Leningrad in 1939 to survey his professional prospects after having suffered ignominious political attack and humiliation, not least of which had been the liquidation of his theatre. It was in Leningrad, in June 1939, that he was arrested on trumped up charges and returned to Moscow, to the infamous Lyubyanka prison where he was repeatedly tortured until he was shot in February 1940. To his dying day, he remained a communist, dedicated to the Soviet Union and to the transformative power of his theatre work for Soviet society.

Theatricality, stylization and the grotesque

These few details of Meyerhold's working biography shed light on the very broad range of his directorial activities, which drove, rather than were driven by, his ceaseless invention of new theatre forms. Meyerhold invented by appropriating fairground, marketplace and other types of popular performances, as did Brecht (see Chapter 4), and by rediscovering lost practices, especially ritual, which he associated with Ancient Greek tragedy, and *commedia dell'arte*, which he unearthed with a commitment outmatched only by Giorgio Strehler after the Second World War (see Chapter 6). Undaunted by the reigning conventions of genre, he merged different performance and visual forms, which entailed close collaboration with architects, designers, painters, sculptors and other practitioners beyond the theatre.

Collaboration of this kind was not only a major source of Meyerhold's inventiveness, but also allowed him to come nearer to the ideal of the 'total' work, as envisaged by Craig, who was Meyerhold's model director-designer. Meyerhold added music to his ambitions for a dynamic interface between the arts, joining up with various composers throughout his career. The most spectacular of them was Dmitry Shostakovich, whom he employed to play the piano in his theatre and whom he asked, in 1929, to compose the music for *The Bedbug* by Vladimir Mayakovsky. Mayakovsky had already made a name for himself as an avant-garde iconoclast, and Shostakovich was well on the way to acquiring notoriety for his rule-breaking compositions. Meyerhold asked the no less radical Constructivist artist Aleksandr Rodchenko – sculptor, graphic designer, photographer – to design the same production: this was Rodchenko's introduction to scenography.

For images of Rodchenko's futuristic design for *The Bedbug*, see http://max.mmlc.northwestern.edu/~mdenner/Drama/plays/bedbug/2bedbug.html.

Meyerhold was the first to direct all of Mayakovsky's plays, and Mayakovsky was the only contemporary Russian author with whom he was in such deep accord artistically and politically that Mayakovsky rewrote his texts without demur to suit his directorial needs.

An earlier collaboration was with Aleksandr Blok, the author of the quasi-mystical, symbolist *The Fairground Booth*, which Meyerhold staged at Komissarzhevskaya's theatre in 1906. A sense of mystery, so different from the clatter and bang of *The Bedbug* many years later, ran in an undercurrent through Meyerhold's highly physical production, to which he contributed his own extraordinarily agile, even balletic, performance as Pierrot. Meyerhold's central focus as a director was not on the production's transcendental dimension, which, in any case, he treated with irony (more so in his 1908 and 1914 versions, this follow-up to his original production indicating its importance for him), but on Columbine, Pierrot and Harlequin and the opportunity they offered for exploring improvisation, puppetry, masks, dance, song and *commedia*-style jest and mime.

The production involved a small fairground booth constructed at the centre of the stage with its own curtain, prompter's box, and so on. When the booth was hauled up into the flies, all the mechanics – ropes, pulleys, wires – were made fully visible to the audience. Furthermore, Meyerhold used the forestage and theatre boxes for play (Harlequin's rapid escape was through one of these boxes), thereby starting with this extension of performance space what was to become nothing short of his obsession with spatial arrangement, each space tailored to the production at hand. In this respect, Meyerhold fulfilled his aspirations to be a director-designer and, more still, a director capable of anything and everything else required. He was to say, in the mid 1930s, that 'a director must be a dramatist and artist [stage designer] and musician and electrician and tailor', and more, besides.[2]

A director's 'musts'

A director must know all the spheres that make up the art of the theatre. I had the opportunity to watch Edward Gordon Craig at rehearsal, and I was always won over by the fact that he didn't shout 'Give me a blue light!' but indicated precisely, 'Switch on lamps No. 3 and 8!' He could even speak professionally with a carpenter, although he probably couldn't build a chair himself . . . When the wardrobe mistress brings the newly finished costumes, the director mustn't hem and haw, 'Here a little tighter, and here a little looser', but indicate precisely, 'Rip out this seam, and put a wire in here'. Only then will lazy assistants not argue that it's impossible to alter anything, as they usually do, and you won't have to take them at their word. Stanislavsky studied pattern cutting in Paris in order to understand the nature of the art of the stage.

> A director must know how to stage everything. He doesn't have the right to be like a doctor who specializes only in children's ailments, or in venereal diseases . . . A director who claims he can stage only tragedies and doesn't know how to stage comedies or vaudevilles, is certain to fail, because in genuine art the high and the low, the bitter and the funny, the light and the dark always stand side by side.
>
> I was an actor with a broad range: I played both comic and tragic roles, and nearly even women's parts. I studied music and choreography. Besides this, I studied law, wrote for the newspapers, and translated foreign languages. I consider myself a litterateur and a teacher. All this has been useful to me in my work as a director. If I knew still other specialties, they would also be useful. A director must know many things. There is an expression: 'a narrow specialty'. Directing is the broadest specialty in the world.
>
> Aleksandr Gladkov, *Meyerhold Speaks, Meyerhold Rehearses*, 126–67

The director Yevgeny Vakhtangov, who was a pupil of Stanislavsky, wrote about Meyerhold in his diary: 'Here is a stage director of genius . . . Each of his productions is in itself a new theatre, each could generate a new trend.'[3] This prescient observation was made in 1921, *before* Meyerhold broke new ground again, first with the exuberant montage that was *The Magnanimous Cuckold* (1922) and then with *The Government Inspector* (1926), a fully fledged episodic structure like no other in his entire career. It came, however, *after* Meyerhold's spectacularly opulent *Masquerade*, his last production at the Aleksandrinsky and the most expensive venture ever undertaken by that theatre. *Masquerade*, a fantasia on Mikhaïl Lermontov's play of high-society intrigue and revenge-murder, opened in February 1917 to gunfire in the streets presaging the Revolution. Its visual splendour, with designs and costumes by Aleksandr Golovin, who had designed for Diaghilev's Ballets Russes, well and truly marked the end of an era.

Meyerhold invented this extravagant genre for spoken theatre (the ballet and opera of the imperial theatres had already made visual magnificence a defining characteristic of their form), but referred in it to the visceral, popular world of *The Fairground Booth*. Towards the end of his elaborate composition, he layered in an unexpected element, the figure of The Stranger dressed in a *commedia*-inspired mask, hat and cloak. More even than in Lermontov's play, The Stranger, for Meyerhold, was a figure of fate with a strong demonic dimension, whom he directed as a conductor might conduct a musical motif. The work certainly demonstrated Meyerhold's capacity to generate 'a new theatre' with every production. Yet, as was noted by Mikhaïl Chekhov, Meyerhold 'could not bear to wait, something inside him kept urging him on';[4] and this prevented him from firmly establishing and consolidating the new trends incipient in his successive productions. Meyerhold's restless experimental energy was such that it provoked even Picasso, whose thirst for experimentation was already legendary, to tell Meyerhold jokingly that he regarded him as a rival.[5] His next shot at 'new theatre' following *Masquerade* was the 1918 *Mystery-Bouffe*, Mayakovsky's satirical parable on the defeat of capitalism by a utopian post-revolutionary future. Meyerhold, the director, was now directed by the turbulent political changes sweeping the country from day to day.

While *Masquerade* and *Mystery-Bouffe* were landmarks in Meyerhold's variegated evolution as a director, *The Fairground Booth*, in its celebration of popular theatre, rejection of literature-oriented textual interpretation, indifference to characterization and exposure of the technicalities of staging, was the first unquestionably successful battle in his lifelong war against the theatre of verisimilitude and illusion, whether according to Meiningen-style naturalism or Stanislavskian realism. It was, in his words, a work of 'pure theatricality' and, having achieved this goal, there was no looking back.[6] Meyerhold's idea of 'theatricality' (*teatralnost*) is specific. It is related to Russian formalist Viktor Shklovsky's notion of *literaturnost* (commonly translated as 'literariness'), which means: qualities intrinsic to literature that make literature uniquely itself; the irreducible essence of literature that is not, and cannot be, a copy, 'like life'. *Teatralnost*, as a parallel term, refers to what makes theatre irreducibly itself, and this principle necessarily involved, for Meyerhold, directing in such a way as to heighten quite deliberately the playfulness, artfulness, artifice and joy of making theatre understood as an activity in its own right. This was an activity other than – different from – 'life'.

Meyerhold also shared with Shklovsky the view that artistic forms could not pretend just to be there, as if they had come into existence by themselves. This dissemblance was unavoidable, as Meyerhold saw it, in the theatre of illusion, which relied on the 'fourth wall'. 'Theatricality', then, was an imperative to show *how* a director was directing, that is, to show the very processes in train when a work was being done. Here Meyerhold was most probably influenced by Shklovsky's idea that literature (Meyerhold's 'theatre') should 'lay bare' its devices of construction and composition. In the case of *The Fairground Booth*, the devices were 'laid bare' when the booth went up into the flies. (Curtains did not come down, for instance, to hide what was happening, as was usual at the time, particularly in naturalist or realist productions.) Where Meyerhold differed from Shklovsky – and this was a huge difference – was his conviction that theatre, like any art, was useful to society. Shklovsky, by contrast, was closer to pre-revolutionary notions of 'art for art's sake'.

The Fairground Booth was such an important incubator of Meyerhold's ideas about himself as a director and the type of work that he wished to direct that, in 1912, he published his seminal essay, called, indeed, 'The Fairground Booth' ('Balagan'), where the phrase 'pure theatricality' first appears. Meyerhold wrote it as a manifesto, where he linked 'theatricality' to what he called, in general, 'the theatre of improvisation' and 'the theatre of masks', and also to puppet theatre and pantomime, among the numerous popular-entertainment forms that he had been using for more than a decade. Thus he related 'theatricality' to vaudeville, as well, where spectators were forced 'to recognize the actors' performance as pure playacting', and to cabotinage, without whose slapstick, farce and physical tricks, including juggling, theatre, to his mind, was simply unthinkable.[7] Cabotinage, Meyerhold insisted, would 'help the modern actor to rediscover the basic laws of theatricality'.[8]

By the same token, Meyerhold linked 'theatricality' to 'stylization', especially of gesture and movement. Increasingly over the years, he related 'stylization' to the kind of 'poetic' understatement he had seen in a Japanese theatre visiting Moscow in 1902, as well as to what can only be called the ellipsis of expression that he so much admired in the performance of the Chinese actor Mei Lang-fan, who also deeply influenced Bertolt Brecht's concept of epic theatre. Mei Lang-fan was in Moscow in 1935, hosted by Meyerhold together with his friend and collaborator, the filmmaker Eisenstein, and his plasticity and articulated movement were integral to the stylization that Meyerhold had defined in his essay, where his example was a puppet weeping: 'the puppet holds the handkerchief away from the eyes'. In the Chinese classical theatre demonstrated by Mei Lang-fan, repeated shrugging of the actor's shoulders suggested weeping. 'Stylized theatrical movement', Meyerhold affirmed, was an 'imaginary gesture' whose aim was 'not to copy, but to create'.[9] In other words, it had nothing to do with rendering everyday actions explicitly, like weeping with 'real' tears.

Finally, Meyerhold linked 'theatricality' to the 'grotesque', which he defined as a device that 'mixes opposites, consciously creating harsh incongruity and *relying solely on its originality*'.[10] He observed some twenty years later that the grotesque was 'not something mysterious. It's simply a theatrical style that plays with sharp contradictions and produces a constant shift in the planes of perception.'[11] Taking *The Fairground Booth* again: its magical dimension was juxtaposed in a calculated fashion against its slapstick; beautiful and sinister effects were constantly in counterpoint. When, subsequently, in 1910, he staged Molière's *Dom Juan*, he used his concept of the grotesque for strong spatial contrasts. He had the actors perform at the proscenium to place it in juxtaposition against both the depth of the stage and the shallow forestage, where actors suddenly stepped out of their characters to expose their make-believe. This spatial play certainly allowed a 'shift in planes of perception'.

He also played with shifts of aural perception in *Dom Juan* by guiding the actors in the roles of Dom Juan and Sganarelle – seasoned Aleksandrinsky actors who first resisted his experiments – to accentuate different speech rhythms, to switch them about abruptly, and to accelerate or diminish tempi and pace, seemingly arbitrarily. These vocal patterns were integral to the musicality of the production as a whole, and musicality – rhythm, timing, phrasing, intonation, cadence of voice, gesture and movement – developed into one of Meyerhold's main directorial principles. In addition, so deeply was pronounced movement indispensable not only for the dynamics of all his productions, but for their very substance as productions, no matter which 'new theatre' they might have been announcing, that movement too became a hallmark of his direction.

The director as engineer: constructivism and biomechanics

His coordination of musicality, movement and architectural and visual structures led Meyerhold easily to Lyubov Popova, a member of the Constructivist group, who designed a complex one-piece set for *The Magnanimous Cuckold* that Meyerhold intended to be compact enough to go out for performances in the streets. Meyerhold, a politically motivated director, wanted his theatre to serve the people; and taking it into the streets was, he believed, the most efficient way of doing this. His enthusiasm for popular theatre became highly ideologically charged and aligned with the Bolshevik cause after the 1917 Revolution. He shared the Constructivists' anti-art sentiments ('art' was 'bourgeois'), which were consistent with the pragmatic ethos of the early 1920s. However, their methods, like his, were not representational but abstract: a horse was not depicted as a horse but, say, as a circle, and principles of montage highlighted the non-representational quality of the images on display. Prevailing ideas of social 'construction', from which the Constructivists took their name, stemmed from the Bolsheviks' policies of social engineering. The Constructivists conformed by identifying themselves as 'engineers' rather than 'artists'.

For an image of Popova's setting for *The Magnanimous Cuckold*, see
www.theatre.ubc.ca/fedoruk/theatrisms/popova1.

Meyerhold, similarly, was attracted by the image of himself as a director-engineer, and he took charge of Popova's abstract, machine-like edifice – a geometric arrangement of multiple levels and planes joined up by stairs, chutes, wheels, passages and platforms – in order to command his actors. They ran, slid, jumped and leapt, performing countless acrobatic stunts and comic turns without make-up and in blue workmen's overalls, which symbolically proclaimed the company's solidarity with the proletariat. The wheels rotated quickly or slowly, in concert with the tempo and rhythm of the acting. Popova's set was too cumbersome to be transferred outdoors easily, as had been intended, although the company managed to transport it onto open-air stages in the parks of Kiev and Kharkov during its 1923 tour. Overall, however, Meyerhold had to settle for bringing workers and Red Army soldiers into theatre buildings.

In the remaining productions of his Constructivist period – the funny *Tarelkin's Death* (1922) and the explicitly political, almost agitprop, *Earth Rampant* (1923), *Lake Lyul* (1923) and *Give Us Europe!* (1924) – Meyerhold directed with a verve that incited audiences to participate in the action: workers interrupted the show with calls or speeches, the Red Army band struck up at moments of particular political significance, and so on, as at a mass rally. A director who had always been concerned with renewing audiences, arguing that spectators were the fourth component intrinsic to the making of meaning in the theatre, Meyerhold was now in his element. The remaining three components were authors, directors and actors.[12]

Meyerhold's efforts to change the social composition of audiences went hand in glove during this period with his formal experiments. In *Tarelkin's Death*, acting space went up and out as the exceptional actor Igor Ilinsky, whom Meyerhold had trained, swung across the stage on a trapeze. Circus techniques joined those of the cinema, including the use of screens. In *Earth Rampant*, machines filled the stage and auditorium in a wide-lens effect: a truck, car, motorcycle, crane; even an aeroplane was envisaged, but proved too difficult to handle. Huge searchlights lit up the space, frequently accompanied by the sound of machine-gun fire. Yet for all their apparent anarchy, these Constructivist productions depended entirely on Meyerhold's directorial precision, and he held them together with the grip that had already earned him the reputation of a director-tyrant who subordinated the will of his actors and collaborators to his vision. They depended, as well, on the 'exposition with utmost clarity' that he believed a director had to '"announce" to the spectator' for the latter to understand what followed. And they relied, as did all his productions across the board, on his fine ear for rhythm, a 'gift for rhythm' being, in his view, 'one of the most important qualities in a director'.[13]

Above all, these productions relied on actors of great physical strength, stamina, agility, flexibility, versatility and coordination – skills developed by Meyerhold's biomechanical exercises. The theory of biomechanics was inspired by the North American Frederick Winslow Taylor who had studied the movements of factory workers to ascertain how they could be more productive. Taylor's time-and-motion studies determined, for instance, that rhythmic motions of the hand were more efficient than ones made in a straight line, and rhythmic movements more efficient than those without rhythm. Breaks between work ensured greater productivity when built into the 'cycles' of work. In practical terms, Meyerhold sought techniques he described as 'efficient' (copying Taylor) to build up the actors' energy and resistance while giving their bodies sculptural form. To this end, he invented exercises like the well-known mime 'Shooting from the Bow'. It involved a three-part sequence: the arm drawing back an imaginary string to engage arm and imaginary object for the action ('reject'), the release of the arrow, which was, so to speak, the kernel of the action ('dispatch') and the action's accentuated completion, like a punctuation mark ('full stop'). The whole exercise was sculpted as in the way a sequence of ballet steps is given clearly defined shape and ends with a pronounced gesture, say, a flourish, to signify its conclusion. The 'Bow' exercise also entailed using the whole body (and not merely the arms), thus encouraging fluidity of movement.

Other exercises stressed partner work – catching a partner on the actor's chest or shoulders, for example, which happened in *The Magnanimous Cuckold*. These exercises were designed to stimulate what Meyerhold called the actor's 'excitability'. It was the outward behaviour or *doing* of this or that action that aroused the emotions appropriate for it. Meyerhold, in other words, countered Stanislavsky's early technique ('affective memory') for arousing emotions through the actor's recall of emotions experienced in the past.[14] Biomechanical exercises had varying degrees of complexity, some developing into comprehensive *études* that fired the actors' creativity. Moreover, they gave Meyerhold's directing greater scope, since developed actor technique was a tool for liberating both the actor and himself. Paradoxically, the rigidity of the theory of biomechanics, with its debt to the 'methods of Taylorism' (see box), gave rise to a disciplined, but free, practice.

> If we observe a skilled worker in action, we notice the following in his movements: (1) an absence of superfluous, unproductive movements; (2) rhythm; (3) the correct positioning of the body's centre of gravity; (4) stability. Movements based on these principles are distinguished by their dance-like quality; a skilled worker at work invariably reminds one of a dancer; thus work borders on art. The spectacle of a man working efficiently affords positive pleasure. This applies equally to the work of the actor of the future . . .
>
> The methods of Taylorism may be applied to the work of the actor in the same way as they are to any form of work with the aim of maximum productivity . . .
>
> The Taylorization of the theatre will make it possible to perform in one hour that which requires four at present.
>
> Meyerhold, 'The Actor of the Future and Biomechanics'[15]

This section cannot end without a brief reference to *The Government Inspector* (1926), a witty production spliced with sinister effects – a grotesque production, in Meyerhold's sense of the word – on which more ink is said to have flown than on any other in Russia. This was so because of Meyerhold's directorial innovations. In the finale, for instance, life-size puppets replaced the characters in an ingenuous trick on the audience (until their heads fell off to reveal the actors' heads). But it was through this production that Meyerhold made good his claim that 'the art of the director is the art not of the executant, but of an author – so long as one has earned the right'.[16] He reorganized scenes in Gogol's play and supplemented it with pieces from his novels. He cut and edited according to his purposes with greater confidence than ever before, challenging the idea that there was such a thing as a fixed, 'true' text. In doing this, and in taking charge of the scenic work as the work of a creator rather than that of an interpreter or 'executant', he behaved as an 'author'. The very notion of the director-author, or *auteur*, to which this book draws attention in a later chapter, has its roots here.

Aleksandr Tairov: aestheticized theatricalization

Vakhtangov's admiration for Meyerhold was outweighed, by far, by Tairov's antagonism towards him. Indeed, Tairov's *Notes of a Director*, which he published in 1921 to stake out his territory in a prolific and competitive field, reads like an open polemic against Meyerhold. It was not that he had any special affection for Stanislavsky, whom he saw as Meyerhold's polar opposite, dismissing him as the primary cause of 'the anti-artistic nature of the naturalistic theatre'.[17] But Meyerhold provoked his ire like no one else because Meyerhold's search for the theatrical in the theatre was in many respects close to his own. Tairov termed his endeavour the 'theatricalization of the theatre'.[18]

Tairov's attack was based only on a part of Meyerhold's work – Meyerhold was in mid-career in 1921 and much more would follow – and this meant that it necessarily focused on Meyerhold's theatre of 'stylization'. The fact that the components of Meyerhold's 'stylization' (figurative expression, pantomime, acrobatics) were similar to those of the Kamerny Theatre ('Kamerny' means 'Chamber'), which Tairov founded in Moscow in 1914, fanned the flames of his criticism, as did Meyerhold's concern to interconnect the plastic and the visual arts. This could not help but bother Tairov, since he too promoted multi-faceted artistic activity, calling his particular variant of it 'synthetic theatre', which 'cannot tolerate separate actors of drama, ballet, opera', but requires a 'master-actor' capable of performing all of them with 'equal ease'.[19]

All questions of rivalry aside, Tairov disagreed with Meyerhold on a matter of substance. What he detected in Meyerhold's conflux of the arts was the latter's control of the actor, to which end, in his view, Meyerhold had elevated the role of contributing practitioners, notably designers, while turning the role of the director into that of a puppeteer. Ironically (given Tairov's dismissal of Stanislavsky), Stanislavsky had also considered in 1905, at the time of the laboratory-studio he had put into Meyerhold's care, that Meyerhold treated actors like puppets who were at the service of his overriding directorial views rather than of their own creative abilities.

Something like a vision of actors banished from the stage haunted Tairov's perception of Meyerhold whom he accused, to boot, of taking emotional content out of the theatre and replacing it with ostentatious, empty forms. The path of the Kamerny Theatre was to be mid-way between Stanislavsky's actor-centred theatre, which, Tairov believed, suffered from the 'dysentery of formlessness', and Meyerhold's 'stylized theatre', which had led to atrophy – 'dead' form, one might say. For this intermediate, third way, Tairov came up with the formula of '*the theatre of emotionally saturated form*', his cue for every production he directed and by which he wanted to identify what could most accurately be called an anti-naturalistic theatre of art with heart.[20]

The director, in such a theatre, was the guarantor of the actor who was 'the sole and sovereign bearer of theatrical art'.[21] Not only did this director secure the creativity of individual actors, coordinating their collective efforts, but he also resolved any disputes between them that might jeopardize the very nature of their work, which was collaborative through and through (see box). The

The role of a director

The art of the theatre is a collective art. Scenic action appears as a result of the very collisions that occur in its process: is a result of interrelations and conflicts which take place between individual 'ones who act' or groups of them. In order that the conflicts not be governed by chance, in order that the scenic action be not chaotic but flow in orderly fashion, that it be cast not in separate and uncoordinated but in harmonious forms which follow one after another in a unified work of theatrical art, it is obvious that *someone* is needed. There must be someone who, creatively striving for this result, regulates and directs the conflicts that arise – softening, strengthening, eliminating, creating – in order to lead all the action to its harmonious conclusion.

This 'someone' is the director.

Insofar as the theatre is a product of collective creativity, it requires a director, whose intrinsic role is the coordination and ultimate harmonization of the creativity of the separate individualities.

Aleksandr Tairov[22]

director in these circumstances was neither an appendage of the process nor its overshadowing force, but integrally related to it. It can be inferred from Tairov's observations that, unlike Stanislavsky, who made the actor sovereign but placed the director in the secondary position of 'midwife' (the midwife, after all, was not the maker of the baby, as Stanislavsky's image indicates), Tairov saw the director as sovereign as well. The director was on an equal footing with the actor. This was possible, for Tairov, because the theatre required mutual trust and interaction between actor and director. In addition, their relations could not be simply practical or formal; they had to be affective, above all else. In Tairov's words:

> The work of the director and actor can produce genuine theatrical art only if they are creatively inseparable – only if from the very first steps of his 'scholastic life' as a student of acting the actor has learned to empathize with the director and the director with the actor. Otherwise they have no business on the same stage together; otherwise there is no esprit de corps, and that means no theatre.[23]

Tairov's emphasis again and again on the word 'art' reveals his predilection for beautiful productions, as his own were always intended to be – refined, polished, finished artefacts that were a far cry from Meyerhold's boisterous, frequently rough nuggets at that time. Tairov built up a coherent grouping of productions, each devoted to the pleasure of the senses, each striking rather than lyrical in its sensuality. And he chose plays that lent themselves to the Kamerny's third way since they resisted daily-life 'naturalistic' treatment, on the one hand, and the extroversion of Meyerhold's 'stylized theatre' (at least in its circus aspects), on the other.

The plays that most deftly served the Kamerny's aestheticized approach were Oscar Wilde's *Salome* and Paul Claudel's *L'échange*, both in the company's 1917–18 season, and Jean Racine's *Phèdre* and Charles Lecocq's opera bouffe, *Giroflé-Girofla*, both mounted in 1922: the formality and calculated speech and gestures of the one was a brilliant foil to the festivity, with its romp-like speed and easy movements, of the other. Tairov also chose Soviet writer Vsevolod Vishnevsky's *Optimistic Tragedy*, which he staged in 1933 – a surprising choice, at first glance, given the text's tendentious character, although Tairov directed it with his usual arresting composition. Tairov's productions may have been excessively concerned with 'look', but they ran on the Kamerny actors' emotional vitality and intensity. *Phèdre*, for instance, with its multi-dimensional space, hieratic positioning of actors, and grand acting, now rhetorical, now incandescent – an explicit style of acting encouraged by Tairov from the earliest rehearsals to the stage – was intrinsic to his conception of 'emotionally saturated form'.

The aesthetic values, even the aestheticism, of the Kamerny, announced without apology by the 1917–18 season, ignited controversy. Its most vocal opponents included Meyerhold and the Proletkult groups ('Proletkult' from 'proletarian culture'), who threw the Kamerny in with everything that they denounced as 'bourgeois'. Their aggression was tantamount to a declaration of ideological enmity in these years of Revolution, Civil War and the First World War. The toll of economic, social and personal hardships in this combination of catastrophes was so immense that exquisite theatre in such times seemed unpardonably frivolous. Yet, whether perceived as lightweight or otherwise, the very fact that theatre productions could give rise to heated debate shows just how central to the ambient social and political struggles the practice of theatre was considered to be.

The 'theatricalization of the theatre' – Tairov's variation on *teatralnost* – demanded of its director scrupulous attention to scenic composition. He rejected two-dimensional space, and so the use of painted backdrops, for three-dimensional space and its multiple planes for action, as envisioned by Adolphe Appia. Not only was Appia his main reference, but so was Copeau whose preference for bare stages accorded with Tairov's view that streamlined space enhanced the actors' play. Costumes, for Tairov, were neither pragmatic nor photographic, but the actor's 'second skin' and 'the visible mask of his scenic figure'.[24] Costumes in *Phèdre*, for instance, were sewn in layers of square, rectangular and triangular panels, all concerned with capturing what he termed the 'essence' of character by strong visual imagery. As a general rule, costumes harmonized with the geometry of the stage design, which invariably displayed steps and flat, angular platforms arranged at different levels to convey depth. (A large circular platform, by contrast, was key to *Optimistic Tragedy*.) Harmony like this featured in all of Tairov's works, facilitated by Constructivist artists, in particular the Sternberg brothers and Aleksandra Exter, and by the avant-garde artist Natalya Goncharova, who had won great renown for her painted backcloths and costumes for the Ballets Russes.

Judging by his observations in *Notes of a Director*, ballet, which held a central role in Russian cultural life, had deeply influenced Tairov. The phenomenal global impact of the Ballets Russes, the company that, for over a decade, had drawn together some of Russia's most remarkable creative talents, must surely have also had an impact on him. The elegance of ballet guided Tairov's directorial work far more than appears to have been recognized by scholars in the Soviet Union, as well as by scholars abroad. He gave priority to the *esprit de corps* between actors and between them and their director, which, in his mind, was analogous to the tight-knit *corps de ballet* and its bond with its *maître de danse*, the dance homologue of a director. Such *esprit de corps* could only come from shared discipline, technique, and artistic principles and objectives, as was the case for ballet and its concept of 'school'. Tairov's recognition of the primary importance of a school for the cohesion of both a ballet company and its work suggests why his understanding of the 'duties' of a director is steeped in his conviction that a director and his/her actors need to fashion their own school.[25]

The idea that a school of technique, thought and value was indispensable for making theatre worthy of the name was not, of course, unique to Tairov. Such was the goal of Nemirovich-Danchenko and Stanislavsky from the very inception of the Moscow Art Theatre, and it continued not only in the official dealings of the MAT, but also in Stanislavsky's five theatre-studios. These studios were veritable seedbeds for like-minded people who garnered the same training and outlook on their craft, performance and professional expectations. And the very principle of 'school' was embedded in Stanislavsky's 'system' in so far as the research constituting this 'system' was meant to help actors work in the unity of a veritable ensemble. Tairov was not a graduate of the MAT or of the studios. Nor was he among the groups Stanislavsky gathered around him in his home (and not at the MAT, from which he now felt exiled) to manage his strained relations with Nemirovich-Danchenko and the MAT. Yet, although Tairov had not been groomed in the Stanislavskian school, as had Meyerhold and Vakhtangov, he was no less aware of its achievements than was the entire theatre community of practitioners, critics and scholars; and he recognized, with them, that this school had given the role of the director institutional legitimacy. Furthermore, Tairov's acknowledgement that a school was indisputably beneficial for the *quality* of work spurred him on to train his actors, exactly as Meyerhold and Vakhtangov were doing, radiating from Stanislavsky.

Yevgeny Vakhtangov: 'festivity' and spectacle

Of the two, Vakhtangov was fundamentally closer to Stanislavsky than Meyerhold – especially in his adoption of the method of *études* – although, like the latter, he had established his own fully distinctive approach. Vakhtangov had participated in the First Studio (1912–24), where he built on Stanislavsky's psychological realism, at first overstressing his master's teachings. And he was in charge of the Third Studio set up in 1920 whose methods he had already begun to flesh out, turning it into a school before it came under Stanislavsky's wing. It was here that he assiduously avoided those reproductive, photographic aspects of naturalism, which by then had become confused with Stanislavsky's project. They were, in any case, identified with the MAT, and, while Vakhtangov declared in his notebook that 'the "slice-of-life" theatre must die', he had no desire to embrace their alleged antithesis in Meyerhold's *teatralnost* blindly.[26] Theatricality, and so Meyerhold's 'stylization' and 'grotesque', were, for Vakhtangov, absolutely necessary for theatre to be theatre, providing that they were not cut off from the vital living force of emotions that only the theatre could explore through psycho-emotionally developed actors. The way to reach 'emotional truth', as he called it, was not to draw up from the depths of human 'nature' – Stanislavsky's touchstone for unaffected, 'natural' acting – but to conjure them up through the imagination so as to configure them as larger than ordinary life. To a period when naming a method or style was a concern, Vakhtangov presented his version of *teatralnost* as 'imaginative realism'.[27] The director in this sphere was 'the sculptor of the stage production'.[28]

It is not particularly helpful to repeat the commonly held assumption that Vakhtangov reconciled the opposing views of Meyerhold and Stanislavsky, since his admiration for the one and his love for the other by no means prevented him from being an independent actor, director and teacher. Moreover, although these views converged in the 1930s, they retained their individuality, as did Vakhtangov's, cut short by his death from cancer in 1922. The three productions that brought him fame, *Erik XIV* (1921), *The Dybbuk* (1922) and his last work, *Princess Turandot* (1922), were crafted with such attention to 'emotional truth' as well as aesthetic innovation and the fantasy of the grotesque, and were motivated with such tact by his sense of social responsibility, that both Meyerhold and Stanislavsky's influence was no longer the issue. What mattered was his idiosyncratic sense of the theatre as a celebration, a holiday. As Vakhtangov noted: 'If there is no sense of festivity, there is no performance.'[29]

'Festivity' in *Erik XIV*, understood as the free play of the imagination, was concentrated in Mikhaïl Chekhov's jarring, jerking but, paradoxically, buoyant performance as the king – structurally offset by Vakhtangov to look like a solo in disequilibrium with the remaining performances. These were Vakhtangov's ploys to have Chekhov exteriorize Erik's insanity while giving it 'emotional truth' rather than verisimilitude. Features such as Chekhov's thick make-up – black zigzag eyebrows, full lips, artificial skin – and peculiar black-on-white costume with a conspicuously jagged, lop-sided collar that framed Erik's madness were Vakhtangov's 'grotesque' alternative to 'slice-of-life' norms.

'Festivity' appeared in the form of dance, music and religious rites in *The Dybbuk*, Ansky's 1914 Jewish mystical play about a bride possessed on the eve of her wedding by the spirit of a man who had believed he was her predestined husband. And here Vakhtangov foregrounded several 'sharp contradictions' (Meyerhold's words), notably between the beggars of his production, whom he presented as a restless huddle of animals – frog, monkey, hyena, pig – with bits of costume and make-up to match, and the staid bourgeoisie who oppress them as much as they oppress the bride. Vakhtangov's contemporaries did not miss his social commentary via this contradiction, and it led to his flamboyant finale, when the bride, in white, hemmed in by sages gesticulating in a stylized manner, dies ecstatically, in anticipation of meeting her groom in the afterlife.

It was *Princess Turandot*, based on Carlo Gozzi's fairytale, that proved to be Vakhtangov's inimitable magical feat; and although its masks, mime, acrobatics and infectious singing, dancing and music (by a mandolin, balalaika, castanets and comb-and-paper orchestra) could be associated with Meyerhold on the one hand, and with Tairov on the other (the production was compared with the operetta-like *Giroflé-Girofla* of the same year), *Princess Turandot* surprised by its joyous inventiveness – the result of streams of *études* and the spontaneity they fostered. Vakhtangov had asked his actors, from the beginning of his first rehearsals, to imagine they were a troupe of Italian travelling players (thus *commedia* players) and to find the corresponding 'Italian' (what he probably meant was 'effervescent') temperament: this would set the tone of the show.[30] The actors pushed through paper walls and built or brought in new 'scenery' in front of the audience. They put up such signs as 'Old China' and 'Peking' to say where the action was taking place, carried in a painted sun, dropped down a moon with the help of a pulley, joked with spectators, quipped and gibed with each other, and indicated in multiple other reflexive ways that all this was 'theatre'. The actors wore brightly coloured paper masks; pieces of shiny cloth were hung on chairs to suggest satin furnishings; strings of black wool were the hair of this or that beauty; long ribbons for moustaches ran from actors' noses to their waists. These few, among countless humorous, often carnivalesque, examples, asked spectators to imagine the stage universe with the actors. In the words of Konstantin Rudnitsky: 'It was as if the festive beauty of the merry spectacle refuted the everyday of Moscow life in the early 1920s, still cold, dark and half-starved.'[31]

For Vaktangov's *Princess Turandot* (1922) see http://upload.wikimedia.org/wikipedia/commons/a/a9/Princess_Turandot_-_1922_-_Adelma_and_Kalaf.jpg.

A good part of the production's success was due to Vakhtangov's direction of his actors and the realization of his idea that

> the most important thing for the director is an ability to find a key to the actor's heart, that is, an ability to tell him *how* to find what is needed . . . He must be shown by simple, ABC methods, just *how* to do so. In most cases things are quite clear – either the actor does not feel the subject, or he organically does not understand the task, or the essence is not strong, or he is word-bound, or far from the motivating action, or he is too tense, and so on.[32]

Chekhov was to corroborate Vakhtangov's words in his reminiscences (1928), referring, as well, to how Vakhtangov directed with a keen sense of the spectators' presence so that the work being created was always dialogical, always alive; this, too, was a strong reason for *Princess Turandot*'s success.

Vakhtangov's 'directing genius'

His talent as a director is known to all, thanks to his stage productions. This was only one of his sides, however; the other side was how his directing genius manifested itself in his work with actors in rehearsals.

The question of the relation between the director and actor is a complex and difficult one. Dozens of lectures can be delivered on the subject, but their result will be nil if the director does not possess a special *sense* and *keen understanding for the actor*. Vakhtangov possessed this sense to perfection. He described it as a feeling that occurs when a person is taken by the hand and carefully, patiently, led to where he should go. He stood invisibly beside the actor, as it were, and led him by the hand. Actors never felt any constraint from Vakhtangov, but they could also not deviate from his conception of the play. When they carried out Vakhtangov's directions and ideas, the actors felt them to be their own. This amazing quality of Vakhtangov eliminated the question of whose voice was the decisive one in interpreting a role: the actor's or the director's . . . In order to become a director like Vakhtangov, one should learn to be more human and attentive towards people in general. Artistic and moral questions thus fuse into one.

Vakhtangov had one more amazing quality: while attending rehearsals seated in the auditorium, he always felt as if the hall were filled with the public. Everything taking place on stage was seen through the eyes of these imaginary spectators filling the hall. He put on his plays *for the public*, and that is why his productions were always convincing and clear. He did not suffer from that director's malady which is so widespread today and which stimulates directors to put on plays only for themselves.

Directors who suffer from this malady do not feel their public and nearly always approach their work from a purely intellectual point of view. They suffer from a special form of intellectual egotism.

Mikhaïl Chekhov, 'About Vakhtangov'[33]

Revisiting Meyerhold: Valery Fokin

Meyerhold's legacy in the Soviet Union was clandestine until his official rehabilitation in 1955, although the process of full rehabilitation was slow, meeting with resistance until the later 1980s, when the last vestiges of opposition disappeared. Even so, the exact nature of his legacy, if palpable to those who were still alive and knew his work, could not be ascertained precisely because the intermesh of the four great strands – Stanislavsky, Meyerhold, Vakhtangov, Tairov – in the living practice of the theatre was so complex by the end of the 1980s that to pull them apart seemed artificial, at best, and, at worst, an impoverishment of the whole. This having been said, it was imperative for the directors, actors, students, scholars, critics, family and friends dedicated to Meyerhold's memory to have his specific contribution properly identified and acknowledged. Two organizations were established in Moscow (the first in 1955) in order to achieve this goal, leading eventually to the foundation of the Meyerhold Centre in 1991. The director Valery Fokin, who had played a significant role in the multiple efforts to rehabilitate Meyerhold, heads the Centre to the present day.

Much as he was involved in the campaign to clear Meyerhold's name, Fokin was not a mere Meyerhold derivative. His directing in various theatres in Moscow, notably at the Sovremennik and Yermolova theatres in the 1970s and 1980s, was marked by pronounced dynamism and theatricality, which, although in the spirit of Meyerhold, had his own individual stamp. Its tone was firm, but not aggressive, despite his desire to draw away from the almost formulaic, domestic realism that had settled into the Russian theatre; and although his choice of repertoire, classic and contemporary, was more or less in line with that of other adventurous directors in the Soviet Union, there was a sense of urgency in his aim to hit the nerve of society and to communicate through strong metaphors with his spectators about their hopes and expectations.

In 2002, Fokin accepted the post of director of the Aleksandrinsky Theatre in St Petersburg, while retaining his position in the Meyerhold Centre in Moscow. It was here, where Meyerhold had captivated the city with *Masquerade*, that Fokin set about rediscovering and reinvigorating the classics through contemporary eyes. His quest for 'new forms' capable of holding new sense was his retaliation against the commercial and celebrity values that had engulfed the New Russia in the later 1990s and had deprived the younger generation of even considering, let alone knowing, the great Russian culture that was their collective heritage. Thus his aesthetic quest was part of his campaign to 'educate' audiences by capturing and sustaining their interest through theatre of the highest quality, avoiding didacticism or blatant propaganda of any kind. His method was typical of Russian directors by now, inherited from the four discussed: continual *études* (thus improvisations), directorial crafting from these *études*, intense director–actor interaction, and ensemble/school cohesion.

Not surprisingly, given Fokin's remit as regards the classics, Gogol, Dostoevsky and Tolstoy are central to his work in St Petersburg, which began in 2002 with an arresting *The Government Inspector*. He directed Khlestakov, Gogol's central character, as a sinister upstart, almost as a pastiche of the mafia-style bosses conspicuous in the country since the advent of the new capitalism. From start to finish, the production was remarkable for its speed, plasticity, pointed references and verbal and visual wit. A reprise in 2008, with a change in cast, saw a slippery Khlestakov. Indeed it contained a whole gallery of slippery opportunists, all of whom – Khlestakov being their epitome – changed as the wind blew, recalling, for spectators, how vulnerable they were to being duped in the instability and uncertainty of their everyday existence. Further, this metaphoric transposition of figures whom spectators recognized only too well from their daily experience implied that the lack of civic responsibility conjured up and exposed on the stage was perilously close to home.

Fokin's *The Government Inspector* is a conscious homage to Meyerhold in several ways: its use of a movement score, arranged in tandem with a musical score written for the show; 'grotesque' juxtapositions; action extended into audience space, along with other means for breaking the barrier between the stage and the auditorium; tight groupings borrowed from Meyerhold's 1926 production; and, as well, a centrepiece foregrounding a staircase and a platform that function as an inn, and 'quote' the set designs of both *Mystery-Bouffe* and *The Magnanimous Cuckold*. Another nod to Meyerhold is his signature on the side of this construction, as are the posters advertising the 1836 publication of *The Government Inspector* pasted on the circular walls of Fokin's 2008 production of *The Marriage* by Gogol.

All in all, Fokin developed his own style of theatricality, which stresses the surreal, as occurs in *The Double*, his 2002 version of Dostoevsky's tale, or highlights the mock-grandiose, as happens in his 2008 *The Living Corpse*, a play by Tolstoy. In the first, for example, a scene opens, to the astonishment of spectators, with male actors in full-body swimsuits and swimming caps immersed up to their waists in water. These strangely impassive figures are like a chorus to the protagonist, who is dressed in an evening suit, wet to his chest. Throughout, a raised wall of dark mirrors revolves as actors dart through them, reflecting – doubling – their vanishing silhouettes. In *The Living Corpse*, an immense cross-like, ornate metal staircase held together by passageways fills the entire stage to showcase the meanderings of its 'lost souls' – another metaphor for the current situation in Russia. The design is by Aleksandr Borovsky, the son of David Borovsky, who made his name in the 1970s designing for director Yury Lyubimov at Moscow's reputedly 'Brechtian' Taganka Theatre. Fokin, in his turn, nurtures the director–designer relationship that had become a feature of the work of Russian directors, seeking, as did Meyerhold, to maximize the actors' active use of design along with its visual impact.

It is, however, *The Marriage* that is Fokin's directorial tour de force. *Teatralnost* is here the reigning principle as the actors skate on ice during most of the performance, playing for laughs, seemingly innocently, as they use the circular space made up of long boards – a skating rink, bullring and circus in one – to show how Gogol's naïve, bitter-sweet characters are enclosed in the competitive spectacle world where they all come a cropper. Even Podkalesin does, the anti-hero, who escapes marriage and ends up slothfully in bed once again, only now with his skates still on. In this bold, effortlessly polished production, where the actors, after only six months of training, skate like virtuosos, Fokin makes his stand for a theatricality that values craftsmanship while it engages in moral and social discourse in the spirit of fun, but with its civic seriousness undiminished.

The politics of theatricality: Ariane Mnouchkine

Specific social conditions profoundly affect how and why particular theatre practitioners influence other practitioners in a defined time and place. Or sometimes it is simply a matter of what could be called the 'dust' of history – particles remaining after the event to be absorbed by x in y circumstances for z reasons. These particles of remaining influence are not necessarily rational or conscious, but they can be detected by spectators and established through research. Meyerhold influenced Fokin directly in so far as Fokin intentionally set about rediscovering Meyerhold; and Meyerhold was also influential indirectly in so far as Fokin was taught in a theatre environment where elements coming from Meyerhold were so well woven into the texture of theatre work across the board that they were no longer obviously 'Meyerholdian'. Further, Fokin adapted Meyerhold-type social commitment to current circumstances, but, as a director, he did not play an agitprop role of the kind engendered by a revolutionary society. Instead, he assumed a discretely educative role in a society struggling to become a democracy.

'Masters'

Meyerhold's influence on Mnouchkine is much more a matter of 'dust' settling on her in another time, place and sociocultural and political space, and it shows primarily in her notion of *théâtralité* (theatricality), which, for her, is synonymous with 'non-realism'.[34] Further: 'Realism is the enemy' because 'theatre is the art of transposition or transfiguration. A painter paints a painted apple, not an apple.'[35] Mnouchkine speaks happily of her 'book masters' – Meyerhold, Copeau, Charles Dullin and Louis Jouvet, who, with Stanislavsky, 'said everything that we need to know about the theatre'.[36]

And she remembered Copeau's advice that a company should have a unique place in which to perform. In 1970, she settled the Théâtre du Soleil, established in 1964 with a group of university friends in Paris, in the Cartoucherie, a disused armaments factory in the forest of Vincennes. Its three enormous hangars with ironwork skylights were to affect how she would work – artistically, certainly, in spatial terms, but also in managerial terms since her administrative offices, carpentry and other workshops, and kitchen and dining area for the whole company would be there. This was no mean undertaking. In 1970, the Soleil comprised some twenty-five actors in a team of fifty. In 2004, there were about thirty-eight actors in a team of seventy-five, roughly the same as today. Moreover, markedly since the mid 1980s, the Soleil actors come from a wide range of nationalities and cultures, making them a fully international and intercultural company.

Her living masters were Jacques Lecoq, in whose classes she was able to spend only six months, and Strehler. Lecoq's physicality and Strehler's development of the *commedia dell'arte*, to which she added the acrobatics of Peking Opera, were her main references in *1789* (1970) and *1793* (1972). The entire promenade organization of *1789*, for instance, where spectators walked about between four platforms showing different scenes simultaneously, called up the squares and marketplaces of *commedia* performances. Characters of all social stations gambolled, skipped and slid about these platforms, nowhere more ostentatiously than when a courtier bedecked in an extraordinarily plumed hat loped onto the stage. In *The Golden Age* (1975), she deployed similar *commedia* techniques, spectacularly in a scene depicting the cramped quarters of North African immigrant workers: a Harlequin, wearing workingmen's trousers and a black mask, 'sleeps' by standing on one shoulder, his legs up in the air. This image fully demonstrates how Mnouchkine not only theatricalizes a character and a situation, but also makes a sociopolitical point indirectly – indirectness also defines *théâtralité* – about a debated issue of the time.

Mnouchkine was, as well, highly receptive to the ideas of Jean Vilar, a director known for his verbally crisp and scenically sparse productions of French and other classics, notably Shakespeare, which he staged to acquaint people, or to remind them, of their world cultural heritage. Vilar was the founder of the Avignon Festival in 1947, and he invited her as-yet emerging company to perform in Avignon in 1969. Mnouchkine had a particular affinity with his democratic vision of a theatre accessible to a wider number of spectators from all social classes rather than exclusively from the middle class, as was the case in France. Vilar's idea of a 'popular' theatre, determined in this way, was to remain Mnouchkine's perennial ideal, as was his argument that theatre was a 'public service'.

It would be a disservice to Mnouchkine to underestimate just how important Vilar was to her perception of her social responsibility as a director, and, like his, her social programme was interconnected with her artistic ventures from the very beginning. Particularly influential was Vilar's conviction that only high-calibre theatre was worthy of the 'popular theatre' economically and artistically accessible to all social classes. Mnouchkine frequently alludes to this as 'elite theatre for everybody'.[37] As good as her word, she has built up a socially diverse audience base, starting early in her career by establishing relations with the industrial and service sectors (hospitals among the latter) whose employees came in groups in buses, organized by the various work associations and unions involved.

Her contribution to democratizing theatre included lowering ticket prices, making inexpensive food available on the premises, especially for the benefit of people coming to the theatre straight from work (precedents set by Vilar), and displaying books and other materials relevant to productions so as to edify spectators. Spectators can, to the present day, read the information open to them before or after a show, or during its relatively long intervals. Time is allowed for eating a meal whose 'theme' reflects the production in hand – Indian food, for example, for *The Indiad or the India of their Dreams* (1987) or for *The Atrides* (1990–92) whose costumes, colours, headgear and dance steps were largely inspired by Kathakali.

The environment is also themed in that the décor of the hangar where the audience gathers to eat and meet captures the essence of the current production. Hundreds of small Buddhas were painted on the vast walls of the Soleil's space, for instance, to convey the Tibetan themes of *And Suddenly Wakeful Nights* (1997), each one lit up by a small lamp beneath it. In a very real sense, Mnouchkine directs the entire space, creating a sensory feast for spectators whom she subtly directs through the space, prompting their reactions with the aid of the numerous stimuli of her magic realm. And this is also a realm of ritual, starting with Mnouchkine's three loud knocks, every night for years on end, from inside the space before she opens its huge and heavy doors to welcome the spectators in. The splendour of it is to remind spectators that they are in a special place, the theatre. The actors 'lay bare' their preparations by warming up, dressing, whitening their faces in the Kabuki manner (for every production), and so forth, in an area open for spectators to see.

Mnouchkine also had countless, often nameless living masters whom she had watched in performance when travelling extensively in India, Japan, Bali, Thailand, Cambodia and elsewhere before founding the Théâtre du Soleil. She involved her actors in her passions by inviting Asian masters to teach them; similarly, by providing the Cartoucherie's facilities for visiting performances. Thus, choosing from later examples, Dolma Choeden from the Tibetan Institute of Performing Arts (TIPA) stayed for three months, teaching the traditional songs and dances required for *And Suddenly Wakeful Nights*. Subsequently, in 2001, a group of Schechen monastery Tibetan monks, who dance, performed on the Soleil stage. Kim Duk-Soo, the renowned master of Korean drumming (*samulnori*), first gave the Soleil actors a master class before they continued intensive six-month training in drumming with his student Han Jae Sok for *Drums on the Dike* (1999). A director with a taste for brio, Mnouchkine had their blazing drumming open and close the production, and mark, as well, several turning points in its dramatic action.

Theatricality, metaphor and the 'East'

The Soleil's space is not only directed – a *mise en scène* that envelops the *mise en scène* performed by the actors. It is also a fully theatricalized space, which, apart from taking spectators out of humdrum reality, concentrates the actors on the *théâtralité* of the theatre they are making. It is, in other words – like the puppets she created for *Drums on the Dike*, one group of actors acting puppets and the other group acting their manipulators – a 'tool', as Mnouchkine says, to 'save the actors, to save us, from the psychological, from realism, from naturalism'. Her task, as a director, is to 'reveal reality theatrically'.[38] Thus the tale of *Drums on the Dike* played by actors, who play puppets playing people, tells of greed and corruption in a mythical Chinese village invented by Mnouchkine and her playwright, Hélène Cixous; and its exposure of the motives of totally unscrupulous developers, who cause a whole village and its people to be drowned, transfigures a 'reality' recognizable to spectators living in the here and now. Mnouchkine, then, transposes metaphorically – and her puppets are metaphors for humans – whatever can be inferred from the production as being relevant beyond the story told, as happens in an allegory, a parable or a fairytale. She concludes, to startling effect, with an inundation made with billowing silk into which the actor-puppets toss miniature puppets – metaphors of themselves – pell-mell.

Theatricality, as Mnouchkine understands it, is rooted in metaphor rather than in straight talking, but, since her 'Kabuki' *Richard II* in 1981, which opened with actors running at top speed down a hanamichi, it has relied heavily on Asian performance forms – the summit of theatricality, in her view. However, these are not authentic Kabuki, Kathakali, Bunraku, and so on, to be replicated by the Soleil actors. They are Mnouchkine's free variations on what really must be called imaginary forms from an imagined East, *l'Orient* being the term she consistently uses instead of *l'Asie* for 'Asia', not without Orientalist overtones. As the subtitle of *The Indiad* implies, this is the India, like the greater Asia, of her 'dreams'.

That Mnouchkine's East is conjured up from her imaginings, however charged up they may have been by the 'real thing', gives her a kind of poetic licence. Yet her flight to Asia is not so much a flight from Europe as an escape from the confines of textual theatre, which, in her view, not only spawned realism, but also, after the Greek tragedies and Shakespeare, killed off the body. Her aim, from the very beginning of the Soleil, was *corporeal* theatre, a theatre of movement, agility, vitality and joy in the flesh. The various kinds of theatre that she had directly experienced in Asia offered her a generic theatre where the actor's moving body, music, sound, richness of colour, texture of costumes, make-up, mask and headdress combined in a sumptuous, sensual whole. It is no accident, given Mnouchkine's belief that Asia is the seat of theatricality, that she frequently cites Artaud, who had discovered *l'Orient* before her in similarly Orientalist hues, and whose mission it also was to restore the supremacy of the body, which a theatre built on words and intent on 'bourgeois' conformity and comfort had driven out.[39]

Mnouchkine, in a paraphrase of Artaud, has never tired of declaring that 'the East is the art of the actor', adding that the West, to paraphrase her, has mastered the art of the text.[40] While this is partisan and oversimplified, it is driven by her certainty that the theatre can and must revolve around the actor (her common ground with Stanislavsky, Copeau, Dullin and Jouvet). Hers is, in other words, an actor-centred theatre whose actors are continually physically stretched by the new forms that they learn. Equally, they have to enter other-cultural worlds imaginatively so as to embody them physically, regardless of the fact that they do not reproduce those worlds; and this obligation arises consecutively with each new production, as is clear when they jump, say, from Tibetan dancing to Korean drumming and 'Japanese'-style puppetry. Mnouchkine's great demands of her actors are an acknowledgement of their agency in the creative process, which, in the Soleil, is firmly based on improvisation, and the shows offered to the public. The actors rehearse in costume, mask or make-up according to their fantasy, none of it particularly related to the production taking shape; and Mnouchkine believes this stimulates improvising. They may rehearse any role they wish. Mnouchkine does not impose roles, but assumes that who is best suited to which part gradually becomes clear not only to her, but to all.

Directing in a collectivity of equals

Indeed, Mnouchkine's affirmation of the actors' pivotal role is evident in how she describes herself as a director, all her terms being more or less collocations of each other. Thus, she, the director, 'offers a tool' so that her actors are not mired in psychology and can also be 'saved from' or helped to 'avoid' dreaded 'realism'; she is 'there for things to happen'; she likens herself to football fans at a match who support, incite and spur on their team; the less a director says the better because directors who impose their ideas on actors are usually anxious, in a hurry, or narcissistic; she does not take pride of place as a director because directors and actors learn from each other, and teach and shape each other.[41] And, then, being a director means 'giving' each actor 'the right horizon and good oars, after which we have to row together'.[42]

This sparse commentary, dating from 2002 and 2003, indicates Mnouchkine's reticence on the subject of directing. A retrospective view helps to fill out some of her silences. Earlier, in 1993, when pushed in an interview, she responded by saying that she was sometimes a 'guide', a 'wall', and even a 'boxer'.[43] Earlier still in 1974, after *1789* and *1793* put the Soleil on the world map, she contemplated, in reply to another interviewer, what being a director meant in a company flagging up its democratic credentials in *création collective* – words that, quite fortuitously, recall Tairov's 'collective creativity'. She felt embattled at this time, since her claim to *being* a director in a collectivity of equals had come into question; and, having considered the issue, she concluded that collective work entailed contribution according to people's tasks and capacities: actors and directors played different parts, and their respective part could not be, nor should be, diminished. In 1993, she attempted to specify how directors differed from other collaborators.

The function of a director

I don't think that we will achieve collective work only when I'm no longer anything because this is also an incorrect attitude. I believe it's a mistake to say that collective work implies the suppression of the specific place of each individual. I'm not talking

> about hierarchy, but about function. I think that the role of the actors will always remain fundamentally different from mine. The only thing – and it is fundamental – is that dialogue should become increasingly rich, increasingly equal, but it remains a dialogue between two people who fulfil two different functions. Perhaps we will need to find a certain democratic centralism. The real problem is not for me to diminish but for each individual to increase, which is in the process of happening. (1974)
>
> The director is the only person in a group who doesn't produce anything in the physical sense of the word. And the relative freedom of their qualities of perception and discrimination may be more developed because they don't have the constraints of the 'instrumentalists' (actors with their bodies, scenographers and their structures and materials). (1993)
>
> *Collaborative Theatre: The Théâtre du Soleil Sourcebook*, 57 and 219

'Collective' in the Soleil's practice embraced improvising and devising, which the company began to do in 1965. However, where its first productions evolved from pre-existing plays, the texts, characters, dialogue, scenes and actions of *1789* and *1793* were all devised: they were *fully* devised productions, and it was this integral devising, followed up in *The Golden Age*, that defined the Soleil as a devising-collaborative and corporeal theatre. But the toll of navigating a large devising company was great, leading Mnouchkine to work with plays that were already there. She thus turned to Shakespeare and then to Aeschylus and Euripides (the *Atride*s tetralogy) and gave Western texts Asian stage forms. To reinforce their Asian quality, she had her composer-musician Jacques Lemêtre play music non-stop through the performances. Lemêtre changed instrument, tone, rhythm and pace according to the actors' play, as he continued to do in her productions afterwards. She then directed Molière (*Tartuffe*, 1995), constructing the production around two plots, as she had done since *1789* – in this case, first, around religious fundamentalism and, second, around the love story of the young protagonists. As always, she did not direct according to a fixed method, but on a try-and-see basis. The 'reality' that she revealed 'theatrically' this time concerned Islamic fundamentalism, which, to her mind, represented fundamentalisms of all denominations. Following this, Cixous started writing for her company with *The Indiad*.

It was not until *The Last Caravanserai (Odysseys)* (2003) that the company resumed textual devising, no longer drawing on Asian forms but, at Mnouchkine's behest, still projecting the emotional states *(états)* intrinsic to Asian theatricality instead of exploring the psychology of characters. *Etats*, for Mnouchkine, are generally recognizable emotions – anger, fear, and so forth; emotions in broad, demonstrative strokes. Once again, the company employed such other components of its theatricality as exceedingly heavy make-up, which functions as a mask.

The Last Caravanserai concerns immigration, a subject of public scandal in the early 2000s (not only in France), and Mnouchkine and her actors researched it at Sangatte, speaking with detainees for hundreds of hours about their experiences. Sangatte was the immigrant detention centre close to Calais from where refugees – Iraqis, Kurds, Afghanis, Chechens – who were largely victims of war and/or political and religious persecution attempted to reach Britain by desperate means. Mnouchkine diverted the actors from working realistically on the material that they had collected by prompting them to improvise analogous or contrary incidents. For the same reason, she had them devise dialogue and events in imaginary cubicles the size of phone-booths. Confined space forced them to be oblique, to imply rather than act out what they had researched. Mnouchkine claims that the actors' devising was so effortless that they simply took the *mise en scène* in hand: albeit with her help, they pretty well directed the production themselves.[44] Here may well be the fruit of that 'increase' of each individual, aware of his or her 'function' in 'dialogue', that Mnouchkine saw in 1974 to be the very stuff of 'collective work' (see box, p. 102).

Mnouchkine introduces, in this production, a novel component of theatricality – dollies, as used in film-making, on which self-contained scenes are played, one after the other, for the entire duration of the performance, and which actors swiftly wheel in and out, virtually hugging the stage floor. She directs each scene with the most economic means possible: the murder of a young woman by Islamic fundamentalists comes as a shock when her caravan on a dollie is suddenly turned around to reveal her hanging body – one of several scenes that break up this story, although all anticipate its climax; speculators in human 'traffic' appear on speeding dollies, and push someone over a barrier, bully someone or count money; running figures attempt to jump on the Eurostar, suggested by wire fences on a dollie and the swoosh of sound; a girl on a bunk weeps. Mnouchkine builds up a sense of urgency in each fragment, even in the comical ones, combining them for her roughly six-hour jigsaw in two parts, epic length having always been typical of her direction.

Collective devising continued for *Ephemera* (2006), a montage of vignettes, which also used dollies to avoid the potential 'realism' of its stories, many quite personal to the actors, some dealing with painful family reminiscences. And it returned for *The Shipwrecked of Mad Hope* (2009), an almost phantasmagorical montage (the dollies had now gone), where the actors play silent-movie actors performing in snippets of various fabricated films. Extravagant, intricate, funny and fun, the production is replete with spoofs of the exaggerated,

4 *The Shipwrecked of Mad Hope* (*Les naufragés du fol espoir*), Ariane Mnouchkine, Théâtre de Soleil, 2010

'theatrical' play of silent movies: overwrought actions display love, villainy, happiness, loss; blizzards are made out of paper and whirring fans, and the characters shiver and bend, accordingly, to the freezing Arctic wind in grey-silver lighting; music mocks action. Within this theatricalization can be detected her homage to her Russian-born father, an immigrant, an exile, who had been a film producer in France.

The personal rarely appears in Mnouchkine's productions for she is a director devoted to pressing social issues, played big. The burning questions of the 1960s found their metamorphosis in the French Revolution, performed with such vitality in *1789* and *1793*. Those to do with the exploitation of labour were first approached in *The Kitchen* (1967) by Arnold Wesker and afterwards in *The Golden Age*. Thereafter she 'spoke' indirectly of war, hunger, genocide, fratricide, matricide, fundamentalism, economic and political oppression, and the fight for freedom, respect and dignity in diverse circumstances. She ran a plot inspired by the contaminated blood scandal of the early 1990s in France and Germany in *The Perjured City* (1994) – and related questions about political, legal and financial corruption – in tandem with a second plot concerning homelessness. The theme of homelessness returned in *And Suddenly*, coupled with that of political exile, and resurfaced in *The Last Caravanserai*. Mnouchkine directed all these productions with her eye on past and present history as a responsible citizen who saw herself in history. In her words: 'The world is my country, its history is my history.'[45]

Mnouchkine's sense of civic responsibility is inseparable from her directing, and, if it appears in the guise of theatricality in her theatre, it is real in her daily life. She is indefatigable in her humanitarian activities of which there are many examples, but one will suffice. In 1996, she provided shelter at the Cartoucherie for several months for some three hundred immigrants threatened with deportation. These *sans-papiers*, thus known because their residence status had not been regularized (some were children born in France so were French citizens by law), had been forced by the police out of the Saint-Bernard church where they had taken refuge, helped by its priest. They came back daily to the Cartoucherie at the end of performances, when its space became theirs. Mnouchkine fought their cause in other ways, through both religious and secular associations, well-profiled humanitarian organizations, and the press. To ignore this hands-on, active dimension of her humanity would be to diminish her sights as a director whose peer in this respect, perhaps her only peer, is Peter Sellars. Sellars, too, provides many examples (not surprising for this admirer of Meyerhold) of which a salient one is *Children of Herakles* by Euripides (2002). The production involved refugees and immigrant youths in non-speaking roles, discussions on US immigration policy and films after performances on how terrorism in the contemporary world, in its many forms, forces people to seek asylum.

Frank Castorf and Thomas Ostermeier: theatricality and violence

Castorf and Ostermeier are complementary figures who tackle a range of questions concerning the state of society and its politics. Castorf grew up in East Berlin, where he was born in 1951, but made his name largely, although not exclusively, outside the city for his bold deconstruction of the classics. Deconstruction was also a vehicle for his outspoken critique of East German repressive control. He became the artistic and managing director (*Intendant*) of the Berlin Volksbühne in 1992, and continues to run this theatre, inviting, as he had done from the beginning, such other non-conformist directors as Christoph Marthaler, Herbert Fritsch and René Pollesch, the latter being particularly close to Castorf's abrasive iconoclasm. His productions at the Volksbühne champion ordinary people who had undergone a confusing, radical life-shift during the process of reunification after the fall of the Berlin wall in 1989, and who had suffered considerable denigration and humiliation at the hands of their 'brothers' from the West.

Even as comparatively late as 2001, when he directed *The Insulted and the Injured* after Dostoevsky, Castorf's stage maintained that the social misery and difficulties of human relations of those early years had not disappeared in post-communist, democratic Germany. The sight of actors falling and picking themselves up again and again onto their skates in a narrow stretch of ice is nothing less than a theatricalized way of saying just how precarious daily life still was in the ex-GDR. The preceding 2000 *Demons* had reviewed, through Dostoevsky's *The Devils*, the contradictions of socialist revolution and how individuals with the desire and power to do evil vitiated its ideologies and intrinsically doubtful ideals (from Dostoevsky's point of view). Although Castorf went on to direct an eclectic range of works, many of them derived from novels, as he had done in the 1990s (among them the super-brash *Clockwork Orange* and *Trainspotting* in 1992 and 1997, respectively), it was with Dostoevsky that he remained in deep conversation, emerging with *The Idiot* (2002), *Crime and Punishment* (2005) and *The Gambler* (2011).

Ostermeier was born in 1968 in what had been West Germany. He made his reputation from 1996 to 1999 at the Baracke, an alternative space in the grounds of Berlin's Deutsches Theater, which, like the Volksbühne, was in the eastern part of the city. Here he staged graphically violent productions of plays by new writers, notably Mark Ravenhill and David Harrower whose London homologues – as with Max Stafford-Clark's direction of *Shopping and Fucking* at the Royal Court in 1996 – looked tame by comparison. So extreme were Ostermeier's stage pictures that they bordered on pornography, not least when they were highly overstated, quasi-parodied versions of neo-naturalism, as was the case of a scene showing broken bottles shoved into a man's anus in *Shopping and Fucking* (1998). The purpose of this pornography of violence was, precisely, to expose not only sexual violence but also all types of violence as social obscenities, engendered by the ruthless and callous mechanisms of everyday capitalism, leaving the young betrayed and in disarray.

In 1999, Ostermeier was invited to run the Schaubühne am Lehniner Platz, made internationally famous by Peter Stein (see Chapter 6). Here he built on his interest in contemporary dramatists, Sarah Kane and Marius von Mayenburg taking pride of place. 'There is a lot of Sarah Kane in everything I do', he was to say in 2011, after his no-holds-barred *Blasted* (*Zerbombt*, 2005) in which the set is blown to smithereens;[46] and time has amply demonstrated that Kane's uncompromising bleak horror suited Ostermeier's penchant for a theatricality which, rather like Castorf's, is steeped in aggression and provocation. In Ostermeier's case, provocation of his audiences in the middle-class area of the Schaubühne has to do with his deep mistrust both of capitalism and of what in 1999, by contrast with socialist realism, he called 'Capitalist realism' and its aesthetics of '"Anything Goes"'.[47] Castorf's provocation is a matter of complicity, of sharing with his spectators a sense of the grit of living and its countless wrongs.

The grit communicated by Castorf's productions is interlaced with Dadaist-style absurdity. His characters do not see this absurdity: they just are, being and doing, warts and all. It is the spectators who see it, increasingly as a play progresses (usually for about five hours); and it plunders such popular theatrical resources as vaudeville, burlesque, clowning, cabaret, clubbing – everything that might belong to the fringes of bourgeois art and society. Castorf by no means seeks Brechtian distancing effects, although Brecht might come to mind because of Castorf's choice of popular theatrical models. On the contrary, he immerses both his characters and his spectators in the popular, which includes pop/rock music, sport and the swagger of street culture. This makes the characters normal urban figures, if quirky or wacky ones, and the spectators neither observers nor empathizers, but something more like companions in arms who are in dialogue with them. Spectators, in other words, see a familiar world in the excessive behaviour of the characters, which, if capable of being perceived in an ironic, satirical or just funny light, is energetic and palpably concrete. It is thus 'real', for all its larger-than-life, over-the-top proportions.

It is in this framework that *The Idiot* trades on everyday vulgarity and kitsch. The General's three daughters, who befriend Dostoevsky's innocent epileptic, dress, walk, gesticulate, chew gum and talk with their mouths full, while food falls out: behaviour common to all the characters. When they do not look like starlets or streetwalkers (this done without any mockery from Castorf or the actors), they appear in denim jeans and jackets, and cowboy hats, as befits the environment created by Castorf's long-term designer Bert Neumann in which the bright neon sign of 'Las Vegas Bar' is prominent. Rows of steep wide steps on which the characters intermittently run up and down are reminiscent of Hollywood-movie stairs for chorus dancing. They disappear and reappear on the vast revolving stage, while other scenes revolve into view, many taking place on the high levels of the tower-like building that constitutes the set. Another tower filled with spectators, also on the stage, mirrors it, placing these spectators both inside and outside the action. Among the scenes turning up to view are the beer bars and *Wurst* eateries typical of former East Berlin.

Castorf's seemingly endless display on this carousel of attractions involves a ceaseless juxtaposition of sightlines. As with Lepage, close shots of scenes videoed in the moment of performance (the cameraman is often visible) are highlighted against the broader panorama. Sometimes events in the chamber spaces of the implied apartment block occur simultaneously with events at ground level. At other times, they are set against each other horizontally as well as vertically: the vertical suggests different floors of the building. The windows/boxes are lit up to show that they are empty (characters come into them to be videoed), or else they hold contrasting fragments of action. Frequently, the video camera zooms in on a particular scene to blow it up, as happens when Rogozhin, who imagines that the Idiot is his rival in love, murders the woman he cannot possess. After this deed, he asks the Idiot to lie by her side while he lies opposite, and then proceeds to deal cards over her covered dead body. The outrageous and the banal, here presented in a matter-of-fact way, are offset, yet again, when the scene shifts, blown up, to the party that the Idiot had left and to which he returns to gorge on food, oblivious to 'reality', as he had always been. Reality, Castorf intimates, is too much to bear.

The murder of an old woman pawnbroker followed by that of a pregnant woman in *Crime and Punishment* (2005) are far more gory affairs, which Castorf directs rhetorically, as if he were shouting, as do, for the most part, his actors when they deliver their lines. The renowned Martin Wuttke, who plays Raskolnikov, strikes with his axe, splattering himself and the walls with blood in a deliberately watch-me fashion. A video tracks the sequences in a possible parody of murder films, and it theatricalizes not so much reality as its imitation. Once again, technology provides Castorf with a tool for theatricality, although this instance is ambiguous, since it is difficult to say whether the brutality captured in close-up can be taken seriously at all. Most likely, and irrespective of how it turns on the themes of poverty and insult and injury, Castorf uses it here for 'purely' vaudeville purposes, which does not make the sequences morally or visually any less repugnant.

In *The Gambler*, Castorf returns to a more benign, but still excessive type of vaudeville, laced with cabaret nonchalance and Dadaist nonsense. Piles of potatoes on the stage over which actors walk with difficulty, a fake crocodile into whose jaws various actors slide their bodies, a gorilla, Little Red Riding Hood in drag and other apparently random actions, images and hysterical outbursts are, together with Castorf's ubiquitous video screening, part and parcel of his trademark theatricality. While Castorf does not ram home a message, topical allusions to Chancellor of Germany Angela Merkel's remarks on how one must work in order to make money, combined with other tit-bits concerning the 2011 euro crisis, generate knowing laughter in the audience.

For all the seeming chaos of Castorf's productions, he directs his ensemble of actors with a cool hand. Most have worked with him for decades, inventively developing their parts with him and generally contributing to the

5 *The Gambler* (*Der Spieler*), Frank Castorf, Volksbühne, Berlin, 2011

Volksbühne's popular ethos which, in its immediate post-wall years, included street theatre, cheaper tickets, free seats to the unemployed and other means for involving the dispossessed, in more senses than one, of the neighbourhood. Ostermeier, in the otherwise 'cool' neighbourhood of the Schaubühne, directs with a cool hand the material that counterpoints his preferred British and German contemporary playwrights. This is, above all, *Nora* (2002, the German name of Ibsen's *A Doll's House*), *Hedda Gabler* (2005), and *Hamlet* (2009), which is Ostermeier's 'middle' Shakespeare, flanked on one side by *A Midsummer Night's Dream* (2006) and on the other by *Othello* (2010).

Ostermeier's theatricality thrives on shock tactics. *Nora*'s end is shocking because she suddenly shoots her husband (whereas Ibsen's heroine slams the door shut behind her). Elsewhere, the actors paddle about in an aquarium in the middle of their expensive living room – conspicuous consumption that Ostermeier hyperbolizes by putting the actors in the water rather than have it there for merely decorative purposes. *Hedda Gabler* ends, too, with a shock partly because Ostermeier directs gamine Katharina Schüttler (also in *Zerbombt*) to play a listless young wife who, without altogether realizing it, is trapped within the glass walls of her yuppie house in which every man who enters feels free to grope her; and this waif-like, lost creature does not appear capable of mustering enough energy to kill herself, not even after her sudden bout of violence, when she smashes Lovborg's computer with a hammer to destroy his life's work. Ostermeier finds in the computer the contemporary equivalent of the manuscript Hedda burns in Ibsen's play. But Hedda's suicide is shocking, in addition, because those nearest to her go about trying to reconstruct draft pages of the manuscript, not bothering in the slightest to check the gunshot they had heard. The revolving stage is a major feature of this production (although Ostermeier, unlike Castorf, uses it infrequently), and, as it turns to reveal Hedda's body slumped against a wall, Ostermeier's reassessment of Ibsen underscores the point that this young Hedda is a trophy wife disempowered by the mores and expectations of affluent society. In this respect, she is a sister of Kane's women.

A moving platform rather than a revolve changes scenes in *Hamlet*. On it is a banquet celebrating Gertrude's remarriage to Claudius. Below it is a field of mud for Hamlet's father's funeral, which takes place in the 'rain' created by a hand-held sprinkler to fall on open black umbrellas and repeatedly throughout the production, on a Hamlet who is as exposed to the elements as he is to the manipulation of all around him. These two playing spaces hold Ostermeier's fundamental conceits for something being 'rotten' not in the state of Denmark but in the contemporary capitalist world where the excesses of food, drink, sex, egoism, narcissism and self-serving politics implode. Von Mayenburg's translation (he is also Ostermeier's regular dramaturge) is racy and provides Hamlet with a series of lewd running commentaries on, for instance, his mother's obsession with sex. Or else Hamlet explains directly to the audience what is happening and why. This showy theatricalization of Shakespeare's plot allows Ostermeier's actors to play with abandon while Lars Eidinger's Hamlet ad libs as he sees fit, clearly encouraged by Ostermeier to overplay the role as far as his laughing audience will let him take it.

The director–actor relationship in *Hamlet*, then, is one of considerable freedom within the production's slapstick parameters. Only six actors play, Gertrude notably doubling as Ophelia, which not only produces titillating moments, some with a whiff of incest, but allows dotty-wig and celebrity-style costume changes in full view. These are meant to be as silly as the drunken faces falling into plates of food or Hamlet's antics, not least his clownish display of the padding around his belly to make him look fat. Ostermeier has Hamlet consistently videoing events and, above all, himself (the production opens with Eidinger/Hamlet videoing his 'To be or not to be') as an additional device for revealing the mechanism of theatre making. Hamlet rolls in mud, covers his face with it, eats it, makes others eat it, and mixes it with blood. The dirtying presence of mud and blood is material (spectators closest to the stage are also dirtied by them), and, as such, it is a reminder that this crazy get-what-you-see theatre is a retort to crazy times; and Hamlet is as mad as you or me.

Eastern European directors: theatricality as resistance

Mnouchkine's metaphoric theatricality is linked to the principle of showing one thing and meaning another so that what is shown both hides and reveals its inner content; and this is the principle of theatricality for Eastern European directors, for whom it was a ruse against censorship when their countries were part of the Soviet bloc, or within the Soviet sphere of influence. Metaphoric theatricality became their weapon of resistance. It was not only a means for speaking up in forked tongues, which interlocutors understood, but also a stratagem for galvanizing opinion covertly where freedom of expression was impossible. In this respect, theatricality in Eastern Europe assumed the role of political critic of regimes and commentator on social matters, which exposed those directors to imprisonment or exile – directors being more vulnerable than actors to such drastic punishment, since they were held responsible for productions. The situation in the Republics within the Soviet Union was comparable, as in Georgia, where the Director of the Shota Rustaveli State Drama Theatre, Robert Sturua, mounted a hard-hitting *Richard III* (1978). The title role was performed with such bravado (an especially hunchbacked Richard strutted and hacked his way across the stage) that it was difficult to tell whether the portrait of tyranny and paranoia was tongue-in-cheek, pure satire or nutty burlesque. This allowed Sturua to deny the production's political slam against the regime as 'only theatre' – unreal.

The politics of theatricality in this context ran dangers Mnouchkine was fortunate not to know, and its methods may have filtered down from Meyerhold, given that older-guard directors such as Sturua either had studied in Moscow or had been in close contact with Moscow-trained teachers. Whatever the case may be regarding Meyerhold's trace in Eastern Europe beyond Russia, it is certain that Eastern European directors established their own tradition of metaphoric theatricality, which was distinguished by its extremely daring, frequently outlandish, devices. These were especially exploited in Poland by directors of Sturua's generation (those born in the 1930s), but the Romanian Silviu Purcarete is an eloquent example among the following generation (those born in the 1950s). Purcarete staged a viciously burlesque *Ubu Rex with Scenes from Macbeth* in 1990 at the National Theatre of Craiova, which played a major role in Romanian theatre. The production was a mixture of Alfred Jarry and Shakespeare, as its title suggests, and a complete showdown, using the Ubu couple of Jarry's play as a jeering metaphor for the political and personal horrors committed by President Ceauşescu and his wife until their demise in 1989, along with the demise of communism.

The semiotics born of communism did not vanish with it, and Purcarete, who has developed from it a veritable style, returned in 2008 to similar themes of power, ruthlessness and violence in *Measure for Measure*, also at Craiova. Here, too, was bombastic, visually strong, theatricality whose asylum/hospital-canteen imagery, featuring a salacious Angelo (rolling eyes, tongue and all-but displayed genitals) and predatory women (even Isabella shows a breast or a leg, adding to the pervasive sexual titillation), targeted the corruption of the power elites of post-communist Romania. Actors continually sweep sawdust and rubbish from the floor – a metaphor for the state of the country. In other words, theatricality here was coupled with its political vocation, as pioneered by Meyerhold, except that, unlike Meyerhold's, it had no revolutionary zeal. The lack of such zeal kept it within the vein of civic-democratic criticism mined by Mnouchkine. Theatricality of this kind returned in Purcarete's *Exit the King* (2009) by Eugene Ionesco, which he directed in French, France having become his country of residence. Once again, the absurdist strain of his work ('absurdist' because images, movements, mimicry and gestures are pushed to the extreme) let loose the production's play on ambiguities where a benign (or crazy) king (or patriarch/patient in a hospital, asylum or nursing home) is indulged by seemingly rational subjects/servants/nurses/toadies whose mannerisms and rhetorical delivery of the dialogue are, at the same time, quite peculiar. All of it was performed in a flamboyant manner, but appeared, paradoxically, unruffled, 'cool'.

The theatricality of political and social criticism, much of it in this kind of absurdist idiom regardless of which play was being performed (frequently it was Shakespeare, so open to metaphorical transposition), became the hallmark of the Eastern European directors who acquired, or were granted, the role of spokesperson for their nations when the latter were under iron control. It is important to note that theatricality as a form of double-talk, which became a necessity under communism, metamorphosed after communism into a highly elaborate aesthetics in which critical perspectives were deeply embedded. Indeed, they were often buried deeply enough in the plethora of startling conceits, tumbling visual and aural images, and movement and dance, which, at first sight, looked fully incongruous, to make them seem totally enigmatic.

The country where this metamorphosis was especially pronounced was Lithuania, in the productions of Eimuntas Nekrosius and Oskaras Korsunovas of the past two decades. Nekrosius, born in 1957, is Korsunovas' senior by twelve years. It suffices to cite from Nekrosius' abundant repertory his 1997 *Hamlet*, an extraordinary kaleidoscope of pieces, each piece diverting the eye while it shocks the mind as it carries both eye and mind through the labyrinthine composition that makes up the whole. In one such fragment a punk Hamlet (played by a national rock idol) is folded, resembling a foetus, into a space the shape of a small box. This image captures his nascent, unprepared state in a sea of change – social change where his father's kingdom is concerned, and spiritual change for him as a human being.

That time passes during terrible strife, leaving behind little of substance, is indicated by the dripping of water off a huge melting block of ice hanging from centre stage; and, apart from creating a dangerous environment for the actors, who slip and slide in the puddles of water forming beneath their feet – metaphorically identifying dangerous Elsinore – this ice, this water, also create something akin to a feeling of desperation, compounded by shards of glass lurking treacherously here and there. A clash of sounds – rock music, electronic effects, indeterminate snatches of noise – layers highly articulated, and sometimes deliberately indistinct speech. Nekrosius' intricate aesthetics places spectators in a position of uncertainty, but, perhaps, in this watery, glassy context is to be found both the trauma of Lithuania's communist history and the trauma of the country's subsequent change. Nekrosius' *Hamlet* is sibylline, and so open to multiple interpretations, but it leaves spectators with the sensation that he directs not only for himself, his actors and his immediate audiences, but in a bigger voice, which may no longer claim to speak for a nation, but has collective resonance, nevertheless.

Korsunovas, whose directorial inventiveness is equally prolific, takes up the existential thread of Nekrosius' production in his 2008 *Hamlet*. (After all, Nekrosius' melting ice can be seen as a conceit for being and nothingness.) However, he knits it firmly into a production possibly concerned above all with social playacting and falsity and how they deceive and betray everyone. This twine of thought wraps itself around every image, each more surrealistic than the next, including that of a person-mouse with a human-size mouse head – surely an allusion to 'The Mousetrap' referred to in Shakespeare's play. In any case, the production's opening scene is provocative enough, showing actors who sit in a row at make-up tables and stare into mirrors asking, then gradually shouting, 'Who are you?' in collective pandemonium. This 'you' is 'I', doubled in the mirror reflection, an 'I' that is somewhere there but invisible, as is Hamlet's father's ghost. The fact that 'Who are you?' is the Lithuanian translation of Shakespeare's first line 'Who's there?', which is addressed to the ghost, enables Korsunovas to suggest that 'You/I' morphs into a ghost. Thus 'You/I' becomes a question of being-but-not-being (and also of suicide), which is

6 *Hamlet*, Oskaras Korsunovas, OKT/Vilnius City Theatre, 2008

embedded in the conundrum of Hamlet's 'to be or not to be', and, as well, in the making of phantasms-illusions of the theatre.

The image of the theatre conjured up swiftly in this way is compounded by the image of death: Hamlet's father's ghost is nothing more than a corpse lying on these same tables. Later, when Hamlet goads Ophelia (Act III, Scene i) and, by this, precipitates her madness, they serve as an altar, or cemetery, adorned with white flowers in white vases in formal, purely perfunctory, gestures of grief. The scene, which, in a surrealistic way, foreshadows Ophelia's death, draws to its end as Hamlet condemns Ophelia to a nunnery while masses of blood-red paper and plastic flat shapes tumble from the flies. The person-mouse surveys the scene as if it were a battlefield, and this very suggestion anticipates the closing scene of the production where these patches of red, still lying on the floor, symbolize corpses.

Throughout the production, Korsunovas implies by his clusters of images, which recur as variations on the theme of artifice, that the mirror of nature that Hamlet says must be held up, is the mirror of our age, a chimera, a falsehood, in which the question 'Who are you?' doubled by 'Who am I?' dissolves into silence. The production's end hovers over the silence of something unfinished, like an instrument that fails to play its last note. *Hamlet* is a confrontation with the troubled times of the twenty-first century proposed by a director who knows that his vision must be strongly personal in order to become personal to spectators: he makes it, but *they* assume it for themselves in their own individual way, freeing him to take up modestly the role of director-spokesperson up front, when iron control is no more, but social snares continue to entrap people and tie into knots the very act of living/being itself.

Further reading

Braun, Edward (trans. and ed. with a critical commentary). *Meyerhold on Theatre*, London: Methuen, 1969

Carlson, Marvin. *Theatre Is More Beautiful than War: German Stage Directing in the Late Twentieth Century*, Iowa City: University of Iowa Press, 2009

Gladkov, Aleksandr. *Meyerhold Speaks, Meyerhold Rehearses*, trans. and ed. with an introduction by Alma Law, Amsterdam: Harwood Academic Publishers, 1997

Tairov, Aleksandr. *Notes of a Director*, trans. and with an introduction by William Kuhlke, Coral Gables, FL: University of Miami Press, 1969

Vendrovskaya, Lyubov and Galina Kaptereva (comp.). *Evgeny Vakhtangov* [Notes by Vakhtangov, articles, and reminiscences], trans. Doris Bradbury, Moscow: Progress Publishers, 1982

Williams, David (comp. and ed.). *Collaborative Theatre: The Théâtre du Soleil Sourcebook*, London and New York: Routledge, 1999

Worral, Nick. *Modernism to Realism on the Soviet Stage: Tairov – Vakhtangov – Okhlopkov*, Cambridge University Press, 1989

Chapter 4

Epic theatre directors

The connections between politics and theatre have always been close in Germany, with its *Intendant* system and the dominance of court theatres during the early nineteenth century (see Chapter 1). It is also no accident that it was in Germany that the first director-impresario emerged – as distinct from the actor-managers who dominated the commercial theatres of England and to some extent North America, or the commercial impresarios (such as the Frohmans) who came to control most of the theatres across the United States.

This highly influential impresario was Max Reinhardt. Starting in Otto Brahm's naturalistic and democratic Deutsches Theater in Berlin, he came to dominate the German stage up to the 1930s, in 1906 taking over the Deutsches Theater – where he established an acting school – while founding the Berlin Kammerspiele for experimental productions: the satire of Carl Sternheim, the expressionism of Richard Sorge, his rediscovery of Georg Büchner or Frank Wedekind's socially explosive plays. He also founded theatres in Vienna and Salzburg, added the huge Circus Schumann building to his Berlin theatrical portfolio in 1918, extended his reach by touring Germany and Hungary every summer, establishing the Salzburg Festival with Richard Strauss in 1920, and mounting vast travelling spectacles like *Sumurûn* or *The Miracle* (London 1911, New York 1924). In a very real sense, then, Reinhardt set the standards for productions across Germany, controlling as he did a significant and highly visible proportion of German-speaking theatre. He epitomizes the socially acceptable and commercial theatre of Germany up until the Nazi era – when his whole theatrical empire was confiscated because of his Jewish heritage – and he can be seen as the symbolic representative of commercial theatre across Europe, England and America (where in the 1930s he produced Hollywood films). Partly because of the responsibilities of managing so many venues, as well as from directing large-scale productions, Reinhardt became the model of the controlling autocrat with meticulously annotated Director's Books covering every move and gesture of the performance, and his work as a director is dealt with in Chapter 5.

At the same time Reinhardt can be seen as the progenitor of epic theatre. Like Brecht, Reinhardt began his independent career in cabaret (*Schall und Rauch, Noise and Smoke*), while his 'Theatre of the 5,000' (the converted Circus Schumann), where big casts and choral movements were required to provide visibility for the huge audience, introduced the exaggeratedly theatrical gestures and moves that can be seen as anticipating Brecht's epic acting style. He also directed highly provocative political works: for instance the German premieres of Gorky's *The Lower Depths* in 1903 or Strindberg's *Miss Julie* in 1904, which led the Kaiser to reject Reinhardt as associated with 'dangerous socialist propaganda'.[1] Indeed, both Erwin Piscator and Bertolt Brecht owed some of their training to Reinhardt, having each spent time as a dramaturge in his Deutsches Theater, while Reinhardt mounted the first Berlin production of Brecht's *Drums in the Night* there. However, with the size and commercial nature of his theatre empire, his repertoire was so eclectic as to be apolitical, whereas epic theatre is explicitly, indeed stridently, ideological.

Opening programme, Wallner-Theater, 1930

Never was it more essential than now to take sides: the side of the proletariat. More than ever theatre must nail its flag fanatically to the mast of politics: the politics of the proletariat. More and more insistent grows the demand: theatre is action, the action of the proletariat. The stage and the masses, a creative unity, not in the 'Drama of Contemporary Life' ('Zeittheater') but in the militant theatre of the proletariat.

Erwin Piscator[2]

Erwin Piscator's political theatre

The theatrical flashpoint of the 1920s was Berlin. War, left-wing revolution and right-wing Putsch, the murder of labour leaders like Rosa Luxemburg and Karl Liebknecht, the aftermath of an increasing polarization of society, inflation and a far deeper financial depression than hit the United States in the 1930s, all exposed the flaws in industrial capitalism. The theatre was also centrally involved since, when war broke out in 1914, Reinhardt along with ninety-two other artists, actors, authors and academics had signed a manifesto pledging support for the national war effort. On the other side of the political fence, in 1919 the playwright Ernst Toller (whose work Piscator was to produce, while Toller was still in prison for his political actions) had been elected President of the short-lived Munich Workers' Republic and, in an iconic image, ran between the opposing lines of troops – his own workers' militia and the regiments of the 'Black Reichswehr' – crying out for peace and national unity. Against that there was the example of Russia, where Lenin had provided an ideal of heroic political action, overthrowing the most repressive autocracy in the northern hemisphere. All this formed a creative ferment that found its expression particularly on the German stage with its traditional claim to be 'a moral tribunal'. The primary challenge was to develop ways of representing a new and distinctively twentieth-century perception of social reality, which led to the development of epic theatre.

> Just the grasping of a new range of material requires a new dramatic and theatrical form. Can we speak about finance in heroic couplets? . . . Petroleum struggles against the five-act form . . . The dramatic technique of Hebbel and Ibsen is insufficient by far for dramatizing even a simple press release.
>
> Bertolt Brecht[3]

Politicized by his war experience, as a very young man in the trenches of Flanders, the director who responded first, and most directly, to this challenge was Erwin Piscator. Yet there seemed no obvious playwrights capable of dealing with this new reality. He had either to develop his own epic material or adapt plays to expand their viewpoint. Even in 1928 Piscator commented: 'The lack of any great imaginative writing that expresses today's world with all its forces and problems, is no accident; it is due to the complexity, dividedness and incompleteness of our period.'[4] For both Piscator and Brecht naturalism inevitably encoded a bourgeois social view, while however political or antisocial its aims, expressionism (which initially attracted Brecht, whose early plays *Baal* and *Drums in the Night* were milestones in the movement) was rejected for its subjectivity and individualism. Apart from *The Threepenny Opera*, Brecht's writing in the 1920s mainly comprised short 'Teaching Plays' (*Lehrstücke*). So Piscator founded a 'dramaturgical collective' to adapt material; and since the focus of the plays they developed was so wide, montage became their standard structure.

Starting from his own agitprop stage, where in the early 1920s he staged politically intense but theatrically simplistic agitprop pieces, Piscator took over a quintessential naturalistic theatre in Berlin, the 'Free People's Theatre' (Freie Volksbühne) founded by Otto Brahm in 1890, which had introduced Ibsen's plays, Zola's principles and Antoine's practices to Germany. Extending the approach of this iconic modern and working-class theatre with contemporary media, Piscator introduced film – for the period, the very symbol of realism – into live stage action. His 1926 production of *Storm over Gotland* by Ehm Welk, a stridently proletarian journalist and writer, provides an example of the technique. The stage action, with live actors, presented the activities of individuals, their singular passions and social commitments, while the film – projected onto a screen filling the back of the stage set – showed the actions of the masses: their vociferous protest against the war, their surging enthusiasm for revolution, their flag-waving triumph. In the finale, huge red flags dropped from the flies. The individual actor was overwhelmed by the power and scale of the cinematic images; and Piscator was dismissed from the Freie Volksbühne, both because Welk himself complained about the extreme changes to his play, by introducing film, and for sacrificing 'artistic' quality to overt propaganda.

Founding his own stage (the Piscatorbühne), he specifically set out to create dramaturgical models for playwrights and other directors to follow: 'the literature that we need is only now coming into existence. We hope that our theatre will give it a powerful stimulus.'[5]

> Tasso's cries strike no echoes in the concrete spaces and steel walls of our century and even Hamlet's neurasthenia can count on no sympathy from a generation of hand-grenade throwers and record-breakers. Will people at last recognize that an 'interesting hero' is only interesting for his own epoch, that the sorrows and joys that were important yesterday, seem a ridiculous irrelevancy to our warring present.
>
> Our epoch . . . has set a new hero high on its pedestal. No more the individual with his private, personal fate; instead, the age and the fate of the masses are the heroic factors of the new drama.
>
> Erwin Piscator[6]

The programme for the 1927–28 season indicates his aims. Anti-war classics deconstructing militarism, Shakespeare's *Troilus and Cressida* and Büchner's *Woyzeck*, were announced together with two other categories of plays. One was a new form: documentary plays – as yet unwritten – *Economic Conditions* (subtitled *Petroleum*, directly picking up on Brecht's point highlighted above) or *Wheat* (a study of stock market manipulation by Brecht that was never completed but formed the basis for his *St Joan of the Stockyards*). These were to deal directly with the unseen forces controlling society. The second was plays analysing the dialectics of history, designed to provide a political perspective on contemporary events: Toller's *Hoppla, We Are Alive!*; or *Rasputin*, a script adapted by Piscator and his 'dramaturgical collective' from what he described as 'a sensationalist potboiler' by Alexei Tolstoy; and an adaptation by Brecht of Hăsek's perambulating novel, *The Good Soldier Schweik*. These form a thematic sequence. As Piscator put it: 'After we had outlined a decade of German history [1917–27] in *Hoppla*, and the roots and driving forces of the Russian Revolution in *Rasputin*, we wanted to illuminate the whole system of war in the spotlight of satire in *Schweik*.'[7] And the staging of *Rasputin* provides a key example of Piscator's directorial approach, as well as the scale of his productions and his use of multi-media.

Political staging: Piscator's Rasputin

Piscator's aim was to develop a new theatrical form that would be both intrinsically political and specifically modern; and as he remarked, looking back at his work:

> Of all my productions the 'Rasputin'-drama had the strongest echo, the most unequivocal effect . . . It was here that I had the opportunity to realize my aims most strikingly and clearly. The motivation for staging this material as well as the purpose and form of the treatment were proved justified through the [political] response to the performance.[8]

Tolstoy's original was a melodrama centred on the monk Rasputin's influence over the Tsarina, and the court conspiracies leading to Rasputin's assassination, ending with the October Revolution of 1917 – which was presented in terms of poetic justice. Piscator habitually changed the scripts of the plays he directed; and the process with *Rasputin* demonstrates his approach. By the time the 'dramaturgical collective' (which included playwrights like Leo Lania, Walter Mehring and Felix Gasbarra as well as Piscator himself) had finished, the number of original scenes had been cut to eight, while nineteen new scenes were added. Tolstoy's naturalistic characters had been multiplied to a cast of thousands: thirty-one actors doubling to play fifty-six named parts plus 'gypsy dancers, soldiers, people' – stage photos show over eighty people on the set, massed both on platforms inside the dome and on the stage around it in the climax, 'Lenin's speech on the occasion of the second Soviet Congress'. Reflecting this change in focus, the title of the piece was expanded to *Rasputin, the Romanoffs, the War and the People Who Rose Up against Them*.

While this extensive revision of the script was being undertaken, Piscator was working with his designers and technical people on the plans for the set. Very early in the process, Piscator had decided the visual concept for the stage: a half globe, representing the northern hemisphere of the world (or rather specifically Germany, Russia and Austria: the focus of the play), which was motorized and could rotate or even split apart.

Everything – plot, scope, perspective – was built around this concept that literally embodied the material of the new scenes, presenting points where global events between 1915 and 1917 intersected with the lives of the historical characters, as well as setting local incidents and individual intrigues in an international context of industrial output and military strategies. Protagonists

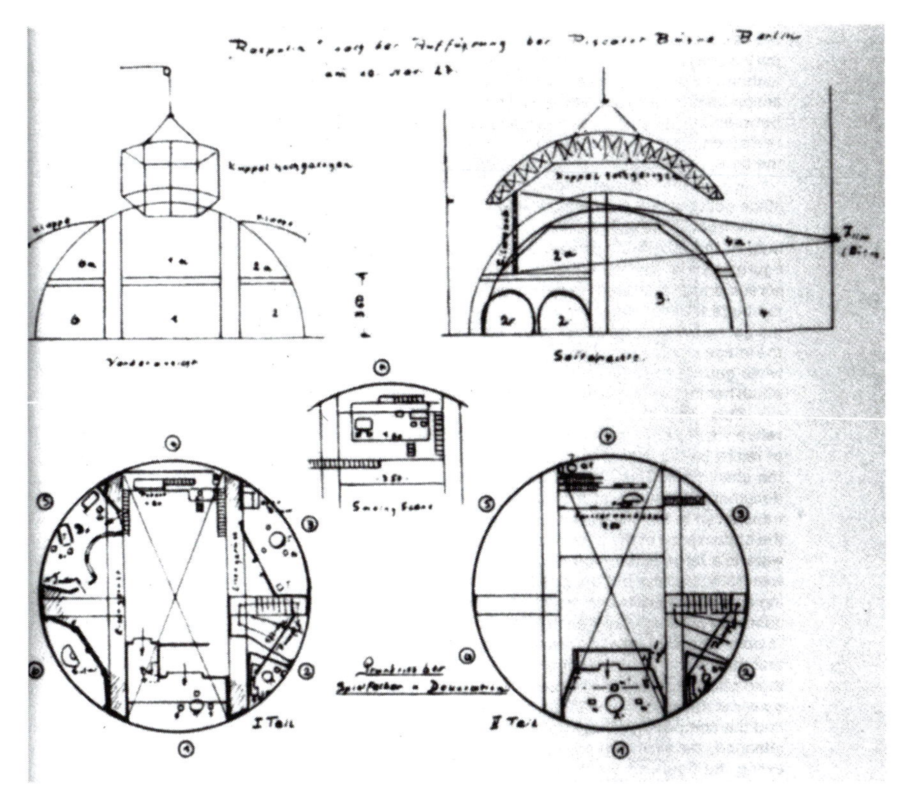

7 Set design for *Rasputin*, Erwin Piscator, Theater am Nollendorfplatz, Berlin, 1927: diagrammatic sections and plans showing use of the hemispherical stage

were transformed into pawns of historical forces, and the overall impression was of inexorably marching events. This net of complex circumstances was seen from a double perspective: triumphantly affirmative for the anonymous masses; tragic for the individuals (emperors and generals) nominally in control. The image of the globe and its potential as an organizing principle determined the way Tolstoy's text was adapted; and its fluidity and movement were essential for handling such a panoramic subject.

Indeed the mechanical nature of the globe was emphasized: the centrefold of the Piscatorbühne programme for *Rasputin* was filled with a photo of the globe, half-opened to show staircases and platforms inside, and the engineered steel-lattice frame of the structure. Around this industrial image were thumbnails of the major characters – identified only by the names of the actors, since their appearance and make-up closely echoed the historical figures they represented, who were rightly assumed to be instantly recognizable to the Berlin audience – the Tsar and Tsarina, Rasputin, the German Kaiser, Lenin. The globe was covered with the stiff, smooth cloth used for the outer skin of Zeppelins (a deliberate reference to machines of war), painted in non-reflecting silver, so that film could be projected onto its curving surface, yet spotlights would not refract off it. The whole structure was 49 feet in diameter, 24½ feet high and weighed over a ton. It was fully mechanized, mounted on a revolve and divided into twelve internal sections, or mini-stages. These had between two and four levels, one above each other, with fourteen different combinations of openings. The hinged sections of the outer shell that covered each section folded back like triangular doors, lifted up like trapezoid flaps, or could be flown – the whole top of the globe lifting up – revealing an acted scene within, or a back-projected screen.

Film and stage

Over 100,000 metres of feature film, in addition to a multitude of newsreels and other documentaries, were screened to select material for the scenes, with many clips taken from a Russian film *The Fall of the House of Romanoff*, which had been compiled from newsreels of the events. Film formed a prologue, tracing Russian history from Ivan the Terrible through a line of crowned heads leading up to Nicholas II, the last Tsar, alternating with repeated film glimpses of masses in revolt and beaten down, sabred and shot, as the timeline progressed through the centuries. During the performance, film was used as a contrast to the individual actions, or commentary – as when in one dome-opening the Tsarina, seated in a lavishly decorated room, ridiculed reports of popular uprisings, while on the 16-foot-high screen immediately above her head shots rang out in a film scene of Bolsheviks executing her together with the Tsar and their whole family at Yekaterinburg barely four years later. The effect was so overwhelming that in each performance, as Tilla Durieux (the Tsarina) recalled, 'I petrified in my role.'[9] There were also times when three different films were projected simultaneously – onto the upper screen, in the background of one of the openings in which actors were performing, and over the curving surface of the dome, allowing additional contrasts.

A further source of commentary was provided through an 8-foot-wide screen running the full height of the proscenium at the right side of the forestage. On these a 'Calendar' of dates and events, plus statements and quotations were projected, as on a continuously rolling vertical band. So, beside

Film and stage

It should be remembered that even in 1927, film was still a relatively new medium, with *The Jazz Singer* – the first movie with synchronized sound – appearing in the same year, so that Piscator's use of film was striking for the time. As the 'Optical Advisor' for the Piscatorbühne described:

> Two projectors were installed next to each other behind the audience ... swivel-mounted on columns with which changes in the height of the instruments could be easily undertaken.
>
> One projected the film onto the entire hemisphere. The other projected the explanatory text onto the respective screen ... A simple machine was used for the reverse projection from the back of the stage ... In order to maintain a uniform film speed when all three projectors were running simultaneously, the speed of the film had to be controlled ... by the use of a clock attached to each projector. Further, as an important innovation, I had a special filter, in the form of a plane-parallel glass of a particular shade, inserted in front of the projector's lens in the path of the light ... This increased the contrast of the image and made possible a less tiring, smoother viewing.
>
> Günther Loeck[10]

each shot of struggling crowds in the Prologue, the Calendar not only listed names and dates of the movements, but made comments like 'BETRAYED BY THEIR LEADERS ... THE SOLDIERS HAD THE GUNS ...', while against each historical Tsar's portrait was an equally laconic notation: 'STABBED TO DEATH ... INSANE, DIED RAVING...' Or during a scene where the Tsar in his headquarters issued patriotic directives while flirting with a nurse, in a series of stark contrasts film showed the corpses of his troops left lying in the mud at the battlefront, while the 'Calendar' cited from one of his letters to the Tsarina, 'THE LIFE THAT I LEAD AT THE HEAD OF MY ARMY IS HEALTHY AND HAS AN INVIGORATING EFFECT', coupled with the actual casualty figures.[11]

The film commented on the acted scenes, the verbal projections commented on both, creating multiple poles within the action that could be played off against each other, offering multiple perspectives and building thematic points out of ironic oppositions. Indeed, since the images on screen were significantly larger than the actors on stage, the comparative insignificance of characters as individual people was underlined. At the same time, the documentary nature of film emphasized the artifice of theatrical conventions, while its impression of actuality was transferred to the historical characters by the correspondence between their physical appearance and their film images. As a result it was not the actors that appeared artificial, but the society they represented, while the film demonstrated how much the characters were out of touch with reality.

Political directing: the Piscator approach

It was this counterpoint and the extension to the stage action provided by the film that Piscator's directorial notes focused on, and made it possible for him to expand the scope of the performance from 'the internal curve of [conventional] dramatic action' to 'the truest and most comprehensive possible epic unrolling of the epoch from its roots to its final repercussions'[12] – in other words from drama to political action. And the way this production, and its documentary nature, touched a nerve and roused passions even a decade after the events portrayed can be seen from the hate mail Piscator received. Ordinary people accused him of defiling the name of Germany, while the ex-Kaiser started legal action for defamation of character in response to a multiple scene where Wilhelm had been shown with Franz Josef of Austria and Nicholas of Russia, in separate segments of the dome, each mouthing the same platitudes. As the legal statement of complaint served on Piscator in 1927 all too revealingly attested:

> The mask by which the plaintiff is portrayed is unmistakable. The plaintiff is clearly associated with the [other] two emperors. The words that the authors set in their mouths express equivalent thought processes. In so far as the erstwhile Emperor Franz Josef is presented as a complete idiot and the Czar Nicholas as a bigoted and characterless fool, one is forced to conclude that the plaintiff too is characterized in a like manner.[13]

Seeking controversy, Piscator printed excerpts in later *Rasputin* programmes (the show ran for over two-and-a-half months – an extremely long period for 1920s Berlin) as an additional form of documentation. And after Wilhelm won an injunction against Piscator, in the 'Three Emperors' scene, Leo Lania (as co-author) appeared on stage – replacing Paul Herm, who played the Kaiser – and read extracts from the court judgment in place of the Kaiser's speeches.

The Piscatorbühne had its own technical office, and their records are revealing. Setting up such a complex mechanized stage, with the technical changes that turned out to be necessary during construction, took 1,690 man-hours (with 1,050 overtime hours); covering the dome alone took 1,122 square metres of material and 246 man-hours; and to finish the set-up in time for the opening sixteen men worked consecutively for twenty-four hours; so that constructing the whole set required a total of 4,516 man-hours. As Piscator's stage-manager wrote in frustration, 'what we need is not a theatre, but a huge assembly-shop with mobile bridges, hoists, cranes . . . with which weights of several tons could be shifted around the stage at the press of a button'.[14] During the performance itself, in addition to the eighty-plus actors in the cast, managing the complex set took twenty-four stagehands, plus film and lighting technicians. Such intensity and scale required an almost military organization – with the director as general officer, orchestrating over a hundred people – and typical photos of Piscator directing scenes show him in a dominating posture, giving orders with arm outstretched in a gesture of command.

His director's notes are almost completely concerned with the movement of the globe-stage, the integration of film, calendar and acted scenes, the choreography of massed actors in the crowd scenes, and the intended effect of each segment. There are relatively few notes relating to the rehearsal or performance of the main actors, reflecting the extent to which all had worked with Piscator over several years. In rehearsal, the first step was clarification of the political significance of their roles. In addition, those actors accustomed to what Piscator dismissed as 'the unmoving decorative scenery of the bourgeois stage' found themselves 'lost in the gigantic mechanical constructions that left them little calm to develop their individual expression', while their roles as such were caricatures, very different from the subjectivity of naturalistic or classical theatre: 'Every role was the sharply delineated expression of a social class. It was not the private characteristics, the individual complexes that were noticeable, but the type; the representative of a particular social and economic viewpoint.' As Piscator commented: 'a great part of rehearsal time was devoted to exploring the political meaning of the text with each of the actors. From this internal command of the material, all by itself, the actors could shape their parts.'[15] So, already aligned with his vision and requirements, his actors were left to fill out their characters and develop their gestures and moves by themselves. At the same time, as Piscator acknowledged, 'the right acting style for the new stage apparatus has not yet been completely worked out'[16] – a problem that was also to concern Brecht.

The Rasputin *production: a model for epic theatre*

This *Rasputin* production indeed was a viable model for epic theatre: not just in its extended scale, but in terms of multiple sources of simultaneous commentary, and the way the use of film exposed individuals as dependent on the wider social context. A conventional dramatic structure of sequential scenes was replaced by synchronous action through the simultaneous presentation of contrasting images and levels of reality. This gave some advantages of the novel in controlling the spectator/reader's judgement, while the ability to show a scene from more than one angle, alter the perspective, or give independent viewpoints, made sweeping vistas of fact possible. In addition, the mechanized context, militaristic impression and modernist symbolism made it a specifically contemporary theatre form.

Piscator's ideal was 'a theatre machine, as inherently technological as a typewriter', which would be emblematic of twentieth-century consciousness, and make it possible to deal directly with the global significance of topical issues. So in his productions, stage machinery was deliberately unconcealed to represent the scientific and specifically contemporary perspective of his theatre – as well as representing reality in performance through the avoidance of illusion. The *Rasputin* globe symbolized this – and although there were continual technical glitches, while the globe rumbled as it revolved so that at times the actors had to shout to be heard, the reverberating ponderousness of its rotation and rackety sense of insecurity must have created a vivid (if unintended) image of a world falling apart, of men at the mercy of machinery.

Mechanical flaws were inseparable from the innovative nature of Piscator's work, and underlined that his was an experimental theatre, forming an atmosphere of creative chaos that almost all the reviewers conceded was electrifying, however much they disliked his ideology. Piscator always associated his epic style with scientific, objective, rational, documentary qualities. Yet his associates, like the political artist George Grosz (who designed costumes for Brecht) and Béla Balàzs (a film reviewer who also wrote the libretto for Bartók's opera *Bluebeard's Castle*), commented on the 'Dionysian' effect of his staging; and Leo Lania's essay in the *Rasputin* programme reminded the audience that they were 'not merely spectators, but participants in the great drama of the collapse of imperialism . . . they form *an undivided unity*, one piece of world history: *the theatregoer of 1927 and – Rasputin, the Romanoffs, the War, and the People Who Rose Up against Them*'. The political rationale for this was to demonstrate that no individual could remain neutral, that the revolutionary forces unleashed by the war were still operating – and indeed the audience were caught up in the epic sweep of events, spontaneously surging to their feet to join with the massed actors on stage in singing 'The International'. Indeed this was a standard response to Piscator's political theatre. In exactly the same way, at the end of *Hoppla*, as the curtain fell on the words of the Mother – 'There is only one way – to hang yourself, or change the world' – the 'proletarian youth' in the balcony spontaneously rose to sing 'The International' to the great disturbance of the paying audience in the stalls.

> This kind of emotional affirmation was 'the sole justification' for political theatre. Aesthetic or artistic qualities were only relevant in so far as they contributed to 'the effect [of] awakening interest and enthusiasm for our political, i.e. *human* goals . . . By itself [political theatre] cannot change the power structure, but it can act as valuable preparation'.
>
> Leo Lania, programme for *Rasputin*

Documentary theatre

Piscator's epic theatre also tended towards extreme realism. This reached its height in his 1929 production of *The Merchant of Berlin* by Walter Mehring, one of the 'dramaturgical collective' – an updating of Shakespeare's *The Merchant of Venice*. A dissection of the hyper-inflation suffered by Germany at the time, this used a revolving stage, two stage lifts or bridges, and two paired treadmills (or rolling bands moving side-by-side in opposite directions – the same structure as had been used by Piscator for Brecht's script of *The Good Soldier Schweik*), on which complete scenes could be mounted, with four screens and a gauze for the projection of both cartoons and a film, specially shot by the designer, Lazlo Moholy-Nagy, together with a complex array of sound effects. As highly mechanized as *Rasputin*, this setting itself became the focus of the production, symbolizing the social mobility and individual restlessness of Berlin society, with the simultaneously rising and falling bridges at the end representing relative changes in social class. As the reviews suggest, this created an astonishingly lifelike picture of life on the streets outside the theatre:

> For our epoch only the *momentary* is living. Newspapers are the history of the moment. On the gauze, film threw whole series of actual news headlines and newspaper clippings of today's events . . . What an apparatus! . . . On it streams the tempo-march of the streets with thousands of steps forward and back, right and left. Troops of soldiers, poor prostitutes, serving men, stock-exchange men, Jewish merchants, swastikas. Traffic intersection on the stage. Reality of the instant. The elevated railway crosses the bridge to the Alexanderplatz station. The underground U sign lights up. Trams sound their bells. Cars hoot. . .[17]

Forced to flee from Germany shortly after the 1933 Nazi Putsch, Piscator found Russia under Stalin even more autocratic than under the Tsar. So he fled (as Ernst Busch once described it) to the United States, where he ran theatre courses for the New School of Social Research in New York, teaching among others Marlon Brando. Then, after the Second World War, he returned to West Berlin to run the Freie Volksbühne, where he developed a contemporary form of documentary drama, showcasing Rolf Hochhuth's attacks on papal responsibility for the Holocaust in *The Deputy*, or British decisions leading to the firebombing of Dresden in *The Soldiers*, and Peter Weiss' *Investigation* about Auschwitz and the Nuremberg Trials. He also reused his 'globe-stage' for his final production: a parallel piece to *Rasputin*, H. H. Kirst's *Uprising of the Officers*, a documentary piece about the Second World War and the attempt by a group of army officers to assassinate Hitler.

Piscator's documentary stagings of the 1960s can be seen as a direct development of his epic work in the 1920s. And while both influenced political theatre world-wide, it was Piscator's early stage experiments that had the most impact, particularly influencing Brecht, who was still working out his theatre theories while collaborating with Piscator. As Brecht was later to acknowledge, Piscator had also developed 'Alienation Effects' in 'a wholly original and independent way. Above all, the theatre's conversion to politics was Piscator's achievement, without which the Augsburger's [Brecht's way of referring to himself] theatre would hardly be conceivable.'[18]

Bertolt Brecht's epic theatre

As we will see, Brecht's version of epic theatre shares many of the qualities of Piscator's work, particularly the aim of creating distinguishable elements of production that would offer multiple viewpoints and internal commentary. It also parallels Piscator in the contradiction between aim (rational, objective) and effect (emotional response). Yet while Brecht takes exactly the same view that the stage should always be recognizably theatrical, undermining standard naturalistic fourth-wall illusion, in sharp contrast to Piscator's complex machinery Brecht's staging was always minimalist – the most mechanized of his productions being *Mother Courage* which used a revolve for the endless travels of her increasingly decrepit wagon. These qualities along with Brecht's montage structure are sometimes attributed to Meyerhold, and indeed, like Meyerhold, Brecht was influenced by the stylized performance of the Chinese actor Mei Lang-fan. But in fact, while Brecht was well aware of Eisenstein's films, also based on a montage structure, the first production by Meyerhold that he saw was in 1930, some time after he had defined his epic theatre.

Brecht's significance was that, unlike Piscator (who commented that 'above all Brecht loved sticking labels onto things before the content was defined'[19]), he contributed the theory for epic theatre, by defining it against the 'dramatic' or 'Aristotelian' theatre. The acting of standard dramatic theatre is set against narration; spectator involvement that negates the capacity for action, against turning spectators into observers and arousing them to act; feeling against reason. While the aim of dramatic theatre is to arouse emotion, the epic aim is to force spectators to make decisions. Where the dramatic theatre works through suggestion, and human beings are represented as already known with fixed personalities, epic theatre works through argument and sees human beings as a subject for exploration, being changeable and changing. In terms of dramatic structure, suspense focused on the ending, with every scene organically integrated in linear progression, is contrasted with suspense during the action, which is a montage of independent scenes, with curvilinear development. All this is premised on the denial of Descartes' iconic statement that 'thought determines being': restated here as 'social being determines thought'. It should be noticed that Brecht's most significant essays – 'The Modern Theatre Is the Epic Theatre' and 'The Literarizing of Theatre' – were written as notes to *Mahagonny* and *The Threepenny Opera*, the folk opera form sharing many of the qualities that Brecht defined as 'epic'.

> The spectator of the dramatic theatre says: 'Yes, I have felt the same. I am just like that. This is only natural. It will always be like this. This human being's suffering moves me, because there is no way out for him. This is great art, it bears the mark of the inevitable. I am weeping with those who weep on the stage, laughing with those who laugh.'
>
> The spectator of the epic theatre says: 'I should never have thought so. That is not the way to do it. This is most surprising, hardly credible. This will have to stop. This human being's suffering moves me, because there would have been a way out for him. This is great art: nothing here seem inevitable. I am laughing about those who weep on the stage, weeping about those who laugh.'
>
> Brecht, 'Entertainment or Teaching Theatre'[20]

It should also be noted that the whole concept of epic theatre is based in spectator theory, precisely because this type of theatre is validated by the public response it can engender.

As Brecht put it in an open letter to the Swiss epic playwright Friedrich Dürrenmatt, 'Today's world is only describable to the people of today, when it is described as a changeable world ... the world of today can indeed be represented on the stage, but only if it is recognized as changeable.'[21] And this is directly reflected in his plays. One of Brecht's songs is titled, 'Change the world. It needs it!' and in play after play, Brecht's characters present the audience with variations on this theme:

> How can a better ending be arranged?
> Can one change people? Can the world be changed? ...
> It is for you to find a way, my friends,
> To help good men arrive at happy ends.
>
> (Shen Te in *The Good Person of Sechzuan*)

> You have seen what is common, what continually occurs.
> But we ask you:
> Even if it is usual, find it hard to explain.
> What here is common should astonish you.
> What here's the rule, recognize as an abuse,
> And where you have recognized an abuse, provide a remedy.
>
> (Final Chorus, *The Exception and the Rule*)[22]

In addition to the call for social change through political action on the part of the audience being directly addressed, this also forms an explicit description of the aims and intended effect of Brecht's epic drama, where spectators are expected to be critical of opinions expressed.

Epic theatre and cabaret

Brecht performed with the comedian Karl Valentin's Munich political cabaret – and there is a well-known 1921 photo of him playing the clarinet in a typical trestle-platform fairground entertainment ('*Bänkelgesang*'), alongside the skeletal Valentin blowing into a tuba. This is an instructive prototype for the basic principles of Brecht's epic theatre.

For a photo of Brecht with Karl Valentin performing a *Bänkelgesang* in Munich, 1921, see www.u.arizona.edu/~chisholm/GER588_files/brecht_valentin.gif.[23]

The third-person narration of a compère, and the obvious gap between 'character' and performer, recurs in Brecht's epic acting principles. His concept of epic theatre where the audience smoked and drank – and were therefore self-aware, automatically critical and not emotionally involved by the performance – is a direct transcription of the circumstances of cabaret. The placard – either giving a title for a scene or critiquing the action – was to become a key technique in Brecht's theatre. The on-stage orchestra of cabaret is an equivalent to Brecht's insistence that the mechanics of performance be exposed to counter theatrical illusion. One of the best-known Brecht songs, 'The Moritat of Mackie Messer' from *The Threepenny Opera*, is precisely the sort of song performed as a 'Moritat' in the fairground cabaret Brecht performed in Munich with Valentin – and it is no coincidence that the Berlin 'Wild Stage' cabaret was where Brecht performed his already notorious song 'Legend of the Dead Soldier', at his first appearance in Berlin. He was whistled off the stage after the third stanza, with the audience shouting insults and throwing their drinking glasses; and provocation remained an essential part of his epic theatre, with the singers in the Baden-Baden premiere of *Mahagonny* being issued tin whistles to respond to audience booing.

> The man he learnt most from was the clown *Valentin*, who performed in a beer-hall. He did short sketches in which he played refractory employees, orchestral musicians or photographers, who hated their employer and made him look ridiculous. The employer was played by his partner, a popular woman comedian who used to pad herself out and speak in a deep bass voice. When the Augsburger [Brecht's name for

himself] was producing his first play, which included a thirty minutes' battle, he asked Valentin what he ought to do with the soldiers: 'What are the soldiers like in battle?' Valentin promptly answered: 'They're pale. Scared shitless.'
Brecht[24]

Indeed, Brecht wrote the script of a short slapstick silent film, *The Mysteries of a Barbershop*, for Valentin in 1923, and Valentin was responsible for Brecht's characteristic technique of chalking his actors' faces in his early epic work. Another influence that Brecht acknowledged was the expressionist playwright Frank Wedekind, although his importance for Brecht was not so much plays like *Spring's Awakening*, but Wedekind's cabaret personality. Wedekind was a long-time performer with the famous Munich 'Eleven Executioners' (*Elf Scharfrichter*) cabaret; Brecht clearly modelled his own harsh singing style – and the musical tone of the operas he wrote with Kurt Weill – on Wedekind; and in a 1918 obituary for Wedekind, Brecht wrote that 'His vitality was his finest characteristic . . . There he stood, ugly, brutal, dangerous, with close-cropped red hair, singing his songs to a guitar accompaniment in a high nasal voice, slightly monotonous and quite untrained. No singer ever gave me such a shock, such a thrill.'[25]

Developing an epic style of staging and directing

While both Piscator and Brecht had the same early training with Reinhardt, Piscator began his career as a director immediately, whereas Brecht started his career as a poet, a cabaret singer and a playwright before beginning to direct. His productions – mainly of his own plays – were almost all co-directed. He participated with Eric Engel on the 1923 Munich premiere of *In the Jungle of Cities*; co-directed the 1926 Berlin version of *Baal* with the actor Oskar Homolka (who also played the title role); assisted Engel with the 1928 *Threepenny Opera*, and in the same year assisted Piscator with his own adaptation of *The Good Soldier Schweik*. His first work as an independent director was his adaptation of Marlowe's *Edward the Second*, at the Chamber Theatre in Munich (1924), followed by his first work with Kurt Weill: the Baden-Baden production of *Mahagonny*, for the Leipzig premiere of which he had been assistant director. Through this process Brecht not only learned directing skills, but also gathered the core of what was to become his own theatre group. *Mahagonny* was Lotte Lenya's first success, while Helene Weigel began her Brecht career with the 1928 Berlin premiere of *A Man's a Man*; Caspar Neher first designed *In the Jungle of Cities*, and went on to design almost every other one of Brecht's plays and operas in the 1920s and 1930s, joining up again with Brecht in Switzerland in 1948 for Brecht's adaptation of Hölderlin's *Antigone*, and at the Berliner Ensemble for

Lenz's *The Private Tutor*. Engel became the continuing director of Brecht's work: from *In the Jungle of Cities*, *A Man's a Man*, *The Threepenny Opera* and *The Rise and Fall of the City of Mahagonny*, to after the war with the 1949 Berlin restaging of *Mother Courage*, which he co-directed with Brecht.

In addition to the cabaret qualities that Brecht integrated into his theatre, which were focused on creating a self-aware – and therefore critical – audience, he also set about completely changing the fundamentals of performance. Following Piscator, but in a minimalist, bare stage manner (which served to emphasize words that Brecht as a playwright valued, and which the Piscatorbühne's elaborate machinery had tended to overwhelm), Brecht changed the whole visual appearance of the theatre by adapting the cabaret genre. Placards introduced scenes; screens behind and above the acting area had text, or cartoons by George Grosz, projected on them (but never moving film, as in Piscator's productions) – all of which introduced contrasting viewpoints or set a specific viewpoint for a scene. At the same time the standard theatre curtain, which covered all scene changes, was replaced with a half-high curtain on a visible wire, while the theatre lighting was always bright (symbolizing a scientific laboratory rather than an impressionistic conjuring space) while – as in *The Threepenny Opera* of 1928 – spotlights were visible above the stage. As Brecht put it in a poem:

> Give us light on the stage, electrician. How can we
> Playwrights and actors put forward
> Our view of the world in half-darkness . . . we need the spectator's
> Wakeful-, even watchfulness . . .
> . . . And please make
>
> My curtain half-height, don't cut the stage off.
> Leaning back, let the spectator
> Notice the busy preparations being so
> Ingeniously made for him . . . And let him observe
> That this is not magic, but
> Work, my friends.[26]

The political premise of Brecht's epic theatre, the intellectual rather than emotional spectator-response, the demystification of performance, and the appeal to the (notional) working-class public's interest in the practical, are all underlined in this poem.

Similarly Brecht demanded a radically different form of acting, which reversed the traditional empathetic performance style. So, in the Berliner Ensemble rehearsals for Lenz's *The Court Chamberlain*, Brecht required his actors to use indirect, third person speech: 'she' instead of 'I' or 'him' instead of 'me'. Alternatively his actors were required in rehearsal to preface each speech with 'the man said' or 'she said' – or to rephrase the speeches into a dialectical 'not / but' formula signifying alternative possibilities (for example, 'she asked him not to move away, but to stand by her'). A way of distancing actor from character – in direct contrast to Stanislavsky – such techniques were also designed to allow actors to create the 'Gestus' of a scene or role: the universalized expression of that particular circumstance.

This was the basis of the alienation effect (or so-called 'V-effect' from *Verfremdungseffekt*) that, rather than corresponding to the psychiatric term, denoted 'distancing' as a shift in vision: making the ordinary/everyday look strange, or showing the hidden reality beneath accepted appearances – ironically very much indeed the same as Wordsworth's nineteenth-century Romantic poetic dictum of 'making the familiar new'. Other techniques for achieving his alienation effect through acting were defined as:

> Translation of speeches into the past tense.
> Including the stage directions and commentary with the speeches.[27]

This was intended to produce a subliminal impression in performance, with the actor's critical approach to the character being portrayed as a way of encouraging an objective view on the audience's part, capable of separating out character from actor and critiquing the character's actions.

The street scene

It is comparatively easy to set up a basic model for the epic theatre. After practical experiments I chose an event which can take place on any street-corner as a representative example of the simplest, that is to say the 'natural' epic theatre: the eyewitness to a traffic accident demonstrates to a crowd of bystanders how the misfortune came to happen. The onlookers either have not seen the accident, or do not share his opinion of it and see it 'differently' – the main point is that the demonstrations of the actions of the driver or of the victim or both are presented in such a way that the bystanders can form a judgement for themselves concerning the accident . . .

Fully decisive is the fact that a major identifier of standard theatre disappears: the creation of illusion. The presentation of the street demonstrator has the quality of a reproduction. The event has occurred, here is the repetition . . . His demonstration for example loses no value if the shock that the accident creates is not reproduced; indeed then it would be less valuable . . .

An essential element of the street scene, which must also be present in the theatre, is the circumstance that the demonstration has practical social significance.

Brecht[28]

However, Brecht's notorious alienation effect was by no means intended to rule out emotional expressivity. Brecht's aim was to get an effect 'not of improvisation but of quotation . . . but with all the undertones, the totally human concrete plasticity of expression'.[29]

Indeed, his lead actors, Ernst Busch – particularly in the leading roles specifically identified with him: Azdak from *The Caucasian Chalk Circle*, the title figure in *The Life of Galileo*, the Cook from *Mother Courage* – and Helene Weigel, who acted the lead roles in most of Brecht's mature work, were by no means unemotional performers. In fact, under its apparently 'cool' speeches, Brecht's theatre is one of extremely violent emotion. So in his 1929 'further attempt at a didactic piece', *The Baden-Baden Cantata of Acquiescence*, spectators fainted when a gigantic clown was sawn into pieces. Or in *The Caucasian Chalk Circle* – directed by Brecht in 1954 – the escape of the innocent Gruscha, carrying a baby and pursued by armoured soldiers, across a rickety bridge over an awesome ravine (in fact suspended bare inches above the stage, in a reprise of Edgar's persuading the blind Gloucester that he stands on the brink of a cliff in *King Lear*) evoked a pure melodramatic response, while the final Solomonic judgment had still more emotional impact:

> AZDAK: The true mother is she who can pull the child out of the circle . . . Pull! (*The* GOVERNOR'S WIFE *pulls the child out of the circle on her side;* GRUSCHA *has let go and stands aghast.*)[30]

In the Berliner Ensemble production, when the young child was torn out of Gruscha's hand, not once, but twice, on the second time the actress gave a tiny cry – and spectators broke into tears. In all these cases, it should be noted that the language is extremely denotative, the stage is almost bare, there are circus elements (clown / tight-rope) or meta-theatrical elements, and the dramatic situation is extremely simple. It is the opposite of the usual rhetorical and intensified appeal to audience emotion. But in a very real sense, less is more.

> It is not the case – however it has been presented – that the epic theatre . . . is in any way simply undramatic theatre, which raises the war-cry 'here reason – there emotion' (feeling). In no way does it reject emotion. Particularly not the passion for justice, the urge to freedom, righteous anger: these . . . indeed it seeks to strengthen or to create. The critical attitude that it aims to evoke in the audience can never be passionate enough for epic theatre.
>
> Bertolt Brecht, conversation with Friedrich Wolf[31]

Directing epic theatre: Mother Courage

Brecht had already shown his capacity as a director with his 1931 staging of *A Man's a Man* with Peter Lorre as the protagonist, Galy Gay. However, it was the 1949 Berlin *Mother Courage* that brought Brecht the reputation of the leading director in Europe, even though the setting and the organizing symbol of the wagon was almost exactly the same as the 1941 Zurich premiere directed by Leopold Lindtberg, since the designer for both was Teo Otto, who also designed the Brecht/Laughton *Galileo*. The director of record may have been Engel, but it was Brecht who rehearsed the actors and coordinated the elements of the production. And since this production was one documented in a published 'Model Record' (*Modellbuch*) – intended as a guide for other directors to stage Brecht's plays – as well as being highlighted in the Berliner Ensemble's *Theatre Work* (*Theaterarbeit*), we have an extensive record of intentions and performance.

Brecht divided his rehearsal and preparation process into fifteen distinct phases. The initial phase of directing the piece – even as its author, and even a decade after he had written the text – was:

1. **Play Analysis**: concentrating the story into less than half a side of writing paper, dividing the action into sections, establishing turning-points, 'finding means and ways to enable the easy telling of the story and to draw out its social meaning'.
2. **Establishing the Setting**: Only after this is the piece
3. **cast**; and the actors' first rehearsal is a
4. **Read Through**: 'with a minimum of expression or characterization ... explanation of the Play Analysis'.
5. **Placing Rehearsal**: 'Main events sketched out in placing and moves, explored in this and that way.'
6. **Set Rehearsal**: 'designs carried over onto the stage . . . everything necessary for acting has to be erected in a usable form (walls, ramps, podiums, windows, etc.). From this point no rehearsal without props.'
7. **Detail Rehearsal**: with 'each detail rehearsed on its own'.
8. **Run-through Rehearsal**: putting episodes into a coherent pattern.
10. **Review and Verification Rehearsal**: repeated explorations of whether the socially valuable recognitions and impulses in the play are being communicated, and if the story is being elegantly and fully told, together with the photographing of all groupings.
11. **Tempo Rehearsal**: fixing speed and length of scenes
12. **Dress and Technical Rehearsal**
13. **Speak-through Rehearsal**: without a prompter, speed-reading of the whole text with gestures.
14. **Preview Performances**: determining reaction of the public, followed by discussion-groups: 'in between the previews Adjusting Rehearsals take place in response to [audience] reactions'.
15. **Premiere**: 'without the presence of the director, so that the actors can perform without restraint'.[32]

Of particular note is the very early introduction of the setting in the rehearsal process, and indications that actors' groupings were based on the designer's sketches. A further technique to note is Brecht's use of photography during rehearsal as a record of gesture and pose. However the most significant phase was the Detail Rehearsal. Echoing the dramatic principles embedded in his play scripts, as a member of the Berliner Ensemble remarks in *Theatre Work*, 'each scene is subdivided into a succession of episodes. Brecht produces as though each of these little episodes could be taken out of the play and performed on its own. They are meticulously realized, down to the smallest detail.'[33] At the same time, when Brecht directed a new production of *Mother Courage* at the Munich Kammerspiele just a year later, basing his staging on the Berlin 'Model' record, he proved open to suggestions from actors and even stagehands, who found that 'Model or no Model, they could show whatever they wanted. If it was good, it was accepted straight away.'[34] This combination of meticulous preparation and improvisation produced a quality of precision together with enthusiasm; rational objectivity superimposed (and thus intensifying) intensely emotional situations. All this added up to a very recognizable Berliner Ensemble style. It also emphasized the visual and physical elements, since Brecht's constant demand was 'Don't talk about it. Act it out for us!' His initial focus in rehearsal was on grouping and gesture, where (as the performance-record photos of the 'Model' clearly show in production after production) Brecht followed the sketches of his designers, particularly Neher, in whose view the stage should be designed as a space for people to experience something, and who therefore included the characters as inhabitants of his set drawings, acting out the key incident of the scene.

Corresponding exactly to his method of dividing scenes into independent episodes, Brecht rejected the conventional type of plot-structure for his plays. As he points out in his 'Short Organum for the Theatre':

> Since the public is not being invited to fling themselves into a story as if into a river, to be swept passively to-and-fro, so the individual events [in a play] must be tied together in such a way that the knots are obvious. The events should not follow one another unnoticeably, but instead make it possible for people to interpose their judgement.[35]

And this carry-over from his dramatic texts into his theatrical presentations means that his plays themselves incorporate a great deal of directorial commentary, illuminating the way Brecht staged his own work. Take one of the key scenes of *Mother Courage*, 'The Stone Speaks', where the last of Mother Courage's children, the dumb Kattrin, awakens the sleeping citizens of a town which is about to be stormed in the night. Faced with the assaulting troops, who silence a group of peasants by threatening their cattle, the Peasant's Wife sets a tone of fatalistic resignation, by urging the agonized Kattrin – who, unable to have a child herself, fears for the lives of the children in the town – to 'Pray, poor creature, pray! Nowt we can do to stop the bloodshed'. But while the peasants sink to their knees:

> *Unobserved, KATTRIN has slipped away to the cart and taken from it something she hides beneath her apron; then she climbs the ladder to the stable roof.*

The action is intensified by its contrast from the bitterly functional tone of the rest of the play; and its emotional power comes from its concreteness, as well as its temporary release from the constrainingly self-centred nature of the narrative as a whole. This is underlined by the opposition between the verbal efforts of the Ensign and his soldiers to stop her, and the eloquent power of non-vocal sound, as Kattrin starts drumming. The set-up emphasizes the expected futility of the action, and (as elsewhere in Brecht's plays) the impact of the scene is only realized after it has apparently finished.

> THE ENSIGN. Set it up! Set it up! (*Calls while the gun is being erected.*) For the very last time: stop drumming!
> KATTRIN *in tears, drums as loud as she can.*
> Fire!
> *The* SOLDIERS *fire.* KATTRIN *is hit, gives a few more drumbeats and then slowly crumples.*
> That's the end of that.
> *But* KATTRIN*'s last drumbeats are taken up by the town's cannon. In the distance can be heard the confused noise of tocsins and gunfire.*
> FIRST SOLDIER. She's made it.

Whether it is her final faltering drumbeats – standing for her ebbing life – that have awakened the town, or the sound of the shot that kills her, Kattrin's unselfish sacrifice, the tension between the Ensign's unfeeling dismissal, the immediate sound of the town's cannon, and the First Soldier's spontaneous admiration for the woman he has just killed, form a clear sequence of emotional manipulation. Even the 'coolness' of the tone magnifies the emotional response.

In fact Brecht's is a theatre of exceptional emotional impact, where the 'A-Effect' becomes an emotional intensifier. Another clear example of this is in Helene Weigel's famous 'silent scream' after being brought the body of her second son. In *The Messingkauf Dialogues* Brecht uses Weigel as an example of the epic playwriting technique:

> The Augsburger cuts his plays up into a series of little independent playlets, so that the action progresses by jumps . . . He does it in such a

> way that each individual scene can be given a title of a historical or socio-political kind . . . The Augsburger filmed Weigel making herself up. He cut the film up, and each frame showed a complete facial expression, self-contained, and with its own meaning. 'You see what an actress she is,' he said admiringly. 'Each gesture can be analysed into as many gestures as you like . . . everything is there for the sake of something else . . .'[36]

And in the 'silent scream' scene, where Mother Courage, unable to acknowledge her own dead son for fear of losing all her goods, dare not openly express her grief, this technique produced devastating impact. Her head thrown back, her mouth opened wide and her eyes screwed shut, Weigel became an icon of immeasurable sorrow – and the fact that no sound came out intensified the

8 *Mother Courage* (Eilif's sabre dance), Bertolt Brecht, Munich Kammerspiele, 1949

emotional transference. At one point Brecht announced that, as a play, *Mother Courage* was intended as a withdrawal course for emotional drug addicts (referring to the rhetorical excess of theatre in the Third Reich). Very obviously avoiding such excess, the unheard ululation echoed in the minds of the spectators, giving far more volume than any actual vocalization might have done. And at the same time – being complicated by the awareness that Mother Courage's dramatic situation makes any expression of grief impossible – this became a *Gestus* focusing audience attention on the inhumanity of the materialist/capitalist system that found its ultimate expression in endless war. Absence of standard expression or rhetoric made the empathy still more powerful. Also, like Kattrin's sacrifice, the essential quality of this 'playlet' was not verbal but physical. And indeed Brecht's theatre was extremely physical in performance. So, for example, in the sabre dance of Mother Courage's eldest son, Eilif, the 'Model Record' photo shows the actor leaping with his feet high above the stage floor. It is a circus leap, showcasing the theatricality that was the essence of Brecht's epic theatre, which is carried forward in the contemporary works of his successors.

The influence of epic theatre

In the 1940s and 1950s Brecht's epic principles were imported into England by the political director Joan Littlewood, who started off with agitprop theatre (as Piscator had done) in Manchester, and created a local equivalent based on music hall – rather than Brecht's cabaret – in productions like the Theatre Workshop's 1963 *Oh What a Lovely War*, a production that also used placards and projections (like Brecht) plus a rolling calendar projecting dates and statistics (derived from Piscator). John Osborne, whose play *Look Back in Anger* gave a new impetus to British drama in 1956 (the same year as the first Berliner Ensemble tour to London), acted the water-carrier in Brecht's *The Good Person of Sechzuan*, and introduced epic characteristics in plays like *Luther* (1961) and, with its music hall frame, *The Entertainer* (1957). Brecht's influence spread throughout British political theatre. The work of playwrights such as John Arden or David Edgar is specifically Brechtian, while Howard Brenton includes a character called Bertolt Brecht in *Berlin Bertie* (1992), and David Hare has adapted both Brecht's *Galileo* and *Mother Courage* (1994, 1995). In addition, directors at the Royal Court (which had more than usual influence as an incubator for new drama), from Lindsay Anderson, George Devine or William Gaskill, to Max Stafford-Clarke, adopted and adapted Brecht's dramaturgical principles. Brecht's influence has been equally present in the American theatre of Sam Shepard and Tony Kushner, and The Wooster

Group. Indeed it would be hard to find a director in British, European or American theatre in the latter half of the twentieth century who had not to some extent been influenced by epic theatre. And it also continues to inform the work of contemporary German directors.

The most striking examples of the way epic theatre has been redefined to express the contemporary post-millennium world are the plays and productions of Heiner Müller (who succeeded Helene Weigel as director of Brecht's Berliner Ensemble), and the productions of Roberto Ciulli at Theater an der Ruhr and in collaboration with theatres outside Europe, indicating the international pull of epic theatre. These follow and build on the development of epic theatre initiated by Brecht and promoted by Weigel and the Berliner Ensemble.

Heiner Müller and post-Brechtian epic theatre

Müller's position in the Berliner Ensemble – from 1992 effectively leading the five-man dramaturgical collective of German theatre directors set up after Brecht's death (which included Peter Zadek and Peter Palitzsche), and appointed its sole director in 1995 – gave him particular prestige. Like Brecht, Müller was a major poet and playwright, as well as a director; and he extended Brecht's dialectics, redefining epic theatre as imaging 'the contradictory nature of the epoch' through 'the contradiction between intention and material, author and reality'.[37] Like Brecht, Müller constructed his plays and productions on the principles of collage and stressed the nature of drama as process by fragmenting the action. But Müller developed this into 'billiard ball dramaturgy' where each scene collides with another; and while Brecht insisted on a non-linear action that proceeds by 'jumps', Müller went further: 'not that one thing is presented after another, as was still the rule for Brecht. Nowadays as many [view]points as possible must be presented simultaneously, if the spectators are to be compelled into choice.' More radically, Müller reinterpreted Brecht's rational, scientific theatre as 'a laboratory for social fantasy'.[38]

An example was his adaptation of Brecht's 'Teaching Play', *The Measures Taken*, re-titled *The Mission: Memories of Revolution*. Müller's title refers to an abortive slave uprising in Jamaica, fomented by revolutionaries from France and abandoned after Napoleon's seizure of power; and the text combines key scenes of Brecht's play with Büchner's nineteenth-century classic, *Danton's Death*, and Jean Genet's *The Blacks*, in a collage around a long stream-of-consciousness dream-monologue in which the unnamed narrator is ascending through time and space in an elevator to be tasked with an important mission by a 'boss' – 'whom I refer to in my mind as No. 1' – which is based on Müller's own personal experience. As he points out in the preface:

> An experience that became a part of this text is one of my approaches to [the East German President] Honecker in the House of the Central Committee, going up in the paternoster. [A primitive form of passenger elevator consisting of a chain of open compartments that move slowly in a loop up and down inside a building without stopping.] On every floor a soldier with a machine gun sat opposite the entrance to the paternoster. The House of the Central Committee was a high security jail for the captives of power.[39]

Müller began directing with a production of this play at the Berlin Volksbühne in 1980, remounting it in Bochum in 1982 where he first came into contact with Erich Wonder, who designed the piece and subsequently worked on the other plays Müller directed, forming an iconic and instantly recognizable visual style. Wonder had been a student of Caspar Neher, and his set synthesized barren urban and industrial streetscapes with forms and colours from such artists as Kandinsky or Rothko, creating independent phantasmagoria that (as one historian of theatre design has pointed out) 'advanced the notion that performance environments were erected not just to illustrate elements of dramatic texts, but indeed, to become texts in and of themselves'.[40]

The importance of designer/director collaboration

One of the key identifying factors in German theatre is the close collaboration between a director and a particular set-designer; begun by Brecht through his career-long association with Caspar Neher, and equally forming the style of contemporary epic directors like Roberto Ciulli, or 'postdramatic' directors such as Christoph Marthaler. It can only be equalled by those *auteur*-directors, like Robert Wilson, who are themselves also designers. Other directors may collaborate with specific playwrights or composers (like Ariane Mnouchkine with Hélène Cixous, or Peter Sellars with John Adams) defining thematic approaches. But the visual continuity provided by specific director/designer partnerships has a distinct stylistic impact.

Stating that Brecht could only be used in contemporary theatre if treated critically, in addition to *The Mission*, Müller wrote several 'counter-texts' to Brecht's plays: revising the 1934 'Teaching Play' *The Horatians and the Curiatians* as simply *The Horatians* (first produced 1973); turning Brecht's 1938 *Private Life of the Master Race* into *The Battle: Scenes from Germany* (1975).

The Battle offers a good example of Müller's revisionist epic style, which treats the theme of fascism in five short 'scenes from Germany', starting with the Night of the Long Knives in 1934 and ending with the Russians handing out bread to the defeated population of Berlin in 1945. The play's focus is the psychological effect of the mechanics of terror on the powerless, and horrors are presented with humour: as when three soldiers, starving in the snow on the Russian front, shoot and eat a comrade in a parody of the Last Supper, and then justify their cannibalism with:

> SOLDIER 1: Now his comradeship strengthens our firepower.

In sharp contrast to Brecht's play, where actions are presented factually and characters behave according to a recognizable (if indefensible) logic, the images in *The Battle* are grotesque and surreal. So in a scene where a butcher kills a downed American airman, then fearing reprisal drowns himself at the urging of his wife, who has sold the chopped up body of the pilot to her customers as pork and now holds his head under water, the mental state of the pair floods the stage in a fevered dream:

> *The inside of an animal / man. Forest of guts. Rain of blood. An over-life-size doll hangs from a parachute, clothed in the stars and stripes. Boar masks in SA uniforms shoot at the doll . . . sawdust runs out of the bullet-holes. The shots make no noise . . . when the doll is empty, it is torn down from the parachute and ripped up. Dance of the boar masks. They stamp the rags into the sawdust.*[41]

What Müller presents are subjective and seductive fantasies of fear, where Hitler's SS appear as angels of death moving with black wings to the music of Wagner; and this emphasis on psychological phantasmagoria carried over into his style of direction. Even more so than Brecht, in staging his plays Müller focused on externals, movements and blocking, rather than on actors' individual characterization. Moves tended to be slowed down, choreography exaggerated, speech chanted rather than expressing individual emotion or thought.

As a result, his staging of *Hamletmaschine* in 1979, with dream elements, slow-motion sequences and fragmented vocalization, appealed to Robert Wilson, who became Müller's partner in several productions that in turn were key in developing Wilson's directorial style. So Müller's 1979 *Gundling's Life Frederick of Prussia Lessing's Sleep Dream Scream: A Horror Story* became part of Wilson's 1984 *CIVIL warS*, and Müller's *Description of a Picture or Explosion of a Memory* became the prologue to Wilson's *Alcestis.* Conversely, Wilson directed Müller's *Quartette* and *Hamletmaschine*, and inserted *Despoiled Shore Medea Material / Landscape with Argonauts* as a prologue to his 1984 staging of Charpentier's opera *Medea*, as well as using parts of Müller's scripts in the collage of *Death Destruction & Detroit II*. It is no accident that Wilson's personal website features a photograph of him together with Müller on its homepage. And it is worth remembering that Wilson has also directed Brecht's *Flight across the Ocean* for the Berliner Ensemble in 1998, and *The Threepenny Opera* in 2007 – which indicates both the convergence of different directorial approaches and styles, and the way the definition of epic theatre has developed in the past decades.

Indeed, Müller's enigmatic, fragmentary pieces are a significant contribution to postmodern drama and post-dramatic theatre. So Müller's significance has been described as replacing the closed didactic form of the Brechtian parable with the 'open' imaginative form of 'synthetic collage', which Hans-Thies Lehman (the definer of post-dramatic theatre) sees as creating multiple meanings through 'montage dramaturgy . . . in which the reality-level of characters and events vacillates hazily between life and dream . . . outside any homogeneous notion of space and time'.[42]

Postmodern epic directing: Roberto Ciulli

Italian in background, which contributes to his wide international perspective (leading to exchange programmes with theatres in Iran, Serbia and Turkey or to his 'Silk Road' project, in which his theatre company performs and trains local actors from Iraq to China), Ciulli began his career as a contract director, working with theatres in Göttingen, Düsseldorf, Stuttgart and Munich as well as at Piscator's Freie Volksbühne in Berlin, before becoming the artistic director of theatre in the city of Cologne in 1972, where he developed his system of 'Work-In-Progress' characterized by improvisation and the free flow of exchange with actors. Like other epic directors, he began working with a particular designer, Gralf-Edzard Habben, who gives his productions extremely vivid visual imagery; and in 1980 Habben, together with Ciulli's dramaturge Helmut Schäfer, joined him in forming a new type of theatre, the Theater an der Ruhr: a limited company owned by them, contracted to perform by the local authority at Mülheim an der Ruhr. Mülheim provided them with an abandoned spa, which they rebuilt as a stage, opening with an adaptation of Wedekind's *Lulu* in 1981. (Following Brecht, epic theatre directors have increasingly seen play scripts as raw material to be used as a basis for new work: Müller operated on the principle of reworking texts, and Ciulli has taken this to its extreme.) As with its organizational structure, Theater an der Ruhr is an unconventional artistic alternative in Germany, which the *Frankfurter Allgemeine Zeitung* has called 'the most unusual non-municipal theatre in the Republic: half strolling players, half permanent independent group'.

Ciulli sees his work as evolving directly from Brecht and Müller. For him, in itself theatre is political: a space for dialogue, an instrument for changing the world. One of his most iconic productions is *The Threepenny Opera* (1987), in which Ciulli himself acted several smaller roles including a cross-dressed prostitute and a clown-like gaoler (with the red nose that is one of the recurrent costume pieces in Theater an der Ruhr productions). Indeed it also became a comment on Brecht, underscoring theatricality by setting the action in a 1920s German cabaret, instead of in early nineteenth-century England (Brecht's original action being specified as on the eve of Queen Victoria's coronation), and presenting Brecht's action as a series of variety acts: skits separated from each other by songs and clown-farce.

Various elements link Ciulli's work with Brecht's epic principles: in particular the revolt against realist presentation, or the concept of spectators as active participants intervening intellectually to imagine alternatives. However, Ciulli is explicitly following Heiner Müller, who is extensively cited in the only extensive analysis of Theater an der Ruhr, as in this passage:

> Brecht focused primarily on enlightenment in the theatre . . . Theatre today is much more about attempting to get the people involved in processes, about participating. As I described it in *The Battle*. The audience should ask themselves, how would I have acted in this situation? And they should realize that in this kind of situation, they too could have been fascists. This I find positive and useful.[43]

So, while asserting that they are following Brecht in provoking spectators' participation, Ciulli's productions build on Müller's aesthetics. His intent is to disturb the standard frames of everyday perception through a style of fantastic realism that illuminates enigmatic and cryptic levels of subjective existence that can only be expressed visually, leading to a 'theatre of images'. At the same time Ciulli's theoretical position privileges both the actor and the audience.

Play texts become raw material to be changed around and shaped according to actors' experience, which Ciulli explores and orchestrates in rehearsal, and are given their final shape by his long-time dramaturge, Helmut Schäfer. Basing his productions on an extended improvisation process, Ciulli himself performs as an actor in most of his own productions: the title figure – as an aged, melancholy and drunken clown – of *The Little Prince* (2005), or a comic white-faced mock-king, seated in a wheelbarrow, for *Trilogy of the Beautiful Holiday* (an improvisation on Goldoni, 2004). In doing so he also plays on his role as a director, bringing out the metatheatrical basis of his work. So in *Everything Goes Ever Better – Ever Better* (a compilation of scenes from Ödon von Horvath's corrosive satires on the proto-fascist Austria of the 1920s) Ciulli played a film director, examining his reels of celluloid images at a decadent café table. Or in Jean Genet's *The Screens* (2003), he guided the audience as a master of ceremonies, dressed in a white rococo costume, through the scenes that he arranged like the snaps in a photo album with 'a lightness of death and grimness of life'.[44] This stylized metatheatre was established early in Ciulli's career, with a production of Horvath's *Casimir and Caroline* in 1985, where Habben's set (in homage to Brecht) represented a complete Oktoberfest theatre, with on-stage Bänkel platform, clowns performing and wandering spectators. As with this metatheatrical continuum, the images which are the expression of Ciulli's work have a recognizable stylistic similarity. At the same time, Ciulli's productions are never thought of as completed at the premiere. During their run – and in many cases continuing through the tours and co-productions of Ciulli's 'Silk Road' project – they are in continual development, like adventure trips into possible imaginary worlds in which Ciulli's troupe of actors are co-authors.

> I promote the theory of the four authors. The first is the playwright, the second is [collectively] the director, the dramaturge and the stage-designer, and the third is the actor. I am convinced that creative activity does not end here, but it continues with the audience, whom I would call the fourth author. The audience should agree to a journey into the unknown. This journey is an obligation to constantly make decisions . . . This is the only way to recognize any change brought about in the individual by the end. Theatre reveals what is behind so-called reality, which the curtain in the theatre represents as a metaphor.
>
> Roberto Ciulli[45]

9 *Danton's Death* (*Dantons Tod*, Act I), Roberto Ciulli, Theater an der Ruhr, 2004

In deliberate contrast to the technological illusions created by modern media, the aim of Ciulli's 'theatre of images' is to bring out 'fissures' in the images on his stage, and thus in the spectator's society, suggesting a world beyond the images. As he has said, 'It makes no sense to raise the curtain on a world one already knows.'[46] Ambiguity and contradiction are Ciulli's and Habben's principles in their visual treatment of dramatic material. So in the staging of Peter Handke's *Kaspar* (1987), the actors present people as macabre puppets with straggling hair, whitened faces and cocaine-chic make-up, or as sinister bureaucrats in black suits and ties, and dark glasses, but with long Pinocchio noses and tiny clown hats attached with obvious rubber strings, or with bowler hats and black eye masks, on an almost empty stage. Or in *Danton's Death* (1986 and 2004), the actors form a chorus of circus monkeys (in full-face monkey masks and red 'majorette' uniforms). Where Brecht's borrowings from cabaret were thematic and structural, Ciulli takes his popular art from the circus, which is presented in explicit visual images, which break the frame of the play text. And one of his pieces, *Clowns in the Night* (filmed for television, 1992), focused entirely on the clown archetype, trapped behind the prison-like bars of a circus ring.

Further reading

Brecht, Bertolt. *Brecht on Theatre*, trans. and ed. John Willett, London: Eyre Methuen, 1964

Plays, Poetry, Prose, trans. John Willett, London: Methuen, 1985

Innes, Christopher. *Erwin Piscator's Political Theatre*, Cambridge University Press, 1972

Kalb, Johnathan. *The Theater of Heiner Müller*, Cambridge University Press, 1998

Piscator, Erwin. *Political Theatre*, trans. Hugh Rorisson, London: Methuen, 1980

Styan, John. *Max Reinhardt*, Cambridge University Press, 1982

Willett, John. *The Theatre of Bertolt Brecht*, London: Methuen, 1977

The Theatre of Erwin Piscator: Half a Century of Politics in the Theatre, London: Eyre Methuen, 1978

Chapter 5

Total theatre: the director as *auteur*

In the contemporary theatre there are directors who overtly strive to create 'Total Theatre'. These are, generally, also directors who create the work they stage – frequently supplanting the playwright – choreograph the movements, design the setting and plot the lighting, and sometimes perform on stage as well, qualifying them as '*auteurs*', a French term developed in New Wave film theory to describe a director who so dominates the film-making process that he or she can be seen as the 'author' because the final product is a personal expression. We have chosen to apply this term to theatre directors who, similarly, embrace the whole creative process.[1] Strikingly, many of these directors are also visual artists; their performances are primarily physical rather than text-based; and they promote a style of 'Total Theatre' that seeks not only artistic unity as in Wagner's *Gesamtkunstwerk*, but also to break through the naturalistic 'fourth wall' and unite performers and audience. In addition, where the structure is primarily pictorial rather than linear, the effect is perceptibly episodic, and the same is true of cinematic structuring. So there is a direct line running from, say, Kandinsky's 1912 play *The Yellow Sound* – where in 'Picture 3' '*Everything is motionless*' until (in a technique paralleling Craig) light brings movement[2] – to Lepage's 1999 *Damnation of Faust* with its multiple cinema frames on stage, or Robert Wilson's *Dream Play* (1998) with its cinematic blackouts or dissolves between vignettes. This episodic quality links these visual directors to the epic theatre pioneered by Brecht; and while the most conspicuous *auteurs* are from the contemporary theatre – Robert Wilson, Richard Foreman or Robert Lepage being obvious examples – the justification for this degree of directorial control has a history going back to the beginning of the twentieth century, where it was first formulated by Gordon Craig.

Gordon Craig and the Artist of the Theatre

The Artist of the Theatre, as Craig outlined the new position, in a 1905 'dialogue' between a stage-director (a usage Craig himself coined) and a playgoer, needs to have expertise in all aspects of production. Technical virtuosity is required in scene and costume construction, lighting design, acting – so that s/he can work out how each element of the performance can be harnessed to express his vision. His or hers is the controlling imagination; and it is the stage-director who also selects and structures the dramatic material. While developed quite independently of Wagner, Craig's ideal shares the qualities of Wagner's 'total theatre' artwork.

The Art of the Theatre and the stage-director

The Art of the Theatre is neither acting nor the play, it is neither scene nor dance, but it consists of all the elements of which these things are composed: action, which is the very spirit of acting; words, which are the body of the play; line and colour, which are the very heart of the scene; rhythm, which is the very essence of dance . . .

If the stage-director was to technically train himself for his task of interpreting the [plays of the] dramatist – in time, and by a gradual development he would again recover the ground lost to the theatre, and finally would restore the Art of the Theatre to its home by means of his own creative genius . . . when he will have mastered the use of actions, words, line, colour and rhythm, then he may become an artist.

Gordon Craig, 'The First Dialogue' (1905; 1911), 138, 146–8

In the designs and essays through which Craig defined his new Art of the Theatre, abstract action became its primary element, the continuity of form and movement its structural principle, spirituality and unity with nature its values. But action he defined as movement, and in his own copy of *On the Art of the Theatre*, where he declares that the theatre of the future will be created 'out of ACTION, SCENE, and VOICE', Craig noted in the margin that the word ACTION related specifically to Isadora Duncan, who embodied the new style of dancing in the early years of the twentieth century.[3] Indeed, movement is also seen as the origin of theatre, with the dancer being the prototype of the classical Greek dramatists, who 'spoke either in poetry or prose, but always in action: in poetic action, which is dance, or in prose action, which is gesture' – and returning to this ideal, Craig argued, would transform theatre into a 'self-reliant' form of expression. The result would be that instead of basing productions on written play scripts, theatre 'must in time perform pieces of its own art'.[4] And for him the key to this Art of the Theatre (the title of his most influential book) was to turn the whole stage into a living entity which he expressed through notional designs for stage productions with images of great flights of steps and shafts of light as the visual equivalents of majestic chords of music.

For an image of Gordon Craig's *Scene* (1907), see http://theredlist.fr/media/database/settings/performing-art/Theatre/1910/024_1910_theredlist.jpg.

What this meant for Craig was the fully articulated moving stage architecture imagined in his 1923 book *The Scene*, which was designed to make the whole stage area the active agent in performance. Although only realized in the shape of model stages, this 'Scene' was designed to create drama out of the play of light and shadow, giving emotional tone to continually moving geometrical shapes: the floor of the stage being divided into squares that could rise and fall as columns of varying width, matched by columns coming down from the flies. While the photographs and designs are restricted to the visual, Craig's vision always included music and vocalization. In addition, it was Craig who (as part of the symbolist movement) first fully articulated the rejection of naturalism that has fuelled so much productive innovation in twentieth-century theatre. As he argued: 'a so-called real room is what we present on stage today . . . real and yet quite dead – expressionless – unable to act . . . so, then, to create a simplified stage is the first duty of a master of the drama'.[5]

Craig notoriously called for the actor to be abolished; and the kind of scenario that Craig envisaged for this new *auteur* theatre appears to be purely abstract. One of his most striking scenarios was simply called 'Motion'.

> The Beginning . . . the Birth . . . we are in Darkness . . . all is still . . .
>
> And from this Nothing shall emerge a spirit . . . Life . . . a perfect and balancing life . . . to be called Beauty . . . the Immortal Beauty of Change Eternal.
>
> A form simple and austere ascends with prolonged patience like the awakening of thought in a dream.
>
> Something seems to unfold, something to fold. Slowly . . . fold after fold loosens itself and clasps another till that which was void has become shapely. And now from East to West, one chain of life moves like a sea before us . . .
>
> Without Architecture we should have no Divine Place in which to praise. Without Music no Divine Voice with which to praise. Without Motion no Divine Act to perform.
>
> 'Motion' (1907)[6]

Yet while it exactly describes what Craig envisaged as the kind of drama that might be realized with his 'Scene', this scenario formed the preface to a portfolio of Craig's etchings, all of which show Isadora Duncan dancing. It is a score for dance, focusing on the inner, imaginary response to movement; and almost all his designs for 'Scene' include human figures – but as archetypal shapes, not as individualized people; as just one element integrated into the whole, not as the 'stars' that characterized the theatre of his time. In fact Craig's ideal 'actors' were puppets. It is worth remembering that the titles of his highly influential theatre journals – all written, as well as edited and published, by himself, which formed the inspiration for the 'New Stagecraft' that swept

North American theatre in the 1920s – were *The Mask* and *The Marionette*. But even though directors like Robert Wilson may treat their actors literally as puppets, for Craig art carried religious connotations which were incorporated in the long tradition of puppetry. Going back to Bunraku puppets and Indonesian or Indian shadow puppets as representations of divine figures, imbued with life by the audience's imagination and beliefs, he explored the idea of spiritual essences inhabiting shaped but inanimate objects.

However, in effect Craig provides the theoretical basis for the modern director as *auteur* – the sole author of the stage work: creating the 'score' (or script), designing the lighting and motions of the physical elements of the stage, coordinating both the soundscape of the piece and the 'puppets' (or figures), and thus controlling the complete audience-response – as well as for the contemporary movement that discards written drama in favour of physical theatre. He was an influential part of the whole rejection of text that characterized the historical avant-garde, and has gained new strength in contemporary theatre. Its most famous formulation may be Antonin Artaud's rejection of words in the theatre; but as Craig had remarked a whole generation earlier, 'Words are a bad means of communicating ideas – especially transcendent ideas – ideas which fly . . . the theatre presents visions through movement which is the very symbol of life.'[7] By insisting on the superiority of physicality over language, and thus diminishing the role of the playwright, again Craig provided theoretical justification for the dominance of the *auteur*-director; and the first to qualify for this title was the German director and impresario Max Reinhardt.

Max Reinhardt: the 'Director's Book'

As we have seen (Chapter 4, pp. 116–17), Max Reinhardt's multi-theatre empire required very close management – in Berlin (Kleines Theater 1900; Neues Theater 1902: Deutsches Theater 1905; the huge 3,000-seat Grosses Schauspielhaus 1919) and across the German European diaspora, in both Budapest (1905) and Vienna (1910), together with touring companies across the continent and in England as well as across the Atlantic in New York, and a Festival Theatre in Salzburg (1920). With twenty-eight different productions, for instance, in 1928 (several of which were mounted to tour with multiple acting companies), the extended repertory theatre that Reinhardt not only produced and managed, but also directed (together with a number of dramaturges, including, as we have seen, Erwin Piscator and Brecht), could only be effectively staged through extremely detailed records of rehearsals. As John

Styan has documented, this led to the development of the *Regiebuch* (the Director's Book), which has since become a standard part of the production material.[8]

Reinhardt's Director's Book for each production gave a moment-by-moment placing of the actors, their moves, gestures, even facial expressions and tone of voice, written in the text or notated on ground-plans of the stage-setting, together with detailed notes on the lighting changes, music and sound effects, in addition to three-dimensional sketches of each scene. Prepared in the minutest detail before the actors were hired or rehearsals for a particular production began, and revised with added notes over the years a production ran, these effectively controlled not only the actors, but every element of a production. Reinhardt's 1916 *Macbeth* was marked up in black and red ink, and red, blue, green and black pencil, reflecting the changes as his vision developed, as well as the conferences with designer and stage manager, which led to further sketches and stage diagrams. Many of Reinhardt's actors also came through the School of Acting he opened on taking over the Deutsches Theater in 1905, which, in imposing a common training, gave additional control, effectively forming the ensemble style that marked Reinhardt's productions. In rehearsal actors were directed to follow each notation, although initially they might have the opportunity to improvise or suggest their own expression. At the same time, Reinhardt kept on introducing changes, cuts or additional details, even in dress rehearsals. Although Reinhardt, in a process of continual renewal and rethinking, kept on inserting and changing notes throughout a production – which could cover several years – his Director's Books also meant that a production could be restaged or brushed up by a stage-manager, while Reinhardt was engaged on a different project.

The Director's Book

Everything has been taken into consideration, from the most important feature to the least: the atmosphere of every scene, or every conversation in that scene, of every sentence in that conversation. Expression, intonation, every position of the actor, every emotion, the indication of every pause, the effect on the other actors – all these details are mapped out in clear, concise words. At the beginning of each scene, there is a minute description of all the decorations, generally accompanied by drawings, together with a sketch of the stage with full explanations; there is an accurate description of the costume for every new actor; all the crossings within a scene are not only detailed but also sketched; the lighting and all the changes in the illumination are described; there are notes on the significance, expression, length and volume of the music; notes on the different noises; and notes on the way in which the change of scene is to proceed.

Heinz Herald, 'Reinhardt at Rehearsal'[9]

Infinitely more detailed than even Stanislavsky's prompt books, Reinhardt's Director's Books served as a model for other directors. Another factor was his preference for large-scale productions: Hoffmansthal's *Everyman* spread out over the old city of Salzburg; the giant thrust stage and acoustical effect of 3,000 people in the auditorium of the Grosses Schauspielhaus drowned out ordinary speaking and demanded heroic acting; perhaps most strikingly, with over 100 performers in Volmoeller's processional religious spectacle *The Miracle* (in London staged at the Olympia Stadium, on its 400 by 250 foot floor space with over 100 foot height to the roof, all transformed into a Gothic cathedral). And like Piscator, faced with the logistics of size, Reinhardt took on military methods of control and coordination. For example, in the New York *Miracle* production, he directed by megaphone from a scaffold in the middle of the audience area, with twenty-two assistants marshalling the actors.[10]

Combining directorial methods: Norman Bel Geddes

Among those heavily influenced by both Gordon Craig (whom he invited to contribute a production for the 1933 Chicago World's Fair) and Reinhardt (whose *Miracle* production he designed for New York, recreating a medieval cathedral in the Broadway Century Theatre) was the American director and entrepreneurial designer Norman Bel Geddes. Like Craig, he planned notional productions: in particular a dramatization of Dante's *Divine Comedy*. But as well as taking up the method promoted by Craig, who relied on costume and stage designs for encapsulating his ideas, Bel Geddes also followed Reinhardt, noting each move and sound with multiple colours and elaborately detailed stage diagrams in a Director's Book. While *The Divine Comedy* was never produced, and the huge domed 'Divine Comedy' amphitheatre designed for the Chicago World's Fair never built, Bel Geddes envisaged every detail of a mammoth spectacle, with over 300 performers occupying a semi-circular stage space 165 feet deep by 135 feet wide with serried rows of steps rising from a central pit to mountainous peaks over 100 feet high.

Using Craig's methods, Bel Geddes designed fantastic costumes and masks – which, like Craig, he exhibited across Europe – and worked out every single move for all the figures on a scale model of the set, as Craig had done for his Moscow production of *Hamlet*, recording the effects with extensive photographs as well as design-sketches. Following Reinhardt's approach he created Director's Books – one for each section of the project – in which he noted the placement of each member of the choruses on every beat of the action, as well as indicating the precise positioning, gestures and postures of his protagonists, the nature and timing of special effects and lighting changes (with notes on intended emotional response), together with graph-paper sketches of all moves and choreography for the 300 performers. As in Craig's vision, too, the stage was to be an active element of the performance, with the 'peaks' being hollow and containing funnels intersected by iron bars for heavy steel balls to run down creating a specific series of sound effects – and, like Craig, while this production was never realized, Bel Geddes exhibited his *Divine Comedy* plans and sketches at exhibitions in the USA and Europe (indeed with a 1922 Amsterdam exhibit impressing Reinhardt who, as a direct result, approached Bel Geddes to design the New York edition of *The Miracle*).

In this *Divine Comedy* project, Bel Geddes also qualified as the archetypal *auteur*. He created the script. He composed his own complete score for continuous abstract music. He choreographed all the moves, and recorded everything. He designed the permanent setting as well as all visual effects and costumes. He designed – and (at least on the model stage) experimented with – the lighting. In addition, he drew up complete architectural plans, elevations and engineering blueprints for the theatre building that was to be dedicated to this production.

Indeed Bel Geddes exercised to some degree the same control in his later Broadway productions, where he acted not only as director, but as his own designer (and lighting as well as sound designer), and also producer. As a result – as intended in the *Divine Comedy* project – Bel Geddes was able to create a unified environment for the audience, most famously with his 1935 staging of *Dead End*. Here the setting was reversed so that the orchestra pit became the East River, into which boys jumped to swim, while surround-sound effects of running water and ship-traffic set spectators imaginatively in the river itself. He also continued to write his own dramatic texts, as he did with his 1934 *Iron Men*: a highly contemporary drama highlighting the workers in the skyscraper boom in New York of the time, where during the performance the cast actually erected the steel frame for two storeys of a building on the stage. And as well Bel Geddes engineered the stage machinery for his shows, as with a 1928 production of *The Patriot* – for which he invented a new system of 'flying' complete scenes into the stage area to allow seamless transitions between scenes without the use of a revolve (which would have meant significantly limiting the acting space for each scene). He even sometimes restructured the whole theatre, as he had with Reinhardt's *The Miracle* and did again to some degree for *Dead End*, and for his 1937 staging of *The Eternal Road*.

The core of Bel Geddes' directorial focus, which inspired all these groundbreaking theatrical interventions, was the integration of audiences into his productions, physically as well as imaginatively and emotionally; and this led him to apply his design and directorial approach to the wider world of society outside the confines of theatre. While continuing with his theatre work, he introduced 'streamlining' as a key architectural and industrial principle of modernism, designing new and specifically modernistic forms of cars, houses, refrigerators and stoves, all of which are standard still today, as well as introducing the classic white kitchen and designing the first motorways. Using theatre as a form of propaganda for his vision, he signally created an interactive exhibit for the 1939 New York World's Fair, where the public were invited to participate in an imaginative airplane trip (this was before commercial air flight became common) right across the American continent. On this journey, where lighting effects took the spectators from broad daylight through night and into a bright dawn on the west coast, they experienced a world of the future – constructed of extraordinarily detailed models, varying in scale according to the distance from the moving aerial seats of the spectators – spread out beneath their gaze, and all embodying Bel Geddes' modern principles.[11]

For a video of Bel Geddes' New York World's Fair exhibit, see www.youtube.com/watch?v=ei3fzdlEJcw.

This was 'Futurama' – one of the most popular exhibits in the whole 1939 World's Fair. A highly theatrical, but purely mechanical display, literally surrounding the audience who were the only actors, this shows the approach of director as *auteur* at its most extreme. At the same time, Bel Geddes' career in carrying theatrical principles into moulding society outside the theatre proper is iconic of the wider potential for theatre – and for the director, as such.

Peter Brook: collective creation versus directorial vision

Peter Brook has had a longer influence on the stage than any other later twentieth-century director. While running a variation on ensemble theatre in Paris, like Craig and Bel Geddes, Brook has sometimes created the designs for his own productions, and even though he has long-term collaborators on the production side (anticipating Katie Mitchell's 'team') Brook's is the vision that determines the productions of his companies. His career falls into two distinct halves. The first is his work in England – from the 1940s up to 1970 – moving from commercial theatre to the major subsidized companies of the RSC and the National, establishing his name largely through productions of Shakespeare; the second, his work based in Paris at his Centre International de Créations Théâtrales (CICT) – from 1971 to his farewell production of Mozart's *The Magic Flute* in 2010 – with his own permanent company (although comprising a very small group of continuing actors) drawn from across the world and representing different theatrical traditions. Towards the end of the earlier period, however, there was a distinct transition, marked by Brook's 1964 experimental 'Theatre of Cruelty' season, where he explored Artaud's concepts of physical theatre in productions of Artaud's own play *The Spurt of Blood* and Jean Genet's *The Screens*. This provoked Brook's hugely influential 1968 book *The Empty Space* – which is 'a bare stage. A man walks across this empty space whilst someone else is watching him, and this is all that is needed for an act of theatre to be engaged'[12] – and led to major political productions like Peter Weiss' *Marat/Sade* and Brook's anti-Vietnam war play, *US* (1964, 1966).

Brook's 1964 season anticipated the widespread adoption of Artaud by the American avant-garde. Artaud's rejection of naturalism and demolition of the text, his search for a return to ritual in performance, and his ideal of a direct and transformative psychological impact on the spectator through a physical assault on the senses (in Artaud's metaphor, like acupuncture through the skin, or the plague), all appealed to the counterculture rejection of established political and social hierarchies by American directors such as Charles Marowitz (with whom Brook collaborated), Julian Beck, Judith Malina or Joseph Chaikin in the late 1960s and 1970s. And like Brook – following Artaud who had declared 'our present social state is iniquitous and should be destroyed' – all identified conventional or naturalistic performance as (in Brook's term) 'deadly theatre': the conformist expression of a commercialized bourgeois society they rejected (Brook referred to the status quo as 'rotten') and sought to change by creating radically new principles of performance.[13]

'Theatre of Cruelty'

I say that the stage is a concrete physical place which asks to be filled, and to be given its own concrete language to speak.

I say that this concrete language, intended for the senses and independent of speech, has first to satisfy the senses, that there is a poetry of the senses as there is a poetry of language, and that this concrete physical language to which I refer is truly theatrical only to the degree that the thoughts it expresses are beyond the reach of the spoken language.

. . .

After sound and light there is action, and the dynamism of action: here the theatre, far from copying life, puts itself whenever possible in communication with pure forces. And whether you accept them or deny them, there is nevertheless a way of speaking which gives the names of 'forces' to whatever brings to birth images of energy in the unconscious and gratuitous crime on the surface.

Antonin Artaud, *The Theatre and Its Double*[14]

Even more so than Gordon Craig, Artaud's reputation came solely through his writings – and primarily through a single slim volume of essays, collected under the title of *The Theatre and Its Double*, published in 1938 and translated into English in 1958 – his work as a director being limited to just three productions at the short-lived, symbolist Théâtre Alfred Jarry in 1926–27. And Brook's translation of Artaud's principles into practical stage terms offers a representative example of the style of directing derived from his theories.

Brook's Theatre of Cruelty season was a training exercise for RSC actors designed to demolish 'the Stanislavsky ethic' through exploring the roots of physical expression. The aim was to create 'a transcendent experience of life' through cries, incantations, masks, shock effects and simultaneous actions 'all flooding one's consciousness simultaneously' in discontinuous rhythms 'whose crescendo will accord exactly with the pulsation of movements familiar to everyone', corresponding with 'the broken and fragmentary way in which most people experience contemporary reality'.[15] The starting point was for each actor to attempt mentally projecting an emotional state, then adding vocal sound or movement, 'to discover what was *the very least* he needed before understanding could be reached'.[16] This was followed by physical improvisations to express emotion: women lashing men with their hair (repeated in a playlet scripted by Brook, *The Public Bath*, where a symbolic scapegoat figure whips a judge as he condemns her, and in his staging of the *Marat/Sade* where Charlotte Corday whips Sade), or Rorschach-like abstract action-paintings (part of *The Spurt of Blood* performance, and reaching full expression in *The Screens*).

Dramatic material was presented as work in progress, rather than a finished product – with texts being brief one-act scripts, or short abstract word-collages by Paul Abelman, Artaud's script for *The Spurt of Blood* being reduced to screams, and only the first twelve scenes of *The Screens* being staged. The emphasis was on collective creation, with short pieces being improvised, and Brook writing down the speeches evolved by the cast, while the authorship of *US* was specifically listed as 'The Collective' in the published text. At the same time, actors were de-individualized, and their personal expression limited: as in *The Spurt of Blood*, where all the performers wore square full-face blank masks with simple holes for eyes, or in *US*, where actors representing the maimed victims of battle wore paper bags over their heads. The stage was bare – even in the *Marat/Sade*, set in the asylum of Charenton – and where there was any form of construct (as in *The Spurt of Blood*, where the acting area was formed out of huge steps and ramps) this was designed to emphasize physical movement. Apart from *Marat/Sade* (where the costuming was clearly nineteenth century, but in general very basic), the actors all wore simple modern clothing. The notional barrier between stage and audience was broken: in *US* the injured soldiers, blinded by the paper bags, stumbled out among the spectators forcing assistance from them – while at the end of *Marat/Sade* a line of capering and chanting inmates surge threateningly down the stage towards the audience, acting out the Marxist image of revolution in one step back, two steps forward.

In Artaud's and Brook's model of 'Total Theatre' – more radically than Bel Geddes – all barriers and separation of functions are broken down. The traditional primacy of text, and verbal language, gives way to physical expression. The focus is on the actors, and on direct involvement of the spectators. In terms of production, less is more – so that while the emotive effect of lighting is (as in Gordon Craig's conception) exploited, there is little in the way of spectacle, scenery or costuming. In addition to uniting all modes of art (the Wagnerian *Gesamtkunstwerk*), a performance unites actors and spectators, stage and society in a transcendental whole. Yet the removal of the author and the privileging of the performer in fact leads to greater directorial control; and Brook's productions all have a completely unique and highly recognizable style. As he has commented: 'By his choice of exercises, even by the way he encourages an actor to find his own freedom, a director cannot help projecting his own state of mind on to the stage.'[17]

Perhaps the best illustration of this – and of Brook's concept of 'the empty space' – is his 1970 production of *A Midsummer Night's Dream*.

For a video selection of Brook's *Midsummer Night's Dream* staging, see
www.youtube.com/watch?v=KYMlylIPkXo (4.40–6.09 minutes).

The stage became a stark white box, highlighting the actors' moves, which being based on circus acrobatics were highly physical. There was no change of scene; omnipresent fairies brought in props or shaped themselves into trees and plants. In poetic passages, Shakespeare's verse was reduced to patterns of sound. The opposing worlds of Athens and the magic woods were united through Theseus doubling as Oberon and Hippolyta as Titania, while Puck literally 'girdled' the auditorium, physically enacting his flight around the world and so bringing the audience physically into 'the magic circle of the play' in which 'the wood and its inhabitants pour forth a primitive wildness which infected all who come into contact with it'.[18]

The same primitivism had been evident in Brook's 1968 staging of Seneca's *Oedipus* (in a modernized version by Ted Hughes) where extreme violence and sexual anarchy were presented ritualistically, with the speeches patterned on

Maori chants and delivered in a depersonalized monotone, together with minimal and formalized movements – as with the blinding of Oedipus, retold by a slave, while Oedipus (John Gielgud) sits completely motionless on the stage.

Ted Hughes, *Seneca's Oedipus*: National Theatre, March 1968 – Director's Book

Suddenly he began to weep everything that had been torment suddenly it was sobbing it shook his	The Slave Narrator
whole body and he shouted is weeping all I can give can't my eyes give any more let them go with their tears let them go eyeballs too everything out is this enough for you you frozen gods of marriage is it sufficient are my eyes enough he was raging as he spoke his face throbbed dark red his eyeballs seemed to be jumping in their sockets forced from the skull his face was no longer the face of Oedipus contorted like	1. Slowly lifts arms
a rabid dog he had begun to scream a bellowing animal anger agony tearing at his throat his fingers had stabbed deep into his eyesockets he hooked them gripping the eyeballs and he tugged twisting and dragging with all his strength till they gave way and he flung them from him his fingers dug back into his sockets he could not stop he was gibbering and moaning insane with his fury against himself gouging scrabbling with his nails in those huge holes in his face the terrors of light are finished for	2. Hooks fingers in front of eyes
Oedipus he lifted his face with its horrible raw gaps he tested the darkness there were rags of flesh strings and nerve ends still trailing over his cheeks	3. Raises arms
he fumbled for them snapping them off every last shred then he let out a roar half screamed you gods	4. Drops arms, X over Box to U/R – stands.
now will you stop torturing my country I've found the murderer and look I've punished him . . .	TIRESIAS rises, X to OEDIPUS. 5. Slave sits as TIRESIAS puts hands on OEDIPUS's eyes.[19]

In *The Empty Space*, Brook rejects the practice of coming to rehearsals with a Director's Book in which all the moves and stage business are already worked out, instead defining a working method where the staging is arrived at during the rehearsal through improvisation with the actors. Yet, as the example from *Oedipus* shows, by the time of the performance every gesture has been noted down – defining the concept expressed by the production. To achieve this minimalist effect, in rehearsals Brook developed exercises from t'ai chi, using gravity as the only source of energy to achieve economy of movement, and led sessions where actors learned to express extreme personal experiences through sounds alone, or through irregular rhythms of breathing based on a recording of a witchdoctor in trance. This drive for ritualistic theatre reached its peak with Brook's production at the 1971 Theatre Festival in the ancient city of Persepolis. A direct rendition of basic myths like the gift of fire, a god eating his children and the Promethean search for liberation through knowledge, the script for *Orghast* was a vocal experiment by Ted Hughes in constructing a universal and organic language out of blocks of sound, where the expressive qualities of tone and rhythm could communicate without the interference of verbal meaning.

> Our work is based on the fact that some of the deepest aspects of human experience can reveal themselves through the sounds and movements of the human body in a way that strikes an identical chord in any observer, whatever his cultural and racial conditioning. And therefore one can work without roots, because the body, as such, becomes the working source.
>
> Peter Brook, Interview, 1973[20]

This search for universal communication, together with the most minimal basis for performance, led to Brook's 1972 theatrical tour through Africa. The ideal of performing on a rug, laid on sand, to an audience who neither spoke the same language nor shared any common theatre traditions, informed this experiment; and from it came the kind of physical theatre embodied in *The Ik* (1975) or *The Conference of the Birds* (1979). At the beginning of *The Ik*, the cast scatter soil over a bare stage, then carefully place stones around, and the performance – based on an anthropological study of the displaced and starving mountain people of Uganda – presents the lives of a tribe at the extreme edge of human existence through the barest of gestures and non-verbal language. To match the extremity of the figures they represented, Brook explored the potential of 'being' instead of 'acting,' by having the actors build and live in an Ik stockade, playing out episodes, many of which never appeared in the script. In the performance there was no attempt to look like the African tribespeople – the actors wore rehearsal clothes without make-up. The focus was on living their behaviour.

The *Birds* illustrates other elements of Brook's directing process. Based on an epic Sufi religious poem from Persia, it was developed over a seven-year exploration, being presented in various improvised forms from 1972 in Africa to 1979, when Brook asked a long-time collaborator, the screen writer Jean-Claude Carrière, to provide a script. So in the first New York production at the Brooklyn Academy of Music in 1973 on a single night there were three completely different retellings of the story – at 8 p.m. an energetic dancing and musical mime; at midnight a ceremonial minimalist and low-key evocation of its religious significance; and at dawn (with Brook himself leading the actors) free-form solo dances, songs and a love story, with the birds only represented by eleven wooden bird-statues, hidden beneath an altar and only revealed at the end. In rehearsal the group focused on improvisations of the many different stories in the poem, and in turning sounds into bird song – with the American composer Elizabeth Swados composing songs for the actors, based on bird calls – or discovering how to move like birds flying. When the scripted *Birds* reappeared at La Mama in 1980 the actors wore ancient and archetypal Chinese masks, or (for the thieves and charlatans) modern grotesque Balinese masks to represent primal forces, together with hand puppets as externalizations of themselves or figures from a different level of reality. (For instance, the birds circle a small Balinese puppet, who, as they land, is replaced by an actor in the Hermit mask). Used to embody character types (Beautiful Princess; Slave; Warrior King) or changes in a character's condition (the Slave's night of love with the Princess, versus his ordinary status), the masks were stripped off when the birds had crossed the desert and arrive in the seven valleys of the spirit, and the Valley of Death was presented through shadow-play projection of three butterflies circling round the light of knowledge, with one consumed by the candle flame as it reaches understanding. The performance was intensely physical, privileging the visual (as with Gordon Craig or Robert Wilson), corresponding to Brook's principle that 'The exchange of impressions through images is our basic language.'[21]

Masks, puppets and shadow-play, together with the symbolic representation of non-human beings, require an abstracted and ritualistic mode of acting, which Brook's troupe had been exercised in over the whole decade. And in the same way, it was largely the long-term unified nature of Brook's acting group that enabled his experimental theatre, where every production was an attempt to change the nature of performance.

Characteristically one of his most recent pieces for CICT was a discussion of the different movements to reform theatre through the twentieth century, as well as bringing in the Japanese tradition that has been so productive for Brook himself. *Why Why* is a monologue that questions texts quoted from Artaud, Craig, Meyerhold and the medieval Noh Theatre philosopher, Zeami Motokiyo. A generic (and unnamed) actress – in fact one of Brook's troupe in the mid 1970s, who had returned for this production – finds herself on the empty stage he has continually called for, and unable to discover a reason for being there, starts to philosophize about the purpose of theatre. The title of the piece echoes Brook's comment that 'the work of a director can be summed up in two very simple words: why and how', while the one-woman monologue highlights his principles and their pedigree, as with a story about Gordon Craig, standing in the wings of a theatre in Germany, noticing a sign declaring 'Sprechen Verboten' (talking is forbidden) and remarking: 'How clever of them to have discovered the true meaning of theatre.'[22]

Robert Wilson: the 'Visual Book'

Where Gordon Craig employed a visual basis for his vision of theatre – as to some degree did Bel Geddes, who began his career as a designer – the contemporary equivalent is Robert Wilson, who creates 'storyboards' (on the line of film-production practice) to define each significant moment of a production before rehearsals begin. As with Craig, too, Wilson's stagings are highly stylized; and where Craig had collaborated with a leading poet of symbolism, W. B. Yeats, Wilson has focused on the linguistic experiments of Gertrude Stein. So, while the way Wilson has extended the notions of interior time and subjective vision that were developed by Maeterlinck or Claudel has been remarked upon by several commentators, linking this to the slowness of movement in his stagings, Wilson's statements about time echo the symbolists: 'Time in the theatre is special . . . We can stretch it out until it becomes the time of the mind, the time of a pine tree moving gently, or a cloud floating across the sky and slowly becoming a camel, then a bird . . . The time of my theatre is the time of interior reflection.'[23]

Wilson began his storyboard method with *Einstein on the Beach*, premiered in 1976. He quickly turned this notation of visual images in sequence into a method by which his sketches, or 'visual books', as he called them, allowed him to perceive the production he would be working on as a coherent whole. To his mind, these 'visual books' in their pictorial form were analogous with the written texts – the dramatic literature – of the Western tradition;[24] and they served him both as a mnemonic and a compass, facilitating as well, as do prompt books, the reconstruction of productions over long periods of time. To this day, whatever the project, whether it is a stage production, an installation, a video portrait, a landscaped garden or any other activity generated by his versatile talent, Wilson is at once its medium, mediator and arbiter. The very fact that Wilson's capabilities are multiple, making him as much a designer and a painter as a director and a performer, and equally adept in the fine arts and the arts of performance, dance and opera included, goes a long way to explaining his ability to take charge of, and channel, the different creative output of his collaborators.

Wilson's way of working is based on the paradox of control and freedom: he is in charge but his composer, costume designer and other collaborators are expected to exercise freely their initiative and individuality in their field of expertise. His assistant director Ann-Christin Rommen is the only permanent member of his various teams. Otherwise, he draws from a pool of collaborators established over the years, selecting them according to each project so as to achieve what could be described as a fruitful balance of creativities rather than their fusion. In this synchronic approach quite different from synthesis, Wilson was inspired by choreographer Merce Cunningham, whose co-creators, notably composer John Cage and painters Jasper Johns and Robert Rauschenberg, developed their material independently. This ensured that they maintained their unique 'voice' in respect of Cunningham's choreography, which, too, took its independent course. Meanwhile, Cunningham crafted movement on his dancers in such a way as to have them follow individual steps and patterns without letting them merge towards a unified, central line of perception. Cunningham's multiple perspectives operating simultaneously in the dance, which destroyed the idea of fixed points in space, were a transposition, in stylistic terms, of the practice of working autonomously, each from his individual perspective, of his colleagues.

Cunningham, having famously initiated these principles together with these same artists at Black Mountain College during the 1950s, consolidated them in the 1960s, the formative decade of Wilson's ideas about how art, and especially theatre, could be constructed. Wilson had a deep affinity with dance, not only Cunningham serving him as an example, but also George Balanchine whose pure lines and non-narrative structures – dance for the sake of dancing, as Balanchine proudly proclaimed – was Wilson's 'legitimation' of his own rejection of narrative and interpretative character-based theatre.[25] Dance, then, whether virtuosic or only implied in the quality of movement, even through the simplest of movements such as walking, was to remain fundamental to Wilson's theatre. This was possible after he had fully asserted its importance in *Einstein on the Beach*, where first Andy de Groat and then minimalist choreographer Lucinda Childs created two twenty-minute dance sequences. These sequences, regardless of their connection to the production's concern with space and time – the velocity of one of them was meant to be associated with a spaceship in flight – held their own as *dance*.

Here, as in the opening scenes, where Childs dances in her idiosyncratic bounce-step manner, the movement component so strongly evident in the production is not subordinated to thematic or design demands. In other words, dance falls in line with Wilson's system of composition by 'separate tracks', as he was to put it several years later, in which – in a clear echo of Craig – the architectural, visual, musical, dance/movement and other streams of the work are believed to be equal, and do not interpret, illustrate or in any way repeat each other but run in parallel. Wilson's directorial task is to arrange the 'tracks', which, as is clear even from his earliest pieces such as *The King of Spain* or *The Life and Times of Sigmund Freud*, both performed in 1969, accentuates the *juxtaposition* of distinctive elements – a *surprising* juxtaposition of surprising elements characteristic of surrealism, to which Wilson's lifelong work can be related.

Where *Einstein on the Beach* was concerned, this system, although it encouraged flexibility, nevertheless required defining the work's basic structural features. Thus Wilson and Philip Glass, whom Wilson had approached to write an opera 'about' Einstein, agreed on several points before they went on to develop their respective parts. The opera would not tell a story about a man who, Wilson thought, was a household name and a myth of the twentieth century, but would deal with the subject nominally and by allusion. The production would be four hours long and in four acts connected by five interludes that Wilson calls 'Knee Plays'. Three visual themes would break up the action – a train, a trial and a field with a spaceship, the latter conveyed figuratively rather than literally through the group dance sequence referred to above. These themes were to combine and permutate differently in visual terms in each act, in tandem with – or in parallel with – the sonic combinations and permutations of Glass' 'additive process and cyclic structure', as Glass describes his musical composition.[26]

For a video showing segments of *Einstein on the Beach*, see www.youtube.com/watch?v=b26E0D2pm1c.

Apart from Wilson, Glass and Childs were the principal drivers of the separate-track process that had evolved with *Einstein on the Beach*, for, unlike Cunningham, Wilson had little need of painters and designers, having formally honed his skills in these areas at the Pratt Institute in Brooklyn. Indeed, so pronounced was the visual quality of this and previous productions that had secured his reputation, *Deafman Glance* (1971) and *A Letter to Queen Victoria* (1973) among them, that his theatre was almost immediately defined as a 'theatre of images' (although his is as much a theatre of sound, as has been finally understood in the twenty-first century).[27] Its visual potency has continued unabated to this day, calling up, en route, such critical remarks as that of the stalwart German actress Marianna Hoppe, who claimed that Wilson was not a director but a lighting designer.[28] At the time, Wilson was directing the octogenarian Hoppe in the title role of *King Lear* (1991), which in his version was virtually a monologue. This was a precedent for Wilson's full-blown monologue *Hamlet* (1995) in which he (like Lepage, also 1995) now played all the roles himself, demonstrating by this, too, how he was more than capable of commanding control not only as a coordinator of others, but as a director-performer operating as a star.

By the time of *King Lear*, Wilson had acquired exceptional lighting skills, both in technical terms, learning from the lighting designers and technicians as he went along, and in terms of the artistic effects to be had from light, Strehler being his admired reference. Typically, Wilson used light as sheets of colour, first for visual splendour in such productions as *the CIVIL WarS* in the 1980s, then subsequently as a tool for articulating emotion by displacing emotion. In other words, light was to place emotion outside what would be a character in psychological theatre, 'embodying' emotion and 'speaking', one might also say, for the 'character' who, in Wilson's productions, is an abstracted figure rather than a lifelike person. *Woyzeck* (2000) provides a fine example of how Wilson uses light not only to convey emotional shifts, but also to evoke emotional responses subliminally in spectators.[29] In his method of abstracting from what is recognizably human rather than rendering this 'human' expressively, Wilson joins forces with Craig, who had rejected the histrionics of actors as a legitimate means for the making of theatre. It may be argued that, like Craig, Wilson asserts his directorial control by effacing the psychological actor, and, indeed, all ostentatious actors who, in their histrionic capacity, dominate the stage.

More connects Wilson to Craig: Wilson, like Craig, explores space and spatial perspectives, and while this involves attention to shape and light, it strongly concerns the architectural dimensions of productions in space, as well as the actual architecture of the places in which the productions are constructed. In addition, Wilson can be compared to Tadeusz Kantor, his senior by twenty-six years, who also deployed his visual-art beginnings in the services of the theatre. Like Kantor, although without Kantor's love of expressionism, Wilson organizes the movements of performers in space down to their smallest gestures and least visible spatial relation to each other so as to make such fine details integral to each 'picture' or frame. These frames build up the work as a whole not so much in cumulative sequences as in the layering and overlap typical of montage.

Also, like Kantor, Wilson places himself as a performer in his arrangement of performance elements not solely for the 'look' of a production, but to highlight a particular component – dance, for instance, in the case of *Einstein on the Beach*, where Wilson's dance solo is prominent. Moreover, the way Kantor and Wilson insert their role of 'performer' in their compositions also shows them asserting their control over the work. Kantor does so frequently with a distancing satirical or reflexive edge, taking in *The Dead Class*

(1975), for instance, the role of observant conductor of events on the sidelines. Wilson performs, for the most part, as a dancer or actor who sees himself as being embedded in the work.

The second of these attitudes belongs to the Cunningham model since Cunningham consistently danced in his own choreographies, integrated in them. Yet, despite the attraction of the Cunningham model, Wilson increasingly set limits on the principle of freedom inherent in it, including the chance element of musical composition to which Cage was devoted and which the independently prepared contributions of Johns and Rauschenberg (as of others who succeeded them) greatly encouraged. Wilson's works of the last decade of the twentieth century and of the opening of the twenty-first – *Woyzeck* (2000), *I La Galigo* (2004), *Shakespeare's Sonnets* (2009) to name but three major productions – avoid anything haphazard, random or purely wilful that might jeopardize the aesthetic equilibrium, from his point of view, of the theatre piece in question. And the exquisite elegance of such pieces links them to the work of the younger Romeo Castellucci (born 1960), another director-designer who, unlike Wilson, seeks the sublime in a spiritual dimension and who, also in this, has deeply marked the twenty-first century.

Increasingly, too, Wilson drew on existing plays rather than on texts devised for the occasion, as was the case for *Einstein*. He used fragments of various plays by Heiner Müller in *the CIVIL WarS* and then staged Müller's *Hamletmaschine* in 1986, subsequently establishing a whole repertoire of productions based in some way on classical texts which he cut, condensed and reshuffled as he thought necessary. His selection includes Shakespeare, as already noted, Büchner (*Woyzeck*, preceded by *Danton's Death* in 1992), Ibsen (*When We Dead Awaken*, 1991, *The Lady from the Sea*, 1998, and *Peer Gynt*, 2005), Strindberg (*A Dream Play*, 1998) and Brecht (the radio play *Ocean Flight*, 1998, and *The Threepenny Opera*, 2007).

His contact with the European dramatic and lyrical canon put Wilson in close touch with dramaturges, whom he incorporated into his successive teams, while maintaining his position as head. A telling example is that of Monica Ohlsson, his dramaturge for *The Three Sisters* (2001) by Chekhov and *Dream Play* as well as *Peer Gynt*. Ohlsson worked together with Rommen on *Peer Gynt*, side by side with Wilson. The two summarized the narrative content of each scene as he asked questions of a factual rather than textually interpretative nature (like 'What time of day was it'?) and visualized his thoughts in drawings. Dialogue was shortened or excised completely as they went. Further textual adjustments and readjustments took place later, according to how Wilson nuanced the performers' movements, gestures and intonations. Meanwhile, Wilson's visual books contained indications about spatial organization: where a painted drop might fall, or a blown-up photograph or a scrim

10 *Peer Gynt*, Robert Wilson, Det Norske Teatret, Oslo, 2005

appear. Details such as the mountainous landscape evoked in *Peer Gynt* were suggested in his visual books by thick jagged lines or geometrical patterns (see figure 10). Figures were occasionally drawn in to show the spatial relations between scenography and performers. Often lines of text would be beneath a drawing, like a legend, or beside it.

All this provided clear-cut frames in which the performers would perform. What the performers would actually do might be hinted at, but was worked out with them in the flesh. What they did was duly noted down by Rommen, who, when required, would replace Wilson in rehearsals, sometimes months after the performers' initial memorization of their moves. Learning the text came last. However, since Wilson's is a non-naturalistic and non-realistic approach, his directorial guidance was and is essentially a matter of instructions as to how to move, or 'place' a gesture, or speed up a voice. These are practical directions that give performers a shape without telling them how to feel it. What Wilson does not control is how they fill it with their presence, that is, how they sense and imagine within themselves the actions that they do. It is this that gives their actions their particular quality and precludes them from becoming mere executants of Wilson's will.

So it is that Isabelle Huppert in the French version of *Orlando* (1993) gave quite a different quality and tone of performance from her predecessor Jutte Lampe in German (1989) or Susse Wold in Danish (1993) and Miranda Richardson in English (1996). The grid or 'mechanical' structure, as she put it, was very much the same in all cases but she 'took possession' of it, while taking her freedom within it.

> Taking your freedom takes time. [Wilson is] the one, nevertheless, who gave me the possibility of taking my freedom when I did. He didn't tell me to take it. But he made it possible for me to do so . . . [B]ecause he put up barriers and constraints, which means that you find your freedom inside them. Obviously, I would have felt much less free without all these constraints. I would have felt lost. Being free does not mean being lost . . . Yes working with Wilson has a quality of its own because he is completely there, and I am completely there. Often, when one works with great directors, the work of the director comes first to the detriment of the person involved. I don't mean the character. I mean the person . . . What I find absolutely extraordinary is that I'm in a production of Bob Wilson where I am totally and completely myself.
>
> Isabelle Huppert[30]

Robert Lepage: cinematic self-directing

Among contemporary directors, Lepage is perhaps the most obvious theatrical *auteur*: a director who writes his own scripts, in which he then performs, having also designed the sets, plotted the lighting and arranged the music or the film clips accompanying the action, extending Robert Wilson's practices, and giving a new meaning to Gordon Craig's 'Artist of the Theatre'. Ranging from highly personal one-man 'chamber pieces' to mammoth, multi-lingual, epic productions, lasting up to nine hours of performance time, his work is highly unconventional stylistically, integrating film with stage action, sometimes combined with puppets or robots, and varying between the two extremes of theatrical presentation: from a bare stage, comparable with Brook's 'Empty Space', to a completely mechanized performance area. Alongside Lepage's standard theatre pieces, there is a mass-market popular line, from designing and producing Peter Gabriel musical performances, to Las Vegas spectacles, and with Cirque du Soleil on a piece like *Totem* (2011 – an exploration of creation-myth through purely physical performance, mirroring and extending the circus concept of Brook's classic 1970 *Midsummer Night's Dream*).

Like Brook, Lepage's aim is to evolve a radically non-traditional form of theatre, and he explicitly based the choreographed mime in *Geometry of Miracles* (1998) on dance-movements created by Gurdjieff, whom Brook acknowledged as his spiritual guru. The connections with Wilson are even closer; and it is striking that both presented solo performances of *Hamlet* in the same year (1995). Like Wilson, much of Lepage's work is self-referential. On another level, Wilson's theatre was hailed by the surviving Surrealists as fulfilling their ideals, while Lepage specifically claims to be the heir of surrealism – particularly of Jean Cocteau, whom he personates in one of his early pieces: *Needles and Opium* (1991).

Lepage's trademark is the use of highly contemporary, cutting-edge technology in his performances. Seeing himself as one of the media generation living in a postmodern age of rootless movement, his characteristic works display a radically non-linear structure. Reflecting these elements, the action of his pieces is aligned with cinematic principles to capture a contemporary mindset. One defining quality of contemporary life is its rapidity: the sheer pace of cultural and scientific change, transcontinental travel and instantaneous communication; and high-speed movement is one of Lepage's central images. For Lepage, movement is both action and metaphor: the geography is psychological, and each journey through space is also simultaneously a move through time, and always a voyage into the depths of the self.

Throughout his career, Lepage has been consciously attempting to reshape the whole theatrical experience. Since today's society has a film education, Lepage insists theatre must 'use the capacity of an audience to read things in fast-forward, jump cuts . . . People have a new language, and it's not all linear.'[31] And on the surface his work presents an audio-visual collage of apparently disconnected images, which deconstructs conventional representations of reality.

A great deal of Lepage's work is inter-textual, in particular the personal, solo-performer works, like *The Andersen Project*, which follows exactly the structure of *Needles and Opium*. Both pieces present artistic figures from the past through an overlapping story of a semi-autobiographical figure in the present (in this case a young author is from Quebec, and has been commissioned by the Opera Garnier to adapt one of Hans Christian Anderson's fairytales into a musical for children). And characteristically, this performance integrates live and filmed performance, the on-stage actor interacting with figures on film, or with film backgrounds into which he steps. In this Lepage is the inheritor of Erwin Piscator's experiments with film and stage; and Lepage also echoes Piscator in his extensive use of stage machinery (aligning with the name of his theatre group, Ex Machina).

From *Polygraph*, one of his earliest works where the stage is conceived as a lie-detector, Lepage has been interested in the interface between machine and mind, technology and thought. As Lepage described it in the programme to *Elsinore*: 'the technology . . . enabled me to "X-Ray" certain passages of *Hamlet*, and while the action apparently only takes place in the protagonist's head, it

11 *Elsineur/Elsinore*, Robert Lepage, Ex Machina, La Caserne, Quebec 1996

occasionally has the look of an electro-encephalogram'. Here the stage is turned into a total machine. In the centre of the acting area stands a circular frame with a square central opening. This revolves horizontally like a great wheel or vertically as a spinning coin – presenting Gertrude's bed when flat, a window or door when upright, a web in which all the characters are caught, with a throne suspended in its centre for Lepage as Claudius, or with white lace stretched across it, through which Lepage puts his arms and head to appear as Ophelia. This revolving central screen is flanked by two others, which can fill the whole stage area, or move into different configurations. Film can be projected onto all three, with which Lepage interacts, as in one sequence where Hamlet is flanked by images of running men echoing Eadweard Muybridge's early motion-capture photography, while two videocam front and back images are simultaneously projected on the side screens, underlining Hamlet's self-consciousness as well as his awareness of being overlooked (see figure 11). There is even a miniature videocam on his sword-point in the duel scene, reflected in a mirror (so that it appears two people are fighting). Indeed, the piece Lepage produced to close the millennium in 1999/2000, *Zulu Time*, is a deconstruction of the high-tech world it showcases.

Performed at Expocité – a vast empty barn, filled with multi-level catwalks and complex machinery – *Zulu Time* featured mechanical robots (with lights in their claws, used to illuminate the performers); and the actors move, in a frenetic, sometimes upside-down dance, on parallel catwalks that rise and descend through a high cage of scaffolding like elevators or moving escalators, to present vignettes of human beings whose actions are channelled and synchronized by their mechanized context. The result of this dehumanization intensifies a yearning for emotional connection that global travel denies. Anonymous sexual encounters are encapsulated in a hotel-room scene where a lonely traveller resorts to pornographic dreams, embodied by a female contortionist whom his lips can never reach in the alienating freeze frames of strobe lighting. Or by flying itself – as individuals launching themselves into the air, with a freedom that the airlines only parody – which here is presented by actors suspended on cords: literally puppets, in an ironic symbol of freedom.

Indeed much of Lepage's work can be seen as a direct interrogation of technology and its impact on contemporary society, with the audio-visual collage of apparently disconnected images in his performance pieces effectively deconstructing conventional representations of reality.

Lepage's progress has been an ongoing search for the kinds of meaning that will both reflect and express contemporary consciousness. And a central aspect of this is the deliberately unfixed quality of his work: performance as process. Only two of his texts have been published; and each theatre piece exists in a state of constant evolution and re-evaluation. *The Dragons' Trilogy* expanded from a ninety-minute performance in 1985, to a three-hour version in 1986, ending up as a six-hour piece in 1987, then reverting to a two-hour touring version (performed everywhere from Bergen to Berkeley and Dublin to Tokyo) between 2000 and 2005, and with a variation, *The Blue Dragon*, mounted in 2008 and restaged in 2010. There are three complete and different scripts for *Needles and Opium*. The seven-hour (but still incomplete) *Seven Streams of the River Ota* is explicitly labelled 'a work in progress' (even though published). And it is this quite deliberate and conscious choice – emphasizing transience and change – that perhaps more than anything else marks Lepage's work. At the same time, his challenging of genres is encapsulated in the transformation of *The Blue Dragon* (set in Shanghai and following the after-story of a character from *The Dragons' Trilogy*) into a manga comic book.

Lepage's directorial approach is complicated by the emphasis on technology, and indeed – with the exception of long-time collaborator actor-dramaturges – the ongoing members of Ex Machina are not actors, but mechanics and carpenters, technicians and administrators: the core production people who make Lepage's working method possible. In contrast to Ariane Mnouchkine, whose long rehearsal periods (sometimes lasting up to three years before the opening of a new show) are her method of training actors, or Brook, whose performances for his Theatre Research Centre may take years to develop (and may be revived again and again in the repertoire) but are rehearsed individually, Lepage prefers to work on up to fifteen different projects simultaneously, developing sequences of actions, interfaces between film and acting, physical images, even storylines. These elements may then become prototypes for other productions; and while many of these projects never reach public performance, working on contrasting material is intended as a learning process for the actors, whose main quality has to be adaptability.

Being conceived, even more than by Brook, as works-in-progress Lepage values and practices what he refers to as creative chaos in rehearsal; and unlike Wilson, who comes to rehearsals with the visual structure of the staging all preset, Lepage has no 'Director's Book' of any kind. In fact there is seldom even a script to work from; and even the mechanical aspect of the setting, so prominent in many of his productions, evolves during the rehearsal process. While for him the major element in a production is the 'picture' (in terms of images constructed with actors, objects and scenic/filmic/mechanized effects) because that is what spectators take away as memories and apply to their own lives, these visual/physical moments emerge from improvisation. In rehearsal, he has sessions with his actors that explore objects, developing (always new) ways in which these might be presented, and how they might become an essential part of an action, and sessions that improvise dialogue, developing not only words and verbal meanings but also tone and expression for different contexts. These are conducted independently, with the expectation that eventually interconnections will emerge. Then, in a process of reduction, it is decided either that the image is more powerful, and the words are cut, or that the image is redundant because in that context words convey the meaning more intensely. While Lepage relies on the input of his actors through the process of trial-and-error that he embarks on, it is always his personal meaning that is the deciding factor in what is kept or rejected. He always has something quite explicit to say, and selects from the actors what improvisations best approximate to his concept.[32] At the same time, because they have been responsible for developing the images and speeches through improvisation, Lepage's actors have the impression that they have a personal stake in the end result.

The basic principle of Lepage's directing comes from his early training with the French director Alain Knapp, a Brechtian disciple who started his career as an assistant for Benno Bessons' 1962 production of *St Joan of the Stockyards*, and made his reputation with *The Exception and the Rule* (1963), *The Respectable Wedding* (1964), *Guns of Mother Carrara* (1964) and *The Life of*

Galileo (1966). While Lepage sometimes refers to his work as corresponding with Brecht's *Verfremdungseffekt* and while his actors – particularly himself in solo performances – tend to be presented as performers, following the epic theatre principle of distancing from the characters they represent, the example Knapp provided was the central significance of the director as the creative artist on any production.

Lepage on Alain Knapp's technique as a director

You write as you perform and you direct as you perform – it was about improvising not just the words, but improvising the *mise en scène*; and that meant having a very strong directorial vocabulary.

Directors/Directing, 126

For Lepage the freedom offered by improvisation is combined, indeed balanced, with the preset structures of forms and expressive concepts learned and developed by the director. In a sense, exactly the same creative balance of restrictions versus concepts characterizes opera production; and it is therefore hardly surprising that Lepage, and all the other *auteur*-directors of total theatre have also been occupied with opera.

Total theatre and directing opera: Robert Wilson, Robert Lepage, Peter Sellars

It is no accident that Gordon Craig began his directing career with three opera productions, Purcell's *Dido and Aeneas* and *The Masque of Love*, and Handel's *Acis and Galatea* (1900–3). Reviving baroque opera for the twentieth century, this (at the time) almost unknown material allowed him to focus on choreography and movement, innovative lighting and visual effects. Combining music, dance and theatrical action with pictorial setting, this was – like Wagner – intrinsically a form of 'Total Theatre'. It was from these productions that Craig developed his concept of 'the Art of the Theatre'; and it is logical to find that almost all the leading contemporary Western directors have turned occasionally to opera, or to various types of musical theatre (Julie Taymor staging Disney's *The Lion King*; Katie Mitchell directing Bach's *St Matthew Passion* for the Glyndebourne Opera; Elizabeth LeCompte adapting *The Temptation of St Anthony* and a version of Gertrude Stein's *Doctor Faustus Lights the Lights* in *House/Lights*). Another who became a leading European opera director was Giorgio Strehler, who began in the 1940s and 1950s with twentieth-century experimental pieces – Honegger, Berg, Prokofiev and Stravinsky (*The History of a Soldier*, which would later become a signature piece for Peter Sellars) – and transitioned through the Brecht/Weil *Rise and Fall of the City of Mahagonny* (1964) to Verdi and Mozart. (He died during rehearsals for *Cosi fan tutte* in 1997 – a production possibly conceived in response to a striking updating by Peter Sellars a decade before.) But this turn to opera has been most marked in those directors who pursue the *auteur* ideal of the complete Artist of the Theatre, or the staging equivalent of total theatre. As with Craig, opera becomes the optimal form for realizing their concept of performance.

Even Brook – despite classifying opera as the most extreme type of 'deadly theatre' in *The Empty Space*, based on his early and unfortunate productions at Covent Garden in the 1940s – turned to opera productions later in his career with a striking chamber version of *Carmen* (1982). A heavily pruned and single piano-accompanied version of Debussy's *Pelléas et Mélisande* (1993) was followed by *Don Giovanni* (1998) and (as discussed in Chapter 6) an equally minimalist *Magic Flute* (2010). And one of the most significant *auteurs* to focus on opera is Robert Wilson.

Visual stylization as musical context: Robert Wilson

Indeed his early approach to the stage was largely defined by his iconic *Einstein on the Beach* (1976 – see above, pp. 162–4), starting a collaboration with Philip Glass that led to *Monsters of Grace* and *O Corvo Branco* (1997, 1998). His range expanded to rock opera with *The Black Rider*, an adaptation of *Der Freischütz* in collaboration with Tom Waits (1990), followed by their 1992 *Alice* as well as their 2002 version of *Woyzeck*, and to Kurt Weill, with Wilson's productions of Brecht's *Threepenny Opera* (Berliner Ensemble 2007, Spoleto Festival 2008, BAM New York 2011). At the same time, Wilson began to establish himself as a leading director of classical opera, focusing on three main lines: the baroque operas of Gluck and Monteverdi (*Alceste* 2003, *Orfeo* 2009, *Ritorno di Ulisse* 2011); Wagner (*Parsifal* 1991, *Lohengrin* 1998, the complete Ring Cycle – Zurich 2000–2) and Romantic opera (including Weber's original *Der Freischütz*, 2009); the nineteenth- and early twentieth-century symbolists. These he sees as his artistic forerunners, starting with Strauss' adaptation of Wilde's archetypal symbolist play *Salome*, and the Debussy/d'Annunzio *Martyre de Saint Sébastien* (1987, 1988), followed by his homage to Eliot in *T.S.E.* (with music by Philip Glass, 1994), and his staging of Maeterlinck's *Pelléas et Mélisande* with Debussy's music (1998), as well as concentrating particularly on Gertrude Stein: *Doctor Faustus Lights the Lights* (1992); *Four Saints in Three Acts* (Houston and New York, 1996) plus a variation, titled *Saints and Singing* (Berlin, 1997).

It was surely his growing familiarity with opera from the later 1980s that sensitized Wilson to conventional drama. After all, opera is built on fixed libretti, obliging Wilson to deal with dramatic structures, narratives, actions, plots and events and their consequences, even though he treated them in his usual highly stylized, hieratic mode. Wilson's visual books proved invaluable for directing opera productions as different as Puccini's *Madama Butterfly* (1993) and Wagner's Ring Cycle. These guides were all the more important for him because operas are large-scale phenomena in large-scale institutions, and require intensive input from their collaborators together with a firm hand to pull the artistic and institutional demands together. On a further level, as the American director Andrei Serban – who sees Brook as his mentor, and (following Brook) turned increasingly to opera – notes, inherent in the genre itself, the production conditions for opera are very much more restricting than for standard theatre.

Directing opera

There is never enough time in opera because after three weeks you start the stage rehearsals with orchestra; and the director's job is almost done because at that point, once the conductor arrives with all the musicians, it's his rehearsal, so everything has to be absolutely fixed; and if you don't have everything clearly enough worked out when you come to the opening rehearsal and first meet the singers, you're in trouble. Plus, singers, unlike actors, don't like to improvise. They move to the music.

Opera theatres have so many productions that they have to plan far in advance; and start constructing the sets so that you have them ready before rehearsals. Since the rehearsal time is so short, all work with the performer is done on the sets – that's the good part of it – but the actual frustration is that two years in advance you have to come up with the vision with the designer. And you have to stick with that vision, even though two years later, you yourself are in another place, with almost certainly quite a different understanding of that material than two years before.

Andrei Serban[33]

Production limitations in staging opera mean directors must appear with a concept already completely visualized, and the rehearsal process focuses on shaping and structure, rather than roles. Intensifying this, the obvious artifice of singing in place of speech, and the symbolic level of many operas, automatically underlines the performative context. As the most meta-theatrical of all forms of theatre, opera has become a prime opportunity for defining new forms of theatre, partly indeed because of the traditional nature of the form in itself, because this highlights innovations by contrast.

While not generally recognized, in all over half of Wilson's directorial work has been in opera; and it is here that his characteristic directing style has reached its full expression. This is clearest in the operas with the most exotic – and so least conventionally realistic – contexts, such as the feudal Japan of Puccini's *Madama Butterfly* and the Pharaonic Egypt of Verdi's *Aida* (2002). Here the physical stasis and extreme slow movement of his other productions becomes a stylized illumination of the well-known music – in Wilson's own view, justified particularly as allowing the singers full vocal rein and focusing the audience on the sound.

In *Aida*, Wilson reduces the Nile to a blue ribbon stretched across the whole width of the rear stage, backed by minimalist black hills, with the sky taking up over two-thirds of the proscenium frame, giving the pre-eminence to the lighting; the protagonists' gestures are hieratical echoes of Egyptian tomb paintings, rigid and simplified. In Wilson's view the three poles of any opera production are music, light and architecture; and while critics admired the exquisitely lit setting and the way its geometry changed with glacial slowness, they found a distinct lack of emotion or personality in the direction since at no point does anyone touch another person.[34] Yet this abstraction emphasized the art of the singers as symbols: a denial of individuality and 'star' essence that Craig would have applauded, emphasized by Kabuki-style facial make-up. Similarly for *Madama Butterfly*, simplicity and stasis were designed to emphasize the singing. Even more minimalist, the lighting in dim colours of blue, grey and gold, with stripped-down gestures and movements suggesting Noh theatre, Wilson's staging deconstructed the emotional kitsch of the original Belasco/Puccini orientalism, challenging his post-colonialist audience's identification with their imperialist past. For the singers, the abstract gestures and slowed-down movements were 'natural' in echoing and following the music.

Cinematic and mechanistic deconstructions of opera: Robert Lepage

Like Wilson, Lepage has also made a significant reputation as an opera director, although it was not until almost halfway through his career that Lepage began to establish his operatic and rock music credentials with the stagings of *Bluebeard's Castle* and *Erwartung* for the Canadian Opera Company (1992), and Peter Gabriel's 'Secret World Tour' (1993). He followed these with experiments in combining theatrical performance with concert-hall classical music, devising an acted accompaniment to Mahler's song cycle 'Kindertotenlieder' (1998), followed by a stage adaptation of Berlioz's 'dramatic legend' *La damnation de Faust* (first produced at the Saito Kinen Festival, Matsumoto, 1999) which became Lepage's introduction to the Met in 2009, and led to his 2010–12 staging of Wagner's Ring Cycle for the Met. With a second rock festival staging, Peter Gabriel's 'Growing Up Live' (2002), and a contra-Brecht contemporary adaptation of Gay in *The Busker's Opera* (2004), together with *1984* (an adaptation of Orwell's novel by Loren Mazel, 2005), Stravinsky's *The Rake's Progress* (2007) and *The Nightingale's Tale* (2009), Lepage's opera productions far outnumber the theatre performances he has mounted since 2000. Lepage's operas display the finished results of his stage experiments.

Thus the psychological focus of Lepage's work was so clearly expressed through his productions of Bartók (*Bluebeard's Castle*) and Schönberg (*Erwartung – Hope*) that they became programmatic, directly dramatizing the subconscious by emphasizing the connection with Sigmund Freud, whose first psychological studies coincided with the original performances of these operas. So Lepage described his aim in *Erwartung* as 'trying to treat [the piece] in a . . . hyper-realistic way, trying to get inside the woman's id, as if it were a close-up of what's inside the singer'. However, where Schönberg's solo for soprano had up to then only been presented as a concert piece, Lepage filled the stage with movement: naked men crawling out of solid walls, the figure of the psychiatrist swivelling his chair to sit at 90 degrees to the vertical, and the woman, presented as a mad Ophelia figure in a straitjacket, rolling down the sharply sloping stage.

Similarly *La damnation de Faust* played strikingly on Lepage's cinematic structuring and the movie-conditioned mindset explored in his plays, through a four-level stage, cut into squares by five vertical columns, presenting a sequence of celluloid strips on an editing machine, where a cast of dancers echo movements from frame to frame, or the departing soldiers march backwards in slow motion away from the girls with their elegantly waved handkerchiefs. Each square frame also contains a screen on which architectural or sky scenes (coiling red clouds for Mephistopheles, cerulean blue vistas for the marching soldiers) are projected; and setting the precisely choreographed action within the ranked squares gives a fragmented, episodic effect. For instance, five Jesus figures are crucified simultaneously on one level, while below bare-chested men writhe in hell, or in another sequence (in an echo of *Elsinore*) multiple images of a galloping horse repeated in each square consciously echo Eadweard Muybridge's well-known 1897 *Horse in Motion*: the first to track movement through still photos one-thousandth of a second apart. As well as corresponding to what Lepage identifies as the contemporary mindset, this also evoked the period when Berlioz wrote *Faust* – Louis Daguerre's 1837 invention of the Daguerreotype coming just seven years before its composition. At the same time Lepage ironicized the image with a live acrobat in each frame, suspended on a wire so that they appear to ride the photos of the horses.

For a video of Lepage's Metropolitan production of *The Damnation of Faust*, see www.youtube.com/watch?v=ScZDA8YOrNc.

This use of acrobats aligns opera with the circus and Lepage's Las Vegas shows, which translate opera into explicitly popular work: Cirque du Soleil's *KA* of 2004, or the 2011 *Totem*, where through-composed music and circus acrobatics combine with highly mechanized performance areas. At the same time, his *Faust* production shows the dominance of directorial concept. The most striking element – as with Wilson – is visual, although here it is intensified by the separation of singers (arranged chorally, together with Faust, on the lower stage) and the active but non-singing figures in the four-level frames above: a technique that is also found in Peter Sellars' productions.

Conceptual politics: Peter Sellars

Where Lepage and Wilson – despite the extent of their operatic work – are primarily recognized for their dramatic stagings, Peter Sellars has focused almost exclusively on opera throughout his career. Of his total output of well over sixty productions from his student days (when he performed four straight plays in 1979) up to 2006, only eleven – less than a fifth of his output – are not musical. As with Wilson and Lepage, Sellars has experimented with staging unconventional music – such as the Weill, Brecht, Balanchine 'ballet chanté' *The Seven Deadly Sins* (1993) – or works on the edge of music, like his production of the Russian futurist Khlebnikov's *Zangesi: A Supersaga in 20 Planes* (1987, originally staged by the constructivist Tatlin in 1923) where words form musical patterns. And he has co-created a number of operas together with his composer/collaborator John Adams, including *Doctor Atomic* (2005–7) where Sellars also researched and scripted the libretto. Significantly, Sellars has also gained the ability to rehearse his opera productions over an extended period through mounting co-productions with multiple European and US opera houses, so that any given cast might be as much as six months in developmental workshops and repeat rehearsals.

Even more than Meyerhold or Mnouchkine, Sellars was influenced by Eastern ritualized performance – being exposed young to Bunraku, trained in Kabuki as a student, and afterwards studying Noh theatre for five years in Japan. His formative period also included experience of Chinese Kunshu opera, from which he derived his version of total theatre: instead of singing, ballet, acrobatics and acting being separate skills, Kunshu offered a model that combined all of these in a highly stylized form. Yet Sellars also emphasizes the importance of Wagner and (like Wilson) symbolist theatre for his work; and he sees himself as in a stylistic tradition developed by Robert Wilson, pointing to Wilson's 'beautiful sense of time, of space, of care of walking, care of a small gesture, in fact, holding a large secret': all qualities that Wilson shares with Noh theatre.[35] In many ways, too, Sellars can be seen as a postmodern director. Irony and pastiche are core parts of his directorial vocabulary, and there is frequently an element of the grotesque (that he defines in ways parallel to Meyerhold, whom he considers to be one of his great influences).

Opera is the most ritualistic, and the most formalized, of Western theatrical forms. This is why it appeals to Sellars with his background in Noh. The music is set and determines the action, yet the traditional conventionality makes any coherent change in vision both provocative and compelling; and Sellars's approach begins with a concept that is generally political. Frequently this takes the form of modernization: Handel with rockets (*Orlando Furioso*, set on Cape Canaveral, 1981), or Mozart set in contemporary America – a stereotypical New England diner during the Vietnam war (*Cosi fan tutte*, 1986), or the newly completed icon of capitalist extravagance, the gold Manhattan Trump Tower (*The Marriage of Figaro*, 1998).[36] Alternatively the opera stage is updated with icons of modern technology: the life-size fuselage of Air Force One at the opening of *Nixon in China* (1987); the Los Alamos atom bomb centre stage in *Doctor Atomic*. This also expresses the significance of politics in Sellars' work – an element that is seldom emphasized among the *auteurs* discussed in this section – which brought him to accept the directorship of the American National Theatre in Washington DC (1984–86) and led to him being fired from the directorship of the Adelaide Festival (2001), as well as being the focus of his teaching at UCLA, where his courses are 'Art as Social Action' and 'Art as Moral Action'. So *Doctor Atomic* draws clear parallels between the development of the bomb, the anti-communist campaign of the time, and the paranoia and public lies of the Bush post-9/11 era – while, like Brook's *Maharabhata*, it also draws on the *Bhagavad Gita* (using the fact that Oppenheimer carried a copy in his coat pocket) and becomes a call for the abolition of nuclear weapons. Indeed his focus on opera itself has a political aspect, where the conditions of operatic performance serve as an example for human advancement.

The politics of opera

What's so liberating about opera is nobody can do it alone. The soprano is dependent on the oboe player, who is dependent on the person whose finger is on the switch on the light board, who is dependent on the person who raised the curtain.

Hello! You're having this total experience. No part of it could ever be isolated – it's only possible because the whole cosmology comes into play. And human beings are doing this astounding thing, which is working together to make something that is way beyond their individual selves, or capacities, and that lifts everybody to a new place.

Peter Sellars, Interview, 2004[37]

Sellars also sees the form of opera itself as an antidote to specific US problems, with its uniting of all the arts – music, dance, poetry, visual art – demonstrating the possibility for people to work together 'in an image of harmony. The deepest contribution we can make at this divided, estranged moment is to say we can work across the divisions, we can work across the differences.'[38]

At the same time, the proponents of total theatre represent a very different line from those directors influenced by Stanislavsky. Sellars makes this explicit, categorizing the earlier twentieth century as 'absorbed in psychology and the self' and rejecting the focus on individual psychology as reductionist: devaluing political commitments, ignoring 'your place in history' and denying community or 'what we are all doing here for each other'.[39] In response his focus is on externals – stylization and structure on stage, and in social/philosophical context in rehearsal. So, for instance, in a production of *The Merchant of Venice* (1994) Sellars, taking account of the founding of the Dutch East India Company as the origin of commercial exploitation in 1602, the same year Shakespeare wrote the play, handed out to his actors copies of economic texts on the way this exploitation worked in the contemporary world: *How Capitalism Under-developed Black America* by Manning Marable, or *Open Veins in Latin America* by Eduardo Galeano. Similarly the performers in *Doctor Atomic* were given such books as the *Bhagavad Gita*, and Robert Jungk's personal history of the atomic scientists, *Brighter than a Thousand Suns*.

Building on this absorption in the contextual material for a piece, Sellars encourages his performers to improvise their roles, while evolving a choreography that becomes the structure for the performance. The moves and gestures are worked out as visual patterns, and not as expressions of personality or feeling. 'The move . . . could be executed with any emotion. It's just a gesture and the gesture doesn't limit the meaning, just focuses it.' His intention is to create a structure of actions freeing the performers to interpret according to their developing sense of character, together with a set of relationships that requires performers to interact: 'the beauty of the choreography is always that

12 *Doctor Atomic* (San Francisco Opera – Act II, the Corn Dancers), Peter Sellars, 2005

it's an empty vessel'.[40] As an example of this structural choreography, in *Doctor Atomic*, with the bare stage representing the New Mexico desert, scenes are included where native corn-dancers wind around the scientists and soldiers. Their duets and arias about nuclear or political challenges are broken up by the choral songs of the dancers as their sinuous line snakes between the groups. At the same time, to approximate his ideal of Kunshu opera in the Western context, Sellars has both dancers and singers in the chorus – choreographing the moves so that, where dancing dominates, the dancers are in the foreground, switching places when the singing rather than movement is primary.

As Sellars points out, his work – and in his view opera itself – is intrinsically Brechtian: 'the beauty of music is that it is a completely abstract formulation, people are singing notes, there is no question that they are just making this up, and you don't confuse the person singing with the role'.[41] While Brecht is dealt with here under the rubric of 'epic theatre', as the author of the works he directed as well as the theoretician who created a new form of acting he would also qualify as an *auteur*. But Sellars' directorial approach also parallels the *auteurs* among his contemporaries. Even though far more realistic than Robert Wilson – his *Don Giovanni* set on a tenement street of New York's Spanish Harlem, littered with trash cans and empty syringes, plastered with graffiti, had the final sextet, naked from the waist protruding from sewer holes in the pavement – the core of Sellars' productions is the visual imagery that defines his directorial concept. Like Lepage's use of improvisation to develop the material for his shows, Sellars allows his performers creative freedom in character development. Similarly, where Lepage has multiple projects all in rehearsal simultaneously, Sellars translates this creative interplay into stage terms, deliberately piling on actions or images to make it difficult for a spectator to catch everything, creating a multivocal theatre.

Sound and space: Christoph Marthaler

Like other visionary directors, Marthaler has turned increasingly to opera, but all his productions are based in musical structures or contain music and songs alongside dialogue. Training in Austria as a musician and then studying in Paris under Jacques Lecoq, he began his career with a 'spectacle', two movement pieces created on the minimalist and repetitive music of Eric Satie, an iconic figure in the early avant-garde: pianist for the famous Parisian Chat Noir cabaret in the 1890s, who had termed himself a 'phonometrician' (someone who measures sounds) rather than a composer. This was followed by a 'Great Word Hymn' – an impromptu for choir, orchestra, six important men and a blind passenger – and a staging of a sound poem by the Dadaist Kurt Schwitters. In addition, one of the first play texts Marthaler directed was Beckett's *A Piece of Monologue*, together (typically) with an adaptation of the short prose piece *Stirrings Still* (1992).

These early works signal the major elements of Marthaler's unique approach to theatre; and although, along with Robert Wilson, he has been hailed as a 'post-dramatic' director, like Wilson, Marthaler clearly draws on the early twentieth-century roots of the avant-garde, while in terms of musical composition the abstract and non-linear qualities of his staging are quite recognizable. So, for example, his first opera production was a strikingly static staging of *Pelléas et Mélisande* (1994). Rhythm, sound, tonality and other musical features of speech and performance are at the centre of the aesthetic organization of Marthaler's theatre pieces.[42] Rather than the narrative features, it is the immediacy, materiality and transience of sound that theatre shares with music, which comes from a compositional approach to the devising and structuring of a piece. And Marthaler's staging follows the lines of a carefully devised spatial, rhythmic and auditory score, encompassing all performance elements, gestures, actions and dancing, speech and singing, playing music and producing sound. He continues to experiment musically, as in the 'Greenland Project', *+ – 0 Subpolar Base Camp* (Vienna Festival, 2011), and has recently taken to working with the contemporary Austrian composer Beat Furrer. As with other theatrical *auteurs*, Marthaler not only adapts classical plays to his own vision, but also compiles the scripts and is listed as the author of over half the theatre works he has directed – frequently alongside the name of Anna Viebrock, his designer, demonstrating the significance of physical context for his work.

Radical and obsessively contemporary – updating almost all his stagings and adaptations of classical theatre, and even operas such as *Tristan und Isolde* (2005), and setting them in ultra-modern settings and costumes – Marthaler rejects all ideologies, but is highly political in his attack on capitalism, bourgeois culture and the materialistic social assumptions of the EU. This is explicit in the titles of his works, from the pseudo-'patriotic play' *Murx den Europäer! Murx ihn! Murx ihn! Murx ihn! Murx ihn ab!* (*Screw the European! Screw Him! Screw Him! Screw Him! Do Him In!*, 1993) marking the occasion of the reunification of the state by a requiem to the German Democratic Republic, up to *Riesenbutzbach. Eine Dauerkolonie* (*Rising Butzbach. A Sustainable Colony*, 2009: 'Butzbach' – a typical meta-theatrical reference in Marthaler's work – being a town in Hessen where the Austrian playwright Thomas Bernhard set his apocalyptic comedy *Histrionics*, *Der Theatermacher*, 1984). In a programme note, Marthaler calls it 'a musical-dramatic contemplation of the last days of consumption'. At the same time, there is no 'story-line' or coherent plot. Here, as elsewhere in Marthaler's work, scripts are constructed mainly for sound, rather than sense, which has led to his productions being compared to modern jazz performances; and the political message comes mainly from the physical attitudes of the performers. Time is elongated, with extreme slow motion movement (though, in contrast to Wilson, there is nothing stylized or aesthetic about the moves) and even actors dozing on the stage for minutes at a time. The atmosphere in Marthaler's works both reinforces and derives from the characterization of his figures, who are worked-out bourgeoisie, despairing proletarians, purposeless office staff: each isolated on stage, but vocally united by joint songs, in a demonstration that all are equally victims of the system. And Marthaler has defined his approach as 'more concerned with the atmosphere and the environment' through which 'one can create space for associations and imagination' than with character or theme.[43]

Marthaler's theatre has two distinct identifiers: one is the dystopian stage space and the other is the slowness of the performance. Anna Viebrock, the stage designer for most of his shows, creates cavernous spaces – a waiting-room (*Murx*), gyms, train stations – sometimes filling complete aircraft hangars (*Groundings*) or a hall in the Rosenhügel-Studios of the Vienna Filmstadt

(*Riesenbutzbach*). But always Viebrock includes some out-of-place element, as if to challenge the audience to imagine other possibilities; so in *Riesenbutzbach* a huge white concrete space labelled 'Institute of Fermentation Industry' contains simultaneously throughout the performance a bedroom, a garage, a bank, a recording studio, a furniture warehouse and a shopping mall in incongruous juxtaposition.

In these vast spaces individual actors feel lost (Butzbach has become a synonym for 'losing one's way'). This emptiness of space corresponds to the emptiness of time in the slow performance pace. So, *Murx* opens with an extremely long and static mute scene. The characters sit, without expression, together but alone, in a vast waiting-room with, on the wall, a broken clock and huge letters spelling out 'So that time never stands still', letters that slowly drop one-by-one to the floor. The isolated people on stage begin their everyday routines: grotesque, even violent, expressing alienation, depression and melancholy. A few times throughout the performance they leave their seats at the sound of a buzzer, line-up in front of an upstage door and wash their hands in the toilet room. These repetitive sounds and actions represent the 'musical bars' of the performance's rhythmical structure, while also creating a collage-effect, which is reinforced by the waiting figures on the stage, isolated even when paired, eyes front, staring silently.

Almost all Marthaler's plays – whether material constructed by him, or scripts adapted from the classics – have been devised performances. And working, as he does, with a core group of actors who have been in his company ever since the beginning of his directing career, he has developed a firm sense of style that all shared in creating. So, in rehearsing, he can leave a great deal of the mechanics to the actors. The rehearsal process is described by his actors as collaborative; and indeed they are given free play with the language and gesture. Yet without narrative through-line, or character individuation – in *Groundings* (2003) the businessmen all carried suitcases containing a dummy head and torso, which eventually replaced them on stage, while *20th Century Blues* (2000) ended with the stage being filled with identical twins – whatever stage business the actors developed in rehearsal remains raw material for Marthaler to create his vision.

Since his aim has never been to interpret a specific dramatic text through his actors, Marthaler has been able to create a consistent and highly idiosyncratic style that applies to all his productions, particularly his own texts (from *Murx* to his attack on the papacy, *Papperlapapp* (Festival d'Avignon, 2010)), but also the most standard works, where his company are not involved (as in his Bayreuth production of *Tristan*). Following the same principle, instead of a Stanislavskian psychological reading of character, Marthaler's actors are required to play only themselves. They are not expected to perform as 'others' – and consequently have been described as automatically conveying a sense of helplessness and resignation that reinforces Marthaler's depiction of an exploitative and repressive society.[44] Similarly Marthaler focuses exclusively on sound and rhythm in the speeches, effectively preventing any individual interpretation of words, and emptying personal meaning from the text.

Early in the rehearsal process, Marthaler gets the cast to sing together in four-part harmony – which requires sensitive awareness and cooperation – yet observers have described Marthaler as imposing 'a highly distinctive style for his singing actors that precludes outward performative "putting over"' and instead gives 'the impression that the performers are being passively ventriloquized by the songs'.[45] And in production, only in song does a common humanity break through in Marthaler's figures, although they generally still stay isolated and physically apart. So even in their climactic love scene, Tristan and Isolde stood side by side apart, eyes fixed front, each undressing themselves as in an auto-erotic fantasy; while in *Riesenbutzbach* the cast gather behind a garage door to let go with the disco hit 'Staying Alive'. As others have noted, 'Singing in Marthaler's theatre occasions acts of collective memory. Mostly sung very quietly, songs grow out of silence bringing individuals from solitude into chorus. They are sung as if half-remembered, very fragile, harmonious and beautiful.'[46] Towards the end of *Riesenbutzbach*, they all sing the 'Prisoner's Chorus', a paean to Liberty from Beethoven's *Fidelio*, conveying a political message in essentially emotional terms, yet still without any emotional expression from the actors. It is a graphic illustration of directorial control. Choral singing demands exact coordination: the director as conductor.

Musical, quasi-operatic theatre is a major factor in the work of such contemporary, cutting-edge directors as Wlodzimierz Staniewski, Grzegorz Bral and Jaroslaw Fret. But since they also illustrate Grotowski's continuing influence, they are discussed in Chapter 7.

Further reading

Dundjerović, Aleksandar Saša. *Robert Lepage*, London: Routledge, 2009.
Holmberg, Arthur. *The Theatre of Robert Wilson*, Cambridge University Press, 1996
Hunt, Albert and Geoffrey Reeves. *Peter Brook*, Cambridge University Press, 1995
Innes, Christopher. *Edward Gordon Craig*, Cambridge University Press, 1983
Designing Modern America: Broadway to Main Street, New Haven: Yale University Press, 2005
Melchinger, Siegfried. *Max Reinhardt: Sein Theater in Bildern*, Vienna: Friedrich Verlag, 1968
Shevtsova, Maria. *Robert Wilson*, London: Routledge, 2007
Sidiropoulou, Avra. *Authoring Performance: The Director in Contemporary Theatre*, New York: Palgrave Macmillan, 2011

Chapter 6

Directors of ensemble theatre

The directors who feature in this chapter have the goal of ensemble theatre, as first envisaged by Stanislavsky, even if all follow their own path to advance the possibilities of directing. This influence has been world-wide. Some, like Harley Granville Barker in Britain in the 1910s, furthered Stanislavsky's principles, not least the principle of ensemble acting, without fully realizing them. Joan Littlewood too promoted ensemble practices in the Theatre Workshop (thus renamed in 1945), drawing on the examples of both Stanislavsky and Brecht that led to productions such as her seminal *Oh What a Lovely War* in 1963; and Peter Hall was inspired by the idea of a creative ensemble when he founded the Royal Shakespeare Company in 1961. Then, too, there are directors who, like Elia Kazan in the United States, have come out of Method Acting, Lee Strasberg's particular take on Stanislavsky's 'system'.

However, ensemble theatre has a particularly firm tradition in Eastern Europe that has continued unbroken to the present in, for instance, the meticulously crafted productions of Krystian Lupa in Poland, where Stanislavsky's legacy as regards ensemble work came via Juliusz Osterwa. Osterwa had come into contact with the Moscow Art Theatre when, in the mid 1910s, he directed in Moscow. The younger generation of Polish directors exemplified by Krzysztof Warlikowski and Grzegorz Jarzyna, both of whom were assistant directors to Lupa before taking off on independent careers, rely on finely tuned ensemble playing for the impact of their productions.

The choice, where ensemble directors are concerned, is broad, but is here restricted to selected key figures of the second half of the twentieth century who are not only representative of the ensemble theme of this chapter, but also important for their explorations and innovations to the history of directing. All but one of the seven chosen directors are still working at the beginning of the second decade of the twenty-first century and are still searching to reinvigorate their craft in the company of others.

Giorgio Strehler, Peter Stein, Peter Brook

Giorgio Strehler was trained as an actor, and, echoing not only Stanislavsky but also Copeau and another actor/director, Jouvet, with whom he had studied briefly in France, he prized acting in the theatre almost above everything else – almost, but not quite, since he was extremely attentive to the smallest details of design and light for the harmony of a production as a whole.[1] So crucial was lighting to him – no wonder that Robert Wilson saw him as his only peer – that he rehearsed light cues even as he rehearsed the actors, constantly stopping them in mid-flight to adjust the light.[2] Still, like Stanislavsky, he placed actors at the heart of the theatre, and believed that 'a real stage director should be as close as possible to his actors' – so much so that, when working with them (just like Meyerhold), he constantly jumped onto the stage to play all the parts.[3] Successive actors working with Strehler over his fifty years with the Piccolo Teatro di Milano until his death in 1997 have consistently reported this trait. His Italian actors have generally accepted it as part of his role of 'a great teacher'.[4] By contrast, the French actors whom Strehler directed in Paris in French in the *Villeggiatura Trilogy* (1978 – three plays by Goldoni structured as one) found his 'always acting it out' to be 'quite difficult'.[5] Strehler may well have 'liked actors who had a creative personality', but they had to struggle for their creative space in his ceaseless 'interference'.[6] While believing in the value of a permanent ensemble, he none the less totally controlled the creative process.

Strehler founded the Piccolo in 1946 with his manager-associate Paolo Grassi as a 'public service', anticipating Vilar, although they stressed, as did their predecessor duo at the Moscow Art Theatre, the 'art' dimension of this theatre that was to be open and accessible to all. His immediate goal was to renew Italian theatre by re-evaluating the plays of Goldoni and the performance style of the *commedia dell'arte*, both of which had fallen into oblivion. He tirelessly foregrounded Goldoni's Venetian vernacular – the latter being essential to 'popular' theatre, as Strehler understood it – his acute insight into class relations and behaviours, and his humour for which the witty resources, verbal, gestural and physical, of *commedia* were indispensable. *Arlecchino, the Servant of Two Masters*, which Strehler first staged in 1949, entailed considerable archival research as well as research into play with masks; and Strehler developed a rehearsal technique of having his actors interpret a text while playing, thereby inculcating in them a sense of space, movement and spontaneity – everything that exploring *commedia* taught them and which they could transfer to any text they performed.

What Strehler did not forgo, however, was the idea that the author's word on the page and the nuances of language were the actors' source and justification for their actions. This is vital for Strehler's direction since *Arlecchino* became his touchstone for his future work: the production was poetic, and not literal, so he transposed the semantic meaning of words into visual, aural and corporeal images. For instance, Arlecchino's obligation to serve two masters, so clearly caught in Goldoni's dialogue, was expressed by Amleto Sartori's extraordinary spinning of plates of food, thrust at him from two directions, sometimes his hands and body almost touching the floor. In the 1977 version (the fifth out of six Strehler productions of this play), two actors, who were exquisitely dressed as servants but who played a door, stood a short distance from each other with lit candelabras in their hands; and they moved, as a door, to be another door in another scene in the second master's 'house' (also an empty space, but for the human 'door'). The formality of their bearing, clothes and movements in a stage awash with golden light mirrored the class status of Arlecchino's masters.

Strehler's poetic direction took a different turn in the *Villeggiatura*, where sonic images capture the meanings of Goldoni's dialogue. The light tread of soft shoes on the floor (the right shoe for the sound was found after hours of rehearsal) was part of a whole musical score of whisperings and tonal and rhythmic variations that communicated what was actually happening between the protagonists of Goldoni's love plot. Musicality, always of uppermost importance for Strehler's direction (and he was a superlative director of opera), was a means for gathering up the themes conveyed in language and harmoniously resolving them. In his posthumously premiered *Cosi fan tutte* (1998), musicality was not only generated by the polyphony of the singing, Mozart's orchestral music (here played by a chamber orchestra) and the singer-actors' mellifluous movements and gestures. It came, as well, from other 'voices' such as the silence of the gliding miniature ship in the scene where the lovers part. The additional counterpoint of this effect of silence, together with the image of the flowing ship, highlights the fact that the characters are thinking their inner thoughts, even as they sing them, much like asides in drama.

The Piccolo was the first ensemble and permanent repertory company in Italy, at odds with the country's actor-manager (*mattatore*) tradition. Unlike Vilar, Strehler and Grassi were socialists, which led Strehler to a lifelong commitment to Brecht; and being as fluent in German as in French he was able to go directly to Brecht's writings. His first attempt at Brecht was his 1956 production of *The Threepenny Opera* whose musical and physical verve and demonstration of class contradictions through clearly articulated *Gestus* delighted Brecht so much (Brecht had come to Milan to rehearsals) that, shortly after his death, the Berliner Ensemble invited Strehler to lead the company.

Strehler refused, his first priorities being social change in Italy and the renovation of Italian theatre through opposing the 'star' individualism, inherited from the *mattatore* system, in the name of the ensemble model exemplified at the time by Brecht's Berliner Ensemble.

It is instructive to pause and consider how the political perspectives of the directors discussed in these pages join their perception of themselves as directors. At the time of Strehler's encounter with Brecht, Peter Brook, his senior by four years, was an establishment director in London. He opened the Bouffes du Nord in Paris in 1974 on team principles for a core group, supplemented by actors according to productions. This could be described as a variant of Stanislavsky's idea of ensemble, although over the years the core became smaller and only a few who had been added along the way returned for chosen pieces. Brook's aesthetic principles evolved through workshops and improvisations during which, when it came to preparing productions, he exercised a director's prerogative, as conceded by himself and the participants, to test, choose and shape the emergent material. His worldview was a humanist one, and remains so. Beneath it lies his personal mysticism – he is a follower of Georgi Gurdjieff – and his affinity with Sufism, as evident particularly in *11 and 12* (2009) about the Mali sage Tierno Bokar.

Peter Stein, Strehler's junior by sixteen years, was a child of the 1960s who fully embraced its left-wing spirit, establishing at the Schaubühne in Berlin in 1970 a company working entirely as a cooperative, down to a voting system on all issues. This included artistic decisions, where everybody's voice from stagehands and technicians to actors and directors was equal. Strehler's vision for the Piccolo was far less radical, by comparison with Stein's, and, after a few years of cooperative experimenting on the cusp of the 1970s he came to the view that the rejection of the director as a 'dictator', which had emerged from the cultural revolution around May '68, was 'an old story that had died decades ago'.[7] When all was said and done, he argued, the director was left with his/her 'extreme responsibility' without which theatre could not operate.[8] Stein was to reach a similar conclusion, modifying the Schaubühne's collectivist practices until, worn down by internal dissension and the institution's demands, he left it in 1985.

The director's responsibility

The director has to be patient and human, has to understand, help, clarify, [and] has to make things harmonious or, often, let contradictions be discovered between him and the actors and among the actors themselves ... I don't know if I am a good or a bad director. I know that I am a good work comrade. A good guide, in the Brechtian sense of the term.

Giorgio Strehler, *Per un teatro umano* (*Towards a Human Theatre*), 139[9]

The comparison between these three directors can be illuminated by analysing their different directorial techniques and stylistic approaches in terms of a single text. Strehler, Brook and Stein each staged Anton Chekhov's *The Cherry Orchard* (1974, 1981, 1989) in sharply contrasting ways iconic of their work. While separated by a gap of seven to eight years, Brook's production can be seen in terms of Strehler's, Stein's in response to Brook's – and all in an implied acknowledgement of the ensemble work pioneered by the original director of Chekhov's play: Stanislavsky.

Three versions of The Cherry Orchard

The stories of plays were, for Strehler, an integral part of society and history, and it was while he was preparing *The Cherry Orchard* (1974) that he came up with his theory of the 'three Chinese boxes' (where one box is inside the next and the next), which was to guide how he directed for the rest of his life.[10] The first box is the box of 'truth', as pertinent to the play: in *The Cherry Orchard*, this is a 'very beautiful human story . . . the story of a family'. The second box 'is the box of History', which, in Chekhov's case, underlies the family story and is barely perceptible in it, but spreads beyond it, embracing a bigger view. The third is the biggest box, the 'box of life' . . . of the 'human adventure from birth to death', which is still a 'political' story, but also has a 'metaphysical' dimension, as if it were drawing the 'arc of human destiny'. In short, what Strehler wishes to convey is the idea that his production (as others to follow) had to embrace all these layers at once, and do so in such a way that the local (first box) did not obliterate the broader 'universal-symbolic' allusions that could be drawn from it.

In order to achieve this interlocking, Strehler avoided the realistic (albeit imaginative) detail that had made Luchino Visconti's 1965 *Cherry Orchard* a landmark of Italian theatre. Instead, he worked closely with his designer-collaborator Luciano Damiani so as to produce a suggestive rather than decorative set. (Strehler worked with the designers and composers of his team from the very gestation of a production to ensure its unity.) He was inspired by Chekhov's letter of 5 February 1903 to Stanislavsky in which Chekhov speaks of *The Cherry Orchard* as having four acts, 'in the first of which flowering cherry trees are seen through the windows, an entire garden of white. And the women will be in white dresses.'[11]

Taking Chekhov at his word, Strehler agreed with Damiani on an all-white stage, or, rather, on a stage in dozens of shades of white, ranging from stark white to faintly pinkish-white, for the duration of the performance; only Dunyasha and Firs are in black. This tonal composition goes from Act I in a white nursery, with white children's tables, study desk, toy train and the big cupboard that Gaev addresses, to Act II whose high, slanted, white rhomboid shape taking the full length of the stage is used by the actors to sit and lie on but which has no markers on it whatsoever to situate it – cherry orchard, grass, river bank, or anything at all. The effect is that of a painting – white on white giving the necessary abstraction from the concrete of Chekhov's play for Strehler's third 'universal-symbolic' and 'metaphysical' box.

In Act III, several white chairs in twos behind each other, as in a domestic theatre (Charlotta also does her tricks here as a show), shape the white space. Lopakhin jumps up on these chairs in irrepressible joy when he announces that he has bought the cherry orchard. The same refrain played off-stage suggests the ball scene in which there is no visible dancing: Strehler focuses entirely on Ranyevskaya's suffering, the latter expressed primarily in the cadences, crescendos and diminuendos of Valentina Cortese's voice in the role, like bel canto. In Act IV, only Firs is in black in a room made sepulchral by a large white object, possibly a grand piano, covered in white for everybody's departure. The floor too is covered in white. Throughout Strehler's pared-back vision floats light, white fabric curled in a loop from above the front of the stage and curving well into the audience. In Act IV it is lowered closer to the stage, suggesting closure, or a shroud. Autumn leaves rather than cherry blossoms float down from it, now here, now there, throughout the performance. The lighting is soft, and barely a shadow falls, unless it darkens completely, as at the end of Acts II and IV.

While insisting that the word on the page, the author's word and the nuances of language were the actors' source and justification for their actions, Strehler's *mise en scène* was poetic, not literal, and so he transposed the semantic meaning of words into visual, aural and corporeal images. For instance, in *King Lear* (1972), one of a number of Strehler's Shakespeare productions – Goldoni, Brecht and Shakespeare were the authors he most frequently directed – a sheet across the stage was torn into two. This was the image for Lear's division of his kingdom. Sheets subsequently became a metaphor of Goneril and Regan's collusion in their father's downfall. The two women folded sheets, helping each other in routine housework while they berated their father and deprived him of his retinue. Always, for Strehler, the text justified the performance conceit. At the same time, the pristine clarity of his productions related to his conviction that the theatre had 'to tell stories' (a Brechtian proposition also reiterated by Brook) and 'succeed in telling a story without telling too much'.[12] Strehler's ability to say less by eliding narrative and illustrative detail accounted in large part for the sheer beauty of his stage work. Elision was also a principle of the actors' play in so far as they sought the inner impulses of their characters' actions so as to externalize ('tell') what was essential about them in the most physically eloquent manner possible.

So, in the gentle, poetic universe conjured up for *The Cherry Orchard*, Strehler harmonizes his actors to play out the drama of quasi-infantile adults locked up in memory (for which white becomes a symbol) and anachronistic perception (they are also locked into inertia in the face of personal and social crisis). Nevertheless, they are held together by their love, for now, if not forever. If white evokes this evanescent moment, this sweet sensation of time passing, like a last Indian summer, Strehler has his actors embody it in the ceaseless flow of their movements and their vocal scores, which he constructs symphonically, each voice a distinctive instrument contributing its unique tone and timbre to the music of the whole.

That this is Strehler's overarching directorial intention is clear from the outset when Cortese as Ranyevskaya returning to Russia and the home of her childhood sets the key, which the other actors modulate according to the modulations of the themes picked out with care by Strehler from the subtext. The subtextual element is especially strong in Act II, when the actors on the rhomboid shape project their characters' underlying dimly acknowledged anxieties – Lopakhin, too, although soon to be a winner, is not free of them; and Cortese's parasol, although telling a story about the summer heat, speaks of Ranyevskaya's endless flight into pain, which, on the surface, looks like flight from it, as she twirls, turns, slides and opens and shuts the parasol, among numerous manoeuvres with it. All of these gestures were made effortless through hours of rehearsal when Strehler explained that 'outer physicality' was to help the actors 'find their inner workings'.[13] Constant repetition, on which Strehler insisted, perfected the smallest movement, like the turn of a parasol, and, as well, relaxed the actor, as do the repeated movements of a dancer, freeing him or her to dance.

It is precisely this combination, which could be described as lyrical realism (flowing from the inner) on the one hand, and lyrical distancing on the other, that illuminates Strehler's claim that his 'vocation' as a director 'lies perhaps in finding a bridge ... between the teachings of Stanislavsky ... and those of Brecht'.[14] Where Brecht is concerned, *The Tempest* (1978) is a fine example in that it is rich in *Verfremdung* devices and their 'gestic effect', the first being Ariel 'hanging from a clearly visible wire ... which made clear from the start the relationship between Prospero and Ariel, between this master and this servant'.[15]

Stein's 1989 *Cherry Orchard*, staged at the Schaubühne to which he had returned for this production in a freelance capacity, is, by comparison, deeply rooted in the realism of setting and action, as might be expected of a director for whom textual exactitude is law – the legacy of his mentor, director Fritz Kortner, whom he had assisted in Munich in the mid 1960s. This applies to each and every production by Stein, as stressed most recently in 2011 by Maddalena Crippa, who has acted with him since 1989 and who was part of the Italian *Uncle Vanya* that Stein brought to the Edinburgh Festival in 1996. Stein by this time had settled in Italy, continuing to work freelance, and directing, among other things, an English-speaking *Blackbird* by the Scottish playwright David Harrower in 2005 for the Edinburgh Festival. Crippa observed that Stein's 'respect for the text, respect for the author' makes him 'go to the text like an archaeologist, with great care to understand what kind of text is at issue'; and he 'does not do this alone, but together with the actors so that they all have the same co-ordinates for the development of their respective characters'.[16] She affirmed, moreover, that 'he never tired of explaining the structure of a scene or an Act', or why an actor had wrongly accentuated a word, since his priority was the 'structure of the text' rather than directorial pyrotechnics. Stein, to emphasize his adherence to the text, asserted that he refused improvisations in rehearsals.[17]

> I do not want to see the *mise en scène* on stage, those kinds of ideas that make themselves important. I'm not interested in the director's art. What I do isn't modern theatre. I try to give Chekhov what he needs, not what I think would be fantastic for me.
>
> Stein, while directing *The Seagull* for the Edinburgh Festival[18]

Stein's archaeological approach shows in his painstaking research to get to the bottom of a text, but also to contextualize it completely both dramaturgically, by consulting available literature (in the case of Chekhov, Chekhov's stories, letters and other writings, and Stanislavsky's production plans), and socio-historically, by digging into archives and other documentation. All of it is veritable intellectual research, undertaken by a hugely erudite and cultivated director whose knowledge of foreign languages, not least of Russian, allows him to check the original sources in his search for the 'truth' of a text. He created an environment for *The Cherry Orchard* that was visually and emotionally recognizable, as he had done for *Uncle Vanya*, and further back, for his extraordinarily evocative *Summerfolk* (1974) by Gorky, in which he planted a forest of birch trees in soil on the stage: this has been described as his aim for 'reality rather than realism'.[19] He took his casts to Russia to places associated with Chekhov and Gorky so that they would fully feel how these life worlds were integral to the imaginative worlds they would perform. Such immersion, while in keeping with Stanislavsky's precepts for truthful acting, was also meant, by its binding shared experiences, to encourage ensemble playing – key to Stein's recall of Stanislavsky.

The Cherry Orchard, then, conjures up the domestic interiors caught with atmospheric simplicity by nineteenth-century Russian painters – spacious rooms, corridors, vestibules and long windows or door-windows in tawny and russet shades, with subdued curtains and wooden floors. Few objects adorn Stein's changing spaces from Act I to Act IV. There is an elegant couch beside the children's table and chairs in brown wood in Act I, and the cupboard, whose brown blends into the wall; seating back-to-back, as favoured in the nineteenth century for conversation, in Act III, which provides respite above all for Ranyevskaya from the ball, where dancing, when it does not flow out of the room in a chain dance in full view, can be glimpsed through three open doors going virtually from the ceiling to the floor; covered stacked shapes in Act IV.

Stein follows not only Chekhov's dialogue, but also his stage directions, carefully placing a billiard room, which is visible through a doorway, to stage right of where Ranyevskaya sits so as to bring out the rhythms of varied speech syncopated against the sound of balls being hit – rhythms to which Chekhov gives great attention. Ranyevskaya's position is equidistant between the billiard room and the ballroom, and this relates everyone in some way to her, whether they are in the background, playing billiards or dancing, or criss-cross her space in the foreground as they speak with her (Anya, Varya, Trofimov, and so on). Only Act II takes place outside, and here Stein has a hillside on which can be seen a bench, a small church and clumps of straw. Telegraph poles spike the horizon – as indicated by Chekhov's stage direction – and beyond them on Stein's cyclorama are hints of a distant town.

Props are few, but enough to offset the spaces around them and permit contrasts of position, movement and tempo between the characters, which indicate their emotional connections to, and disconnections from, each other. Act IV is particularly telling in this respect in the scene when Lopakhin is expected finally to propose to Varya. Stein usually marks action coming from and going somewhere quite decisively, and this, besides drawing the spatial perspectives that help to structure his productions, partly accounts for the strong sense of purpose that characteristically emanates from them. Varya rushes in from somewhere beyond a doorway, heading straight to the suitcases at some distance from her; and her purposefulness betrays her frustration and anxiety. She all but trips over one suitcase, looks into another and rummages about in a third, and puts off by her busyness an already reluctant lover who is confident in his new ownership of the estate and wants a lady of the house more than a housekeeper.

The scene is played crisply, with no hint of pathos, not even in the fleeting moment when Varya appears to offer her lips to Lopakhin, and, for a split second, it seems that he might just kiss her. The second passes, but there is no hint of comedy here, either. In his attentive, analytical way, Stein manages to have the actors communicate the emotional charge of the unarticulated, unresolved relationship between their characters. And typical of Stein's direction here is the space he allows spectators to observe and catch what is at stake. This is the respect he believes must be shown to spectators who, moreover, take from a show what is right for them – and they are always right, he maintains, even if they leave, dissatisfied, before its end.[20]

Stein's focus on precise detail of both acting and physical context extends to lighting and music. White fills the long windows of Act I from behind, suggesting the cherry orchard in blossom – noted in Chekhov's opening stage direction and referred to in dialogue. In Act II, light records day going to dusk, while in Act IV shutters drawn for departure shut out the day. Music for the ball of Act III is historically accurate, as is the series of ballads Epikhodov sings in Russian in Act II, accompanying himself on a guitar as he comes in and out from behind the hill. This Act, unlike the others, is episodically structured, its characters almost pointedly taking their scenes two by two and going out. Gradually, the entire picture with its obtrusive telegraph poles and its characters' timed exits and entrances looks hyper-real rather than merely real, strange in its exactitude. This effect was to recur in Stein's *Uncle Vanya*, highlighted when imaginary bird droppings, indicated only by the actor's gesture of looking upwards, suddenly makes the real of the stage seem totally fake. Stein directs Act II in this manner quite consciously, creating a Brechtian-style distancing effect, but, possibly, also engaging in an internal dialogue with Stanislavsky on constructions of reality.[21] He made a similarly hyper-real and reflexive gesture by unexpectedly producing a real-life car on the stage towards the end of *Blackbird*.

If this device permits stepping back, even to survey critically in the manner of Brecht – Stein was hardly immune to Brecht's legacy to the German theatre – it also has the punch of a *coup de théâtre*, precisely as had occurred at the very end of *The Cherry Orchard*: Firs emerges from a hidden corner in the dark and, after his last speech, a tree comes crashing in through the window to the sound of splintering wood and glass. The shock of the event cannot help but force spectators to consider how his masters had inadvertently, but cruelly, abandoned Firs after decades of his devoted service to them. But Stein's *coups de théâtre* do not always elicit critical reflection. In *The Broken Jug* by Kleist, for instance, which Stein directed for the Berliner Ensemble (2008), the punch has a different quality: the roof of Judge Adam's house lifts up into the flies (meanwhile he has jumped out of a window to escape retribution) to reveal him being chased around a tree by his victims in the snow. At this moment of closure, Stein turns his neatly crafted comedy of deceit into a children's picture book. *I Demoni* (2009) with Italian actors, which he adapted from Dostoevsky's eponymous novel, is different again, ending on a tragic note with a sudden pistol shot as Stavrogin kills himself. Stavrogin's death happens in the book, but nothing in Stein's production leads spectators to anticipate this conclusion.

Twelve hours long, *I Demoni* demonstrates Stein's capacity for holding attention in works on a large scale, which are only as long as he needs for his 'respect for the text' (Crippa above). Nothing is superfluous, whether in his early six-hour *Peer Gynt* (1971), his ten-hour *Oresteia* in Russian (1994, with his own acclaimed translation from Ancient Greek into German at hand), or his twenty-one hour *Faust*, performed at the Hanover Expo in 2000. Stein's directorial eye for scale resulted in riotous mob scenes in *Julius Caesar* (1992) performed by two hundred extras in modern dress on a 45-metre stage – a far cry from his *Cherry Orchard*, but his sense of the real on the verge of the hyper-real was right there.

Stein's may have been a retort to Brook's 1981 *Cherry Orchard*, where Brook avoids verisimilitude of setting, preferring the associative style that was customary at the Bouffes du Nord. The theatre itself, left by Brook in the dilapidated state in which he had found it in the early 1970s, albeit with some adjustments, was Ranyevskaya's house.[22] The Bouffes was Brook's ideal 'empty space', the nearest thing to Shakespeare's theatre, as he perceived it, and his model for a place where spectators conceived the whole life of a performance in their imagination. The doors of the playing space were opened and closed, but gave no depth or perspective. Performance was in the central, open space and occasionally went upwards to the stairs against the back wall, and, in Act IV, to the first and third balconies of the theatre; the latter balcony served Anya as an attic. An armchair and a few chairs made their appearance in Acts I and III (and a cupboard in Act I). Otherwise the actors sat on the floor in various positions, sometimes stretched out, as well – trademarks, by now, of Brook's directing. All in all, Brook used his space organically, as he had begun to do with *Timon of Athens*, which had inaugurated the Bouffes in 1974.

Several screens broke up the space for the ball scene of Act III, which they purportedly hid from view. As in Strehler's production, there was no dancing to be seen, and the music was also periodic, seemingly coming from behind the screens. Stein's orchestra, by contrast, played virtually non-stop, holding its own against speech in what was a polyphonic composition.

Brook concentrated on streamlining in every respect and especially as regards the acting, which was natural, non-theatrical, unforced. If this recalls Stanislavsky, it is crucial to observe that, unlike Stanislavsky, he did not provide an environment to sustain the actors; further, his pace was fast, contrary to that of Stanislavsky's 1904 production of *The Cherry Orchard*, which, like Stein's, took well over three hours to perform.

In the bare walls of the Bouffes, the actors, together with the spectators, had to imagine what the words referred to but was not shown (the cherry orchard, the telegraph poles, and so forth); and, because they had to spin everything out of themselves, as if spontaneously – this was part of the 'natural' of playing, which Stanislavsky had also sought – their performance was lively and fresh. Yet, although the onus was on the actors to do the work – the key to Brook's directing, which was enabling, regardless of his reservations about 'knowing' directors (see box) – they were helped, nevertheless, to get hold of their characters by their exquisite, simple costumes. Designed by Chloe Obolensky, these costumes evoked the turn of the twentieth century without detracting attention away from the play.

The director as imposter

It is a strange role, that of the director: he does not ask to be God and yet his role implies it. He wants to be fallible, and yet an instinctive conspiracy of the actors is to make him the arbiter, because an arbiter is so desperately wanted all the time. In a sense the director is always an imposter, a guide at night who does not know the territory, and yet has no choice – he must guide, learning the route as he goes.
The Empty Space, 43–4

Helpful, too, in orienting the actors was the Persian carpet that covered the floor. This carpet – if a movable feast, gracing *Conference of the Birds* (1975) and *Pelléas et Mélisande* (1993), Brook's heavily pruned and piano-accompanied version (instead of full orchestra) of Debussy's opera – implied for *The Cherry Orchard* a house that had known better days. A carpet of whatever shape or size in each production has, since, become Brook's signature. In *Hamlet* (2000), for instance, a small, bright orange rectangular rug served the purpose of 'carpet'. In *A Magic Flute* (2010), after Mozart, in another of Brook's pared-away operas, the 'carpet' is a symbolic gesture in the form of a shawl thrown on the floor for sitting; and this patch of bright colour, when it happens, throws into relief the strangely mysterious 'forest' of fine vertical metal rods that, in their abstract, non-representational quality, serve as markers of various different places throughout the production's narrative, as, indeed, does the carpet in most of Brook's works.

The point, for Brook, was that a carpet signified storytelling, the principal vocation of theatre, in his view, which he tested in his 1972–73 journeys to Africa with a team of actors.[23] Wherever they travelled, the actors laid down a carpet as a signal to villagers that a story was about to be told (performed); and the experiences of these carpet shows – the proof, to Brook's mind, that stories well told could communicate across cultures – remained firm in Brook's direction hereafter, most notably in how he stripped down plays to their fundamental

13 *A Magic Flute* (Bouffes du Nord), Peter Brook, 2010

storyline and used the most economic of means to perform it. The presence of a carpet in his productions thus had particular resonance, involving, as well, Brook's idea that the theatre was an intimate relationship between performers and spectators. It was to this end that the Bouffes du Nord's playing space was made to be a semi-circle on the same level as the spectators, the closest of whom sat on cushions, cheek by jowl with the performers.

Storytelling, intimacy, natural acting and unadorned action – these basic principles of Brook's directing were at the heart of *The Cherry Orchard*, facilitated by the spatial organization of the Bouffes, which he reproduced in the theatres where his productions were performed on tour, or had specially built for him. Brook's improvisation techniques (see Chapter 7) helped the actors, in the words of his assistant on the production, 'to move and react through the text in complete freedom', a quality evident, for instance, when Lopakhin tells Ranyevskaya that he has bought her cherry orchard, not quite daring to look into her eyes.[24] Niels Arestrup in the role sweeps joyfully across the space before Lopakhin's excitement overcomes him and he jubilantly orders the (invisible) orchestra to play; Natasha Parry as Ranyevskaya turns her head in profile and weeps.

The dialogue adapted by Jean-Claude Carrière, Brook's long-term collaborator, sounds like normal speech, thereby countering the extant literary-sounding French translations, which betray Chekhov's straightforward *spoken* Russian. Carrière had the language come off the tongue like contemporary French, much as he had done with Shakespeare's English in *Timon of Athens*. However, he and Brook refrained from making the kind of major cuts that had simplified the plot and content of *Timon*, as of the remaining Bouffes Shakespeare productions, *The Tempest* (1990) and *Hamlet*.[25] Brook sought revitalization for Chekhov on the stage, as he did for Shakespeare, which, in his view, could only be achieved through deliberate intervention.

> When I hear a director speaking glibly of serving the author, of letting a play speak for itself, my suspicions are aroused, because this is the hardest job of all. If you just let a play speak, it may not make a sound. If what you want is for the play to be heard, then you must conjure its sound from it. This demands many deliberate actions and the result may have great simplicity. However, setting out to be 'simple' can be quite negative, an easy evasion of exacting steps to the simple answer.
> *The Empty Space*, 43

Lev Dodin and Anatoli Vassiliev: continuing Stanislavsky's principles

Dodin and Vassiliev are inevitably steeped in the Stanislavsky tradition, given that the cult of Stanislavsky propagated during Stalin's regime held fast in the 1960s, their formative years. Yet they are thus immersed primarily because their respective teachers – Zon for Dodin and Knebel for Vassiliev (noted in Chapter 2) – came in an unbroken line from Stanislavsky, transmitting to them, orally and by physical demonstration, the fundamentals of their teacher's teachings. Not only had Zon and Knebel made the latter their own, but Dodin and Vassiliev were to do the same, for only in this way could heirs to Stanislavsky avoid the deathly grip of his canonization and find what was alive in his work; and only in this way could each produce, from the same source, his/her different and distinctive theatre. Knebel was considered by her contemporaries to be a remarkable director, as well as an exceptional pedagogue, and her pupil Vassiliev, while absorbing her heritage, together with her heritage from Stanislavsky, rejected psychological realism without rejecting Stanislavsky. Dodin, by contrast, embraced that realism, excavating the inner recesses of the human heart, which, he believes, is the very subject of the theatre as such.

Dodin – director-pedagogue

Dodin first learned about that most quintessential of Stanislavsky's precepts, the necessity of an ensemble, from the teacher of his early youth, Matvey Dubrovin, who had learned from Meyerhold; and, as Dodin observes, 'Meyerhold himself was a pupil of Stanislavsky.'[26] In the course of his training as an actor and director in St Petersburg, before his fifth and final director-training year, he came to the conclusion that Vakhtangov's model of the continuum school-studio-company – a variation on Stanislavsky's idea of the optimal conditions for actor development – was the most organic and efficient way of building up and sustaining an ensemble.[27] Thus Dodin integrated into the Maly Drama Theatre, after he became its artistic director in 1983, his pupils at the St Petersburg Academy of Theatre Arts, as it is known today. *Gaudeamus* (1990), which was their graduation production, together with *Claustrophobia*, devised by the same group four years later, constituted what was called a 'student' ensemble within the company, and was, in effect, Dodin's 'studio', the base for their collective experimentation.[28]

Yet, 'student' was inaccurate since most of this third generation of Dodin's Academy pupils destined for the Maly had graduated, and a good number of them were performing with company actors in *The Devils* (1991, from the same Dostoevsky novel as Stein's *I Demoni*). Later, in the 2000s, Dodin simply cast his pupils in major roles straightaway, alongside the experienced Maly actors: this was the case for Lear's daughters in *King Lear* (2006) and for both male and female roles in *Life and Fate* (2007), devised by the company from Vasily Grossman's novel. His reasoning was that the trainee actors should be challenged by demanding roles and by their interaction with the older actors, both spurred on by each other to make new discoveries.[29]

Where the idea of the studio was concerned, Dodin was finally able to realize his goal in 1999, when a refurbished space was dedicated to small-scale experimental work directed by the Maly actors who had trained, or were still training, as directors with Dodin. In Dodin's pedagogical system, as generally in Russia, prospective directors undertake the actors' course (previously four years, five in the later 2000s, at Dodin's behest) before studying for an additional year to become directors. Dodin prizes pedagogy, which he sees as a matter not so much of 'teaching' as of 'possibilities to learn', and claims that he 'would have been finished both as a director and a human being long ago' without it.[30]

As this implies, Dodin the director cannot be separated from Dodin the pedagogue. Everything that makes up his school – shared values, perceptions, thoughts, attitudes and objectives, as well as methods of training, skills and techniques – provides a common 'language' for the Maly and is the very material, embodied by his actors, with which he directs. This 'language' binds the company, making it an ensemble in the strongest sense of the word. Similarly, it integrates Dodin in the group without diminishing his status as its leader, as the term 'director' has indisputably implied in Russian culture since Stanislavsky. This 'language' is continually maintained by the voice, dance and music teachers, who, having taught the former students at the Academy, train them, together with the entire company, as they rehearse and when they are on tour. Training, in other words, never stops, and, for Dodin, actors must train their entire life.[31] Such training is integral to their growth not only as artists, but also as human beings, since the dimensions of their artistry are tied to their dimensions as living beings. This process of learning and change, this 'journey without end', which is Dodin's mantra, is, for him, the very condition of the theatre – and so, too, of the director – as of life itself.

It is in rehearsals where Dodin's directing has particular force because of their length, intensity and improvisational method. *A Play with No Name* (1997), after Chekhov's *Platonov*, underwent some five years of work with *études*, much of it with the *Gaudeamus* cast while the production was on tour.[32] In 1996, the company began to analyse the play, during which time the actors tried out roles and scenes according to the Maly ethos of working on their feet. As Dodin observes: 'We never break down a text without trying it out . . . [and] we must check everything that we find with probes' [*proby*].[33] Dodin also participated in the process, as he usually does, checking findings against himself as an actor and checking again on the actors as a director; he does not tell them what to do, but will suggest what might be worth trying out. As a director, he gradually cuts, culls, selects and puts bits and scenes together and, then, eventually, the whole piece. The continual flow of improvisation in *études*, together with the constant change generated by an open imagination sharing the same 'language', accounts to a large degree for the organicity of the work, upheld by Dodin's – call it –'editing' directorial method in which he seeks the beating pulse of what is being worked. Dodin's task is to keep a watch so that this organic, living quality is never lost for a moment in the production that is finally performed to audiences.

A Play with No Name was premiered in Weimar – a testimony, in the production's six and more years of development, to Dodin's by then established practice of letting a work absorb the layers and layers of tries or probes that go into its making over time. But Dodin pitches his sights to Stanislavsky's 'discovery' that 'theatre is a constant search for the ideal, a striving for perfection'.[34] Dissatisfied with sections of *A Play with No Name*, Dodin deleted them from the production on the very eve of its premiere in Weimer. He reworked it again in St Petersburg because he found its ending too abrupt. In the Weimer version, the performance ends with Platonov sprawled on stairs at the edge of a lake of water in which, throughout the performance, the actors dive, swim, dialogue and play musical instruments. The St Petersburg version ends with the same image, but is followed by one of harmony in which the protagonists, other than Platonov, sit still at a table on a platform while cleansing rain falls. This tableau alternates three times with blackouts, closing a tragedy of disoriented people with a vision of community and hope. The effect is powerful, like an aftershock, which is not unique to this production. The six-hour long *Brothers and Sisters* (1985), the first of Dodin's 'theatre of prose', heralded what has since become a familiar trait of Dodin's direction – his capacity to build up a ground swell of intense emotion that, while ebbing and flowing from scene to scene, hits spectators with full force just as a production draws to its end, or has just finished.[35]

Not all Dodin's productions have as long a gestation period as *A Play with No Name*. *King Lear*, Dodin's first Shakespeare production, only took two years of preparation, allowing, in the customary Maly manner, various actors to play the same role until Dodin makes his choice (Dodin rarely casts before rehearsals begin). *Uncle Vanya* (2003), on the other hand, took only three months, as did *The Three Sisters* (2010); and Dodin accounts for this relative speed by saying that the company had been so profoundly immersed in Chekhov's universe that *Uncle Vanya* came to them quickly. *The Three Sisters* was subsequently to benefit from their accrued experience.[36] Moreover this production had so deeply absorbed the company's principles of acting as regards internally focused emotion, so suitable for Chekhov, that it is physically minimalist, all action being in the intensity of the emotions themselves.

It must be remembered that the 'universe' to which Dodin refers concerns not only the long haul of *A Play with No Name*, which, being in repertory, was consistently performed (and still is, as is *Uncle Vanya*), but also *The Cherry Orchard* (1994) and *The Seagull* (2001). It ought to be observed that Dodin's *The Cherry Orchard* is the dark counterpart of Strehler's white production. Screen-windows, like triptych icons, have dark panes to which branches of cherry tree are attached from behind, and they shape the space. Dodin directs his actors in this sombre setting, fixed until the end, to play seamlessly so that each action-event initiates the next. Thus, for example, a rifle shot from an eccentric, whimsical Charlotta sparks off and immediately merges into the laughter and music of the ball. Dodin regularly seeks this type of chain-effect when he puts together the performance material generated in rehearsals.

One of Dodin's major directorial principles concerns the maturation of a work, and this means that his directing is ongoing: no production in the repertoire is

14 *The Three Sisters*, Lev Dodin, Maly Drama Theatre of St Petersburg, 2010

finished and done with. Contrary to Meyerhold, who said a production begins to die the minute it goes on the stage, Dodin believes that its real birth starts with this very moment.[37] From here on, the production grows, mutating with the actors' growth as artists and people. The salient example of this symbiosis is *Brothers and Sisters*, which, in its twenty-fifth year in repertory, is still performed by many of the actors who first played in it. Some have matured physically into their roles, now being closer to the age of their characters. Others have become older than their characters, but play them with the freshness that comes from complete ease in a role. In all cases, however, their performances benefit from what might be called the hindsight of experience – the experience the actors have accumulated along the way playing Chekhov and Shakespeare, which colours *Brothers and Sisters* differently.[38] Dodin channels the nuances they bring, without changing the structure and overall 'drawing' of the work.

The maturation undergone by *Brothers and Sisters* enhanced the physical and emotional vitality of an already intoxicating piece, which ends on an elegiac note as imaginary cranes fly past in the sky. In the case of *Uncle Vanya*, maturation brought out the production's tragic undertow, a quality that Dodin had nurtured during rehearsals without forcing it into the open. In one of its funniest scenes, Vanya, who is clutching a bunch of flowers for Yelena, Serebryakov's wife, comes upon Astrov kissing her. Five years into the production's life, a moment that had blatantly exploited vaudeville was now still funny, but was also impregnated with deep pain: that of Vanya's unrequited love for Yelena, Yelena's sublimated love for Astrov and Sonya's hopeless love for Astrov. It also showed Yelena's involuntary avowal of her feelings when, a few seconds before discovery, she unexpectedly kisses Astrov. Dodin had retained this action from *proby*, while eliminating others, but it took time and countless performances before it yielded its full potential. And the fact that he kept it demonstrates Dodin's keen sense, as a director, of dramatic turn-around. Five years on, the same moment also captured Vanya's terrible insight into the waste that was his life. Dodin and the actors prised open this existential dimension of Chekhov's play after *King Lear*, where Sergey Kuryshev (Vanya) and Pyotr Semak (Astrov) perform Gloucester and Lear, respectively, and plumb the depths of Shakespeare's riddles on existence.

Continuity and close proximity make Dodin's and the Maly's relations like those of a family, and, in the footsteps of Stanislavsky, along with other Russian directors, he speaks of his 'theatre-home'. But he also sees himself, as a director, as someone who undertakes an expedition whose end point is not clear at the outset (see box).

Who are you as a director?

I like to know, to think, to get to know the theatre, and I seek to draw the company into this knowing. Some sort of leadership arises from this act of drawing people into an expedition. It's a relatively risky thing because ... you are drawing people in when you yourself do not know the road or where you will arrive. Yet, it seems that everyone must assume that you know both the road *and* the destination. If the road changes, then everyone has to see it as a discovery and not as a defeat...

Many underlying aspects emerge from your being a director. You become a pedagogue, an organizer, a friend, a psychologist and often a psychiatrist because the profession has its maladies and sometimes you have to have real insight into why somebody finds a task difficult; and people's lives are complex.

Lev Dodin, *Directors/Directing*, 61

Vassiliev's laboratory

Anatoli Vassiliev shares with Dodin the view that actors must work on a text in actual space and on their feet, rather than analyse it intellectually before they start to act. This is fundamental to the Method of Physical Action elaborated by Stanislavsky in his last studio, the Opera-Dramatic Studio (1935–38), in which Knebel had participated. What distinguishes Knebel from her colleagues at the Studio is the fact that she clarified and *systematized* Stanislavsky's Method of Physical Action for her directing students at GITIS (State Institute of Theatre Art), among whom, from 1968 to 1973, was Vassiliev; and she adapted it as 'Action Analysis', thus putting her stamp on the approach. What distinguishes Vassiliev from directors contemporary to him in Russia, Dodin included, is his own systematization of everything that he had learned from Knebel. He was to systematize, as well, everything he was to learn from his research, for which teaching actors was indispensable. More than any other director, Vassiliev is a rigorous theoretical thinker, formulating his method in theoretical terms in strict conjunction with practical work. His conditions for this type of research are those of a laboratory and a monastery in one, entailing years of seclusion, with few demonstrations and workshops to show the research, and even fewer productions. These productions, like their director, are unthinkable without the long process of pedagogical, collaborative research.

Vassiliev made his reputation in Moscow with several productions in the 1970s, but it was *Cerceau*, staged at the Taganka Theatre in 1985, after three years of rehearsal, that was a major breakthrough in his attempts to put psychological realism behind him. The play was written by Victor Slavkin in collaboration with Vassiliev, and its theme was not so much the search for happiness as the attraction of this very idea. Several people randomly meet in a house inherited by Petushok from his grandmother. They read her letters and imagine her vanished world, symbolized by the game of hoopla that they play, twirling and tossing illuminated rings from the end of sticks. They also imagine that they can live together peacefully in a community, until their utopian dream vanishes when they discover that the house does not, in fact, belong to Petushok, and is bought by one of their group. Their failed quest does end, however, not on a nostalgic note, but on a graceful, matter-of-fact one that implies acceptance. This is 'fate' without fatalism.

Vassiliev's spatial arrangement was unusual – an oblong house at a slant, placed towards the centre-back of the stage, which allowed spectators to see the actors through its windows. The performance was light and elegant as the actors sat, talked, read, laughed and played without too much emotional investment, which, in turn, curtailed any potentially excessive empathy on the part of spectators. The magic that they generated contributed to the production's diaphanous beauty, defined by the *Times* critic, Jeremy Kingston, when *Cerceau* started its two-year international tour in London, as 'lighting up the world' (17 July 1987). Vassiliev, in order to achieve this lightness of being, had initially asked his actors, when rehearsing, to dance their parts. The point was to avoid the tensions and conflicts to which the actors, steeped in realistic theatre, automatically tended to revert. Yet he had used the method of *études*, the mainstay of psychological realism and, as well, of Knebel's Action Analysis. In Vassiliev's practice, this method can be summed up as follows: the actors quickly agree on what they will be doing, but this must be related to the text to be worked on actively, in action; they do it; they come back together to assess; they do it again; and so on, until they have gone through the whole text. Vassiliev's intention, in using *études*, was to have the actors grasp the processes of textual composition. '*Etudes*', he says, 'are training in dramatic construction.'[39]

Cerceau could be seen as Vassiliev's test case for what he calls 'play structures' or 'ludic structures', which he differentiates from 'psychological structures' with their focus on characters, mimetic behaviours, social situations, actor identification and/or symbiosis with character, and so on.[40] He set about exploring his new method in the School of Dramatic Art, which he founded in 1987, bringing to it the ensemble of *Cerceau*. The School's course of five years was destined not for beginners (as was Dodin's programme at the Academy in St Petersburg), but for trained actors, a number of whom had already worked in the theatre. It was effectively a master class, and it encompassed Vassiliev's Pirandello period (1987–91) which, incorporating *Six Characters in Search of an Author*, the School's inaugural production, led to occasional workshop demonstrations while maintaining its laboratory-monastery vocation.

It was in 1991 that Vassiliev with a group of his actors, who were 'unveiling' their research in Italy, spent time at Grotowski's Workcenter in Pontedera.

And that Vassiliev should claim Grotowski as his last mentor is significant. (In Russia, apart from Knebel, his mentors were his other GITIS teacher Andrey Popov and the directors Oleg Efremov and Anatoly Efros). It not only signposts his own commitment to laboratory work, together with the ensemble principle that laboratory practice necessarily implies, but also suggests his attitude to directing, that is, as a spin-off of research rather than its purpose.[41] Research, in other words, has priority over directing. Even so, unlike Grotowski, who had abandoned directing altogether, Vassiliev was to continue making productions, however infrequently, the last of which, counting retrospectively from 2011, was *Uncle's Dream*, after Dostoevsky's novel, in Budapest in 2009.

Six Characters in Search of an Author was a perfect vehicle for Vassiliev's 'ludic structures', and the following, briefest of summaries of his theoretical-practical principles, while drawing on the above production, holds for subsequent productions up to and including *Uncle's Dream*; and the synopsis is relevant, regardless of Vassiliev's considerable shift in genre (although not of underlying principles) with *The Lamentations of Jeremiah*, premiered in Moscow in 1996. Five main points defining 'ludic structures' need to be observed. First, the very subject matter of *Six Characters in Search of an Author* – the existence of characters *outside* an author, who ask this author to imagine them – corresponds to Vassiliev's search for actors who find their characters outside themselves rather than from within their inner psycho-emotional constitution. In other words, the Vassiliev actor invents images rather than reconstructs sensations for characters from within 'affective memory'. Vassiliev's affinity, on this point, is with Mikhaïl Chekhov, who had profoundly disagreed with Stanislavsky, insisting on the crucial importance of having images come, like visitations, to actors.

Second, in 'ludic structures' character and actor are two separate entities: the fusion between them typical of the Stanislavsky actor is thus impossible. Freed from psycho-emotional bonds, the Vassiliev actor is able to step outside his/her character, although not in Meyerhold's sense of 'de-familiarization', or Brecht's *Verfremdung*, but for the sake of playful creativity and playfulness as regards this character: hence Vassiliev's emphasis on the ludic rather than representational quality of playing.

Third, the very notion of 'character' is put into question – and this is central to *Six Characters* – since psychological definition, development and conflict, which are quintessential to 'psychological structures', no longer pertain. In 'ludic structures' actors do not incarnate people, but, paraphrasing Vassiliev, are meant to incarnate ideas.[42] They are not this particular mother, or father, or daughter – Pirandello's dramatis personae in *Six Characters* – but figures, and so ideas, incarnate of Mother, Father, Daughter. These actors, since they are no longer obliged to enter into the hearts and minds of 'real' people, can hold back from their performances, as a 'tease' might do when promising to give more than is actually delivered. Spectators, in this kind of playfulness, are also held back so as to observe the play with greater lucidity.

None of this is to say that 'ludic structures' are devoid of emotion. Emotion here is neither emotive nor expressive. What Vassiliev is after – and this is the fourth point to be noted – is a contained internal process ('the way in which a role can be realized') that is more or less invisible, but sustains everything that is externalized in play.[43] He, the director, pulls the internalized and the externalized aspects together (see box); and he does this by intentionally and systematically inverting Stanislavsky's approach to texts. Stanislavsky always started from the 'initiating event', working his way through a text to its end point in the 'principal event'. Vassiliev always starts with the 'principal event', working his way backwards. As a consequence, since everything is seen from the end point and thus known from the beginning, he and his actors are able to by-pass the exploration of character, the conflict between characters, and the linear development of cause and effect fundamental to 'psychological structures'. Everything, then, is held off – outside, at a distance – because the stakes are connected not to life, but to how composition is composed. In other words, the actors play what they know as a piece of composition, as *art*, and not as a paradigm for life.

The director's craft

For me, the director's craft begins with the study of internal movements. Finding the reason, constructing the genesis of play, giving the code [and] the rules – all this comes from the act of creation. Analysis of internal structure gives birth to conditions, form. The director is the person who engenders the fruit. Someone who is sterile cannot become a director.

The process of creation occurs in two stages. The first concerns the internal life of a role. The second concerns its external life. Then the two are put together.

The director sees what is hidden in a text; he reveals it: it is like a leaf through which the rays of the sun shine, and all its filaments appear. Then he transmits these hidden characteristics to the actors. It is up to the actor to play all that – that is his craft, but if he has another idea, let him follow it.

Anatoli Vassiliev, while directing Mikhaïl Lermontov's *Masked Ball*[44]

Vassiliev's concern not with the life-social force of theatre, but with its art and aesthetics yielded, in *Six Characters in Search of an Author*, experimentation with space. Actors and spectators occupied exactly the same space, some actors performing sitting among spectators, others standing closely beside them, and still others speaking dialogue across them. All of this ambiguously implied both

15 *Six Characters in Search of an Author* Anatoli Vassiliev, 1987

the collapse of the 'fourth wall' and an even more radical erection of it, since the actors' exclusive focus on each other, together with their highly stylized play, shut spectators out completely. Furthermore, this paradox generated a sense of mystery, of something that was there but transcended everyday reality because, ultimately, it was out of reach. In this respect, Vassiliev was already anticipating his quasi-sacred *The Lamentations of Jeremiah*, where monk-like hooded figures in gentle groupings repeated movements ritualistically, now chanting, now in silence, the whole belonging to the Mysteries of antiquity or of the Middle Ages, or to some sort of non-denominational liturgy. Vassiliev the director, in this arcane, anonymous universe, seemed to have all but disappeared, replaced not only by a theatre ensemble but, in addition, by a veritable, seemingly self-propelled *community* – as, indeed, any congregation is a community – although he had trained and watched over it, and had created a composition with it.

Meanwhile, in the earlier 1990s,Vassiliev had begun to work with actors on Plato's dialogues so as to explore better his conception of the non-character, the figure-idea incarnate. The dialogues provided Vassiliev with philosophical argument and the interchange of reasoned ideas by speakers interested only in the impersonal debate between them. By focusing on what they offered as thought, he also foregrounded the significance of the Word. He shifted accentuation and intonation, stressing first syllables when normal speech would stress the second or third, and found countless other means through diction and vocal rhythm, cadence and punctuation to transform and even disfigure normal speech patterns. This intense verbal work resulted in workshops based on Plato and productions as different as *Mozart and Salieri* by Pushkin (2000), *Medea Material* by Heiner Müller (2001), *The Iliad, Twenty-Third Canto* by Homer (2004) and *Medea* by Euripides (2008).

Apart from the fact that the Word here reigned supreme – the contours of words were so pronounced as to make them appear hewn in stone – these productions were united by their luminous visual beauty (configuration of bodies, space, light, costume) and their beauty of movement: *The Iliad*, for instance, was shaped by t'ai chi and dance sequences that were like incantations in movement rather than in sound. It was clear from their highly 'finished' quality that Vassiliev had fashioned these productions with the patience and care of a director who was a master craftsman. It was just as clear, most notably in the methodically acquired vocal range, agility, pulsation and vibration of Valérie Dreville, the prominent French actress whom he had trained in Moscow to perform *Medea Material*, her every word a rock flung out to kill, why Vassiliev claims that the 'best directors' seek to 'control the method concerned with the process of playing'.[45]

Katie Mitchell and Declan Donnellan: adapting Russian ideals of ensemble

British directors do not have the opportunities open to Vassiliev to train actors thoroughly in specific ways of performing ('method concerned with the process of playing'). This is so mostly because British theatre culture has not been conducive to the development of schools in which such methods can be elaborated. Nor has the Stanislavsky model of ensemble practice within a permanent repertory company taken root. The idea of such an ensemble, envisaged early in the twentieth century by Granville Barker, partially pursued in mid-century by Brook, as well as by Peter Hall, who had founded the Royal Shakespeare Company with these goals in mind, and re-appropriated by Mitchell and Donnellan at the end of the century, has been more of an *ideal* than a concrete reality.

It was precisely because of her need to grasp the workings of 'ensemble' and how directors operated within such a system that Mitchell undertook a five-month study tour in 1989 to Russia, Poland, Lithuania and Georgia.[46] The latter two countries were well versed, at the time, in the precepts of Russian theatre, which were part of the cultural hegemony of Soviet political control. In Russia, Mitchell had access to Vassiliev's School of Dramatic Art, and was able to observe Dodin in action with the young actors of his school. Dodin was her conduit to Stanislavsky's teachings, from which, she claims, come most of her 'tools'.[47] It must be said that she adapted and modified Stanislavsky, and interpreted Dodin's teaching in class as well, according to her lights, updating what she took from them both as she went. In Poland, she worked with Wlodzimierz Staniewski and his group Gardzienice, which he had formed in 1976, after he left Grotowski. His, like Grotowski's, were ensemble principles that were not bound by texts or representational theatre. Text and representation, on the other hand, were integral to Mitchell's directorial idiom, and they have remained to this day, regardless of her more recent interest in Pina Bausch, who is well and truly an ensemble choreographer-director. She continued her acquisition of Stanislavskian 'tools', mainly through director Elen Bowman, a pupil of Sam Kogan, who had been a pupil of Knebel at GITIS and who founded, in London, the School of the Science of Acting in 1991. She learned from Tatyana Olear, an actor in Dodin's company, who ran workshops on her visits to the capital.[48] Mitchell was, in addition, influenced by Mike Alfreds, another 'Stanislavskian' British director committed to the idea of permanent ensemble companies.

Mitchell moulded the Russian ensemble ideal to the conditions available to her by casting as many of the same actors as suitable over time. Take, for instance, Kate Duchêne who performed in her *Iphigenia at Aulis* by Euripides (2004), *Waves*, devised from the novel by Virginia Woolf (2006), *Attempts on her Life* by Martin Crimp (2007), her second version of *Women of Troy* also by Euripides (2007, the first in 1991), and *A Woman Killed with Kindness* by Thomas Heywood (2011). Yet even relative continuity of this kind has not always proved possible; and Mitchell has essentially been obliged to adapt the idea of 'ensemble', focusing on actors, to that of a stable production 'team' of stage-designer Vicki Mortimer, lighting designer Paula Constable and sound designer Gareth Fry. Where actors are concerned, she is well aware, sometimes painfully, that they come from different acting horizons and that she must accommodate these as efficiently as she can while striving for the unity necessary for a successful production. From this stems the urgency of her instruction to young directors in *The Director's Craft* to introduce 'the actors to your language from the first day of rehearsals and stick to that language until the last night'.[49] In the absence of a common language, verbal as well as in terms of artistic training, it is imperative, she believes, that a director be absolutely clear as to what he/she means; and this is a rule that she follows strictly (see box).

> Actors will walk into your rehearsal room speaking many different languages about their craft. These languages will reflect their training and working experience. When you introduce them to your language (and the process it describes), do not do so in a way that suggests it is the only way of talking about acting because it is not. Rather, assure them it is one of many languages but that these words will help everyone work together if they all agree to use it for the duration of the job.
>
> Katie Mitchell, *The Director's Craft*, 125

Among Mitchell's 'tools' is the basic one she calls 'back history' with which she helps actors to construct biographies for their characters.[50] Taking *The Seagull* as her case study, she advises actors to separate their material into 'facts' and 'questions'. The aim, when they compile each list, is not to confuse what can be verified through the text with what is not clear from it and needs further research. 'Facts', Mitchell maintains, 'are the non-negotiable elements of the text. They are the main clues that the writer gives you about the play.'[51] Questions, by contrast, 'are a way of notating the areas of the text that are less clear or that you are simply not sure of', and she proceeds to demonstrate by asking what had happened to Konstantin's father and where Sorin's estate was in Russia. Mitchell's could be described as a pragmatic approach, and indeed her own production of *The Seagull* shows a director concerned with neatly ordered actions, reactions, movements and consequences – so much so that the logic of her exposition of actions, and so forth, looks like a series of practical solutions to problems that she had set beforehand. The production, in other words, is not so much organic as predetermined, and concentrated on what she calls, citing Chekhov as her example, her 'forensic' attention to detail.[52]

'Forensic' is apt for Mitchell's way of directing because she is interested, above all, in behaviour – in how characters actually behave in different circumstances rather than in how they emotionally experience their situation or relation to others in that situation. Consequently, although she draws, in rehearsals, on Stanislavsky's idea of 'affective memory', she is interested less in the affective aspects of the tasks the actors carry out – thus less interested in the interior life of characters – and more in the visibility of the mechanics of their bodies. The example she selects from *Iphigenia at Aulis* is telling in that, when asking 'the actors to think of a situation in their own lives when they were afraid', she asked them to observe 'how the actors' bodies behaved as the frightening stimulus hit them'.[53] Her emphasis, during rehearsals, on 'people's physicality' rather than on 'psychological analysis', which she actively discourages, was incarnated on the stage in the sharp jumps and jolts of the actors articulating fear, among them Duchêne as Clytemnestra. Mitchell confirms her intention to make such behaviours quite noticeable when she points out that the 'physical frame' she had devised for Achilles for the moment when he was told he was to be married was 'a three-metre leap backwards in surprise at the news'.[54] In other words, what mattered here was the *physiological* reaction to a stimulus. Mitchell puts it succinctly when she specifies that she is after the 'precise physical shape of a certain emotion'.[55]

It is in this area of dispassionate 'science' that she places the younger Stanislavsky whom she prioritizes – the Stanislavsky who had read the physiologist-psychologists Théodule Ribot and William James in order to understand better the workings of emotions so as to teach his actors how to convey feelings more accurately. But she goes beyond this to the writings of neuroscientist Antonio Domasio who 'defines an emotion as a change in the body'.[56] Achilles' 'three-metre leap backwards' illustrates how Mitchell had absorbed Domasio's research,

She follows up Domasio's investigations in *A Woman Killed with Kindness*, where tempi are widely disparate as characters walk up and down stairs and in and out of doors, all in counterpoint. It is evident in this production that Mitchell had directed her actors to move at a tempo that corresponded to the bodily changes their characters were presumed to be undergoing in response to whatever stimulus – word, event, threat – had triggered off the change. At one particular point, then, the adulterous wife of Heywood's play meanders down the stairs while her lover saunters about at ground level, her servant scurries towards a back door and various others, snappy males who appear to be clones of her husband, hurry out of rooms on the upper floor to descend rapidly down the stairs. The effect is quite surrealistic, and is reminiscent of *A Dream Play* (2005) – Strindberg re-written by Caryl Churchill – with its Bausch-like, dance-like sequences. Elsewhere, as in *Waves*, or *Attempts on her Life*, or *After Dido* (2009) based on the opera *Dido and Aeneas* by Henry Purcell, Mitchell is a director adept in technology. She uses film cameras, video cameras, sound recordings (as for a radio play) and multiple screens, often simultaneously, to bring what faces and bodies are doing close up, as they are being filmed. These are behaviours under a microscope, one might say, and reflect her meticulous and patient approach.

The director as long-term thinker

Rehearsals should allow the actors to build things step by step over time, gradually and slowly. The mind skills required from the director are patience and long-term thinking. Even if you are rehearsing for only two weeks, the process should be one that evolves carefully and gently. It is like building a house in which different materials are laid down layer by layer from the foundations to the roof. The materials must be put into place carefully and in logical order, or the building will not

> stand up properly . . . Actors need time to build their characters and to practise what they have to do in the scenes. They cannot always respond to an instruction with an immediate solution or result. If you wait a couple of days you may well see the outcome unfold. If not, simply keep giving the instructions until it does. Similarly, if there is a problem in the scene, do not think you have to solve it in one go. Instead, chip away at it over time.
>
> Katie Mitchell, *The Director's Craft*, 115

Mitchell's concern with the behavioural surface of both characters and actors has little in common with Donnellan's attention to their 'outside'. Donnellan's 'outside' is a matter not of behaviour but of seeing – of an actor really seeing what the character needs from his/her partner and letting spectators see what that is. Very often, this translates, in Donnellan's directing, into spacing the actors out so that they are physically at some distance from each other, all the better to see and be seen, the eyes leading to what is at stake between them. His 'outside' is opposed to the psycho-emotional 'inside' that might motivate characters, and, in his step away from introspection, from the 'I' of the actor and the 'I' of the director, he takes a step away from Stanislavsky and the latter's preoccupation, even compulsive preoccupation, with emotional density and the means for expressing it. Donnellan's goal for his productions is emotional lightness, which has to do not with superficiality or lack of substance, but with a lightness of touch that brings forth comedy, pathos and tragedy but is captive to none.

Donnellan does not speak of such lightness in *The Actor and the Target*, but it is actually behind his idea of 'target' with its stress on the objective that the character has to reach at one particular moment, and then the next and the next.[57] Meanwhile, the target shifts with the circumstances rather than with the character's inner feelings and the actor's attempts to embody them. Donnellan's book is not a manual for actors, but it is a conversation with them to stimulate their creativity. It might be described as a soft-core variation on training, especially given his declaration that he is 'more interested in training the actor than in imposing specific interpretations of a play' (*Daily Telegraph*, 4 May 1999). This, by his own admission, 'is something else I have in common with the Russians'.

Donnellan's Russian journey started before he and his partner-designer Nick Ormerod founded Cheek by Jowl in 1981 on ensemble principles. This was a national touring company with an international brief. Its 1991 all-male *As You Like It*, which travelled the world, was a huge success in both Moscow and St Petersburg, where Donnellan and Ormerod renewed their contact with Dodin and the Maly Drama Theatre, having met them at various international festivals. They had also seen *Brothers and Sisters* in St Petersburg in 1986 and were completely bowled over by it, not least by its ensemble strength.[58] Dodin's practice of following a production years into its development coincided with Donnellan's with Cheek by Jowl: Donnellan stayed with a production on its tour, right through until it was performed no more. His growth as a director depended very much on this continuity of observation, which also sensitized him to the actors' need to renew their individual creative powers within a collective. Similarly, he became more acutely aware of the responsibility of a director not only to understand the ensemble spirit, but also to nurture it without interruption.

In 2000 Cheek by Jowl was given its Russian double by a group of Russian actors under the name of the Chekhov International Theatre Festival, designed also to be a touring company. It is a repertory company, as well, which is not the case of Cheek by Jowl, whose productions die when touring ends, as happens with those of Brook. The Russian company's inaugural production was Pushkin's *Boris Godunov*. Donnellan initially had misgivings about how these actors from various companies would come together.[59] But, in fact, he had underestimated the potency of the values of the 'Russian school', as Vassiliev calls the particularity of Russian training as a whole.[60] Consequently, he had underestimated the capacity of his Moscow 'independent stars' to knuckle down to ensemble work, which is there in abundance in the production.[61] Donnellan exercised the cool wit that had become a feature of Cheek by Jowl productions, turning this tragedy of the usurpation of power into boardroom wrangles over politics whose protagonists recall contemporary Russian politicians. Ensconced within this political allegory is a scintillating scene in which the Pretender to Godunov's throne and Marina, the Polish princess for whom power is nothing less than an aphrodisiac, seduce each other in a tank of water. Here, as in the political tussles, Donnellan's directorial hand is light, allowing these scenes to gather their own momentum.

He directed the Russian actors rather as if they were actors of Cheek by Jowl, warming up with games, insisting on the ambiguity of feelings and actions – summed up in *The Actor and the Target* as (to paraphrase), 'Juliet loves and does not love Romeo' – and achieving scenic simplicity with directness of play and minimal décor and props. Pyotr Semak of the Maly recalls that, when Donnellan directed *The Winter's Tale* (1997) for the company – the 'taster' before Donnellan's engagement with his Moscow actors – he not only had the Maly actors playing 'children's games'. He also went to great lengths with them to work out the size of Leontes' army, the place of his kingdom on a map, and other military details destined to situate Leontes in a context accustomed to violence.[62] Donnellan employed *études* to establish Leontes' relations with his family, courtiers and army, leaving Semak to draw on his Maly training to understand his character's eruption of jealousy from within. Donnellan meanwhile urged him and the other Maly actors to look outside their characters.[63] Donnellan: 'Seeing specifically what is outside will send the actor deeper into the character than thinking what is inside.'[64]

Donnellan characteristically directed Cheek by Jowl productions on a neat, often geometric grid formed by how he blocked the actors, and *The Winter's Tale* fell into this pattern, while *Boris Godunov*, coming later, was in a more fluid arrangement. The purpose was to provide the spatial possibilities for that distance of seeing referred to above; and Donnellan seems to have believed that this distance helped actors to play tension and conflict – in short, to play the opposites epitomized by Juliet's loving and not loving at the same time, which, in his view, are the very drama of any and every play. His layout, often marked scenographically with flagpoles (pronounced in *As You Like It* and *Much Ado About Nothing*, 1998) or chairs (a recurrent feature), permits concurrent action. Such simultaneity occurs whether he combines the past and the present or presents separate events, which from a narrative point of view supposedly take place sometime and somewhere else.

The device of tableau-freeze, in this frame, suited Donnellan for indicating that actual, recounted and fabricated events were occurring simultaneously. In *Othello* (2004), for instance, Cassio and Desdemona sit frozen with their backs to the audience as Iago lies to Othello about her (false) sexual encounter with Cassio. Frequently, as in *Othello*, all characters are on stage, frozen when not acting, but signifying that they belong to the whole story of the play. Such simple methods for storytelling, which Donnellan had always admired in Brook, who, he claims, was a great influence on him, also appear in the several productions he has staged in French, the last of which is Racine's *Andromaque* (2007). To make the story transparent, he turns Astyanax, Andromaque's son, into a character, whereas Astyanax is no more than a reference in Racine's play. That the child was performed by a grown man and was occasionally held on the lap of another man is a typical Donnellan joke on gender, gender-play being the main feature of *As You Like It*. In *Twelfth Night* (2003) with his Russian company, Donnellan gives another of his directorial grins by ending the production with three marriages instead of two, the third being between Antonio and Feste. By such means, he emerges as a director-champion of gay rights, having already flown his colours when he staged Tony Kushner's two-part *Angels in America* at the National Theatre in London in 1992 and 1993.

Twelfth Night was the second of four touring productions with the Chekhov International Theatre Festival, the most recent being *The Tempest* in 2011. The latter was the nineteenth of Donnellan's Shakespeare productions, by which he could be said to be a Shakespeare director, and it followed *Macbeth* with Cheek by Jowl in 2010. *Macbeth* is a study in testosterone dressed in black leather, a macho affair in which the Macbeth–Lady Macbeth duo, juxtaposed against a phalanx of men, are bound to each other sexually very deeply. This palpable sexuality makes Donnellan's *Macbeth* uncommonly human: these are Macbeth and Lady Macbeth in love rather than merely partners in murder, and such a perception of them, unusual, to say the least, in the Shakespeare canon, comes from Donnellan's consistently fresh interpretations of Shakespeare. Antonio and Feste's marriage apart, *Twelfth Night* is at its most original in Malvolio's tragic dimension. Malvolio, when reading the letter supposedly from Olivia, weeps on his knees for joy, convinced that Olivia loves him. When he discovers that Sir Toby has tricked him, he breaks down, sobbing: this moment is all the more cruel for the lovingness of the letter scene. The actor was here, in Donnellan's word, 'experiencing' the situation, and Donnellan's recourse to this Stanislavskian notion suggests that a more emotionally engaged layer had now entered his structures of ambivalence ('Juliet loves and does not love Romeo').

> When I first started thirty years ago, I was much more controlling, having an end-game plan, and thinking how I wanted things to come out: how it should finally look, how it should feel, what effect it should have. But slowly I learned to work in a different way ... Increasingly it seemed to me that what is important is to reflect as much as possible the actual experience, however unpredictable, uncomfortable, or unexpected that might turn out to be. Recently there has been a slight shift in how I see the work that we do. I always thought that there was 'text' and that, underneath the text, there was 'story'; and that text and the story were often different. It's like in real life, where somebody says one thing, but does something else, and this conflict is often deeply painful ... It's what a person does that really matters. So it's the situation, it's the *story* that really matters because a text can mean one thing, or something else. Now it seems to me that there is something else buried underneath the story: there is a deeper layer. The story is actually made up of fragments of experience.
>
> Declan Donnellan, in *Directors/Directing*, 74–5

The Tempest shows quite clearly how liberating for him as a director Donnellan's experience with his Russian company has been. Not only is his dual position unique – a British director with a permanent Russian ensemble – but also his cross-cultural venture has been enormously fertile. It has generated the continuity he could not sustain with Cheek by Jowl, on the one hand, and has provided him with a wealth of directorial possibilities, on the other. The sheer facility and panache of the actors' performances, as if they were improvising on the spot, give a glimmer of the never-ending stream of inventiveness that must have been their rehearsals. They also suggest that these actors provided great support for Donnellan's direction – something that may only be possible in this intensive way in ensemble practice. In fact, so rich is the flow of their performances that Donnellan may well have taken his cue from *them* rather than they from him.

Among the many scenes that could be cited is the end of Act IV, Scene i, where Ariel and his spirits conjure up splendid clothes for Trinculo and Stefano. This scene turns brilliantly into a duty-free store, where New Russian, mafia-style Trinculo and Stefano, who are bejewelled in gold and sport sunglasses and mobile phones, go mad with clothes racks, shopping bags and credit cards, accompanied by gags on how unused they are to using them. Caliban, meanwhile, is a 'dude' accomplice whom the burly actor in the role (Aleksandr Feklistov) has prancing about like a fairy, as he had done in Act I, when Trinculo's wine had inebriated him. Donnellan's greatest discovery in this *Tempest* is the close relationship between Caliban and Miranda. When she leaves the island, she lurches back towards him with a sharp cry, for he had virtually become the mother she had lost. The production is remarkable in more ways than one, and testifies to the subtle harmonies of play that can be achieved through ensemble playing in which all the players are sensitive to the work of each, striving for something bigger than their individual self.

Further reading

Brook, Peter. *The Empty Space*, Middlesex: Penguin Books, 1973

Dodin, Lev. *Journey without End*, trans. Anna Karabinska, and Oksana Mamyrin, London: Tantalus Books, 2006

Donnellan, Declan. *The Actor and the Target*, London: Nick Hern Books, 2nd edition 2005

Hirst, David L. *Giorgio Strehler*, Cambridge University Press, 1993

Mitchell, Katie. *The Director's Craft: A Handbook for the Theatre*, London and New York: Routledge, 2009

Patterson, Michael. *Peter Stein: Germany's Leading Director*, Cambridge University Press, 1981

Shevtsova, Maria. *Dodin and the Maly Drama Theatre: Process to Performance*, London: Routledge, 2004

Chapter 7

Directors, collaboration and improvisation

Improvisation or devising, as a collective process, raises questions about the nature of directing, its limits and responsibilities. The staging of theatre is always to some degree a group activity. Even where a director is an *auteur*, like Gordon Craig and Robert Wilson, or the sole performer, as with Robert Lepage's monodramas, there are technical or dramaturgical staff who contribute to the final shape of a production. However, in an ensemble style of theatre, where it is the performers as a group who evolve the material, develop their own styles of presentation and/or structure the production, the role of the director changes. In such a context, to what extent does a director control or guide the process? What is the director's function? As we shall see, there is a wide range of possible variations within the frame of improvisational theatre. Improvisation is closely related to physical theatre, and, at its extreme in Paratheatrical projects, claims to deny any directorial role. Yet even here in the examples analysed, there is always a director in some form. Any hierarchical structure contains a political position; and in theory, at least, improvisational theatre is a paradigm of democracy in so far as it projects an image of artistic equality.

Signally it is a director with an extremely marked theatrical and performative style, Roberto Ciulli (see above, pp. 143–6), who has defined a theory of improvisation. And, for the form to mirror content, this is expressed not through a manifesto or a book (like Brook's *The Empty Space*), but through a series of unstructured conversations with one-time members of his acting troupe.

Theory and politics of improvisation

For Ciulli, who once wrote a doctorate on the subject, the relationship between the individual and the state defines his ongoing approach to theatre, the key to which is his insight that the 'contrast between the unpredictable vitality which inheres in art and the predictable actions of the social being forms the coordinates among which theatre moves today'.[1] Following through this dialectic, theatre becomes a working model and indeed essential catalyst in the political process.

Theatre as a political tool

The ideal laboratory for working on the problems associated with the building of a society and for the social formations we have to invent so that a more humane society may emerge is the theatre. What we encounter there all the time is the dialectical relationship between the freedom of an individual and the order of the state, and the search for the maximum degree of freedom within a state, which is to say inside a prison.

Roberto Ciulli, *On Improvisation*, 39

In theatre terms, the individual capable of exercising freedom is the actor, while the repressive order of the state is represented by the structure of the play or performance itself. Because any text, or even any agreed-on sequence of actions, represents a marked-out area, whether dictated by a director, or still with a collaborative process, limited by the confines of the story or the emotional focus of the acting group, a theatrical performance can be seen as a sort of prison: a metaphor for the state. At the same time, Ciulli sees improvisation not simply as a theatrical technique, but defining people's behaviour: 'Human beings improvise all the time.'[2]

As Ciulli points out, even improvisation in rehearsal leads to the creation of an imprisoning box. In terms of performance itself, creating a complete drama out of improvised actions expressing the individuality of the actors is essentially no different from using actions to illustrate a text that is not essentially altered in the production. So to keep the tension inherent in this political dialectic, there need to be two distinct uses of improvisation. The first is the collective creation of the play to be performed (which, once completed, itself forms the 'prison'); then during the performance itself the actors have to find 'free spaces within the framework, within the given constraints so that individual creativity can unfold'. Reconstructing improvisations is the opposite of improvising – rather the actors must discover ways of improvising every night of a performance if the lines spoken or the gestures enacted are to come alive: a procedure illustrated by The Wooster Group (see p. 226).

So improvisation is presented as the true basis for 'the craft of acting' that consists in 'an actor finding his own means of expression, for himself, what is in him'. Further, Ciulli presents improvisation as the essential link uniting the contrasting acting theories of Stanislavsky with Meyerhold and Brecht. Improvisation, in stage performance as much as in the political sphere, forms 'moments when a human being has the sense of being at a distance from the situation – that is the true [Brechtian] alienation', while simultaneously improvising is not simply physical: its effectiveness depends on the quality of feelings involved in the process and the emotional expression created by the actions.[3]

What of the role of the director in this collaborative process of collective creation? As Ciulli describes his own practice, while he discusses ideas and content with his actors – and relies on a group whose long-term experience with him, his dramaturge and his designer has evolved a coherent style over many productions – he never speaks about the way these concepts might be expressed. Unlike Robert Lepage or Simon McBurney, each of whom also works collaboratively with a stable acting group, but also acts as the lead performer (thus defining tone and focus through their own improvisation), Ciulli performs only minor roles in his productions. He sees rehearsals as a process of mutual improvisation, where a director takes ideas and actions from the actions improvised by the actors, improvises conceptually and passes the images of action that emerge (while avoiding any suggestions about how these might be expressed) back to the group 'in an associative way . . . so that the actor does not begin to think: this is how he wants it, so this is the way I shall have to do it'. His aim in putting a production together is to create the free spaces in the framework that will allow continued improvisation in performance. Without 'collective work . . . nothing is being created in the minds of the audience'. With standard directing, 'What is being produced is dead theatre.'[4]

As Ciulli emphasizes, improvisation incorporates this vitality and communicability because the form of a theatrical production (in contrast to film or other forms of storytelling) forms a mirror for the political situation of society. It encourages spectators as well, through the example of actors exercising the freedom to make individual decisions within the set structure of the performance. Improvisation on an artistic level is a demonstration of the ability to take individual decisions that translates directly to politics. For audiences as for the actors: 'It is a question of not simply allowing oneself apathetically to be oppressed by life but of becoming aware not only of one's lack of freedom but also of one's inner freedom – that is what will enable one to change and to survive.'[5]

Physical theatre: Simon McBurney

Simon McBurney defines himself as 'an actor first and foremost . . . a director by chance rather than design' and rejects directing as 'a kind of fake job . . . without real function'.[6] Working, as he does, primarily with mime and wordless action automatically privileges devising; and in his training he was particularly fascinated by the improvisation taught by his mentor, Jacques Lecoq, whose influence largely defined his theatrical approach. Improvisation forms the basis of a very physical theatre, in which the body is used to express emotion; and the name of his acting troupe itself underlines the centrality of a communal nature of theatrical performance for McBurney. Following the principles expounded by the Ecole Jacques Lecoq: *le jeu* (playfulness), *complicité* (togetherness) and *disponsibilité* (openness), the original title of 'Théâtre de Complicité' – changed in 2006 to the simplified Complicite – focuses on the relationship between spectator and performer, which McBurney has described as a 'partnership'. McBurney was also influenced by Brook's concept of the ensemble, incorporated in his Centre for Performance Research, attending all their dress rehearsals while in Paris. And indeed one of the defining productions for Complicite, *The Three Lives of Lucie Cabrol*, has been compared to Brook's 'Empty Stage' performances, such as *The Ik* (1974).[7]

At the same time, the influence of *commedia dell'arte* – derived again from Lecoq – can be seen in the characterization of his pieces, particularly in his early work. This adoption of iconic figurations forms a convenient basis for actors to experiment with material, but, together with physical clowning, it also prevents any Stanislavsky-like building of a role; and indeed McBurney believes that the function of a performer is not to experience a feeling, but to transmit the emotion to spectators, which is precluded to the extent that the actor is carried away. In addition, McBurney is frequently the lead performer in the pieces Complicite produces. The movements in his staging may be worked out by individuals in the group, yet the effect in performance is always choreographed.

More recently he has come to use workshops through which his company play with potential material that attaches to no particular story or dramatic project, although for instance very general workshop explorations of memory and its biochemistry eventually fed into *Mnemonic* (1999). And in his standard way of approaching a production, while he may collaborate on developing a story with a member of his troupe, it is his invention or concept that is the catalyst for rehearsals during which the piece evolves. His working approach always starts with an image, or an object, while rehearsals help to define a single moment that the action of a show revolves around; and the story is then expanded into a full-length piece. Typically the stories McBurney stages tend to reject linear narrative in favour of circular progression or regression, so that his devised pieces come to be built out of repetitive acts, which have been developed by the company.

Complicite rehearsals are designed to produce a large number of fragmentary actions, that McBurney integrates and arranges – but in working with an author, like John Berger (*The Three Lives of Lucie Cabrol*, 1994, or *The Vertical Line*, 1999), McBurney writes a scenario, which the author uses as a basis for creating possible words to speak, out of which dialogue emerges. With Berger this text became a series of one-line sentences on cue-cards that McBurney brought with him to the first rehearsals. In other works, for example *Mnemonic* where McBurney derived the central image from a book written by the Austrian archaeologist Conrad Spindler, *The Man in the Ice*, McBurney develops the complete story. Led by his experience of visiting the shattered Sarajevo immediately after the Yugoslav civil war, which seemed to correspond with the violent history of the prehistoric Iceman, McBurney combined the Iceman with a book from his childhood: Rebecca West's 1955 memoir *Black Lamb and Grey Falcon: A Journey through Yugoslavia*, recording her travels in 1937 on the eve of the Second World War. West's reflections on the history of Europe as 'a vast Kossovo, an abominable blood-logged plain' linked up specifically with Sarajevo having sparked the carnage of the First World War, to provide an overlapping palimpsest of violence over the millennia and ending with a present-day love story centred on a girl's search for her missing father.

16 *Mnemonic*, Simon McBurney, 2002

In both pieces, once the overarching story had been set, rehearsals were then devoted to evolving a physical *mise en scène*. Based on these one-liners or on readings of the source books, the cast devised actions to express the elements of the story. As rehearsals progressed the actions developed by the actors, singly and in groups, were noted down in sketches or brief descriptions pinned up randomly on the walls or recorded on video clips. Then the company returned to the opening of the story, and worked through, selecting specific actions from the multiple choices, and developing links to form a coherent sequence.

The rehearsal process is echoed in the dramatic material evolved through it, as illustrated by the Director's Note in the programme for *Mnemonic*.

> We live in a time where stories surround us. Multiple stories. Constantly. Fragmented by television, radio, print, the internet, calling to us from every hoarding and passing by us, by our every street corner. We no longer live in a world of the single tale. So the shards of stories we have put together, some longer some shorter, collide here in the theatre, reflecting, repeating, and evolving like the act of memory itself.
>
> Simon McBurney, 'Collisions'[8]

In performance, like much of McBurney's other work (and echoing Robert Lepage's defining technique), *Mnemonic* combined video with the live acted scenes. Integrating such technology requires the exercise of a single vision. And indeed McBurney sees himself as the person who puts all the fragments together. Even if the group evolves the elements of the whole piece, there is still an overarching vision, which is McBurney's. Emphasizing musical rhythms as the shaping force of Shakespeare's texts, he talks of 'hearing' the structure of a piece while acting in it, and compares the dramatic form to architecture.

His approach is a unique combination of overarching vision with collaboration. The actions, gestures and even dialogue evolve from the group, with different elements contributed by the other performers. At the same time McBurney – whether in *Lucie Cabrol* or *Mnemonic* – generally plays the central role, particularly in his earlier work, although from 2000 on he has functioned more as director than actor, even in key pieces such as *The Noise of Time* (2000), *Vanishing Points* (2005) or *A Disappearing Number* (2008). But in those pieces where he performs, it is McBurney's presence that determines the overall reception of the piece. The effect is demonstrated by one of the reviews for *Mnemonic*:

> His solo prologue to the twin narratives that are interlaced in *Mnemonic* is utterly compelling ... presented as it is by a character so touchingly

> human, manic with ideas that range from the philosophical to the absurdly mundane. It is an engagingly anarchic rant by a man desperate to communicate his feelings; a man rendered vulnerable because he is unreservedly open to feelings, cultural ponderings and, above all, personal memory. A man who cares, and is trying to make sense of experience in a world of forgetting; a world that deprecates the sensual experience in favour of materialism.[9]

As this indicates, McBurney is also politically engaged. The essence of his staged stories is a developed, if partially disguised, critique of contemporary civilization; and his working relationship with a strongly socialist author such as Berger, whose critique is expressed in theoretical writings (and television serials) about art history, as well as novels, is telling.

This political stance is also embodied in the expressionistic style he has developed with his acting company. Surfacing most clearly in his 1992 *Street of Crocodiles* (adapted in collaboration with the writer Mark Wheatley from the stories of Bruno Schulz), it is equally present in McBurney's 2010 production of the Russian opera *A Dog's Heart* (derived from Mikhail Bulgakov's 1925 novel).

Based on the life and stories of the 1930s expressionist writer and painter, shot by the Nazis in Poland in 1942, the staging of *Street of Crocodiles* brilliantly mirrored in physical terms the hallucinatory phantasmagoria of Schultz's writings. Centring the story on Schultz's relations with his reclusive father, a failed shopkeeper fascinated by birds and with a whole aviary in his attic, who spent his final years in a lunatic asylum, McBurney and his actors created distorting perspectives, where (as the father comments), 'Matter is in a constant state of fermentation' and books turn into fluttering birds, while actors become furniture and inanimate objects, like rolls of cloth, take on a life of their own, accompanied by the ominous sound of marching boots. McBurney described the style as 'the drama of twilight: of shifting colours and juxtapositions of movement'.[10]

In *A Dog's Heart* the effects are very similar, although Bulgakov's satire of Soviet manipulation is manifested by different means: with a puppet (the dog, as it is transformed into a monstrous human by organ-transplant surgery, manipulated by a trio of on-stage puppeteers), distorted projections of Soviet graphics, film clips and photos from the era, masks and the shifting geometry of the set. However, McBurney managed to evoke intensely physical performances from the singers, leading several reviewers to compare this piece with *Street of Crocodiles*; as one described: 'Peter Hoare turns in the performance of the night as he squeals his way from scream to growl in a master-class of grotesque acting, singing and (often literal) scenery-chewing.'[11]

Indeed, expressionism, as revived by McBurney from the 1920s and 1930s, corresponds well with the soul-searching, hysteria and sense of crisis in contemporary society. And the Complicite style of physical performance, focusing on bodies in movement through almost bare stages and minimal props, has had significant influence on contemporary British theatre. McBurney effectively redefines the role of playwright as a deviser in a poetic drama where gesture and movement communicate more directly than speech, and redefines the role of director as the organizing consciousness structuring the results of group improvisation – although by defining (unlike Elizabeth LeCompte) the initial images or impetus for a performance, McBurney serves as a playwright of physical theatre.

The Wooster Group: media(ted) improvisations

Improvisation of various kinds has been key to The Wooster Group since Elizabeth LeCompte founded the company and directed *Sakonnet Point*, her directorial debut, in 1975. She had come out of the 'cool' aesthetics emerging from the 1960s, which referred to its own processes of making rather than claiming to be 'about' something or taking strong positions regarding the social and political issues of the day. This aesthetic was the antithesis of firebrand politics and so of the 'hot' performance style adopted by Julian Beck and Judith Malina who ran the Living Theatre, or of the more didactic Luis Valdez who nurtured the Chicano theatre, El Teatro Campesino (and, in the 1970s, influenced Peter Brook). Thus it was aligned with the early work of Wilson, Cunningham and Meredith Monk and with the non-narrative ballets of George Balanchine, all of which LeCompte admired, as well as with the quirky pieces by Richard Foreman with whom she was to collaborate briefly in the later 1980s.

LeCompte's background was in painting and photography rather than theatre, and her visual-arts perception of the world brought her closer, on the one hand, to Wilson's understanding of stage space as an open field for construction and, on the other, to the feel for the painterly quality of a canvas promoted by such painters as Jasper Johns. Johns never tired of saying that his paintings were about painting, and while LeCompte appears not to have avowed any special affinity with him, her declaration that 'the piece is about the making of the piece, always' – this on her 1988 *Frank Dell's The Temptation of Saint Antony* – holds tight throughout her creative endeavours.[12] Her task as a director is to put a work-in-the-making 'on its feet', and, while doing so, she also shows precisely what moves are being made to get it there.[13] In this respect, her contribution as a director is to ensure that the stage work is a matter not of interpreting, or glossing, or psychologically embellishing meaning, but of physically, visibly, *doing* something as an action in and of itself. Ari Fliakos, one of her more recent collaborators who plays in *Hamlet* (2006), calls this 'executing a series of actions', which are a means 'to be actively doing something in performance as opposed to be pretending to be doing something'.[14] Such active doing, in full view, is a way of being about the 'making of the piece'.

The drive to be doing something, and, moreover, to be observed by spectators to be doing it, is one significant feature of what is probably best described as the *sensation* of improvisation given by a Wooster Group work – the sensation that it has not come ready-made to the stage but is being fixed as it goes along, literally improvised on the spot. But this is not quite the truth, or at least it is only half deceptive in so far as the Group's every work treads on the borders between the rehearsed and the structured, and the spontaneous and the risky. The second coupling is the factor that makes the work look and feel improvised, regardless of whether it actually *is*, there and then, in the very moment of doing/performing. When action is, in fact, improvised spontaneously, it occurs nevertheless in a structure that took time and effort to prepare and organize: this is the rehearsed side of the border, and, in being structured into the composition, the 'rehearsed' requires vigilance during runs of performances, night after night, so that it does not disintegrate and fall away, exposing spontaneous improvisation to chaos.

These remarks are a preamble to a point that needs to be stressed, namely, that The Wooster Group relies on three types of improvisation: the sensation that the work is in-the-making and about itself, as just discussed; the processes of improvisation set into train during a work's preparatory period; the improvisation that actually occurs during public performance. Of great importance for all three is the fact that works are never considered to be 'finished'. Not only does the Group prefer to show parts of work-in-progress to spectators, absorbing responses in its review of the work, but LeCompte also continues to change the work after it has been 'released', so to speak, to the public. LeCompte adjusted *Poor Theater* (2004), for example, after having solicited spectators' commentaries with a suggestion box on the production.[15] Fliakos notes that LeCompte is often not able to correct problems until they reveal themselves several years later.[16] A work then shifts accordingly. Similarly, the performers do not rest on their achievements. Kate Valk, who has performed with the Group for more than twenty years, affirms that LeCompte 'wants to see us growing and changing over time'.[17] All this indicates how LeCompte directs her productions while giving her performers ample freedom to play as they will. The main issue, where her directing is concerned, is her need 'to work from watching the performers' rather than decide anything in her head.[18]

The material with which the performers play is gathered, improvised upon and chosen collectively during the preparatory periods; and all material is considered, whether it involves costumes, props and records or video tapes from earlier productions that are subsequently recycled and transformed, or whether it is found for the first time, prompted by the new production. Material can be visual, sonic, gestural, kinetic or verbal, and if established classical texts are points of departure – for instance, Chekhov's *The Three Sisters* for *Brace Up!* (1991) or Racine's *Phèdre* for *To You, the Birdie! (Phèdre)* (2001) – they are spliced and reconfigured in relation to the performance material amassed from all the contributing components during the course of improvisation. Since LeCompte does not make a hierarchy of components, they are all, in her word, 'texts' to be combined.

> Well, you have to be careful when you say 'improvise'. We don't improvise texts. The texts are there. They're like a guide for us. When I say 'texts', I mean both physical and written texts. Our improvisation has to do with how we combine texts. We improvise around how our physical text will meet our oral text. I'll take a piece of music, a text, and a physical thing on the TV and I'll say, 'Ok, you have to do all these three things together'. The performers take all these texts and make the associations, and they take off of them. They don't make anything up on their own out of thin air. The way they combine the material is the way they make something up on their own.
>
> *Directors /Directing*, 129

The Wooster Group's approach to improvisation is quite different from the kind of improvisation practised by McBurney or Lepage with their successive actors, or by Mnouchkine's Théâtre du Soleil where things evolve out of stimulated imaginings, with prompts from historical and contemporary events. Improvisation, as practised by The Wooster Group, relies above all on the combinatory ingenuity of all its participants. Furthermore, since it is tightly connected to the use of technology and, more still, to an intermesh of media, its technicians are also improvisers of both the work in process in rehearsal and the work still in process shown to spectators. *Hamlet* amply demonstrates this principle in that, being 'taken' or played 'off of' a film, the production depends on the technicians. It is they who run the film, and how they stop or start it, or fast-forward or make an error with it, either by mistake or as a deliberate provocation to the performers, affects, sometimes considerably, the way the production is performed; and the same is true for all technological media, like the videos, monitors and computers always used by the company.

When Scott Shepherd expressed his desire to perform *Hamlet* with himself in the title role, the whole company rallied round, undertaking extensive research into available recorded versions, including audio tapes and films in archives in London. LeCompte finally settled on the performance by Richard Burton, which John Gielgud had directed on Broadway in 1964, the film of the live production having been shown across the United States in 2000. The Wooster Group imitated this *Hamlet*, imitation or simulation being typical of its performance mode. Martha Graham and Cunningham dance was imitated highly skilfully in *To You, The Birdie!* and Valk and Shepherd were nothing short of virtuosic in their mimicry, in *Poor Theater*, of Grotowski's iconic 1962 work *Akropolis*, as well as of choreography by William Forsythe, the one layered on top of the other.

The imitation in *Hamlet* was done directly from tapes playing on various monitors. These were placed in various spots in the space according to where the performers would be and see them best; and it resulted in a compelling play of gazes going up, looking down, or traversing the stage from several angles. All of it played on the idea of random gazing, while at the same time glimpses of the Burton film, some of them ghosted in fading double image as occurs in early films, indicated to spectators that the performers were themselves copying and doubling the tape. The trajectories of gaze were not in fact by chance, but structured.

Visually, all this created a tapestry of images, which layered the levels of movement and sound so characteristic of the texture of LeCompte productions. It is in this multi-layered universe of *Hamlet* that the spontaneous improvisation referred to above takes place. Shepherd may decide to omit a section, as happened in a performance when spectators heard him telling the technicians to 'skip to the book', that is, to Hamlet's speech 'Words, words, words'. This meant not only Shepherd's rapid readjustment to the altered composition, but also that of the other performers to each other: their dealing with each other in the moment, often in a surprise fashion, is an integral aspect of their improvisation in general. Shepherd's call here, as on other occasions, is 'a way of Hamlet orchestrating the making of the piece'.[19] More still, it is a way of showing how that orchestration is done, thereby also involving the technicians in the process as performers.

The same holds when it is the technicians who make a sudden decision about an audio or visual tape, or accidentally make a mistake. Sometimes the performers ignore the glitch and take the risk to catch up, or to pick up the cue elsewhere. Or else they request a re-run, as occurred when Shepherd asked the technicians to re-play a section they had lost regarding Ophelia so that he could actually do it. Mistakes like this are random events to be distinguished from technical mistakes that occurred in rehearsals but were retained as residual directorial decisions, made then, on the spot, by LeCompte.

The use of technologies not merely as enabling tools but as integrated features of a given work has become more common since the company consolidated its operations in this way in the 1980s. Apart from small-scale groups like Forced Entertainment, which, consciously or not, follow in the steps of The Wooster Group, there is the large-scale Toneelgroep Amsterdam which is worthy of comparison. Directed by Ivo Van Hove, the company has harnessed diverse technologies to provide constitutive compositional elements for its productions, of which *Roman Tragedies* (2006) is a brilliant example. Even so, none has made of technology a deeply embodied principle of improvisation, as The Wooster Group has done, and in this it is unique among performance groups for which improvisation is their basis.

The paradox of improvisation: Jerzy Grotowski and Eugenio Barba

The paradox of improvisation and direction raises many questions, not least the one asking what the role of the director can be in the collective development of a piece from inception to presentation by a whole group. This paradox is pronounced in the case of The Wooster Group, where the actors' authorship is paramount but where LeCompte can and does intervene at any moment, 'compromising' that authorship to some extent. In this way, she maintains her directorial role without querying its legitimacy – any more than do her collaborators. The contrast with Mnouchkine on this very point in the early improvisation-centred days of the Théâtre du Soleil is striking (see Chapter 3); and the paradox of directorial authority in individual and group creation appears in the quite different 'holy'/ritual theatre of Grotowski who, as in the Polish and Russian schools, was trained as an actor before being trained as a director, and whose practice has been taken up and varied by a range of contemporary European directors, selected as examples for the remainder of this chapter.

The Grotowski paradigm

Reinvigorating the existent Theatre of Thirteen Rows in Opole as of 1957, on the invitation of Ludwig Flaszen who was to become his literary adviser/dramaturge – it was to be renamed the Laboratory Theatre when the company moved to Wroclaw in 1965 – Grotowski and his actors formed an intimately connected performing group. This was an ensemble following both Stanislavsky and Nemirovich-Danchenko's model (Grotowski had studied for a year at GITIS with Stanislavsky's pupil Yury Zavadsky) and its remodelling for Poland by Osterwa and Mieczyslaw Limanowski, who founded the laboratory theatre Reduta in 1919. Working with his team, among them the now legendary Rena Mirecka, Ryszard Cieslak and Zygmunt Molik, Grotowski discovered 'that to fulfil myself was far less fruitful than studying the possibility of helping others to fulfil themselves'. In doing this, he was always present: 'I myself am there, guiding the work, and I say to the actor: "I don't understand" or "I understand" or "I understand but I don't believe".'[20] Such a director-helper-guide has to be as invested in the process as the actor from the fullness of his inner being (Grotowski's 'plenitude').

The director and reciprocal guidance

An actor can only be guided and inspired by someone who is whole-hearted in his creative activity. The producer [that is, director], while guiding and inspiring the actor, must at the same time allow himself to be guided and inspired by him. It is a question of freedom, partnership, and this does not imply a lack of discipline but a respect for the autonomy of others. Respect for the actor's autonomy does not mean lawlessness, lack of demands, never ending discussions and the replacement of action by continuous stream of words. On the contrary, respect for autonomy means enormous demands, the expectation of a maximum creative effort and the most personal revelation. Understood thus, solicitude for the actor's freedom can only be born from the plenitude of the guide and not from his lack of plenitude. Such a lack implies imposition, dictatorship, superficial dressage.

Jerzy Grotowski, *Towards a Poor Theatre*, 258

Grotowski's reflections on what it means to be a director are few, since, as is well known, his energies were devoted to the development of a new type of actor, the 'holy' actor, in the framework of ritual theatre, which, opposed to the theatre of illusion and thus also to Stanislavsky's psychological realism, emphasized the irreducible importance of the actor's 'total act'.[21] By this, Grotowski refers to the actor's uninhibited openness to his/her deepest 'innermost core', which is an act of 'self-penetration', 'self-donation' and readiness to 'give his all in the context of his own experience', not as an acting 'mask' but (to paraphrase Grotowski) as a human being who becomes transparent, transformed by the ecstatic, Dionysian liberation of body and soul.[22]

What does Grotowski as director do in such a personal and profoundly intimate journey, which is also a private transgression of limits that, in the moment it is communicated to somebody else, director or fellow actor, is made public, and is then re-made publicly again in front of spectators? The answer can probably only be in Grotowski's 'helping others to fulfil themselves' since the actor 'fulfils' him/herself by gradually developing his/her 'score'. Grotowski, while indebted to Stanislavsky and Meyerhold for this term, radicalizes the practice behind it in that the 'score' is a notation fully *in the body* of the actor's impulses. Such impulses are, in effect, movements of the soul that take unprecedented (because so personal and unplanned) forms of vocalization and physicalization in the quick of being done. This does not happen in free fall, which, for Grotowski, runs the danger of becoming 'hysteria' and 'narcissism'.[23] It necessarily depends on the tension in the actor between 'spontaneity and discipline', which, for Grotowski, 'mutually reinforce themselves' and are essential for the actor's creativity.[24]

This may sound more like a personal spiritual process of discovery (which it certainly is) than a matter of improvisation. And yet, improvisation, when understood as development from *études* (as with Dodin's and Vassiliev's actors, see pp. 199–200, 204–5 above), can be a significant part of structuring a performance through defining its agreed frames – agreed, that is, by actors and director. From his Meyerholdian constructivist *Mystery-Bouffe* in Opole (1960) to *Apocalypsis cum figuris* in Wroclaw (1969), the production to close Grotowski's Theatre of Productions phase, *études* appear to have provided Grotowski with the principle of improvisation grounded in the 'spontaneity and discipline' from which his director/actor 'partnership' was inseparable. It can be inferred from Flaszen's reference to Grotowski's 'instruction of the actors' that Grotowski channelled, if not controlled, his actors' 'scores'.[25] 'Instruction' for *Forefathers Eve* (1961) after the play by Adam Mickiewicz, and *Kordian* (1962) from the play by Juliusz Slowacki, both from the Polish Romantic canon, prepared the way for *Akropolis* (1962), which had its 'score of actions' built up 'through improvisational work in rehearsal'.[26]

Akropolis, from the play by Stanislaw Wyspianski, another canonical drama, was a montage of scenes and fragments of texts, like the other two productions. What distinguished the production was its theme concerning Auschwitz, transposed to the terrifying level of myth, which rejected empathy but implied the complicity of all present, the living *and* the evoked dead. The actors used a minimum number of objects – a wheelbarrow, stove-pipes, bits of metallic rubbish, oversized heavy shoes and sackcloth for clothes – for multiple suggestive purposes, including to suggest that a stove-pipe was a bride. As Grotowski notes, also because of the tightly squeezed space of performance, 'We didn't build a crematorium but we gave spectators the association of fire.'[27] Associations of this kind, together with the movement dynamics and the incantation or other vocalization realized through association, evolved from improvisations. And while in *Akropolis* its momentum materialized in

17 *Akropolis*, Jerzy Grotowski, 1962

a finished piece, in *The Hamlet Study*, which followed (1964) and was based on Shakespeare together with Wyspianski's makeover of the play, it led to what could be described as a suspended improvisation. In fact, it was probably meant to be more of an *étude*, given the word 'study' in its title, than a production. In Flaszen's words, other than being an exploration and improvisation of 'entire scenes', it was, as well, 'a study on the theme of acting method and collective direction'.[28] 'Collective direction' can here mean nothing other than the making and structuring of the piece by the group as a whole.

The Hamlet Study may have been a stepping-stone to the greatly celebrated and much written-about *The Constant Prince* (1965) with Cieslak in the title role. There is no evidence to prove that the two are linked by the same collective working method, although they are thematically linked by the figure of the individual-martyr of each work, crowned by the actor-martyr in *The Constant Prince*. The big shift where the director–collective paradox discussed in these pages is concerned took place with *Apocalypsis cum figuris*. Unlike the preceding productions, this did not use pre-existing texts as a point of departure, but worked on and 'settled' the action first before adding passages from various written sources chosen by the actors (Dostoevsky, the Bible, T. S. Eliot, Simone Weil). This change of order went hand in glove with Grotowski's change of approach. According to Flaszen, Grotowski, who 'previously . . . really was a dictator', 'discovered another way of work and who he was in the work'.[29] Instead of instructing, he 'sat silently, waiting, hour after hour', and *Apocalypsis* was 'something we arrived at during rehearsals, through flashes of revelation, through improvisations'.

The actor Stanislaw Scierski recalls that, at one stage in the production's three-year genesis, the 'collective search' via *études* 'was in Grotowski's hands'. 'He helped the "studies" to develop, respecting our right to take risks: he selected them; very often he inspired them in their entirety; in short – he watched over the collectively emerging outline.'[30] Perhaps the key phrase here is 'collectively emerging outline' because it echoes the collective 'we' and the organic 'arrived at' noted by Flaszen, which suggest that the director and collective improvisation can co-exist. But then comes Flaszen's sting in the tail. He states that 'at that point' (when Grotowski sat silently, waiting), 'there was no more theatre, because theatre to some extent requires dictatorship, manipulation'.[31] In 1970, one year after the premier of *Apocalypsis*, Grotowski, in the prophet-like manner he was known to adopt, announced that 'we are living in a post-theatrical epoch'.[32] He was then already preparing to embark on his Paratheatrical research.

Paratheatre (1969–78) was Grotowski's attempt to transcend theatre (perhaps already implicit in the 'holy actor'); to supersede the director as manipulator; to abandon all notions of art and aesthetics for the sake of 'meetings' in which people come face to face in a state of simplicity possible only when all social roles and masks are dropped. These meetings appear to have been for him akin to a state of grace, even to a primeval sort of innocence that allowed people quite different from each other, and from different countries and cultures, to come together in what must surely be called utopian communities, however brief their duration. The utopian character of the ventures, albeit on a broad geographical scale – Paratheatrical events occurred in Poland, the United States and Australia – was reflected in the pastoral environment selected for each occasion: forests, fields, farms and, in one instance, a hilltop with the ruins of a castle to fill out the quasi-idyllic scene. And the people turning up from all over the world eventually swelled to over 4,000 of them in Wroclaw in 1974.[33]

The members of Grotowski's Laboratory team, Molik and Cieslak among the founding group, and newcomers, among them Wlodzimierz Staniewski (who was to leave in 1976 to start up the Gardzienice Theatre Association), discretely kept the meetings in check so that their group dynamics did not disintegrate. They were referred to as 'guides', the notion of guidance being already familiar from Grotowski's days as a director, although it was now called upon with a different intention.[34] Or else they were described as 'leaders' of 'projects' and 'workshops', the latter vocabulary being meant to preclude any reference to 'theatre' and 'directors'. Mirecka and Zbigniew Cynkutis, another of the Laboratory founders, ran a project called 'Event', for instance, while Molik worked on 'Acting Therapy' to help participants remove blockages of one kind and another. The point, too, was to be inclusive, replacing 'spectators' with active participants, who were all performers. It can be seen that, in this dimension of Paratheatre, Grotowski, aided by his team, was extending the experiments with space of *Kordian*, for instance, where spectators sat on the beds that indicated the asylum in which the performers performed, right next to them, sharing the same space. The aim there was also close inter-human contact – a 'meeting' by another name through the theatre.

Grotowski's Paratheatre world of non-theatre and non-directors contained the transcultural elements (by virtue of its mixture of nationalities) that characterized the period of the Theatre of Sources (1976–82) with which it overlapped by a number of years. Robert Findlay, a participant, observes that, from 1977 to 1980, Grotowski 'worked with a multi-national group of 36 people representing such diverse cultures [*sic*] as India, Colombia, Bangladesh, Haiti, Africa, Japan, Poland, France, Germany and the United States'.[35] The reason for such diversity was to discover what Grotowski called the 'different techniques of sources', that is to say, Sufi techniques, shamanism, yogic practices, including those of the 'yogi-bards from Bengal in India', and Haitian voodoo.[36] In short, Grotowski sought practices that were bound to tradition; and, in researching them either with a small group or as part of his individual studies in lone travel to India, Haiti, and so on, his emphasis was not on appropriating them for the creation of theatre (let alone of the intercultural type) but 'on witnessing some performative approaches and on possibilities for entering into direct contacts [*sic*] with the strong human examples of the holders of ancient tradition'.[37]

Grotowski's own account of Theatre of Sources is rather nebulous, but it can be inferred from it that he exchanged his directorial role for that of a pupil learning from the 'holders of ancient tradition' (the notion of tradition is stressed in his account) in preparation for becoming a pilgrim-teacher-mentor – a non-director – not of how-to-do something, but, one might say, of how-to-be.[38] This could well be nothing less than a spiritual path that eventually led to Art as Vehicle, the last phase of Grotowski's research (1986–99), and to the Workcenter of Jerzy Grotowski at Pontedera in Italy. It was here that he guided Thomas Richards and Mario Biagini, his successors (Richards' name was added to the institution's title in 1996) to find deep within themselves and in their respective song traditions – Afro-Caribbean for

Richards, Italian for Biagini – as well as among other traditions, another way of performing for the 'post-theatrical epoch'. It was not that his distant Afro-Caribbean heritage provided Richards with a ready-made culture. His life experiences were such as to make him unfamiliar with it, and ethnic memory, a kind of pre-given cultural capacity by sheer dint of ethnicity or ethnic background, does not exist, since cultural practices (thus also art practices) are learned and acquired. Richards had to approach his ancestral sources – 'source' in Grotowski's vocabulary now also referring to personal origins – as he would any foreign culture.

Ang Gey Pin found herself in a similar situation when she explored her Chinese ancestral past at the Workcenter, developing from this internal itinerary towards the 'source' from 1998 to 2002 six versions of the piece known as *One breath left*. Her score evolved from her itinerary, as did that of her co-performers from their own material. Even so, the meticulously probed and meticulously chartered type of improvisation practised at the Workcenter did not appear to have killed off the idea that the 'director' still had some kind of function, however altered it may have been by an alternative way of performing, which meant the creation of *performances* rather than productions. It is not surprising, then, that Richards was described as the 'co-director' of, for example, *One breath left – Dies Irae* (2003, with subsequent developments) or that Biagini, the director of the Open Programme project ('project' belonging to Grotowski's lexicon), should be billed as the director of the four performances that came out of that project and were shown at the Zero Budget Festival under the auspices of the Grotowski Institute in Wroclaw in 2009.

Eugenio Barba: improvisation and 'dramaturgies'

The Workcenter's particular alternative way is not the way of Barba – without whose devotion and prodigious promotional skills, when Barba was Grotowski's apprentice in Opole during the years 1962–64, it is doubtful whether Grotowski's achievements with the Laboratory Theatre would have spread so rapidly beyond the frontiers of Poland.[39] Poland was then a communist country, although not as sealed off as others, as indicated by Grotowski's individual travels during communist rule. Entry back into Poland having been refused to Barba after his journey to Kerala in India (his visa had run out), Barba went to Oslo where, in 1964, he formed Odin Teatret with a bunch of 'rejects', as he likes to call, in his many writings, those who were neither accepted nor fitted into the established theatre institutions. The image of the outsider is one Barba has maintained throughout his working life; and it has sustained the complex of activities, including publishing and international seminars, that grew with Odin after it had moved to the rural environment of Holstebro in Denmark in 1966. Barba's image holds as much for the laboratory-style, closed-door rigorous physical and vocal training undertaken by Odin actors in the first ten years of its existence (most of them were 'outsider' autodidacts), as for the small-group, independent 'third-theatre' example set by the Odin and whose emulators proliferated throughout the world, especially in the 1970s and early 1980s, continuing into the twenty-first century.[40]

The greatest effect of third theatre was probably in South America – Peru, Venezuela, Argentina, Brazil, among other countries – mainly because the social conditions here were ripe for the guerilla-type role of sociopolitical intervention that such groups frequently filled; and this role was not only non-institutional, but, more important, anti-institutional in all senses of the word, including its non-alignment with political parties. Augusto Boal had already developed his more explicitly political Theatre of the Oppressed in Brazil in the 1960s (third theatre, by contrast, functioned more with subterfuge than with open fire). What Barba added was the concept of an archipelago of 'floating islands', as Barba, with a mythologizing streak similar to Grotowski's, defines those theatre groups that share values, perspectives and modes of behaviour and so form veritable communities. What, in his view, identified these islands was not their indigenous cultures, but their gravitation around 'theatre-culture', which Barba perceived as a culture defined not by national identifications but by groups of people devoted to the making of theatre per se, giving them the status of self-regulated entities – or (ornamenting Barba's metaphor of 'islands') of kingdom-islands.[41]

What the place of a director on such islands might be is a pertinent question, as it was for Grotowski's Paratheatre. There are similarities between them: their motivation to meet and mingle with others, and their multi-national and multi-cultural character. Yet Paratheatre is multi-cultural by virtue of the culturally diverse people who were active in its events. The archipelago requires multi-cultural islands but, when the archipelago's performing groups come together, its character morphs into a celebration of, in Barba's words, 'theatre-culture' as such. The groups' diverse cultural provenances are part of the plan, and are evident – this group is from Chile, that one from Italy, and so on – but they are of subsidiary importance to the primary intention of the gathering, which is to produce *theatre*. In other words, third theatre was always meant to be theatre, and even up to today Barba has never lost sight of this term. (Barba's emphasis assumes, of course, the – debatable – idea that theatre transcends cultural influences.)

Who and where, then, was the director in the floating-island alternative to the large (or not so large) houses that sheltered conventional, often text-based theatre? The question has to keep in mind the fact that this theatre of contestation was to a great extent founded on a collectivist ideal and so on the practice of improvisation that almost invariably went with it. Barba, as can be deduced from how he works with Odin, reinvented the director's role. Such reinvention, in a collectivist setting, necessarily involved confronting the issue of directorial control.

An anonymous participant in a 1980 workshop led by Barba for directors records Barba saying that

> People allow themselves to be manipulated if they aspire to give their maximum and have reciprocally chosen each other. In this case, manipulation is an agreement, an acknowledgment of an affinity aiming at independence.[42]

Barba not only accepts the manipulation that Flaszen repudiated – in Grotowski's Laboratory, too – by recasting it as a matter of 'agreement' and 'affinity' (although the Laboratory Theatre could not have functioned without these, as well). He also embraces the director's power and authority, to which he brings a significant nuance by calling it 'power, or authoritativeness' (see box). Barba's 'or' is decisive because it shifts the emphasis away from the idea of power as control to that of power as the capacity to incite for positive ends. The latter, positive impetus is integral to 'authoritativeness' and, given Barba's notion that 'manipulation' is agreed upon, 'authoritativeness' must operate in this consensual context. Further, he nuances the issue by observing that 'you lead small groups' (here echoing Paratheatre vocabulary) because 'you do not have the defences of the directors of a "normal" theatre: economic hierarchy, cultural prestige and contractual guarantees'.[43] A leader, in Barba's framework, is a director of a small group: distinguished only from directors of 'normal' theatres by the lack of institutional advantages that small, so-called alternative or independent groups, which are usually embattled economically, cannot hope to have.

The director's power to incite

The power of the director is that of the example. I don't believe in a director chosen democratically by the group. Some of you said: 'I would like to be an actor but my group needs a director. So I sacrificed myself.' But how can this be possible? If you feel the need to be an actor, you don't become a writer just because the group needs a play. What is the particular trait of a director? A personal need which makes him choose a role of power: the ability to make decisions, to implement them and take responsibility for them. This entails commitment and effort.

> I know I have great power. Everything I do leaves traces: how I speak, with whom I speak, if I keep silent, if I smile or am serious. With a word or a grimace, I can depress a person for a whole month. If I allow my personal problems to take over, these will spread like an epidemic.
>
> Power, or authoritativeness, is necessary for the director to incite, not subdue. To create mutual stimuli. I must be fascinated by an actor, admire his tenacity or naivety. Not for his physical beauty or talent, but for his will to work, to make sacrifices, for his desire to change and, by doing so, to change me. This is the mutual stimulus.
>
> Eugenio Barba, *On Directing and Dramaturgy*, 152

It is clear how Barba identifies himself as a small-group/third-theatre director, but the next step is to see what he does. Barba starts with what he calls the 'actor's dramaturgy', which is the vocal and physical 'score' (the term from Grotowski via Stanislavsky–Meyerhold) elaborated through actions by an individual actor during repeated improvisations. According to his long-standing collaborator Julia Varley, such a dramaturgy comprises three levels: the narrative level (which, glossing Varley, is the story made up by the actor to which she/he refers inwardly as the score is being elaborated); the organic level (which is the physical or movement dynamics of the actor); and the evocative level (which, again interpreting Varley, is made up of the images, associations and allusions deployed by the actor and which channel his/her emotions, evoking by their perceptibility reactions from spectators).[44]

By and large, the actors work alone on their improvisations, which include verbal texts, whether personally devised or pre-existent, before Barba works with them; and this is usually separately with each actor rather than together with them as an ensemble (contrary, say, to Brook's or Dodin's practices, where improvisation is a matter of constant bouncing-off of one another). His reason for his individual-focused rather than interactive approach is that two or more actors improvising together 'live in real time' and their 'natural tendency is to adapt themselves to what their companions are doing, turned towards the outside in order to understand what is happening and behave accordingly'.[45] Contrastingly, his purpose is to have the actor undertake a personal, in effect also private, journey. Despite this, Barba's *productions* are made up of exteriorized actions that allude to that journey (often cryptically, from the spectator's point of view) rather than being expressions of it; and in this they are noticeably different from Grotowski's inner-driven works.

Barba is quite clear that actors have to learn to repeat their individual improvisations and fix them;[46] and this, of course, actually turns these improvisations into scores, as in music, to be played thereafter. He intervenes 'once the actors had improvised and flawlessly assimilated their improvisations', noting that 'then my own improvisation as director began'.[47] By calling his activity an 'improvisation', Barba draws attention to the non-premeditated, spontaneously reactive and so desirably organic nature of his actions, which wend their way through 'a wealth of signals' emitted by the actors. These 'signals' refer to meanings that the actors have attributed to their own associations and evocations but to which Barba does not necessarily have any privileged access. As a consequence, Barba interjects through his reactions, which can call up his own associations and allusions, and through his own 'story' at the narrative level of his 'own improvisation'. While the process may sound indeterminate, it is nothing of the kind. Barba likens his actions to those of a surgeon 'cutting and sewing skin and human flesh', and, while his actors know that he is a 'surgeon, expert in techniques and different ways of operating', they are also aware that his 'know-how' does not 'guarantee the result'.[48]

Varley refers to how Barba 'cuts, mixes and edits my improvisations and materials', noting that commentators who have queried this process see 'the director who models my actions as a sculptor sculpts stone'. However, they do not 'perceive the opportunity offered to me by the obligations to refuse banality, dig deeper to face other limits and to constantly give the maximum of myself'.[49] Iben Nagel Rasmussen, another long-term member of Odin, reflects on how the Odin actors have learned to 'compose, improvise and fix scenes' over time, thus becoming more independent of the director and more capable of alternating between 'doing one's own thing' and 'being led' by him.[50]

Barba, when it comes to bringing improvisations together to make productions, changes his metaphor of surgeon and speaks of himself as 'orchestrating the actors' dramaturgies'.[51] The resultant 'montage', the term he frequently uses to describe both the procedure employed for the composition and the type of composition being made, is his 'dramaturgy of dramaturgies'.[52] This directorial 'dramaturgy' might well be described as a syncretic action that interweaves different entities while retaining their individual character, instead of merging or synthesizing them. Syncretism is, indeed, a feature of montage.

Individual dramaturgies also lead to individual pieces, usually solos, performance-demonstrations, or straight demonstrations with commentary. These are, among others, Roberta Carrera's *Traces in the Snow* (1988), Nagel Rasmussen's *White as Jasmine* (1993) and Varley's *The Dead Brother* (1994). In the latter, Varley shows how specific associations gave rise to her gestures and movements, and then to actions filled with intentions, and how, afterwards, Barba remodelled them, changing the direction of an action, or shortened or lengthened it, or stressed the opposition between actions, and so forth. Her annotated demonstration sheds light on Barba's 'dramaturgy of dramaturgies' approach, which, although elaborated over the years, during which time it also found its name, has fundamentally held fast from the early Odin landmark *My Father's House* (1972–74) to Odin's most recent production *The Chronic Life* (2011).

The Chronic Life is a vivid demonstration of Barba's 'dramaturgy of dramaturgies'. The production has seven characters for whom the actors had crafted individual dramaturgies, all set in the future in 2031 after a fictive civil war. The action takes place simultaneously, purportedly in different countries in Europe, including Denmark, and the production's linking thread on the narrative level (which is in fragments rather than a continuous storyline) is war, the aftermath of war, and death. There is thus a Chechen refugee as well as the widow of a Basque fighter, both of whom come in and out of the scenic picture and whose paths cross, here and there; and also a young Colombian boy who has come to Europe in search of his father. There is a (feckless) Danish lawyer, brandishing a notebook with an empty page, and a rock musician who, together with the lawyer-turned-guitarist, sings pointed ditties: the lawyer, for instance, about the poor becoming poorer while the 'rich get rich'. A Romanian housewife in a blonde wig and a parodic costume hanging with tea towels perpetually cleans invisible glass windows, and bursts into Louis Armstrong's 'What a Wonderful World'. This is Carrera's individual dramaturgy, and her chosen song, although optimistic, is ironic in the given circumstances. Barba's dramaturgy highlights its irony with the entrances and exits of two silent soldiers in fatigues and balaclavas.

Strong visual images abound. Huge butcher's hooks hang from the back enclosing 'wall' of the narrow stage space, flanked by spectators on either side (and they echo the fate of the army officers who plotted to kill Hitler in 1944). A puppet the size of a small boy hangs sideways from them, as does, frontwards, a block of ice that had served as a pillow for a dead body. Several characters also place themselves among the hooks, as if hanging from them when they do not simply lean against them. The prop at centre is a grave alternately filled and unfilled by the puppet and the young boy at different intervals, while, eventually, another puppet lying at the bottom of the grave becomes visible – all this suggesting layers of the dead. For the most part, this grave is covered, whether by a cloth or by a door-like object beneath it, whose carved-out squares are filled with coins – as spectators discover unexpectedly. The door represents a cross when it is 'worn' on a character's back. Meanwhile, showers of coins cascade twice across the stage, alluding, perhaps, to squandered abundance, or to the rich who 'get rich'.

A violinist who is the double of the Colombian boy enters, playing, towards the end of the performance, and these two representatives of the younger generation run off, laughing, through the door whose key (a symbolic father?) the boy has at last found. Spectators can patch together all these and many more fragments and details, as they will. But Barba the director interweaves them and their story-threads syncretically, careful not to fuse them in any way so that they retain their autonomy. The actors, too, do not connect (their aloofness from each other is noticeable) but intersect in what can be described as an apocalyptic view where the door opening for the young might be a chink of hope in and for an indeterminate future. Or it may simply be a door into perpetual darkness.

Wlodzimierz Staniewski (Gardzienice); Anna Zubrzycki and Grzegorz Bral (Song of the Goat)

The Grotowski line of collaborative-improvising-devising work being traced in these pages shows Barba at the first branch of its genealogical tree. However, Staniewski also belongs here, for, although he came to Grotowski and his core actors (Mirecka and others already cited) a good decade later than Barba, he is nevertheless from that first generation of practitioners who reflect Grotowski's direct influence while striking out on their own, often producing, like Barba, quite different work. Some of Grotowski's generation, artistically speaking, perhaps most noticeably Mirecka, inspired and helped such other practitioners as (in the late 1970s and early 1980s) Stacy Klein, founder of Double Edge Theatre in the United States (1982), with whom she is still in contact, offering workshops at Double Edge. Klein has also worked closely with Staniewski, and his example may well have influenced her choice of a home in the country in Ashfield, Massachusetts – the Farm – for the company.

Staniewski's greatest impact has, however, been in Poland, to which he has attracted various international collaborators. Having founded Gardzienice in 1977, he was joined soon after by Anna Zubrzycki, from Australia of Polish parents, who stayed with the group for sixteen years in its rural outpost in eastern Poland by the village from which it took its name. Zubrzycki together with Grzegorz Bral, who joined Gardzienice in the later 1980s, left to found Song of the Goat Theatre in Wroclaw in 1996, thus forming a second generation now further removed from Grotowski and more interested in consolidating new principles than in mining older ones, including those of Staniewski. Even so, Zubrzycki favours the notion of genealogy evoked above, stating that 'the genealogy is our strength' because:

> We know where we come from. We know where we're going. We come from a family. We have a point of reference ... I think it's crucial because it's not working in a vacuum. There's a real thought process behind the work we do and there's a real process in the work that Wlodek [Staniewski] did and Gregorz does. A real thought reference point to practitioners and it gives a sense of real stability. You know that it's embedded, and its fine, and you just keep going with it.[53]

Staniewski was less willing to acknowledge genealogy and, if anything, hoped to cut his ties with the Grotowski legacy. Yet it is inherent in the way he used the term 'expeditions', born of Paratheatre, as he set out with his troupe on their research journeys. The purpose of the expeditions was to come close to the peoples in the eastern border territories of present-day Poland – Poles, Ukrainians, Belorussians, Lithuanians, Lemkos in the Carpathian Mountains – not for anthropological reasons (although there was certainly an anthropological participant-observer dimension to Gardzienice's penetration of these ethnic groups), but from a desire to recover, to know and even to preserve the cultures of the 'people'. And these are the same 'people' or rural 'folk' venerated by nineteenth-century Polish Romantics, Mickiewicz at their helm, who saw in them the hope of Poland's freedom from successive foreign occupiers. However, rural populations, when Staniewski turned to them, had been thinned out not only by decaying farms and the old age of inhabitants, but also by migration to the cities where a living could be earned through industrial work.

One would be hard pressed to attribute a political dimension to Staniewski's position (as being against the communist drive to industrialization, for instance), although there is a political residue in his search for cultures that represent ancient identities and traditions putatively 'lost' under communist rule. More likely Staniewski had a deep personal affinity with the songs, music, religious ceremonies and stories of these peoples, and felt artistically inspired by them. Expeditions, in his words, are a 'pre-performative process', not only for collective gathering of the material offered, but because they 'embrace the life of the participants and the creative theatrical process'[54] (see box). They are a 'process of journeying, of "pilgrimage"' – perhaps not solely to founts or 'sources' of human expression, but to some kind of cleansing of the pilgrims. The leader of the pilgrimage is also its 'expedition director' (in Staniewski's vocabulary) who is responsible for the breakfast table as well as for the moment when eating becomes a 'ceremonial, artistic situation', or a rehearsal, or a piece of performance.[55] In short, the borders between performing and living fall away, and the director is omnipresent. Omnipresence, however, can be oppressive, even if the totalizing living-artistic experience is meant to be conducive to the creativity of the individuals within the group, and to the group as a whole.

The leader-director

This sort of journey, which I call expedition, has to have rules. It has to be framed, otherwise the intentions of every participant can pull it in different directions. There has to be one leader. It is not about authoritarianism. It is about accepting extreme responsibility for other human beings. It is more than just a theatre director rehearsing a play five or six hours a day, as in administrative theatre. This is someone who directs life twenty-four hours a day. The art of theatre and cultural activity is a segment in the greater plan for survival ... in homogenous societies the leader remains in that position as long as she or he proves they have the ability to deal with people's passions, imagination and creativity. Someone who is able to shape, to carve and to tune them. To direct means to make sublime in the chemical sense: to transform from one state to another. Metaphorically, it means to 'make poetic'.

Wlodzimierz Staniewski, with Alison Hodge, *Hidden Territories*, 40–1

Musicality is key to this creativity because it is a matter not of technical knowledge of how to sing or play an instrument, but of fathoming, in the case of song, the inner emotions that surge forth and fill the song. As Staniewski explains, when referring to the polyphony of *Avvakum* (1983), he asked the actors to 'look for these sounds in their hidden emotions'.[56] The search, frequently arduous, cannot dispense with intensive vocal training (not to be mistaken for mere acquisition of technique). This process of 'sounding', as Staniewski calls it, is strengthened by the type of improvisation done by the group that Zubrzycki likens to jazz.[57] In other words, voices come in when they sense it is the appropriate moment; and an acute intuition of the right moment comes from continual repetition not only of singing, but of playing instruments and movement work as well, in the course of their daily life together. Sensing of this kind is also stimulated by night running, a practice key to Gardzienice that Staniewski developed to awaken the actors' awareness of each other in the dark, all the better to sharpen their community responsiveness, also in performance conditions.

All of this articulates Staniewski's idea of 'musicality', which, he stresses, cannot simply be let loose, but 'has to be framed'.[58] Limits, too, have to be set in agreement with individual actors when emotional probing can cut too close and possibly be damaging to them. His example of working on the subject of hysteria with an actor, which was potentially harmful, calls forth the observation that his task then 'as the director' was to keep the work within a preventative, mutually defined 'map of reference points'.[59]

Gardzienice's practice raises the issue of where the boundaries between life and performance begin and end, and how, in such circumstances, a director such as Staniewski, who feels 'extreme responsibility for other human beings' (see box), risks controlling lives. Barba, in similar circumstances, felt from the very beginnings of Odin that he was obliged to guarantee the livelihood – the financial base – of his actors. However, the actors themselves made sure that they led their own lives by also engaging in other work that was their very own, even if it was under the umbrella of Odin's myriad activities. It is precisely because of her concern that actors should not dry up and wear out under the demands of collective training, improvising and devising – demands on which Gardzienice's work relied – that Anna Zubrzycki stresses the importance of their freedom to invent within the collaborative artistic processes of the group and to choose how else to expand their personal abilities outside it.[60]

Musicality

Since expansion entails outside professional engagements, it brings up the question of how independence sits with loyalty in a tightly knit group like Song of the Goat, and how possible conflicts of loyalties can be resolved without tearing the group apart. A clash of loyalties, not necessarily acrimonious, involves changes in group composition. It happens, too, that former members return to perform pieces they had helped to devise. Such has been the case for reprises of *Chronicles – A Lamentation* (2001), the multi-prize-winning work that established Song of the Goat. This work also marked out the company's principles, garnered both from heritage (like Gardzienice actors, Goat actors also undertake expeditions, which started with Greece and Albania instead of covering the border territories) and from cumulative experience in which, contrary to Gardzienice, improvisatory freedom is central. Zubrzycki takes the word 'leader' for herself as co-founder and co-artistic director and manager of the company, leaving the title of 'director' to Bral, since he is responsible for pulling performances together. Bral concedes that, as a director, he is a 'conductor'[61] (see box). Zubrzycki adds that the actors improvise (she is one of them), whereas Bral's role is to 'be our sounding board, a mirror, to lead us deeper and deeper into the material'.[62]

A director who is not one

I see my role as being really important because I bring the idea, I bring inspiration, I bring the corrections. I bring some kind of judgment on the work but, actually, the whole work – everything that you see in the performance – is produced by actors, not by me . . . I never say to the performer, 'Do it like this.' Occasionally, I may correct something when the performance requires me to say, 'Look, if you three go simultaneously, that will give you something additional.' So I am just trying to be supportive, but I'm not really a director. I never was.

Grzegorz Bral[63]

Bral foregrounds the fact that the actors generate the production, thus calling to mind how Brook, when discussing *The Tempest* (1990), also gave precedence to his actors' 'countless ways' of improvising: so rich was it that even the 'actors lost their way, and the role of the director is to keep track of what is being explored and for what purposes'.[64] If Brook observes that the 'energy' of improvisation 'produces a vast amount of raw material out of which the final shapes can be drawn', Bral focuses on how such material can be consistently coordinated by the actors, who finely tune in to each other, body and soul, throughout the process. It is in this absolute coordination between them, comparable to how instrumentalists coordinate in a 'concert' or 'symphony' (musical analogies to which Bral frequently refers), that his identification of himself as a conductor takes its full meaning.

Yet coordination involves more still. Song of the Goat is song-theatre, having started its life-path with polyphonic singing and, especially, lamentations, perhaps the most elemental and potent form of singing in Europe. (The company's name refers to the choral hymn, the dithyramb, sung and danced in Ancient Greece to honour Dionysus, the god of ecstasy, wine and fertility.) Mixed polyphonic songs, some from the repertoire of the male-singing Corsican group A Filetta, were the basis of *Macbeth* (2008). In this production, however, and contrary to the Corsican tradition, the women of Song of the Goat also sing these songs. Song, Bral claims, 'opens something internally', thereby releasing the energy and imagination necessary to 'explore the world of its sounds'.[65] In doing this, song allows the singer to travel deeper inwards (Zubrzycki's notion of finding 'a connection in your very own self' or 'psycho-emotional connection').[66] At the same time, this singer is keenly listening to the next singer, coordinating not only sound to sound, but how it is produced: one singer might move closer to another, or bend forward behind another, or perch near somebody else according to the sounds needed; and groupings of voices change according to the spirit of the song in a ceaseless flow of sound and motion.

Song, then, is the motor of this theatre and, in *Macbeth*, the type of intimate listening and body-placing required for polyphonic singing, lamentations or not, profoundly affects the performers' work with language. Shakespeare's text, when not chanted or intoned, is not quite spoken and not quite sung (the case particularly with dialogue between Lady Macbeth and Macbeth). The rhythms, intonations and cadences emerging from this treatment blend into the sound patterns of the whole. For Bral, Shakespeare's play is a concise musical composition, which he likens to the music of Bach: the words, like notes, provide emotional keys, assonances, dissonances and echoes, as do 'witch' and 'which' in *Macbeth*.[67] The actors build up counterpoint from the text, which they contrast with song or incantation, as in the production's opening scene. Here they chant, tightly grouped together, the speeches of Shakespeare's witches in fast crescendo, setting the pace of the production, which ends in Zubrzycki–Lady Macbeth's powerful lament not only for her husband, but for all the dead. Her voice filled with pain and compassion tells the spectators that these dead are part of her, and she of them.

The tremendous sense of unity and unison communicated by *Macbeth* comes from the subtle coordination of its musicality, certainly, but it equally comes from the coordination of all its elements: the kayagum, a Korean stringed instrument, between whose notes the actors weave their sounds and movements (many derived from the *kata* of Japanese martial arts); light (including candle light); costumes (reminiscent of Japanese Samurai skirts, which facilitate the jumps and other sharp movements of the legs); and props (wooden swords, whose thrusts give sounds). All these elements and more work closely in relation to each other and reflect the strong sense of collaborative endeavour emanating from the work of the performers. According to Zubrzycki, 'what Grzegorz tries to do as a director is open up fields and possibilities for us', and this must surely facilitate the group's explorations together.[68]

Jaroslaw Fret (Teatr ZAR): choral collaboration

Song is also not only at the heart of Teatr ZAR, it *is* Teatr ZAR, the most profoundly sonar of several third-generation groups descendent from Grotowski; and the fact that choral singing, an ensemble form par excellence, totally defines ZAR makes this group fully representative, even emblematic, of the very process of artistic collaboration itself.

Fret had spent a year and a half with Staniewski in the early 1990s, although, as a university student in Wroclaw, he had previously been part of a loose association of friends of Gardzienice and so was familiar with the company's all-round activities. He was also involved in the milieu of Grotowskians and their workshops (notably run by Mirecka and Molik), continuing these links after his return from Gardzienice to Wroclaw to work in the very place where the Laboratory Theatre had made its home (then known as the Grotowski Centre: today the Grotowski Institute, which Fret directs). Fret came into contact with Grotowski when Grotowski visited Wroclaw from Pontedera in 1991 on a formal occasion, and met him again informally several times in the mid 1990s.[69] It was he, together with Kamila Klamut, co-founder of Teatr ZAR, who repaired and reopened Brzezinka, the seat in the forest from which Paratheatre had radiated into the wider world. Fret and Klamut worked with Zubrzycki and Bral in Song of the Goat from 1996 to 1999.

This very brief historical sketch indicates that a network of connections to Grotowski, mostly indirect, was available to young practitioners who sought collaborative body-and-voice work not to be found in mainstream schools. Fret took his research further afield, going in 1999 with Klamut to Georgia, Armenia and Iran because of what he calls an 'intuition' rather than a will to make performances.[70] This was the first of four expeditions (the term and the thinking behind it definitely came from Staniewski) until 2002, when, as Fret recalls, nine people who would make up Teatr ZAR in 2003 travelled together. Fret's primary intention was to seek out the earliest song sources of Christianity – a desire that had its roots in his family history and Catholic upbringing.

Fret found in Svaneti, in the northwestern mountains of Georgia, the Orthodox communities of the Svan people who sing polyphonic songs in three-part harmony thought to be some 2000 years old, possibly the oldest polyphonic songs in the world. Among these songs sung in a language that was no longer spoken or understood was Zar: a funeral song, sung predominantly by one family for hours on end to send the soul of the deceased person safely on his/her journey into the afterlife. Fret and his companions decided that this song with its simple but irreducible, unfathomable sonorities, old beyond imagining, was to give its name to the company that they inaugurated in 2003 with *Gospels of Childhood: Fragments on Intimations of Immortality from Recollections of Early Childhood*. In 2007, *Caesarian Section: Essays on Suicide* followed, and *Anhelli: The Calling* in 2009. All three, developed without haste, as is evident from the time taken between them, made up a triptych (the reference here to icons being perfectly intentional) that could be performed as one whole or in separate sections.

Gospels is steeped in Svanetian polyphony and also in liturgical chant learned at the Sioni Church in Tbilisi, the capital of Georgia. The remaining pieces of the triptych draw on these vital sources within a wider range – polyphonic songs from Bulgaria and Corsica in *Caesarian Section* (together with Erik Satie's *Gnossiennes*), and, in *Anhelli*, paschal chants from the

Castelsardo brotherhood in Sardinia together with Orthodox hymns. All were learned during expeditions. Fret may not have set out to create performance pieces, but create them he did, expanding with collaborators who did not necessarily share his religious background, which increasingly became the case after 2005 as the group became more international. The generic 'Christian', which he continues to be, superseded any religious confession or denomination. Furthermore, the triptych, by the very nature of its singing, opened up a space for listener-spectators that can be defined as 'spiritual' without committing it to an institutionalized framework of belief of any kind. Fret is quite adamant that the group did not set out to be 'spiritual' when ZAR was founded; nor do its members discuss 'spiritual' issues.[71]

ZAR extended its brief to workshops, lecture demonstrations and related dissemination, which appear to be a hallmark of small-scale collaborative performance groups issuing from the Grotowski nexus and which, in this same context, justify the name of 'project leader' that Fret uses to identify the many-sided 'functions' (Fret's term) that he fulfils in the ZAR group. This name (as noted above) emerges from Paratheatre and post-Paratheatre perception that directors and productions necessarily belong to 'theatre' – indeed, essentially to literary theatre – while 'projects' are beyond 'theatre', in the realm of what Grotowski called the 'post-theatrical'. Yet Fret does, in fact, direct. He does so not by imposing, but by proposing 'hunches', 'intimations', 'ideas' (among various terms), associated with the tangle of memories and impressions accumulated during ZAR's expeditions, as well as by 'editing' (Fret's term) the material devised collaboratively by his companions.[72] It can be said, as seems to be characteristic of collaborative improvising-devising groups in general, that, for the triptych, the material of the process becomes the composition of the performances.

The tone and temper of the triptych modulate according to whether its sections are played together or singly. *Anhelli*, for instance, which has the softness of a prayer when it completes the triptych, is a more energetic, extroverted piece when performed alone. This fluidity has to do with how the three works, although conceived in the spirit of music and the spirit of liturgy – Grotowski's 'holy' theatre here finds a fitting incarnation – are not meant to replace either church singing or church ritual, but to be *theatre* in which what can be construed as sacred – and, indeed, is sacred because of the sacral quality of ZAR's song and singing – goes together, side by side, with the secular. It goes together, for example, with the rape at a wedding alluded to in *Gospels*, or with the suicide attempts of *Caesarian Section*, one of which, gently humorous, involves a small mandarin tree and a large rope with a loop that Klamut holds in each hand, standing on a chair; another, in a fragment closing the work, involves Klamut failing to hold a plastic bag – a banal item from any kitchen – out of which scatter numerous bright oranges. The startling colour of these oranges, together with the sound of their falling and their movement as they roll, counterpoints the startling stupor that Klamut conveys, which turns, at play's end, into a silent scream. The counterpoint of song, sound, silence, imagery and movement pithily caught in this fragment recurs throughout the triptych.

The theatre dimension of ZAR performances is constant, bringing together sonic and visual imagery, movement dynamics (which, in any case, is inherent in the breath and sound of singing), and shards of narrative that, by being non-linear, displaced and decontextualized, are elusive and allusive, often disorienting the spectators' perception of where and how they fit. Pieces from the story of Lazarus, Mary and Martha in *Gospels* are a case in point. A mound of earth, loud knocking on a table (possibly associated with knocking on a grave to awaken Lazarus from the dead) and actions of giving birth, the washing of feet and other biblical allusions, not only to the resurrection of Lazarus but also to the birth and death of Christ, permeate the production as song fills it. This process of envelopment, from which arises the production's sonosphere, shows that song is the baseline triggering off the type of action to be performed, its tempo and rhythm, and its quality or 'feel', or, as Fret aptly says, its 'temperature'.[73]

Blackouts counterpoint the presence of light – predominantly candle light – and accentuate, through an absence of seeing, the sounds of singing, of musical instruments, of objects (wine spilling, glass breaking, earth falling, water running) and of bodies (the slap of hands on the floor, the stamp of feet, the thud of a fall). Towards the end of *Gospels*, the group evokes Christ's resurrection of Lazarus by singing Zar in total darkness. The sound here, as Fret observes, 'is the image'.[74] Indeed, to have added a layer of visual or movement imagery would have been superfluous, and, of course, hopelessly literal in what, in biblical terms, is a mystery and, in dramatic terms, is meant to be mysterious. Furthermore, Zar sung here as both a farewell and a call for the resurrection of the soul, as it is by the Svan, requires something akin to deep respect, which, in terms of theatre, is arguably communicated with the greatest sensitivity through darkness. The group was taught Zar by the family who sings it, and this oral transmission, given with the family's permission for the purposes of theatre, is also treated respectfully with ambient darkness.

ZAR always develops its movement-visual 'score' (now also Fret's term) separately from the singing, in parallel with it rather than as an illustration or extension of it; and group improvisation relies on whatever stimulates the imagination, including bits of text – non-fiction, novels or poems – and is done with little talk so as not to rationalize creativity or block its openness. As the work advances, Fret's role is to hold together the different energies of its different components. Yet the energy-charge of singing is such that, while it embraces everything happening in the performance, as with an invisible thread, it threads together the performers and the listener-spectators. In this threading of oneness lies too, for spectators, the space of the 'spiritual', and the potential, for them, of a spiritual experience from a theatre performance.

Fret provided much less in the way of suggestions for *Caesarian Section* and *Anhelli* than he did for *Gospels*, which was so personal to him. Nevertheless, he continued to suggest the 'subject' of each new sequence of work from its beginning. Thus for the 'subject' of falling in *Anhelli*, for example, he asked the men to fall in numerous different ways.[75] The production shows that his purpose was not so much to see as to *hear* and *listen to* different falling, and because ZAR, for Fret, is above all a matter of listening, he timed visual-sonic actions very precisely: he asked that one (for example, falling) last a minute and forty seconds, another, a minute and forty-five seconds, and so on. He arranged the order of sequences of actions as the material emerged, his ear consistently open to the overarching timing of their combination. It really could not be otherwise in a theatre for which the time and timing integral to music and song is crucial.

Fret can be said to direct like a composer and choirmaster in one, and, since he also sings in this extraordinarily powerful choir of eleven people, he occasionally conducts it from within, sometimes using the least perceptible of gestures, while at others (notably in *Gospels*) they are quite evident and strong; but he always uses his breath to mark and measure time. A sharply drawn-in breath, an exhalation, or a gasp of air by the whole group makes breath inseparable from the composition and is meant to be noticed by the listeners, as if they were noticing their own breathing. Sound by such means, together with voiced polyphonic sound, which is multi-layered, adding further layers through overtones, creates compactness of sound. Fret calls it a 'column of breathing', referring here, as well, to the idea of the 'vertical' created through singing (the purpose of Zar), which is the path upwards to the divine.[76] ZAR's singing also expands what Grotowski in his practice with song in Art as Vehicle described as 'vibratory qualities which are so tangible that in a certain way they become the meaning of the song'.[77]

ZAR's themes are simple, transported by its songs: birth, life, death and resurrection. Resurrection is not envisaged in *Caesarian Section*, which focuses on the pain of living. In *Anhelli*, by contrast, the hope of resurrection is expressed as the work closes with the Orthodox hymn from the Byzantine liturgical tradition known as an *irmos*. The singers here ask God to 'receive my soul'. The hymn comes at the end of a voyage suggested from the very beginning by a white canopy that lightly floats up and down: it breathes with the breath of song and of the motion of long poles, reminiscent of oars, moved by the singers. The hymn is preceded by the heavy fall of five men, who pick themselves up, tear away the boards from the floor, and fall again and again. By a collocation of associations, the gaps in the floor recall the grave, implied by piled-up earth, in *Gospels*. In this way, anterior work was remembered, perhaps subliminally, during the devising of *Anhelli*.

Anhelli remembers the past in yet another way since it borrows Slowacki's poem of this name for inspiration, several lines from it being spoken in an otherwise wholly sung performance. Slowacki, as ZAR knows well, was central to Grotowski's universe. *Kordian* is by Slowacki, and Grotowski used Slowacki's version of *The Constant Prince* by Calderon de la Barca. Encrypted, perhaps, in ZAR's *Anhelli* is a tribute to Grotowski but it in no way affects the power of the trope of the journey in this production. Slowacki's Anhelli travels to the Holy Land on a mission that he fails to accomplish. ZAR's *Anhelli* is a vehicle for the group's meditation on life's journey towards death. The bells that gave such sonic texture to *Gospels* are replaced, in *Anhelli*, by the majestic beat and resonance of a large Persian drum played by Fret, who is hidden in the shadows. Hidden but present, and providing the beat: this description is apt for Fret's part in collaborative work whose freedom lies in voices that sing.

18 *Anhelli: The Calling*, Teatr ZAR, 2009

Further reading

Barba, Eugenio. *On Directing and Dramaturgy: Burning the House*, London and New York: Routledge, 2010

Bartula, Malgorzata and Stefan Schroer. *On Improvisation: Nine Conversations with Roberto Ciulli*, Brussels: P. I. E.-Peter Lang, 2003

Grotowski, Jerzy. *Towards a Poor Theatre*, New York: Simon and Schuster, 1968

Savran, David. *Breaking the Rules: The Wooster Group*, New York: Theatre Communications Group, 1988

Schechner, Richard and Lisa Wolford (eds.). *The Grotowski Sourcebook*, London and New York: Routledge, 1997

Staniewski, Wlodzimierz with Alison Hodge, *Hidden Territories: The Theatre of Gardzienice*, London and New York: Routledge, 2004

Notes

1 Traditional staging and the evolution of the director

1. For a discussion of the Greek chorus, see Josh Beer, *Sophocles and the Tragedy of Athenian Democracy*, Westport, CT: Praeger, 2004, 45–6. For a discussion of the *Choregus*, see 32ff.
2. The overriding significance of the chorus and the dithyramb are documented by Beer, *Sophocles*, 14–16.
3. *Trinummus* (Threepence) by Plautus (date unknown).
4. For more detailed information on the staging of Roman theatre, see William Beare, *The Roman Stage*, London: Methuen, 1968.
5. This sketch, attributed to Henry Peacham, has been widely reproduced: for instance in *William Shakespeare: The Complete Works*, ed. Stanley Wells and Gary Taylor, Oxford: Clarendon Press, 1988.
6. The suggestion comes from Peter Thompson: entry on Masque, *The Cambridge Guide to World Theatre*, Cambridge University Press, 1988, 625. Another suggestion attributes the origin of the proscenium arch to the Teatro Farnese in Parma; but although this is the first permanent building to have a frame separating the audience from the stage, it was only completed in 1628, and initially was not designated for dramatic performances.
7. Kalman Burnim, *David Garrick: Director*, University of Pittsburgh Press, 1961.
8. Burke's epitaph is reproduced in George Stone and George Kahel, *David Garrick: A Critical Biography*, Carbondale: Southern Illinois University Press, 1979, 648.
9. Denis Diderot, *The Paradox of the Actor* (1770–84), in *Selected Writings on Art and Literature*, trans. Geoffrey Bremner, Harmondsworth: Penguin, 1994, 120.
10. John Hill, *The Actor*, London: Printed for R. Griffith, 1750; New York: Blom, 1971, 239. Macklin advised Garrick for his famous 1741 performance as Richard III and Garrick acted under him when Macklin was stage-manager of Drury Lane Theatre.
11. Leigh Woods, *Garrick Claims the Stage*, Westport, CT: Greenwood Press, 1984, 13.
12. Garrick mounted a Shakespeare Jubilee at Stratford in 1769, which he then produced as pageants at Drury Lane, where he delivered an Ode to Shakespeare. Even so, he was also capable of cutting Shakespeare (omitting both Ophelia's madness and the gravediggers from a 1772 production of *Hamlet*), using Nahum Tate's notorious version of *King Lear* and making his own adaptations of *Antony and Cleopatra*, *The Winter's Tale* and *The Tempest*.

13. What is known of Garrick's settings comes largely from contemporary stage-paintings by Benjamin Wilson, who may have made the scenery more realistic than it actually appeared.
14. Anon., *The Case of the Stage in Ireland – Wherein the Qualifications, Duty and Importance of a Manager are Carefully Considered*, Dublin, n.d., 37.
15. See Charles Knight, *London*, London: Henry G. Bohn, 1851, V, 287.
16. John Davis Batcheleder, *Henry Irving – A Short Account of his Public Life*, New York: William S. Gottsberger, 1883, 149–50.
17. Edward Gordon Craig, *Henry Irving*, London: Dent, 1930, 55.
18. Henry Irving, *The Drama: Addresses*, London, 1893, 157 and 55.
19. Batcheleder, *Henry Irving*, 153.
20. *Ibid.*, 152.
21. Quoted in Bram Stoker, *Personal Reminiscences of Henry Irvine*, London: Macmillan, 1906, I, 147.
22. Edward Gordon Craig, *Index to the Story of My Days*, New York: Viking, 1957, 156, 159–60.
23. The popularity of the post in 1815 was as a form of censorship in reaction against the threat to established hierarchies by the defeated Napoleon – and the *Intendant* system is sometimes blamed for the widespread decline of German theatre in the 1830s and 1840s: see Eduard Devrient, himself an *Intendant* (1848–74), in *Geschichte der deutschen Schauspielkunst*, or for example, Simon Williams, *Richard Wagner and Festival Theatre*, Westport, CT: Greenwood Press, 1994, 36–7. At the same time not all *Intendants* were by any means establishment figures: Heinrich Laube, for instance, had been jailed for his part in Junges Deutschland in 1837, being released from prison just five years before his appointment to the Burgtheater. However, they became an important source for theatrical innovation.
24. For a discussion of the role of the dramaturge, see Mary Luckhurst, *Dramaturgy: A Revolution in Theatre*, Cambridge University Press, 2006.

2 The rise of the modern director

1. See Christopher Innes (ed.), *A Sourcebook on naturalist Theatre*, London and New York: Routledge, 2000, 77.
2. Ellen Franz having maintained a close youthful friendship with Cosima Liszt: first married to the musician Hans von Bülow, whom Duke Georg appointed to lead the Meiningen court orchestra. Notoriously von Bülow's enthusiasm for Wagner's work led to Cosima's scandalous affair with Wagner, her 1869 divorce and remarriage to him – and in 1876 the Duke and Ellen attended performances in Bayreuth while Wagner came with Cosima to conduct his own work in Meiningen in 1877.
3. Stanislavsky had seen the Meiningen's 1890 Moscow production of *Julius Caesar* – and was also impressed by their staging of *The Merchant of Venice*, which was added to their repertoire for the 1895 tour.

4. 'Naturalism in the Theatre', trans. Albert Bermel, in Eric Bentley (ed.), *The Theory of the Modern Stage*, Harmondsworth: Penguin Books, 1976, 359, 364–5.
5. Bibliothèque nationale de France, Manuscrits, NAF 10345, ff. 14–15.
6. 'Naturalism in the Theatre', trans. Bermel, 369ff.
7. Antoine criticized the Meiningen crowds because their costumes were accurate for time and place, but not for the texture of their lives, being too new and clean. See Jean Chothia, *André Antoine*, Cambridge University Press, 1991, 61.
8. Many of the details of Antoine's staging and directorial practices are informed by Chothia's *André Antoine*: here 7–10.
9. See Chothia, *André Antoine*, 14.
10. J. T. Grein, see Michael Orme, *J. T. Grein: The Story of a Pioneer, 1862–1935*, London: Murray, 1936, 70.
11. See, for instance, Chothia, *André Antoine*, 132.
12. The productions for which these screens were used included Yeats' *The Hour Glass* (1911) and *On Baille's Strand* (1914).
13. For a discussion of the stage effects created by Lugné-Poë, see Bettina Knapp, 'The Reign of the Theatrical Director: Antoine and Lugné-Poë', *The French Review*, 61, no. 6 (May 1988), 871f.
14. Ideas expounded by Wagner in 1849 essays, 'Die Kunst und die Revolution' and 'Das Kunstwerk der Zukunft', and elaborated in *Oper und Drama* (1851).
15. Richard Wagner, *Gesammelte Schriften und Briefe*, ed. Julius Kapp, Leipzig: Hesse and Becker, 1914, IX, 21.
16. Even though this was not the first design of this kind, since there was at least one earlier example, at the theatre in Riga where Wagner had been conductor 1837–9, and which served to some extent as his model, the Bayreuth Festival Theatre proved the success of this form and was by far the best known example.
17. Richard Wagner, *Das Bühnenfestspielhaus zu Bayreuth* (Leipzig, 1873), see Herbert Barth, *Der Festspielhügel*, Munich: List Verlag, 1973, 11. For a fuller discussion of the Bayreuth Festspielhaus and its stage, see Williams, *Richard Wagner*, 117ff.
18. The total number of theatrical productions Appia directed was only five: two one-act pieces (given a single private performance in Paris, 1903), *Orfeo*, with Dalcroze at Hellerau (1912–13), *Tristan* (1923) and a patriotic pageant at Geneva (1925) – and in addition to the two parts of the Ring directed by Oskar Wälterlin, his designs were used as settings for just two further productions, *Tidings Brought to Mary* staged by the author Claudel himself (Hellerau 1913) and Aeschylus' *Prometheus* (Basle 1925), also directed by Wälterlin.
19. For a more detailed discussion of Appia's connection to symbolism, see Richard Beacham, *Adolphe Appia: Theatre Artist*, Cambridge: Cambridge University Press, 1987, 3–5. Beacham also offers an extensive analysis of Appia's relationship to Bayreuth, 150ff.
20. 'Actor, Space, Light and Painting' (Ts. c.1920, 105) and 'Eurhythmics and the Theatre' (Ts. c.1911, 74), trans. Walther Volbach (Appia Coll. Bieneke Library, Yale University).

21. 'Ideas on a Reform of our Mise en Scène' (Ts., 28), trans. Walther Vollbach (Appia Coll. Bieneke Library, Yale University).
22. Souvenir programme, Bayreuth: see Karl Reyle, 'Adolphe Appia and the New Stage', *American-German Review*, Aug.–Sept. 1962, 19.
23. Jacques Copeau, 'L'art et l'œuvre d'Adolphe Appia', *Comoedia*, 12 March 1928.
24. In addition, he worked briefly with Otto Brahm and Max Reinhardt in Berlin, designed productions for the great Italian tragedienne Eleonora Duse and for the poet W. B. Yeats, and also designed backdrops and lighting for Isadora Duncan's pioneering modern dance performances.
25. While Grotowski referred to Stanislavsky in various texts and especially in his lectures and other oral presentations and commentaries, arguably his richest reflections about the Russian practitioner are to be found in his speech published as 'Reply to Stanislavsky', which, unfortunately, appears not to be available in English, but can be consulted in the Italian translation from the Polish, 'Risposta a Stanislavsky' in *Opere e sentieri. Jerzy Grotowski, tetsi 1968–1998*, II, ed. Antonio Attisani and Mario Biagini, Rome: Bulzoni Editore, 2007, 45–64. Similarly, Barba's writings offer a range of observations about this one of several of his 'masters', but none, perhaps, as succinct as his remarks in the interview 'Eugenio Barba in Conversation with Maria Shevtsova: Reinventing Theatre', *New Theatre Quarterly*, 23, no. 2 (2007), 99–114. Peter Brook, always shy in his books about his influences, incorporates Stanislavsky as a figure who cannot be ignored in his two treatise-like productions *Qui est là?* (*Who's There?*, 1996) and *Warum, Warum* (*Why? Why?*, 2010) compiled from texts largely by Zeami, Artaud, Craig and Meyerhold. In any case, Brook, like his direct influence Grotowski, ascribes to the laboratory, actor-centred concept of theatre, and in this is indirectly linked to Stanislavsky.
26. Chekhov became the anglicized 'Michael' after he came to teach acting at Dartington Hall in England in 1936.
27. Jean Benedetti (selected, ed. and trans.), *The Moscow Art Theatre Letters*, London: Methuen, 1991, 225; italics in the original.
28. *Ibid.*
29. Trans. and ed. Jean Benedetti, London and New York: Routledge, 2008.
30. *My Life in the Russian Theatre*, trans. John Cournos, London: Geoffrey Bles, 1968, 155.
31. *The Moscow Art Theatre Letters*, 165.
32. Konstantin Stanislavsky, *Zapisnye Knizhki*, Moscow: Vagrius, 2001, 196, trans. Maria Shevtsova.
33. *Ibid.*, 172–3.
34. *Ibid.*
35. *The Moscow Art Theatre Letters*, 33.
36. *Ibid.*, 64.
37. *Ibid.*, 120.
38. *Ibid.*, 185 and 186.
39. *Ibid.*, 37.

40. Wilson's commentary on juxtaposition is in the video by Mark Obenhaus, *Einstein on the Beach: The Changing Image of Opera*, Obenhaus Films/Brooklyn Academy of Music, 1985.
41. The phrase is to be found in Konstantin Stanislavsky, *An Actor's Work*, trans. Jean Benedetti, London and New York: Routledge, 2008, 99 in the chapter 'Concentration and Attention', 86–118.
42. S. D. Balukhaty, ed. and trans. David Magarshak, *The Seagull Produced by Stanislavsky*, London: Denis Dobson, 1952, 174–5. For the Russian text see S. D. Balukhaty, *Chaika v Poctanovke Moskovskovo Khudozhestvennovo Teatra, Rezhisserskaya Partitura KS Stanislavskogo*, Leningrad: Isskustvo, 1938, 166–7.
43. *Ibid.*, 259; Russian text, 261.
44. *Ibid.*, 278–79; Russian text, 282–5.
45. David Richard Jones, *Great Directors at Work*, Berkeley and Los Angeles: University of California Press, 1986.
46. O. A. Radishcheva, *Stanislavsky i Nemirovich-Danchenko: Istoria Teatralnykh Otnoshenyi, 1909–1917*, Moscow: Artist Rezhisser. Teatr, 1999, 19.
47. Quoted in Jean Benedetti, *Stanislavsky: His Life and Art, A Biography*, London: Methuen, 1999, 124.
48. Quoted in *Stanislavsky i Nemirovich-Danchenko*, 20, trans. Maria Shevtsova.
49. *My Life in Art*, 114.
50. *Ibid.*

3 Directors of theatricality

1. Aleksandr Gladkov, *Meyerhold Speaks, Meyerhold Rehearses*, trans. and ed. with introduction by Alma Law, Amsterdam: Harwood Academic Publishers, 1997, 176 and 173 for 'instantaneous inspiration'. Gladkov, who was a pupil of Meyerhold, also observes that 'in essence, Meyerhold played all the roles in all the plays he staged', 174.
2. *Ibid.*, 132. The Russian word *artist* means both 'actor' (also *aktyor*) and 'stage designer' and here refers to the latter. Hence the correction above to the English translation of Gladkov's Russian text.
3. Quoted in the introduction by Alla Mikhaïlova to Alla Mikhaïlova *et al.*, *Meierkhold i Khudozhniki/Meyerhold and Set Designers* [a bilingual publication], Moscow: Galart, 1995, 61.
4. *Ibid.*
5. Letter of 16 December 1928 by Zinaida Raikh, Meyerhold's favourite actress and wife, in *Teatr*, 2 (1974), 34.
6. Meyerhold in Edward Braun (trans. and ed. with critical commentary), *Meyerhold on Theatre*, London: Methuen, 1969, 125.
7. *Ibid.*, 122–8. Strictly speaking, a 'cabotin' (French word) is a strolling player. Meyerhold's spirited defence of 'cabotinage' here focuses on the type of play done

by strolling players, but it is also an attack on the MAT's pejorative understanding of the term, which equates 'cabotinage' with third-rate or ham acting.

8. *Ibid.*, 126.
9. *Ibid.*, 129.
10. *Ibid.*, 138. Meyerhold's emphasis.
11. Gladkov, *Meyerhold Speaks*, 142.
12. In another seminal essay, 'First Attempts at a Stylized Theatre' (1907), Meyerhold speaks of the assumed 'theatre-triangle' of current practice in which the director is the apex of the triangle of the theatre event, flanked by the author and the actor in the two remaining corners. He replaces this model with a straight horizontal line featuring the author, director, actor and spectator, who together define the theatre. See this essay in Braun, *Meyerhold on Theatre*, 50.
13. Gladkov, *Meyerhold Speaks*, 121 and 126.
14. 'The Actor of the Future and Biomechanics' (1922) in Braun, *Meyerhold*, 199. Meyerhold's stress on how outward actions stimulated emotions is the antithesis of the early Stanislavskian approach, which Stanislavsky subsequently revised through the method of physical action, as observed in the preceding chapter.
15. Meyerhold cited in Braun, *Meyerhold*, 198–9.
16. *Ibid.*, 209.
17. Aleksandr Tairov, *Notes of a Director*, trans. and with introduction by William Kuhlke, Coral Gables, FL: University of Miami Press, 1969, 107.
18. *Ibid.*, 143.
19. *Ibid.*, 54.
20. *Ibid.*, 47 and 65 (Tairov's emphasis).
21. *Ibid.*, 90.
22. *Ibid.*, 90.
23. *Ibid.*, 131.
24. *Ibid.*, 125.
25. See especially 93–4 of *Notes*; 90 for 'duties'.
26. Lyubov Vendrovskaya and Galina Kaptereva (comp.), *Evgeny Vakhtangov* [*Notes by Vakhtangov, Articles and Reminiscences*], trans. Doris Bradbury, Moscow: Progress Publishers, 1982, 140 for the citation.
27. *Ibid.*, 156–8. This could also be translated as 'fantastic realism'. See 153 for the phrase 'emotional truth'.
28. *Ibid.*, 138.
29. *Ibid.*, 37.
30. *Ibid.*, 251; commentary on *Turandot* by Boris Zakhava, one of Vakhtangov's most important actors, who performed in the production. See also Yury Zavadsky, *Uchitelya i uchineky (Teachers and Pupils)*, Moscow: Iskusstvo, 1975, 202–3.
31. *Russian and Soviet Theatre: Tradition and the Avant-Garde*, trans. Roxane Permar and ed. Lesley Milne, London: Thames and Hudson, 1988, 55.
32. *Evgeny Vakhtangov*, 121–2.

33. Mikhaïl Chekhov, in *Evgeny Vakhtangov*, 208–10.
34. David Williams (comp. and ed.), *Collaborative Theatre: The Théâtre du Soleil Sourcebook*, London and New York: Routledge, 1999, 173. It is important to note that the final 'é' of *théâtralité* is the exact linguistic equivalent of the Russian 'nost' of *teatralnost*, which suggests an exact parallel in usage.
35. Ariane Mnouchkine, *Entretiens avec Fabienne Pascaud: l'art du présent*, Paris: Plon, 2005, 58. All translations from French are by Maria Shevtsova except in the inserted box.
36. *Ibid.*, 77.
37. *Ibid.*, 82.
38. *Ibid.*, 173 and 68.
39. *Collaborative Theatre*, 173 for reference to Artaud. See Antonin Artaud, *The Theatre and its Double*, trans. Mary Caroline Richards, New York: Grove Press, 1958, 74–88.
40. Maria Shevtsova, 'A Theatre that Speaks to Citizens: Interview with Ariane Mnouchkine', *Western European Stages*, 7, no. 3 (1995–96), 9. See also *Entretiens avec Fabienne Pascaud*, 162 and *Collaborative Theatre*, 217.
41. *Entretiens avec Fabienne Pascaud*, 15, 173 and 162; 93; 138; 17; 25, respectively, for each identified point.
42. *Ibid.*, 201.
43. *Collaborative Theatre*, 219 and 56 for the earlier interview.
44. *Entretiens avec Fabienne Pascaud*, 70.
45. *Ibid.*, 60.
46. Interview with Andrew Dickson, *The Guardian*, 13 November 2011.
47. Quoted in Marvin Carlson, *Theatre Is More Beautiful than War: German Stage Directing in the Late Twentieth Century*, Iowa City: University of Iowa Press, 2009, 166.

4 Epic theatre directors

1. See Georg Fuchs, *Revolution in the Theatre*, trans. Constance Connor Kuhn, Ithaca, NY: Cornell University Press, 1959, xvii.
2. *Blätter der Piscatorbühne Kollektiv*, no. 8. Berlin, April 1930, 12.
3. Bertolt Brecht, *Schriften zum Theater*, Frankfurt-am-Main: Suhrkamp, 1967, 192. (All citations from this source trans. Christopher Innes.)
4. Erwin Piscator, 'Das politische theater', *Die Rote Fahne*, 1 January 1928, 53.
5. Manifesto for the Piscatorbühne, 1927. (All translations from Piscator are by Christopher Innes.)
6. Piscator, *Das politische Theater*, Reinbeck bei Hamburg: Rohwolt, 1963, 132.
7. *Ibid.*, 179.
8. *Ibid.*, 172.
9. See 'The Piscator Section', *Drama Review*, 22, no. 4 (December 1978), 92. There are numerous photos from the production reprinted in this issue of *TDR*.

10. 'Die Filmprojektion im Theaterstück "Rasputin"', Film Supplement of the *B.Z am Mittag* (no date) Steinfeld Archiv, Cologne.
11. Quotations from *Rasputin* are taken from the Piscatorbühne prompt book, Akademie der Künste, Berlin.
12. *Das politische Theater*, 161.
13. Excerpt from Leo Lania's script, Akademie der Künste, Berlin, reprinted in *Das politische Theater*, 177.
14. Julius Richter, '*Rasputin*/Nach der Aufführung der Piscatorbühne', *Die Scene 2*, (1928), 40f.
15. *Das politische Theater*, 151–3.
16. *Ibid.*, 152.
17. Bernhard Diebold, *Frankfurter Zeitung*, 11.9.1929, reprinted Günther Rühle (ed.), *Theater für die Republik*, Frankfurt am-Main: Fischer Verlag, 1967, 962ff.
18. Brecht, *The Messingkauf Dialogues* (1965: trans. John Willett) in *Bertolt Brecht: Plays, Poetry, Prose*, London: Methuen, 1985, 69.
19. *Ibid.*, 181.
20. Brecht, *Schriften zum Theater*, 63–4.
21. *Ibid.*, 8–9.
22. Brecht, *Parables for the Theatre* (trans. Eric Bentley and Maja Applebaum), New York: Grove Press, 1961, 96; *The Jewish Wife and Other Short Plays* (trans. Eric Bentley), New York: Grove Press, 1965, 143.
23. The Compère, in top hat, frockcoat and white gloves, is the well-known comedienne Liesl Karlstadt in drag. Pinned to the curtain is a caricature of a sneering bourgeois; in front of the performers is a stand on which large roll-down placards can be successively shown during the presentation. The one on display depicts a car knocking down a circus strongman – clearly the topic of the presentation.
24. Brecht, *The Messingkauf Dialogues*, 69–70.
25. *Brecht on Theatre*, trans. John Willett, London: Eyre Methuen, 1964, 3–4.
26. Brecht, *Gedichte*, trans. John Willett, see *The Theatre of Bertolt Brecht*, London: Methuen, 1967, 161.
27. *Schriften zum Theater*, 109–10.
28. *Ibid.*, 90–3.
29. *Ibid.*, 110.
30. Brecht, *The Caucasian Chalk Circle*, trans. Eric Bentley, New York: Grove Press, 1965, 126.
31. *Theaterarbeit*, Berlin: Henschelverlag, 1967, 254.
32. *Ibid.*, 256–8.
33. *Ibid.*, 14.
34. *Ibid.*, 315. (Given the divided state of Germany, the ensemble in East Berlin were not permitted to act in the West, so a completely new cast had to be rehearsed for Munich.)
35. Brecht, 'Kleines Organum' #67, *Schriften zum Theater*, 166.
36. Brecht, *The Messingkauf Dialogues*, 75.

37. Heiner Müller, interview with Horst Laube, *Theater Heute*, Sonderheft, 1975, 121.
38. Müller, in *Theater der Zeit*, 3, no. 8 (1975), 58–9.
39. *The Mission*, in *Theatremachine*, ed. and trans. Marc von Henning, London and Boston: Faber, 1995, 60.
40. Chris Salter, *Entangled: Technology and the Transformation of Performance*, Cambridge, MA: Massachusetts Institute of Technology, 2010, 63.
41. Müller, *Die Schlacht*, in *Theater Heute*, Sonderheft, 1975, 120, 130, 131.
42. See Jonathan Kalb, *The Theatre of Heiner Müller*, Cambridge University Press, 1998, 19.
43. Müller, see Frank M. Raddatz, 'Botschafter der Sphinx: Zum Verhältnis von Ästhetik und Politik am Theater an der Ruhr', *Theater der Zeit*, Sonderaufgabe, 2006, 135.
44. Ulrich Deuter, *Süddeutsche Zeitung*, 22 October 2003.
45. Roberto Ciulli, see Raddatz, 'Botschafter der Sphinx', 98.
46. *Ibid.*

5 Total theatre: the director as *auteur*

1. The source of the term 'auteur' is dealt with in more detail by Avra Sidiropoulou, in *Authoring Performance: The Director in Contemporary Theatre*, New York: Palgrave Macmillan, 2011, 1–3.
2. *Theatre of the Avant Garde, 1890–1950: A Critical Anthology*, Bert Cardullo and Robert Knopf (eds.), New Haven: Yale University Press, 2001, 176.
3. Craig's personal copy of *On the Art of the Theatre* is held at the Harry Ransome Humanities Research Center, Austin, Texas. Craig had an intimate relationship with Isadora Duncan, and served as her designer and manager.
4. *On the Art of the Theatre*, 148, 144.
5. *Craig on Theatre*, ed. J. Michael Walton, London: Methuen, 1983, 51.
6. Gordon Craig, 'Motion. Being the Preface to the Portfolio of Etchings', Nizza-Firenza, 1907.
7. Daybook 2 (1910–11), 165 (Harry Ransome Humanities Research Center, Austin, Texas). While Craig never actually staged his ideas, like Yeats, Terence Gray (Cambridge Festival Theatre) was extremely interested in Craig's theories. His biographer, Peter Cornwell, suggests that 'Gray was the total uncritical disciple who wanted above all else to reproduce Craig's ideas at the Festival Theatre. Gray's personal contribution would be in the actual demonstration of Craig's theories in the living theatre' (Peter Cornwell, *Only by Failure: The Many Faces of the Impossible Life of Terence Gray*, Cambridge: Salt Publishing, 2004, 138).
8. See John Styan, *Max Reinhardt*, Cambridge University Press, 1982, 120ff.
9. See Oliver M. Sayler, *Max Reinhardt and His Theatre*, New York: B. Blom, 1924, 118.
10. See Norman Bel Geddes, *Miracle in the Evening: An Autobiography*, ed. William Kelley, New York: Doubleday, 1960, 296ff.

11. For an extended discussion of Geddes' theatre and its relation to industrial design, see Christopher Innes, *Designing Modern America: Broadway to Main Street*, Newhaven, CT: Yale University Press, 2005.
12. Peter Brook, *The Empty Space*, Harmondsworth: Penguin Books, 1973, 11.
13. Antonin Artaud, *The Theatre and Its Double*, trans. Mary Caroline Richards, New York: Grove Press, 1958, 42; and *The Empty Space*, 36.
14. *The Theatre and Its Double*, 27, 37, 82.
15. Peter Brook and Charles Marowitz, *Sunday Times*, 12 January 1964, and Charles Marowitz *et al.*, in *Drama Review*, 11, no. 2, 156.
16. Marowitz *et al.*, 155 (my italics). See also Brook in *The Empty Space*, 55–7.
17. *The Empty Space*, 68–9.
18. John Kane, *Sunday Times*, 13 June 1971.
19. *Seneca's Oedipus*, Director's notes, Act 5 (pp. 49–52 of the published text). National Theatre Archives.
20. Peter Brook, in *Drama Review*, 17, no. 3 (1973), 50.
21. *The Empty Space*, 87.
22. *Ibid.*, 44.
23. Wilson cited in Arthur Holmberg, *The Theatre of Robert Wilson*, Cambridge University Press, 1996, 162.
24. Wilson in Robert Enright, 'A Clean, Well-lighted Grace: An Interview with Robert Wilson', *Border Crossings*, 13, no. 2 (1994), 18.
25. Balanchine in Lincoln Kirstein (ed.), *Portrait of Mr B*, New York: The Viking Press, 1984, 32.
26. Philip Glass, *Opera on the Beach*, London: Faber, 1988, 58. For a detailed study of *Einstein on the Beach* see Maria Shevtsova, *Robert Wilson*, London and New York: Routledge, 2007, 83–117.
27. Thus the essays that subsequently gave Bonnie Marranca (ed.), *The Theatre of Images*, Baltimore, MD: Johns Hopkins University Press, 1996.
28. Quoted in Holmberg, *The Theatre of Robert Wilson*, 138.
29. *Ibid.*, 67–9.
30. Isabelle Huppert, see Maria Shevtsova, 'Isabelle Huppert Becomes Orlando', *TheatreForum*, 6 (1995), 74–5.
31. Lepage, see John Lahr, *New Yorker*, 28 Dec. 1992, 190.
32. For instance, see *Directors/Directing: Conversations on Theatre*, Cambridge University Press, 2009, 129.
33. Andei Serban, interview with Christopher Innes, New York 2005 (unpublished).
34. For a review, see www.guardian.co.uk/music/2003/nov/10/classicalmusicandopera1.
35. Peter Sellars, interviewed by Christopher Innes in *Directors/Directing*, 211.
36. For a detailed description of the staging in Sellars' updating of Greek tragedy as well as Mozart and Wagner operas, see Tom Mikotowicz, 'Director Peter Sellars: Bridging the Modern and Postmodern Theatre', *Theatre Topics*, 1, no.1 (1991), 86–98.
37. Interview, www.pbs.org/wgbh/questionofgod/voices/sellars.

38. Interview, Bob Graham, *San Francisco Chronicle*, 28 February 1999: www.sfgate.com/cgi-bin/article.cgi?file=/chronicle/archive/1999/02/28/PK1001.
39. Interview, www.pbs.org/wgbh/questionofgod/voices/sellars.
40. *Directors/Directing*, 228.
41. Peter Sellars, see Richard Trousdell, 'Peter Sellars Rehearses Figaro', *Drama Review*, 35, no. 1 (Spring 1991), 67.
42. David Roesner has analysed Marthaler's work in musical terms. See *Theater als Musik*, Tubingen: Gunther Narr Verlag, 2003.
43. Grigolli, in Klaus Demutz (ed.), *Christoph Marthaler*, Salzburg and Vienna: Residenz, 2000, 152.
44. As David Barnett points out in Maria M. Delgado and Dan Rebellato (eds.), *Contemporary European Theatre Directors*, London and New York: Routledge, 191.
45. Nicholas Till, 'On the Difficulty of Saying "We"', *Contemporary Theatre Review*, 15, no. 2 (2005), 227.
46. Benedict Andrews, 'Christoph Marthaler: In the Meantime', at www.realtimearts.net/article?id=8246.

6 Directors of ensemble theatre

1. Giorgio Strehler, *Per un teatro umano*, ed. Sinah Kessler, Milan: Feltrinelli Editore, 1974, 133–4 for his discussion of his 'masters'.
2. Robert Wilson, Preface to *Strehler dirige: le tesi di un allestimento e l'impulso musicale nel teatro*, ed. Giancarlo Stampalia, Versiglio: Marsilio Editori, 11–16.
3. *Giorgio Strehler ou la passion théâtrale/Giorgio Strehler or a Passion for Theatre: Proceedings of the Third Europe Theatre Prize* [bilingual volume], Catania: Prix Europe pour le Théâtre, 2007, 44. Those who have observed Strehler's rehearsals, as has done the writer of these lines, concur that he was a great actor.
4. Valentina Fortunato speaking in *Giorgio Strehler*, 311.
5. Nada Strancar in *Giorgio Strehler*, 362.
6. Renato Carmine in *Giorgio Strehler*, 288 and Gérard Desarthe speaking of his work with Strehler on *L'Illusion* (Pierre Corneille's *Illusion comique*, which Strehler staged in French in Paris, 1984) in *Giorgio Strehler*, 299–300.
7. *Per un teatro umano* (*Towards a Human Theatre*), ed. Sinah Kessler, Milan: Feltrinelli Editore, 143. All translations from the Italian here and below are by Maria Shevtsova.
8. *Ibid.*
9. *Ibid.*, 139.
10. *Per un teatro umano*, 260–1.
11. Anton Chekhov, *A Life in Letters*, ed. Rosamund Bartlett, trans. Rosamund Bartlett and Anthony Phillips, London: Penguin Books, 2004, 510.
12. Giorigo Strehler, 196.
13. Ludmila Mikaêl in *Giorgio Strehler*, 333 and 338.
14. *Ibid.*, 236.

15. David L. Hirst, *Giorgio Strehler*, Cambridge University Press, 1993, 84.
16. 17 April 2011, trans. from Italian by Maria Shevtsova. Crippa was speaking at the symposium in honour of Peter Stein, who was awarded the fourteenth Europe Theatre Prize, this edition held in St Petersburg.
17. Stein on 17 April 2011, as above.
18. Stein quoted in *The Telegraph*, 11 August 2003.
19. Michael Patterson, *Peter Stein: Germany's Leading Director*, Cambridge University Press, 1981, 7.
20. Stein in St Petersburg, as above.
21. For a discussion of how Stein dialogues with rather than emulates Stanislavsky, see Maria Shevtsova, *Sociology of Theatre and Performance*, Verona: QuiEdit, 2009, 87–91 and 96–7.
22. On the space of the Bouffes, see Jean-Guy Lecat and Andrew Todd, *The Open Circle: Peter Brook's Theatrical Environments*, London: Faber, 2003.
23. See John Heilpern, *Conference of the Birds: The Story of Peter Brook in Africa*, Harmondsworth: Penguin Books, 1979.
24. Maurice Bénichou speaking in *Peter Brook: A Theatrical Casebook*, comp. David Williams, London: Methuen, 1992, 326.
25. See Maria Shevtsova, 'Peter Brook' in John Russell Brown (ed.), *The Routledge Companion to Directors' Shakespeare*, Abingdon: Routledge, 2008, 16–36.
26. Lev Dodin, *Journey without End*, trans. Anna Karabinska and Oksana Mamyrin, London: Tantalus Books, 2006, 17.
27. Dodin in Shevtsova and Innes, *Directors/Directing*, 41.
28. For a detailed account, see Maria Shevtsova, *Dodin and the Maly Drama Theatre: Process to Performance*, London: Routledge, 2004, 101–24.
29. *Directors/Directing*, 55.
30. *Puteshestviye Bez Kontsa (Journey without End)*, St Petersburg: Baltic Seasons, 2009, 232. This book in Russian is more comprehensive, by far, than the collection in English with the same name cited above.
31. *Ibid.*, 178.
32. *Journey without End*, 164–5.
33. *Puteshestviye*, 88.
34. *Journey without End*, 17.
35. For a detailed account of *Brothers and Sisters* and the notion of 'theatre of prose' see *Dodin and the Maly*, 63–100.
36. *Directors/Directing*, 49; and personal communication, 15 April 2011.
37. *Puteshestviye*, 93.
38. *Ibid.*, 228.
39. Jeanne Pigeon (ed.), *Anatoli Vassiliev, maître de stage: à propos de* Bal masqué *de Mikhaïl Lermontov*, Carnières-Morlanwelz (Belgium): Lansman Editeur, 1997, 70 (edited workshop held by Vassiliev, 17–25 February 1992 in Brussels, translator not cited).
40. For a full account see Anatoli Vassiliev, *Sept ou huit leçons de théâtre*, trans. Martine Néron, Paris: POL, 1999, especially 17–77.

41. On Grotowski, mentorship and other material relevant to these pages see 'Anatoli Vassiliev in Conversation with Maria Shevtsova', *New Theatre Quarterly*, 25, no. 4 (2009), 324–32.
42. *Anatoli Vassiliev, maître de stage*, 13.
43. *Ibid.*, 34 for the quotation.
44. Pigeon (ed.), *Anatoli Vassiliev*, 34–5 (trans. from Russian not cited; trans. from French by Maria Shevtsova).
45. *Ibid.*, 97.
46. *Directors/Directing*, 181–2.
47. *The Director's Craft: A Handbook for the Theatre*, London and New York: Routledge, 2009, 2.
48. *Directors/Directing*, 189.
49. *The Director's Craft*, 125.
50. *Ibid.*, 12.
51. *Ibid.*, 11 and also for the next quotation.
52. *Directors/Directing*, 198.
53. *The Director's Craft*, 154 and for the next quotation.
54. *Directors/Directing*, 190.
55. *The Director's Craft*, 156.
56. *Directors/Directing*, 190.
57. *The Actor and the Target*, London: Nick Hern Books, 2nd edition 2005.
58. Unpublished interview with Maria Shevtsova, London, 30 December 1998.
59. *Directors/Directing*, 81.
60. *New Theatre Quarterly*, as above, 328–9.
61. *Directors/Directing*, 81 for the quotation.
62. Maria Shevtsova, 'Pyotr Semak' in John Russell Brown (ed.), *The Routledge Companion to Actors' Shakespeare*, Abingdon: Routledge, 2011, 217–18.
63. *Ibid.*, 219.
64. *The Actor and the Target*, 242.

7 Directors, collaboration and improvisation

1. Ciulli, in Malgorzata Bartula and Stefan Schroer, *On Improvisation: Nine Conversations with Roberto Ciulli*, Brussels: Peter Lang, 2003, 112.
2. *Ibid.*, 11.
3. *Ibid.*, 38, 25, 48.
4. *Ibid.*, 78–9.
5. *Ibid.*, 29 (see also 52).
6. Simon McBurney, Interview in Shevtsova and Innes, *Directors/Directing*, 165.
7. See Christopher Innes, *Modern British Drama: The Twentieth Century*, Cambridge University Press, 2002, 538.
8. *Mnemonic* Programme: John Jay College Theatre New York, 2001.

9. Jackie Fletcher, *The British Theatre Guide*, 2002: www.britishtheatreguide.info/reviews/mnemonic-rev.htm.
10. McBurney, Interview in *The Tribune*, 21 April 1992.
11. Mark Valencia, *What's On Stage*, 21 November 2010.
12. LeCompte quoted in Susan Letzler Cole, 'Elizabeth LeCompte Directs *Frank Dell's The Temptation of Saint Antony*' in *Directors in Rehearsal: A Hidden World*, London and New York: Routledge, 1992, 96.
13. The quotation is from LeCompte in Shevtsova and Innes, *Directors/Directing*, 113.
14. In an unpublished interview with Elizabeth LeCompte, Scott Shepherd and Ari Fliakos by Maria Shevtsova at the Gdansk Shakespeare Festival, 5 August 2009.
15. LeCompte in *Directors/Directing*, 108.
16. Unpublished interview, as above.
17. *Ibid.*
18. LeCompte quoted in David Savran, *Breaking the Rules: The Wooster Group*, New York: Theatre Communications Group, 1988, 195.
19. Fliakos in unpublished interview, as above.
20. *Towards a Poor Theatre*, New York: Simon and Schuster, 1968, 213.
21. *Ibid.*, 35–6 and 41 for 'holy actor'; 123, 125 and 131 for 'total act'.
22. *Ibid.*, 37–8.
23. *Ibid.*, 246.
24. *Ibid.*, 125–6 and 121.
25. Ludwig Flaszen, 'Conversation with Ludwig Flaszen (reported by Eric Forsythe)', *Educational Theatre Journal*, 30, no. 3 (1978), 324.
26. Jennifer Kumiega, *The Theatre of Grotowski*, London: Methuen, 1987, 60, Kumiega's observation.
27. Grotowski cited in *ibid.*, 61.
28. Flaszen cited in *ibid.*, 74.
29. Flaszen, 'Conversation with Ludwig Flaszen', 325 for this and the following quotation.
30. Cited in Kumiega, *The Theatre of Grotowski*, 89.
31. Flaszen, 'Conversation with Ludwig Flaszen', 324.
32. Cited in Zbigniew Osinski, *Grotowski and His Laboratory*, New York: PAJ Publications, 1986, 120.
33. Richard Schechner in Richard Schechner and Lisa Wolford (eds.), *The Grotowski Sourcebook*, London and New York: Routledge, 1997, 212. The dates of Grotowski's different work periods are generally agreed and are well marked and well presented in this book.
34. Grotowski in *The Grotowski Sourcebook*, 229.
35. Robert Findlay cited by Schechner in *The Grotowski Sourcebook*, 213.
36. Grotowski in *The Grotowski Sourcebook*, 259 and 267.
37. *Ibid.*, 269.
38. See also Grotowski's 'Holiday' in *The Grotowski Sourcebook*, 215–25.

39. Observed by many, notably Osinski in *Grotowski and His Laboratory*, 76 and 80. See also Eugenio Barba, *Land of Ashes and Diamonds: My Apprenticeship in Poland*, Aberystwyth: Black Mountain Press, 1999, especially 68–74.
40. Ian Watson notes that Barba came to the concept of third theatre in 1976. See Ian Watson and colleagues, *Negotiating Culture: Eugenio Barba and the Intercultural Debate*, Manchester University Press, 2002, 197.
41. See *The Floating Islands*, Odin Teatret Vorlag: Holstebro, 1979 and *Beyond the Floating Islands*, New York: Performing Arts Journal, 1986, especially its 1979 article 'Theatre-Culture', 195–212.
42. Eugenio Barba, *On Directing and Dramaturgy: Burning the House*, London and New York: Routledge, 2010, 165.
43. *Ibid.*, 153.
44. Julia Varley, *Notes from an Odin Actress: Stones of Water*, London and New York: Routledge, 2011, 139.
45. *On Directing*, 162.
46. *Ibid.*, 26 and 29.
47. *Ibid.*, 53, and for the next quotation.
48. *Ibid.*, 54.
49. *Ibid.*, 77.
50. *Ibid.*, 76 and 77.
51. *Ibid.*, 57.
52. *Ibid.*, 204.
53. Personal communication, 3 June 2011.
54. Wlodzimierz Staniewski, with Alison Hodge, *Hidden Territories: The Theatre of Gardzienice*, London and New York: Routledge, 2004, 39 and 40 for the following quotation.
55. *Ibid.*, 41.
56. *Ibid.*, 66.
57. Personal communication, 3 June 2011.
58. *Hidden Territories*, 65.
59. *Ibid.*, 69.
60. Personal communication, 3 June 2011.
61. 'Finding the Musicality of the Text: The Art and Craft of Coordination: Anna Zubrzycki and Grzegorz Bral in Conversation with Maria Shevtsova', *New Theatre Quarterly*, 26, no. 3 (2010), 256.
62. *Ibid.*
63. *Ibid.*
64. *There Are No Secrets: Thoughts on Acting and Theatre*, London: Methuen, 1993, 109, and for the next quotation.
65. 'Finding the Musicality of the Text', 257.
66. *Ibid.*, 254.
67. *Ibid.*, 251–2.
68. *Ibid.*, 260.

69. Jaroslaw Fret interviewed by Maria Shevtsova (unpublished), 10 December 2010.
70. Fret interviewed by Maria Shevtsova (unpublished), 3 July 2010.
71. 10 December 2010.
72. *Ibid.*
73. 3 July 2010.
74. *Ibid.*
75. 10 December 2010.
76. 3 July 2010 for 'column of breathing'.
77. 'From the Theatre Company to Art as Vehicle' in Thomas Richards, *At Work with Grotowski on Physical Actions*, London: Routledge, 1995, 126.

Select bibliography

Anon. *The Case of the Stage in Ireland – Wherein the Qualifications, Duty and Importance of a Manager are Carefully Considered*, Dublin, n.d.

Artaud, Antonin. *The Theatre and its Double*, New York: Grove Press, 1958

Balukhaty, S. D. *Chaika v Postanovke Moskovskovo Khudozhestvennovo Teatra, Rezhisserskaya Partitura KS Stanislavskovo*, Leningrad: Isskustvo, 1938

The Seagull Produced by Stanislavsky, ed. and trans. David Magarshak, London: Denis Dobson, 1952

Banham, Martin. *The Cambridge Guide to World Theatre*, Cambridge University Press, 1988

Banu, Georges *et al. Giorgio Strehler ou la passion théâtrale/Giorgio Strehler or a Passion for Theatre: Proceedings of the Third Europe Theatre Prize* [bilingual volume], Catania: Prix Europe pour le Théâtre, 2007

Barba, Eugenio, *The Floating Islands*, Holstebro: Odin Teatret Vorlag, 1979

Beyond the Floating Islands, New York: Performing Arts Journal, 1986

Land of Ashes and Diamonds: My Apprenticeship in Poland, Aberystwyth: Black Mountain Press, 1999

On Directing and Dramaturgy: Burning the House, London and New York: Routledge, 2010

Barba, Eugenio and Nicola Savarese. *A Dictionary of Theatre Anthropology: The Secret Art of the Performer*, London and New York: Routledge, 1991

Barth, Herbert. *Der Festspielhügel*, Munich: List Verlag, 1973

Bartula, Malgorzata and Stefan Schroer. *On Improvisation: Nine Conversations with Roberto Ciulli*, Brussels: Peter Lang, 2003

Batcheleder, John Davis. *Henry Irving – A Short Account of his Public Life*, New York: William S. Gottsberger, 1883

Beacham, Richard. *Adolphe Appia: Theatre Artist*, Cambridge University Press, 1987

Beare, William. *The Roman Stage*, London: Methuen, 1968

Beer, Josh. *Sophocles and the Tragedy of Athenian Democracy*, Westport, CT: Praeger, 2004

Bel Geddes, Norman. *Miracle in the Evening: An Autobiography*, ed. William Kelley, New York: Doubleday, 1960

Benedetti, Jean (selected, ed. and trans.). *The Moscow Art Theatre Letters*, London: Methuen, 1991

Stanislavsky: His Life and Art, A Biography, London: Methuen, 1999

Braun, Edward (trans. and ed. with critical commentary). *Meyerhold on Theatre*, London: Methuen, 1969

Meyerhold: A Revolution in Theatre, London: Methuen, 1995

Brecht, Bertolt, *Parables for the Theatre*, trans. Eric Bentley and Maja Applebaum, New York: Grove Press, 1961

Brecht on Theatre, trans. and ed. John Willett, London: Eyre Methuen, 1964

Schriften zum Theater, Frankfurt-am-Main: Suhrkamp, 1967

Plays, Poetry, Prose, trans. John Willett, London: Methuen, 1985

Brecht, Bertolt *et al. Theaterarbeit*, Berlin: Henschelverlag, 1967

Brockett, Oscar. *History of the Theatre*, Boston: Allyn and Bacon, 1968

Brook, Peter. *The Empty Space*, Harmondsworth: Penguin Books, 1973

The Shifting Point, New York: Harper and Row, 1987

There Are No Secrets: Thoughts on Acting and Theatre, London: Methuen, 1993

Brown, John Russell (ed.). *The Routledge Companion to Directors' Shakespeare*, Abingdon: Routledge, 2008

(ed.). *The Routledge Companion to Actors' Shakespeare*, Abingdon: Routledge, 2011

Burnim, Kalman A. *David Garrick: Director*, University of Pittsburgh Press, 1961

Cardullo, Bert and Robert Knopf (eds.). *Theatre of the Avant Garde, 1890–1950: A Critical Anthology*, New Haven: Yale University Press, 2001

Carlson, Marvin. *Theatre Is More Beautiful than War: German Stage Directing in the Late Twentieth Century*, Iowa City: University of Iowa Press, 2009

Carnegy, Patrick. *Wagner and the Art of the Theatre*, New Haven, CT: Yale University Press, 2006

Carnicke, Sharon Marie. *Stanislavsky in Focus: An Acting Master for the Twenty-First Century*, London and New York: Routledge, 2009

Chekhov, Anton. *A Life in Letters*, ed. Rosamund Bartlett, trans. Rosamund Bartlett and Anthony Phillips, London: Penguin Books, 2004

Chothia, Jean. *André Antoine*, Cambridge University Press, 1991

Christoffersen, Erik Axe. *The Actor's Way*, London and New York: Routledge 1993

Copeau, Jacques. 'L'art et l'œuvre d'Aldolphe Appia', *Comoedia*, 12 March 1928

Craig, Edward Gordon. *Henry Irving*, New York: Longmans, Green, 1930

Index to the Story of My Days, New York: Hulton Press, 1957

On the Art of the Theatre, New York: Theater Arts Books, [1911] 1960

Craig on Theatre, ed. J. Michael Walton, London: Methuen, 1983

Delgado, Maria M. and Dan Rebellato (eds.). *Contemporary European Theatre Directors*, London and New York: Routledge, 2010

Devrient, Eduard. *Geschichte der deutschen Schauspielkunst*, Munich and Vienna: Langen Müller, 1967

Diderot, Denis. *The Paradox of the Actor* (1770–84), in *Selected Writings on Art and Literature*, trans. Geoffrey Bremner, Harmondsworth: Penguin, 1994

Dodin, Lev. *Journey without End*, trans. Anna Karabinska, and Oksana Mamyrin, London: Tantalus Books, 2006

Puteshestviye Bez Kontsa (Journey without End), St Petersburg: Baltic Seasons, 2009

Donnellan, Declan. *The Actor and the Target*, London: Nick Hern Books, 2nd edition, 2005
Dundjerović, Aleksandar Saša. *Robert Lepage*, London: Routledge, 2009
Enright, Robert. 'A Clean, Well-lighted Grace: An Interview with Robert Wilson', *Border Crossings*, 13, no. 2 (1994), 14–22
Filipowicz, Halina. 'Gardzienice: A Polish Expedition to Baltimore', *Drama Review*, 31, no. 1 (T113, 1987), 131–6
Flaszen, Ludwig. 'Conversation with Ludwig Flaszen (reported by Eric Forsythe)', *Educational Theatre Journal*, 30, no. 3 (1978), 301–28
Foulkes, F. J. *Lessing and the Drama*, Oxford: Clarendon Press, 1981
Fuchs, Georg. *Revolution in the Theatre*, trans. Constance Connor Kuhn, Ithaca, NY: Cornell University Press, 1959
Gladkov, Aleksandr. *Meyerhold Speaks, Meyerhold Rehearses*, trans. and ed. with introduction by Alma Law, Amsterdam: Harwood Academic Publishers, 1997
Glass, Philip. *Opera on the Beach*, London: Faber, 1988
Grotowski, Jerzy. *Towards a Poor Theatre*, New York: Simon and Schuster, 1968
'From the Theatre Company to Art as Vehicle' in Thomas Richards, *At Work with Grotowski on Physical Actions*, London: Routledge, 1995, 113–35
Opere e sentieri. Jerzy Grotowski, testi 1968–1998, vol. II, trans. and ed. Antonio Attisani and Mario Biagini, Rome: Bulzoni Editore, 2007
Heilpern, John. *Conference of the Birds: The Story of Peter Brook in Africa*, Harmondsworth: Penguin Books, 1979
Hill, John. *The Actor*, London: Printed for R. Griffith, 1750; New York: Blom, 1971
Hirst, David. *Giorgio Strehler*, Cambridge University Press, 1993
Holmberg, Arthur. *The Theatre of Robert Wilson*, Cambridge University Press, 1996
Hopkins, D. J. *City/Stage/Globe: Performance and Space in Shakespeare's London*, New York: Routledge, 2008
Hunt, Albert and Geoffrey Reeves. *Peter Brook*, Cambridge University Press, 1995
Innes, Christopher. *Erwin Piscator's Political Theatre*, Cambridge University Press, 1972
'The Piscator Section', *Drama Review*, 22, no. 4 (December 1978), 83–98
Modern German Drama, Cambridge University Press, 1979
Edward Gordon Craig, Cambridge University Press, 1983
Avant Garde Theatre: 1892–1992, London and New York: Routledge, 1993
(ed.). *A Sourcebook on Naturalist Theatre*, London and New York: Routledge 2000
Modern British Drama: The Twentieth Century, Cambridge University Press, 2002
Designing Modern America: Broadway to Main Street, Newhaven, CT: Yale University Press, 2005
Irving, Henry. *The Drama: Addresses*, New York: Tait [1892]
Jones, David Richard. *Great Directors at Work*, Berkeley and Los Angeles: University of California Press, 1986

Kalb, Johnathan. *The Theatre of Heiner Müller*, Cambridge University Press, 1998
Kiernander, Adrian. *Ariane Mnouchkine and the Théâtre du Soleil*, Cambridge University Press, 1993
Kirstein, Lincoln (ed.). *Portrait of Mr B*, New York: The Viking Press, 1984
Knapp, Bettina. *The Reign of the Theatrical Director: French Theatre, 1887–1924*, Troy, NY: Whitston, 1988
'The Reign of the Theatrical Director: Antoine and Lugné-Poë', *The French Review*, 61, no. 6 (May 1988), 866–77
Knight, Charles. *London*, London: Henry G. Bohn, 1851
Koller, Anne Marie. *The Theater Duke: Georg II of Saxe-Meiningen and the German Stage*, Stanford University Press, 1984
Kosinski, Darius. 'Songs from Beyond the Dark', *Performance Research*, 13, no 2 (2008), 60–75
Kumiega, Jennifer. *The Theatre of Grotowski*, London: Methuen, 1987
Leach, Robert. *Vsevolod Meyerhold*, Cambridge University Press, 1989
Lecat, Jean-Guy and Andrew Todd. *The Open Circle: Peter Brook's Theatrical Environments*, London: Faber, 2003
Letzler Cole, Susan. 'Elizabeth LeCompte Directs *Frank Dell's The Temptation of Saint Antony*' in *Directors in Rehearsal: A Hidden World*, London and New York: Routledge, 1992, 91–123
Marowitz, Charles, Robert Bolt and Kelly Morris. 'Some Conventional Words: An Interview with Robert Bolt', *Drama Review*, 11, no. 2, (winter 1966), 138–40
Marranca, Bonnie (ed.). *The Theatre of Images*, Baltimore, MD: Johns Hopkins University Press, 1996
Meierkhold, Vsevolod. *Stati, Pisma, Rechi, Besedy, Chast Pervaya, 1891–1917*, Moscow: Isskustvo, 1968
Stati, Pisma, Rechi, Besedy, Chast Vtoraya, 1917–1939, Moscow: Isskustvo, 1968
Melchinger, Siegfried. *Max Reinhardt: Sein Theater in Bildern*, Vienna: Friedrich Verlag, 1968
Merlin, Bella. *Stanislavsky*, London and New York: Routledge, 2003
Mikhaïlova, Alla *et al. Meierkhold i Khudozhniki/Meyerhold and Set Designers* [a bilingual publication], Moscow: Galart, 1995
Mikotowicz, Tom. 'Director Peter Sellars: Bridging the Modern and Postmodern Theatre', *Theatre Topics*, 1, no. 1 (March 1991), 87–98
Milne, Lesley (ed.). *Russian and Soviet Theatre: Tradition and the Avant-Garde*, trans. Roxane Permar, London: Thames and Hudson, 1988
Mitchell, Katie. *The Director's Craft: A Handbook for the Theatre*, London and New York: Routledge, 2009
Mnouchkine, Ariane. *Entretiens avec Fabienne Pascaud: l'art du présent*, Paris: Plon, 2005
Müller, Heiner. Interview with Horst Laube, *Theater Heute*, Sonderheft, 1975, 119–23
Theatremachine, ed. and trans. Marc von Henning, London and Boston: Faber, 1995

Nascimento, Claudia Tatinge. 'Of Tent Shows and Liturgies: *One breath left: Dies Irae*', *Drama Review*, 54, no. 3 (T207, 2010), 136–49
Nemirovich-Danchenko, Vladimir. *My Life in the Russian Theatre*, trans. John Cournos, London: Geoffrey Bles, 1968
Obenhaus, Mark. *Einstein on the Beach: The Changing Image of Opera*, Obenhaus Films/Brooklyn Academy of Music, 1985 (video)
Orme, Michael. *J. T. Grein: The Story of a Pioneer, 1862–1935*, London: Murray, 1936
Osinski, Zbigniew. *Grotowski and His Laboratory*, New York: PAJ Publications, 1986
Patterson, Michael. *Peter Stein: Germany's Leading Director*, Cambridge University Press, 1981
Pigeon, Jeanne (ed.). *Anatoli Vassiliev, maître de stage: à propos de Bal masqué de Mikhaïl Lermontov*, Carnières-Morlanwelz (Belgium): Lansman Editeur, 1997
Piscator, Erwin. *Political Theatre*, trans. Hugh Rorisson, London: Methuen, 1980
Porubcansky, Anna. 'Song of the Goat Theatre: Artistic Practice as Life Practice', *New Theatre Quarterly*, 26, no. 3 (2010), 261–72
Raddatz, Frank M. 'Botschafter der Sphinx: Zum Verhältnis von Ästhetik und Politik am Theater an der Ruhr', *Theater der Zeit*, Sonderaufgabe, 2006
Radishcheva, O. A. *Stanislavsky i Nemirovich-Danchenko: Istoria Teatralnykh Otnoshenyi, 1909–1917*, Moscow: Artist Rezhisser. Teatr, 1999
Raikh, Zinaida. Letter of 16 December 1928, *Teatr*, 2 (1974), 34
Richards, Thomas. *At Work with Grotowski on Physical Actions*, London: Routledge, 1995
Richter, Julius. '*Rasputin*/Nach der Aufführung der Piscatorbühne', *Die Scene*, 2 (1928)
Roesner, David. *Theater als Musik*, Tubingen: Gunther Narr Verlag, 2003
Rohmer, Rolf von. 'Autoren-Positionen: Heiner Müller', *Theater der Zeit*, 30, no. 8 (1975), 55–9
Rudnitsky, Konstantin. *Meyerhold the Director*, ed. Sydney Schultze and trans. George Petrov, with introduction by Ellendea Proffer, Ann Arbor, MI: Ardis, 1981
Russian and Soviet Theatre: Tradition and the Avant-Garde, ed. Lesley Milne and trans. Roxane Permar, London: Thames and Hudson, 1988
Rühle, Günther (ed.). *Theater für die Republik*, Frankfurt-am-Main: Fischer Verlag, 1967
Salter, Chris. *Entangled: Technology and the Transformation of Performance*, Cambridge, MA: Massachusetts Institute of Technology Press, 2010
Savran, David. *Breaking the Rules: The Wooster Group*, New York: Theatre Communications Group, 1988
Sayler, Oliver M. *Max Reinhardt and His Theatre*, New York: B. Blom, 1924
Schechner, Richard and Lisa Wolford (eds.). *The Grotowski Sourcebook*, London and New York: Routledge, 1997

Senelick, Laurence. *Gordon Craig's Moscow* Hamlet, Westport, CT: Greenwood Press, 1982
The Chekhov Theatre, Cambridge University Press, 1997
Shevtsova, Maria. 'Isabelle Huppert Becomes Orlando', *TheatreForum*, 6 (1995), 69–75
'A Theatre that Speaks to Citizens: Interview with Ariane Mnouchkine', *Western European Stages*, 7, no. 3 (1995–96), 5–12
Dodin and the Maly Drama Theatre: Process to Performance, London: Routledge, 2004
'Eugenio Barba in Conversation with Maria Shevtsova: Reinventing Theatre', *New Theatre Quarterly*, 23, no. 2 (2007), 99–114
Robert Wilson, London and New York: Routledge, 2007
'Anatoli Vassiliev in Conversation with Maria Shevtsova: Studio Theatre, Laboratory Theatre', *New Theatre Quarterly*, 25, no. 4 (2009), 324–32
Sociology of Theatre and Performance, Verona: QuiEdit, 2009
Shevtsova, Maria and Christopher Innes. *Directors/Directing: Conversations on Theatre*, Cambridge University Press, 2009
Sidiropoulou, Avra. *Authoring Performance: The Director in Contemporary Theatre*, New York: Palgrave Macmillan, 2011
Staniewski, Wlodzimierz with Alison Hodge. *Hidden Territories: The Theatre of Gardzienice*, London and New York: Routledge, 2004
Stanislavky, Konstantin. *My Life in the Russian Theatre*, trans. John Cournos, London: Geoffrey Bles, 1968
Zapisnye Knizhki, Moscow: Vagrius, 2001
An Actor's Work, trans. Jean Benedetti, London and New York: Routledge, 2008
My Life in Art, trans. Jean Benedetti, London and New York: Routledge, 2008
Stoker, Bram. *Personal Reminiscences of Henry Irvin*, London: Macmillan, 1906
Stone, George and George Kahel. *David Garrick: A Critical Biography*, Carbondale: Southern Illinois University Press, 1979
Strehler, Giorgio. *Per un teatro umano*, ed. Sinah Kesler, Milan: Feltrinelli Editore, 1974
Styan, John. *Max Reinhardt*, Cambridge University Press, 1982
Symons, James M. *Meyerhold's Theatre of the Grotesque*, Cambridge: L. Rivers Press, 1973
Tairov, Aleksandr. *Notes of a Director*, trans. and with introduction by William Kuhlke, Coral Gables, FL: University of Miami Press, 1969
Zapisi Rezhissera, Stati, Besedy, Rechi, Pisma, Moscow: Vserossiiskoye Tetaralnoye Obshchestvo, 1970
Trousdell, Richard. 'Peter Sellars Rehearses Figaro', *Drama Review*, 35, no. 1 (spring 1991), 66–89
Varley, Julia. *Notes from an Odin Actress: Stones of Water*, London and New York: Routledge, 2011
Vassiliev, Anatoli. *Sept ou huit leçons de théâtre*, trans. Martine Néron, Paris: POL, 1999

Vendrovskaya, Lyubov and Galina Kaptereva (comp.). *Evgeny Vakhtangov* [Notes by Vakhtangov, and Articles and Reminiscences], trans. Doris Bradbury, Moscow: Progress Publishers, 1982

Wagner, Richard. *Opera and Drama (Oper und Drama)*, trans. Edwin Evans, London: W. Reeves, 1913

Gesammelte Schriften und Briefe, ed. Julius Kapp, Leipzig: Hesse and Becker, 1914

Watson, Ian. *Towards a Third Theatre: Eugenio Barba and Odin Teatret*, London and New York: Routledge, 1996

Watson, Ian and colleagues. *Negotiating Culture: Eugenio Barba and the Intercultural Debate*, Manchester University Press, 2002

Whyman, Rose. *The Stanislavsky System of Acting: Legacy and Influence in Modern Performance*, Cambridge University Press, 2008

Willett, John. (ed. and trans.). *Brecht on Theatre*, London: Eyre Methuen, 1964

(ed.). *The Theatre of Bertolt Brecht*, London: Methuen, 1977

The Theatre of Erwin Piscator: Half a Century of Politics in the Theatre, London: Eyre Methuen, 1978

Williams, David. (comp.). *Peter Brook: A Theatrical Casebook*, London: Methuen, 1992

Williams, David. (comp. and ed.). *Collaborative Theatre: The Théâtre du Soleil Sourcebook*, London and New York: Routledge, 1999

Williams, Simon. *Richard Wagner and Festival Theatre*, Westport, CT: Greenwood Press, 1994

Wilson, Robert. Preface to *Strehler dirige: le tesi di un allestimento e l'impulso musicale nel teatro*, ed. Giancarlo Stampalia, Versiglio: Marsilio Editori, 11–16

Woods, Leigh. *Garrick Claims the Stage*, Westport, CT: Greenwood Press, 1984

Worral, Nick. *Modernism to Realism on the Soviet Stage: Tairov – Vakhtangov – Okhlopkov*, Cambridge University Press, 1989

The Moscow Art Theatre, London and New York: Routledge, 1996

Zavadsky, Yury. *Uchitelya i uchineky (Teachers and Pupils)*, Moscow: Iskusstvo, 1975

Zola, Emile. 'Naturalism in the Theatre', trans. Albert Bermel, in Eric Bentley (ed.), *The Theory of the Modern Stage*, Harmondsworth: Penguin Books, 1976, 351–72

Zubrzycki, Anna and Grzegorz Bral in Conversation with Maria Shevtsova. 'Finding the Musicality of the Text: The Art and Craft of Coordination', *New Theatre Quarterly*, 26, no. 3 (2010), 248–60

Index

Cambridge Introductions to ...

AUTHORS

Margaret Atwood Heidi Macpherson
Jane Austen Janet Todd
Samuel Beckett Ronan McDonald
Walter Benjamin David Ferris
Lord Byron Richard Lansdown
Chekhov James N. Loehlin
J. M. Coetzee Dominic Head
Samuel Taylor Coleridge John Worthen
Joseph Conrad John Peters
Jacques Derrida Leslie Hill
Charles Dickens Jon Mee
Emily Dickinson Wendy Martin
George Eliot Nancy Henry
T. S. Eliot John Xiros Cooper
William Faulkner Theresa M. Towner
F. Scott Fitzgerald Kirk Curnutt
Michel Foucault Lisa Downing
Robert Frost Robert Faggen
Gabriel Garcia Marquez Gerald Martin
Nathaniel Hawthorne Leland S. Person
Zora Neale Hurston Lovalerie King
James Joyce Eric Bulson
Thomas Mann Todd Kontje
Christopher Marlowe Tom Rutter
Herman Melville Kevin J. Hayes
Milton Stephen B. Dobranski
George Orwell John Rodden and John Rossi
Sylvia Plath Jo Gill
Edgar Allan Poe Benjamin F. Fisher
Ezra Pound Ira Nadel
Marcel Proust Adam Watt
Jean Rhys Elaine Savory
Edward Said Conor McCarthy
Shakespeare Emma Smith
Shakespeare's Comedies Penny Gay
Shakespeare's History Plays Warren Chernaik
Shakespeare's Poetry Michael Schoenfeldt
Shakespeare's Tragedies Janette Dillon
Tom Stoppard William W. Demastes
Harriet Beecher Stowe Sarah Robbins
Mark Twain Peter Messent
Edith Wharton Pamela Knights
Walt Whitman M. Jimmie Killingsworth
Virginia Woolf Jane Goldman
William Wordsworth Emma Mason
W. B. Yeats David Holdeman

TOPICS

American Literary Realism Phillip Barrish
The American Short Story Martin Scofield
Anglo-Saxon Literature Hugh Magennis
Comedy Eric Weitz
Creative Writing David Morley
Early English Theatre Janette Dillon
The Eighteenth-Century Novel April London
Eighteenth-Century Poetry John Sitter
English Theatre, 1660–1900 Peter Thomson
Francophone Literature Patrick Corcoran

German Poetry Judith Ryan

Literature and the Environment Timothy Clark

Modern British Theatre Simon Shepherd

Modern Irish Poetry Justin Quinn

Modernism Pericles Lewis

Modernist Poetry Peter Howarth

Narrative (second edition) H. Porter Abbott

The Nineteenth-Century American Novel Gregg Crane

The Novel Marina MacKay

Old Norse Sagas Margaret Clunies Ross

Postcolonial Literatures C. L. Innes

Postmodern Fiction Bran Nicol

Romantic Poetry Michael Ferber

Russian Literature Caryl Emerson

Scenography Joslin McKinney and Philip Butterworth

The Short Story in English Adrian Hunter

Theatre Directing Christopher Innes and Maria Shevtsova

Theatre Historiography Thomas Postlewait

Theatre Studies Christopher B. Balme

Tragedy Jennifer Wallace

Victorian Poetry Linda K. Hughes